The Foreign Relations of Iran

A Developing State in a Zone of Great-Power Conflict

SHAHRAM CHUBIN *and* SEPEHR ZABIH

The Foreign Relations of Iran

A Developing State in a Zone of Great-Power Conflict

With a Foreword by Paul Seabury

UNIVERSITY OF CALIFORNIA PRESS
Berkeley • Los Angeles • London

University of California Press
Berkeley and Los Angeles, California

University of California Press, Ltd.
London, England

ISBN 0-520-02683-7
Library of Congress Catalog Card Number: 73-91677
Printed in the United States of America

For Nassrin and Abdolhossein   For Joan, Ramin, and Leyla
              Sh. Chubin   S. Zabih

CONTENTS

FOREWORD

No state would seem more unfortunately situated than a small power set adjacent to a superpower with a reputation for aggressive, expansionist behavior. Such a state, lacking the force to guarantee its own sovereignty, confronts several options. It may choose to place itself at the mercy of its strong neighbor. It may opt for a course of agile diplomacy, seeking to solicit limited aid from remote powers to redress the imbalance. Or, as in the instance of Castro's Cuba, it may choose the hegemony of a distant power in preference to that of its immediate neighbor. None of these courses of action is without risk and penalty. The first may lead down a slippery slope from dependency to subjugation to actual extinction of independence. The second and third risk trading one form of dependence for another. In all cases, however, success requires a high degree of centralization of authority over foreign policy, and strong political will. Foreign policy dictates its necessities to domestic policy. The grim fate of eighteenth-century Poland, faced by such a dilemma, in large measure sprang from its internal constitutional weakness.

But excessive centralization of control, while it may ensure firm command, is not without its own risks. It may bring into being a brittle authority which, out of caution and anxiety, may conceal its purposes in secrecy and refuse to share and diffuse knowledge and responsibility in decision-making. The absence of a domestic consensus thus places a premium upon the survival abilities of its current leadership.

In the present work Professor Zabih and Dr. Chubin focus upon Iran to illustrate these classic dilemmas of such a small power. Situated for more than a century in a zone of great-power rivalry, Persia (subsequently Iran) has experimented with all of these options and risks in its diplomacy. Fortunately, like the Abbé de Sieyès through the French Revolution, it has managed to survive. Yet in surviving it continues to confront the dilemmas which such a situation entails. Iran today has, for the time being, attained a surprisingly high level of autonomy, and now plays an increasingly influential role in the affairs of the Persian Gulf. But, as the authors point out, one condition of such success has been the dynamic will, and skill, of its hereditary ruler. It lacks a stable polity in which foreign policy might command broad understanding and support. In a time of super-power detente, uncertainties have arisen about the dependability of the countervailing influence of the United States in the region.

A fine book appearing at the right time combines merit with good fortune. The October War of 1973 and the world energy crisis have lent great importance to Iranian regional and economic policies. The role of Iran in relations between oil-producing countries and advanced industrial societies is as critical as its stabilizing, or destabilizing, role in the Middle East.

The multi-dimensioned character of this book makes it a timely and invaluable aid not just to scholars but also to political leaders and opinion-makers who seek to comprehend the changing essence of power politics in the 1970s.

Paul Seabury

PREFACE

Experience in teaching and research as well as work at the United Nations over the last ten years have convinced the authors of the need for a comprehensive and systematic analysis of Iran's foreign relations, especially those of the recent decade. The unevenness, both in quality and scope, of the literature on the post-World War II era has been a further incentive. Available works on the earlier part of this era have treated the subject matter either from a primarily international cold-war angle or exclusively from the narrow perspective of Iran's relations with one or another major power. The rise of Iran's influence in the Persian Gulf, beginning in the early 1970's, and the dynamics of oil politics in the region as a whole, have reinforced the need for completing this study.

In a sense the genesis of this project dates back to the authors' initial contact in 1965, when they met in the department of government at Oberlin College in Ohio. Since then they have both participated in research and writing on this subject. During his years at the Middle Institute and department of political science at Columbia University (1966–1973), Dr. Chubin has pursued his interest in international politics, particularly the study of Iran's foreign relations. In addition, his advisory work at the Permanent Mission of Iran to the United Nations (1969–1973) has given him an insight into Iran's diplomacy in a multilateral forum. A considerable portion of the present study is an outgrowth of his research on this subject while completing his doctoral dissertation at Columbia University.

As a guest scholar at the Center for Advanced Study of the Brookings Institution, Washington, D.C., in 1969, Professor Zabih conducted initial research in Washington in support of a related study of de facto nonalignment in the Northern Tier countries of the Middle East, as well as field work in Iran. As a research scholar at the Institute of International Studies, University of California, Berkeley, since January 1972, he has done research and field work on a study of Soviet foreign aid to selected non-Arab Middle Eastern countries. Of particular value was the time he spent in the spring of 1973—while visiting in the government department of the University of Texas in Austin—at the Lyndon B. Johnson Library, with its valuable collection of data and research material covering United States foreign relations during Mr. Johnson's presidency.

This study is thus the result of a fully collaborative relationship in which both authors, though emphasizing particular chapters, have contributed to the entire book.

Many individuals have lent a helping hand at various stages of this study. James Bill of the University of Texas; J. C. Hurewitz, Donald Puchala, and Annette Baker Fox of Columbia University; and John Badeau of Georgetown University have read all or parts of an earlier draft of this work and made many useful suggestions. Equally helpful have been Iranian government officials, including Prime Minister Amir Abbas Hoveyda, Court Minister Assadollah Alam, and Foreign Minister Abbasali Khalatbary, who granted frank and comprehensive interviews in the course of their field work. They are grateful to Paul Seabury of the University of California at Berkeley for consenting to write a foreword to the book.

Dr. Chubin wishes also to acknowledge his gratitude to Ambassadors Mehdi Vakil and Fereydoun Hoveyda and members of the Iranian Mission to the United Nations, as well as to Douglas McArthur III, the former American ambassador in Iran; Timothy W. Childs and Martin Hertz of the U.S. State Department; and Richard Peyer and Colonel John A. Reed, Jr., of the U.S. Defense Department, for their generous time and valuable cooperation. In addition, he wishes to single out his friends Nancy and Basil for the encouragement and understanding they provided during the course of this long and at times arduous enterprise.

Professor Zabih is indebted to Ahmad Ghoreichi, dean of the faculty of law of the Danashgahe Melli Iran, and Jahangir Tafazzoli, Iranian ambassador to Afganistan, for their valuable suggestions and keen insights as well as their hospitality, which made his field work so enjoyable and rewarding. Harold Saunders of the White House National Security Council and Theodor Eliot, Jr., former country director for Iran at the State Department and the present Ambassador to Kabul, were most generous with their time and cooperation while he conducted research in Washington. Responsibility for the content of this study, however, belongs to the authors exclusively.

The *Middle East Journal* and *World Politics,* in which Professor Zabih published some of the preliminary findings of this study, have granted permission for the use of parts of the material therein.

In the absence of a standard method of transliteration of Persian, Arabic, and Russian names and titles, a fairly simple formula has been used to permit their reasonably accurate pronunciation by those unfamiliar with these languages. Occasional exceptions are due to the retention of different styles of transliteration used in various citations. Primary sources in non-Western languages are translated in the bibliography.

INTRODUCTION: THE ANALYTICAL FRAMEWORK

The evolution of Iran's foreign relations since the end of World War II accurately reflects the transformation of power relationships in the Middle Eastern region and the shift in the international political system as a whole. It also reflects major developments in the Iranian political system which have either generated that evolution or benefited from it. The nature and intensity of the interaction between domestic and foreign political developments account for the essence of this evolution which, in about a quarter of a century, has ranged from the struggle for Iran's survival as an independent state to its emergence as a dominant regional power whose interests and aspirations may exercise considerable influence on both regional and, to a lesser extent, international politics.

Chronologically the postwar era represents several distinctive phases. During the immediate postwar years to 1953, the major objective of Iran's foreign policy was to liquidate the consequences of wartime occupation by the Soviet Union and Great Britain. The Iranian political system of this period could be characterized as a quasi-parliamentary regime with a multi-party system that rendered the task of forming a stable cabinet immensely difficult. Thus between 1941 and 1953 Iran was ruled by 19 cabinets with an average life span of about 7½ months. During this period the Shah did not exercise a powerful role in Iranian political evolution; he reigned rather than governed. Effective power belonged to the landed aristocracy, which controlled the Iranian parliament, particularly its lower house, the Majlis.

Nevertheless Iran achieved remarkable success in restoring its territorial integrity and sovereignty against formidable odds. This was possible mainly because the open and clear Soviet threat to Iran's sovereignty generated strong nationalistic resistance among most of the country's politically articulate. The paramount danger in their eyes was Soviet desire to extend its influence into Iran, through Sovietization or, failing that, through economic and political concessions. Thus it was Iranian policy to rely on whatever external support it could muster to offset this. In this period the majority of successive governments and nationalist political groups, though disagreeing on means and methods, recognized the priority of frustrating the threats to Iran's sovereignty from a proximate power like the Soviet Union. It was hoped that a subsequent effort drastically to reduce British economic and political influence could presage a posture of neutralism toward both powers.

The first objective was fully achieved by late 1947, when the Soviet-supported separatist regime in Azarbayjan collapsed and a treaty for a vast oil concession to the Soviet Union was rejected by the Iranian parliament. Having attained the primary goal of regaining Iran's sovereignty in the face of open Soviet design, foreign policy was focused on the second objective, vastly more complex than the first.

The influence of Great Britain in Iran was more subtle and disguised, and the struggle to reduce it to manageable proportions was prolonged and difficult. The Soviet danger could be dealt with in the context of the cold war; British influence could not. However, Iran's efforts to lessen the British presence culminated during the period of the nationalist movement (1950–1953), when Prime Minister Mohammad Mossadegh dealt a severe blow to British economic power through nationalization of the Anglo-Iranian Oil Company.

As leader of the small parliamentary group *Jebhe-ye Melli* [National Front], Mossadegh had persistently advocated a policy of resistance to both Great Britain and the Soviet Union, even during the wartime occupation (1941–1945). Indeed it was he who had authored and successfully initiated a parliamentary move to prohibit any new oil negotiations with foreign companies, when both Soviet and American companies approached Iran in late 1944. The successful implementation of this policy, which came to be known as *Siyasate Movazenehe Manfi* [negative equilibrium policy], required even-handed treatment of Britain and the Soviet Union. When Mossadegh became prime minister in April 1951, the thrust of his foreign policy gained a pronounced Anglophobic accent. Although the oil nationalization was legally successful when the International Court of Justice at the Hague refused to adjudicate the Anglo-Iranian dispute in July 1952, the political and economic ramifications of the Western oil companies' boycott of Iran's nationalized oil negated that success. A number of external and internal factors combined to cause the collapse of the Mossadegh regime and inaugurate a new era in the country's foreign policy.

The first causal factor in the downfall of the nationalist regime was the emergence of the United States as the dominant power in the region, replacing Great Britain in the traditional Anglo-Soviet rivalry which had dominated Iran's foreign policy responses and objectives for more than a century. Although initially sympathetic to the nationalist aspirations of Mossadegh's regime, the United States ultimately reversed its stand and coordinated its policy with Great Britain, as well as with Iranian opponents of Dr. Mossadegh, to bring about the downfall of his regime. The persistence of cold-war considerations in the overall American conception of international allegiances in the early 1950's, coupled with the looming shadow of the Korean war, were chiefly responsible for this policy change. Iran's desire for a nonaligned posture toward Britain and the Soviet Union had to be subordinated to the broader bipolar cold-war exigencies.

A second factor contributing to the demise of Mossadegh's regime was the serious threat to Iran's internal security posed by social and economic chaos, and its exploitation by a revived communist movement. Many who had originally believed in "negative equilibrium" sensed in renewed communist activity a threat to their earlier success in reducing Soviet encroachment.

Finally, unlike the struggle against the Soviet threat, attempts to undermine British influence entailed tremendous economic hardships which weakened the regime's ability to withstand the combined pressures from internal and external opponents.

The overthrow of the nationalist regime in August 1953 by a royalist military-civilian uprising signaled the end of the first phase in Iran's foreign policy. It had attempted to strike a balance between the diametrically opposed aspirations of interested powers, to rely on international organizations and, somewhat ambivalently, to rely on United States support in order to adopt a nonaligned stance in the international system.

In the period between 1953 and the early 1960's the Iranian political system experienced a radical transformation which significantly altered Iran's foreign policy priorities and objectives. The crux of this transformation was total abandonment of the quasi-parliamentary system of the previous period and the ascendancy of the Shah in the country's political hierarchy. Reigning and ruling became indistinguishable as the monarch consolidated his position at the apex of that hierarchy.

Iran's international posture and specific actions in foreign policy soon began to assume a pronounced pro-Western course. This can be attributed to several causes: first, failure of the earlier "negative equilibrium" policy and the quest for other feasible alternatives; second, the need of the reinstated regime of the Shah for internal security and new sources of support; third, the replacement of British power by the United States, which made pro-Western alliance appear less a reinstatement of traditional British influence; fourth, American initiative, which sought to complete a chain of anti-Soviet defense pacts by linking the three Middle Eastern countries on the southern periphery of Russia to existing NATO and SEATO treaties. This new defensive alliance, also known as Northern Tier Defense, gradually interested Iran.

As for the first factor, the Shah viewed the failure of "negative equilibrium" as only the most recent example of a small power's inability to cope with security dangers posed by a proximate great power. Thus memories of wartime occupation and its concomitant internal upheaval were revived to reinforce the case for alliance policy. The government pointed out that a policy of neutralism, faithfully adhered to by the late Shah on the eve of World War II, did not keep Iran out of the hostilities. These two experiences proved that a strategically located country such as Iran, which lacked the military power to conduct independent foreign policy, had no choice but to ally itself with those states whose interest dictated the maintenance of her sovereignty, even if this entailed the acceptance of political and military commitments.

This line of argument was closely linked with a second factor, that of the regime's internal security. Because the security of the Shah's regime and the state as a whole were equated, foreign policy was expected to strengthen the internal and external requirements for stability and survival of the regime. This meant a concerted search for external sources of military support from those powers which accepted this equation of regime security and were able and willing to support it.

The absence at that time of any serious alternative to the United States which could satisfy both these requirements made the choice of pro-Western alliance easier. This choice was also calculated to pave the way for substantial economic aid from the U.S. and other interested Western powers. A third argument in its favor was that, as the United States was a distant power without a tradition of imperialistic goals toward Iran, alliance with it did not entail restoration of a dominant Western power in the country.

Finally, mention should be made of American initiative in convincing Iran of the wisdom of her policy choice. In fact, this might be regarded as the single most determinant factor, for the United States was diligently seeking to complete a chain of defensive pacts around the Soviet Union. With the failure of such alternative projects as the Middle East Defense Pact involving the whole region, the U.S. State Department seemed bent on realizing the Northern Tier Defense concept. Iran, while responding affirmatively to American urgings, did endeavor to secure maximum concessions in return. The main thrust of these efforts, which did not terminate with the conclusion of the Baghdad Pact, was to seek reassurance that the United States' overriding concern in the region also extended to the survival of the Iranian regime.

Having decided on the necessity for reinforced United States commitment, the Iranian government set out to explore American-Soviet rivalry and mutual distrust in order to stimulate a positive U.S. reaction. Ideally, Iran would have liked the United States to formally join the Central Treaty Organization, believing that a treaty obligation approved by the U.S. Senate would elevate the commitment to the level enjoyed by NATO members. The fact that Turkey already enjoyed this type of American protection strengthened this Iranian conviction. As an alternative, Iran aimed at a bilateral mutual defense treaty similar to that between the United States and Japan, hoping this would maximize American commitment.

Toward the end of this phase, Iran's efforts to use the potential of a rapprochement with the Soviets in order to consolidate the American commitment to Iranian security generated a major crisis in Iran-Soviet relations. However, by the fall of 1962 a considerable shift toward normalization of relations between the two countries became apparent. The fact that this coincided with a series of more drastic government-sponsored economic and social reforms in Iran facilitated the Soviet task of rationalizing this change in attitude.

The third phase began in 1963, when a marked trend toward disengagement from a rigid pro-Western posture had become visible. The decade since 1963 has also witnessed significant changes in Iran's internal political development. After long hesitation, the Shah set in motion a series of socioeconomic reforms, including a three-stage land reform project, designed to broaden the base of his support. Along with these measures Iran's economic development was greatly accelerated by the steady increase in oil revenue. However, the basic feature of the political system—namely, the concentration of all legitimate power in the institution of monarchy—remained unchanged. If anything, these reforms, which have since been labeled the White Revolution, or the Shah and People Revolution, reinforced the claim that the centralized authority of the Shah was indispensable to the task of rapid modernization.

The principal ramification of the new foreign policy orientation is the acceptance of the logic of nonalignment, so roundly rejected in the second phase. This fundamental change in Iran's foreign policy was firmly reinforced by the second Kashmir war in 1965. Just as the Iraqi revolution in 1958 had demonstrated the inadequacy of the Baghdad Pact to insure the survival of the regime of a member state, the second Kashmir war shed serious misgivings on the regional reliability of bilateral agreements with the United States when the territorial integrity of another member state was endangered by a stronger proximate power other than the USSR.

The emergence of the Soviet Union as a chief intermediary for the termination of this war lent weight to the impression that the Soviet Union had changed into a status-quo power which, far from seeking to exploit national and social conflicts on its periphery, utilized its power and influence in the opposite direction.

The Iranian outlook toward the international system therefore underwent a number of significant changes in the mid-sixties. The premises of this new outlook were that: (1) the intensity of the bipolar system manifested in the cold war had radically abated; (2) the Soviet Union, though not formally abandoning its world revolutionary aspirations, had become at least a selective status-quo power in terms of its foreseeable objectives toward such countries as Iran and Turkey; (3) U.S. involvement in Southeast Asia, and China's dispute with the Soviet Union, had rendered a large number of bilateral and regional issues far less significant than they were in the mid-fifties.

From these premises the Iranian regime formulated a concrete set of conclusions for its foreign policy, since labeled *Siyasate Mostaghele Melli* [independent national policy]: (1) The cold-war decline rendered a rigid pro-Western posture superfluous, for the West neither needed nor benefited from automatic adherence of its allies to a prescribed position on every international issue. (2) The experiences of Irano-Soviet relations since 1962 meant that the Soviet Union, at least for the foreseeable future, no longer constituted a clear and present danger to the regime's security and existence. (3) The American attitude toward Pakistan during the second Kashmir war, as well as the third

Indo-Pakistan war in 1971, made the diversification of military supply sources indispensable for a more independent foreign policy.

The attraction of these new concepts was due largely to a mood of confidence that the regime manifested in its own ability to cope with internal and even regional threats to its security. Neither the bloody riots of June 1963 nor the assassination of Prime Minister Hassanali Mansur, and an attempt on the life of the Shah himself, two years later, indicated any visible weakening of the regime. Hence, military support from external powers no longer had to be viewed primarily in the context of the regime's survivability. Even the military establishment, which had earlier espoused a policy of pro-Western alliance, chiefly in the hope that it would fulfill the dual aspirations of coping with the Soviet threat and strengthening the army, accepted the logic of the new foreign policy.

However, the need for nonalignment stemmed from new domestic economic and political needs as much as from new external conditions. It was hoped that material economic aid could be obtained from both sides: a Soviet alternative would help relations with the West, just as a Western alternative would help divorce economic ties with the Soviet bloc from political subordination. Furthermore, an independent foreign policy could be presented as inherently nationalistic, since it reduced the dependence of Iran on either of the superpowers. It guaranteed a wider range of choice in terms of satisfying Iran's requirements for military and economic supplies. Diversification of their sources also meant fewer strings attached to them and more freedom in their utilization. Inasmuch as U.S. interest was geared to the maintenance of territorial status quo in the region anyway, Iran's alignment seemed less valid—for any alliance between a superpower and a small one contains an element of subordination, however sincere its intentions.

In effect, postwar Iranian foreign policy has come full circle, from rejection of an alliance policy in the first phase to acceptance in the second, and finally to a de facto nonalignment within the pro-Western alliance that characterizes Iran's contemporary international posture. Throughout this historical evolution Iran's foreign relations have been vulnerable to transformations in the main international system. Some of the transformations have had immediate ramifications for all small states; others have more directly affected a strategically located state such as Iran.

Chief among the more general transformations has been the emergence of many new actors participating fully and independently in a global system. The homogeneous European-centered system has now expanded into a heterogeneous world system. The tight bipolar pattern imposed on international politics by the rivalry of the superpowers at the height of the cold war submerged the impact of these new actors on world politics (except as symbolic allies) and stimulated little scholarly attention to the conduct of their foreign policies. Many of the new actors are also new states (e.g., Pakistan, Israel); some are fragments of older multi-national states (e.g., Turkey, Iraq); some are new entities, aggregations of tribal polities (e.g., Ghana, Nigeria, the Persian Gulf states), or simply large and complex aggregations (e.g., India). Several new actors are "older" states that participated, if at all, only peripherally in international politics in the past, usually as objects of European imperialism (e.g., Iran [Persia], Thailand [Siam], Ethiopia). Some are states that were colonized (Algeria), or controlled or protected by imperial states (Egypt, Morocco). These states range in size and population from India to Mauritius, and share in common the negative attribute of being non-Western states and the disadvantage of being nonindustrial states, for the most part dependent on the export of primary commodities. With the possible exception of India, their "underdeveloped" economies are usually matched by equally underdeveloped bureaucracies and political institutions. There are many differences between the states sometimes vaguely referred to as the "Third World." The presence or absence of a colonial tradition and the geopolitical location of the state, in particular, appear to account for the varying responses of these states to the cold war.

Our focus is on the foreign policy of one non-Western small state which is not a new state, but which shares with many of these states both a history as an object of imperialism and a contemporary condition of underdevelopment. Unlike many of these states, its experience has not been solely with the Western variety of imperialism. There is consequently little disposition for the government in Tehran to succumb to the notion that imperialism is exclusive to any one type of great power. Indeed, the primary and conditioning element of Iran's foreign policy has been its contiguity to the Soviet Union.

THE SINGLE CASE-STUDY APPROACH

Students of international politics have long had to grapple with problems of reconciling the level of analysis. Either they have chosen the wider perspective given by a general systems approach, at the cost of losing the rich detail that comes from single-country studies; or, emphasizing the national level, they have obtained deep insight into the foreign-policy processes of a single state at the expense of a wider overview. The attempt to bridge these levels has led some scholars to suggest that comparative foreign policy may be the necessary link between the two levels, and to argue that the distinction between national and international systems is in any case a false one, given the penetration of most polities in single or multi-issue areas.[1]

This study is concerned with the foreign relations of a single state. It is intended as an analysis of the salient aspects of Iran's foreign relations, with emphasis on tactics, levers, and arguments in a shifting international context.[2] We hope thus to facilitate theorizing about the behavior of a certain category of small states. The dearth of studies on contemporary Iranian foreign policy has necessitated some emphasis and attention to detail, but it is hoped that this has not been at the expense of the analysis.

Not only is there a scarcity of detailed studies on many states, but there still exists no common or generally accepted theoretical framework which is manageable for one student to utilize in a single case study. The author of a recent monograph has concluded that, given this situation, the possibility of comparative analysis

depends less on the use of a common framework than on the willingness of writers of case studies to put their conclusion in the form of general hypotheses, using well-known, loosely defined variables capable of easy translation from one study to the next.[3]

This study will proceed on a similar assumption.

We are also cognizant of James Rosenau's views about individual, role, governmental, societal, and systemic variables which serve as causal agents in foreign affairs.[4] However, operationalizing Rosenau's five sets of variables is extraordinarily difficult in the case of Iran. This is due partly to the type of government system in Iran and partly to the dearth of reliable evidence available for all five sets of variables. Individual, role, and governmental variables are virtually indistinguishable from the Shah as a person and institution. The societal variable is also difficult to discern and weigh, in its nonmaterial

---

[1] James N. Rosenau is one of the prominent scholars in the field. See especially his *The Scientific Study of Foreign Policy* and Rosenau (ed.), *Linkage Politics: Essays on the Convergence of National and International Systems.*

[2] See Rosenau, *Linkage Politics*, p. 75, and *Scientific Study of Foreign Policy*, pp. 77, 100–103.

[3] Franklin B. Weinstein, "The Uses of Foreign Policy in Indonesia: An Approach to the Analysis of Foreign Policy in Less Developed Countries."

[4] Rosenau, *Scientific Study of Foreign Policy*, pp. 108–116. For a useful and comprehensive discussion and outline of relevant variables, see David O. Wilkinson, *Comparative Foreign Relations: Framework and Methods.*

or value manifestation, although it is doubtless partly reflected in the general attitude of the attentive public (which is largely coterminous with the elite). The systemic operational environment is the most easily focused upon. As a result, our primary emphasis in the following chapters is on the content and outcome of foreign policy rather than on the perceptions, motivations, and decision-making process giving rise to it.

The Shah's unique characteristics as an individual, official government roles, and the government structure are inextricably bound together in contemporary Iran. His Imperial Majesty, the Shah, makes every major foreign policy decision and most of the minor ones. No one occupies a public position except at the tolerance of His Majesty, and all are dependent directly or indirectly on the monarch for continuance. There exists no formal policy-making process as that term is understood in the West, nor are there any interest groups, lobbies, associational groups, or mass media that influence the content or conduct of foreign policy. The formal governmental structure has no relevance at all to the content of Iran's foreign policy. Insofar as societal values are known, they serve as general constraints on Iran's foreign relations. This section will attempt to substantiate and enlarge on these assertions.

An American confidant of the Shah, E. A. Bayne, has attested to the monarch's primacy in Iran's foreign policy.

As diplomats in Tehran know, Iranian foreign policy is largely personified in the king. . . . The personal nature of Iranian foreign relations is its chief characteristic, and what the monarch believes is of primary significance.

Nevertheless, the Iranian Foreign Office is not a nonentity in the management of foreign relations, although it must be regarded as an extension of the Shah's personal direction of policy. . . . The Shah is his own foreign minister, his policies deriving from a personal synthesis of diverse views held within the structure of national power.[5]

The present foreign minister recently described his role thus: "I am honored to be executing Iran's foreign policy. The Imperial Government's overall policies are worked out by the Shahanshah. He decides the principles, all the broad outlines. We carry out his policies to the best of our abilities.[6] It is what Bayne calls a "personal synthesis of diverse views held within the structure of national power" that is the most puzzling aspect of decision-making in Iran. One specialist,

---

[5] E. A. Bayne, *Persian Kingship in Transition: Conversations with a Monarch Whose Office Is Traditional and Whose Goal Is Modernization,* pp. 197–199.

[6] Abbas Khalatbari, *Keyhan International,* Sept. 11, 1972.

Marvin Zonis, has written that the Shah's *divide et impera* policy toward the Iranian elite has fractured and discouraged their ability to work together in groups, and that the phenomenon of institutionalized *immobilisme* and the "irrelevance of institutions" has severely curtailed their ability to formally affect policy decisions in Iran.[7]

Less clear is the pattern of informal decision-making that has resulted. Bayne agrees that "position and privilege in the hierarchy depend on the king's favor" and observes that there is a substantial lack of communication between the monarch and the elite. He suggests that this may be partially due to the Shah's "reluctance to share his responsibilities as a decision-maker, a reluctance which is understandable in an Iran where power must be served assiduously by those who hope to survive in a changing society." But Bayne does not elaborate how a "personal synthesis of diverse views held within the structure of national power" is possible in this situation, or how it takes place. Clearly it is not through any policy process so much as through informal contacts with confidants:

Bayne: Who reaches you with the proper information? Who can tell you that something is not working well? Who *dares* to tell you?

H.I.M. the Shah: I have my information sources. And in addition I have my valet. My valet, my gardener—all those people.[8]

Zonis, in his study of the contemporary Iranian political system, has observed:

The system is highly conducive to the avoidance of assuming responsibility for any bureaucratic act. Conflicts are pushed ever higher in the bureaucracy for resolution. . . . One result is a continued reinforcement of the tendencies of the elite to avoid challenging others and the system." [9]

One consequence of this is a diminution in the possibility of any bold, imaginative, or novel suggestions that might serve as useful inputs into the formulation of policy.

Since politics is seen as a zero-sum game in Iran, with self-advancement as the goal, substantive policy suggestions or criticisms of public policy are viewed and evaluated as motivated by personal gain, and treated accordingly. One result is that discussions inside the bureaucracies, including the foreign ministry, are seldom based on facts

---

[7] For a comprehensive discussion of this, see Marvin Zonis, *The Political Elite of Iran*, pp. 191–202, esp. 196–197 *et seq.*; 314–319; *et passim*. See also James Alban Bill, *The Politics of Iran: Groups, Classes and Modernization*, pp. 39–49.

[8] Bayne, *Persian Kingship*, pp. 234–236. (Emphasis in original.)

[9] Zonis, *Political Elite*, pp. 334–335.

or reasoned analysis, and the weight given to a particular view reflects the weight of the person advancing that view.[10] Similarly, to enhance effectiveness frequent references are made to the Shah's speeches and writings. It is hardly surprising, given the political culture, that the foreign ministry's suggestions, when they are elicited by the Palace, tend to be a repetition of His Majesty's last public utterance on the subject.

The foreign ministry is not very different from other bureaucracies. Perhaps because of the *apparent* lack of expertise required in this field (compared to, say, development economics), the Shah has dominated every facet of its activities. Although the members of the ministry are on the whole better educated than their counterparts, the "education" consists mostly of memorization and an emphasis on static principles (often outdated) rather than the dynamics of recent history, modern concepts, or analysis. Since loyalty and longevity are valued over merit and expertise, there has been little incentive until recently to recruit qualified personnel. Like other institutions, it primarily implements policy in whose formulation it had scant participation.[11]

If the role of the executive branch in foreign policy-making is weak, that of the legislature is still weaker. Writing in the early 1960's, when the monarch's role was less solid than it was by the end of the decade, Leonard Binder observed: "Constitutionalism as presently maintained in Iran is a farce." [12] Ann Tibbitts Schultz, a student of the lower house of Iran's parliament, the Majlis, has noted that its power is "far from being significant relative to the power of the Shah and his cabinet," and that loyalty to the Shah is the main factor in the choice of a legislator. The legislature's role is somewhat different from that of a check or balance on the government's *poli-*

---

10 Leonard Binder writes of the non-Western states that one consequence of their attitude toward foreign policy is the "continuation of the presently low incentive to train good diplomats and to give such men important responsibilities. There is, after all, little sense in training men to gather the facts and report on the background of important international issues if the facts do not matter. Area specialists need not be trained if the only countries that count are those visited by contemporary leaders during their school days." Binder, "The New States in International Affairs," p. 206.

11 For comparative figures on education levels in government ministries, see Bill, *Politics of Iran*, p. 64, also p. 105. See also Binder, "New States" pp. 208, 210–211; and *U.S. Army Area Handbook for Iran* (Washington: U.S. Govt. Printing Office; D. A. PAM, Nos. 550–568, 1971), pp. 300–302. The latter describes the foreign ministry as it is thought to function.

12 Leonard Binder, *Iran: Political Development in a Changing Society*, p. 85.

cies: "Because Majlis deputies are primarily chosen by the Shah, efforts of the Majlis to exert control over the government are roughly synonymous to the efforts of the Shah, in cooperation with less powerful groups, to control the established political elite." [13]

Despite the fact that the foreign affairs committee is considered an important one in the Majlis, the legislature's impact on Iran's foreign relations is minimal for a number of reasons: (1) Most policy decisions are made before legislation reaches the Majlis or can be referred to committees. (2) Consultation between a committee and the ministry takes place at the ministry. (3) The ability of the Majlis to contribute constructively is weakened by the committee's lack of resources, personnel, or private sources of information. (4) Floor debate is monopolized by the committee chairman and the relevant ministerial representative. (5) "Debate" generally involves long speeches "directed to an external audience." (6) High turnover in the Majlis' leadership posts "inhibits the development of expertise." (7) Parties in Iran serve as "personal recruitment organizations" rather than aggregates of people agreed on basic principles of public policy or similar philosophy.[14]

The weakness of contemporary political institutions is partly accounted for by Iran's historical experience. The maintenance of Iran's nominal independence in the nineteenth and early twentieth century was at the cost of fracturing and undermining the indigenous institutions, which were thoroughly penetrated by Britain and Russia.[15] The wartime occupation of Iran by the Allies further weakened these institutions, and the postwar world saw a new government, the United States, penetrating Iran's politics on many issue areas. The impact of the U.S. penetration on Iran's political system has been a pervasive and generally acknowledged, though probably declining, fact.[16] There is little concrete evidence as to the impact this penetration

---

13. Ann Tibbitts Schultz, "The Recruitment and Behavior of Iranian Legislators: The Influence of Social Background," (Ph.D. diss., Yale University, 1969), pp. 34–36, 42, 48, 19.

14 *Ibid.,* pp. 205–243.

15 This concept is used in James Rosenau's sense: The existence of a penetrated system is determined by the presence of nonmembers who participate directly in a society's politics and not by their affiliations and responsibilities. A penetrated political system is one in which "nonmembers of a national society participate directly or authoritatively, through actions taken jointly with the society's members, in either the allocation of its values or the mobilization of support on behalf of its goals." *Scientific Study of Foreign Policy,* pp. 130, 127–128.

16 Numerous examples of British and Russian penetration can be found in any

has had on the content of Iran's foreign policy, although it can be hypothesized that its impact on Iran's cold-war posture has been more far-reaching than on its regional foreign policy. The Iranian government's cold-war orientation had a profound impact on Iran's domestic politics in the early 1960's. To the extent that this affected what Rosenau terms the "societal" variable—i.e., its values—it has provided a parameter beyond which the Shah has not lightly ventured.

There is also evidence that the issue of foreign military aid to Iran is frequently perceived by the elite "as not serving the purpose of helping Iran protect itself from foreign aggression but rather as maintaining the power of the regime." [17] The identification of the regime with its foreign mentor, and vice versa, gave Iranian dissidents a convenient method of criticizing the Shah's government by focusing criticism on foreign countries.

This critical attitude toward the regime had two manifestations: criticism of the United States and support for the USSR. Zonis' study is particularly useful in the case of the regime's relationship with the United States. He found a tendency among the elite to "lay responsibility for the major policies of their own government on the United States," and observed that "xenophobia in Iran has far-ranging connotations for domestic politics, connotations that imply dissatisfactions with the contemporary balance of political power within Iran. . . ." He found the better educated, younger members of the elite most actively opposed to "the association of the Shah with foreign governments and the nearly pervasive intervention of foreigners in Iranian affairs."

Dissatisfaction with the regime and criticism of its western patron, the United States, have also been reflected in the attitude of the regime's opponents to the USSR. The communist movement in Iran served as an umbrella for many groups opposed to the regime; it was, in Binder's phrase, a "negative protest party." Thus the foreign power supporting, or identifying with, the regime became a focus of hostility; and the power opposing the regime, a force to support.[18]

---

standard history of Iran. For examples of U.S. penetration since World War II, see Bayne, *Persian Kingship*, pp. 152, 153, 157, 191–196, 202–205; Zonis, *Political Elite*, pp. 294–311, *et passim;* Bill, *Politics of Iran*, pp. 121, 126; Schultz, *Recruitment and Behavior of Iranian Legislators*, p. 26.

17 Zonis, *Political Elite*, pp. 304–325.

18 See Sepehr Zabih, *The Communist Movement in Iran*, pp. 246–247, *et passim;* Binder, *Iran*, p. 328; and Chapter II below.

The impact of Iran's foreign policy is not difficult to discern. The relationship between the regime and its domestic opponents, and the government's attitude toward the U.S. and the USSR, have undoubtedly influenced Iran's foreign policy to the extent that strong opposition to one foreign power has prevented too open or blatant an identification with any one power. It has thus given the Shah every incentive to assume the pose of the supreme nationalist, pursuing an independent, national foreign policy, and to cultivate such societal values as independence, nationalism, and glorification of the Iranian past.

It has also been a steady incentive for the Shah to normalize relations with the USSR—and later, China—to diversify his sources of arms supply, and to balance—at least by visits—the U.S. and the USSR. Values such as the glorification of Iran's "historic role" also in part account for the pursuit of a foreign policy of prestige, and an emphasis on style, over the more difficult and elusive concentration on the quality of foreign policy.[19]

The interaction between discontent with the regime and criticism of its foreign policy has probably been recognized by the regime and used to externalize energy, as a safety-valve. In the early 1960's the National Front was given one seat in the Majlis, although its degree of influence on policy remained limited. In the mid-to-late 1960's, when the Shah had consolidated power, the Pan-Iranist party, a right-wing party with claims to an authentic nationalist ideology and expansionist in its foreign policy goals, particularly in the Persian Gulf, was permitted in the Majlis. Its right-wing foreign policy goals were tolerated by the government (until 1970), but on domestic issues "the Pan-Iranists follow the other . . . parties in trying to be the party most closely identified with the 'Shah-People Revolution.' " [20] The displacement of political energy on foreign policy has been permitted, but it should not be viewed as a *constraint* on the leadership's ability to follow its own foreign policy goals. To the extent that the Pan-Iranists and other groups became constraints on specific issues of Iran's foreign policy in the late 1960's (e.g., on Bahrayn and the Gulf islands), it was at the sufferance of the government. It is essential to establish time boundaries when discussing the Shah's control of for-

---

19 Binder briefly alludes to the relationship among "certain domestic problems," "keeping up a nationalist front," "prestige," and Iran's "international claims." *Iran*, p. 331. For a discussion of quality in foreign policy, see Wilkinson, *Comparative Foreign Relations*, pp. 21–22.

20 Schultz, *Recruitment and Behavior*, pp. 117, 123.

eign policy. During the 1953–1963 period, when the monarch's position was weak and the cold war was as its height, the Shah was both
more vulnerable to nationalist attacks and more dependent on the
United States. The consolidation of the Shah's position since 1963 has
coincided with a decline in the intensity of the cold war, an improvement in relations with the USSR, rapid growth in Iran's economy,
and an increasing salience in regional issues, all of which gave the
Shah increased latitude in handling foreign policy. This is particularly true in regional affairs, which have not had the domestic political connotations associated with Iran's cold-war orientation.[21]

If the basic orientations of the elite, or society's values, have provided a general but declining constraint on the Shah's management
of foreign policy, this is scarcely a quantifiable variable. More concrete limitations have been imposed by budgetary constraints, the
requirements of development, the balance of foreign trade, and dependence on foreign sources for weapons, training, spare parts, and
credit. And these in turn have partly revolved around the availability
of trained manpower and its ability to assimilate these weapons. The
United States' earlier advocacy of "restraint" in arms purchases (see
Chapter II), in addition to material and manpower constraints, has
also constituted a further influence on Iran's foreign policy, to the
extent that it has shaped military capabilities.

As observed above, formal political institutions are weak, and group
activity discouraged, in contemporary Iran. As a result personal and
informal politics prevail. It is difficult to assess the degree of influence
of nonassociational groups (families), or informal groups of friends
[dowreh], on the making of Iran's foreign policy decisions. It is known
that the Shah makes many decisions after informally and privately
consulting with various confidants. But the nature of evidence available on the systematic inputs into the formulation of foreign policy
is anecdotal and noncumulative.[22] The Shah meets with the State
Security Agency (SAVAK), foreign ambassadors, personal envoys, confidants, members of the armed forces, the prime minister and cabinet
and a skeletal cabinet known as the High Economic Council.[23] But

---

21 For some pertinent comments on the orientation of the elite toward Europe and
the United States and the lack of contact with Islamic countries, see Zonis, *Political
Elite*, pp. 185–186, 149–150.

22 The sorts of questions one would pose in a comprehensive study of decision-
making which are discussed in Wilkinson, *Comparative Foreign Relations*, pp. 101–
134, cannot easily be answered in a system of informal and secretive politics.

23 For an imaginative attempt to conceptualize the informal, nonhierarchical
"Pahlavi web-system" of politics, see Bill, *Politics of Iran*, pp. 39–49.

it is not known to what degree any or all of these, or other sources, are consistently influential in the making of foreign policy. In the absence of detailed studies of decision-making in Iran, the key concept in regard to influence over the monarch is the degree of "access" to the Shah enjoyed by officials.

In the past an extraordinary dependence on foreigners, particularly the American and British ambassadors, was maintained. In the perennial dispute between the monarch and strong prime ministers of the pre-1953 era such as Ali Soheili, Ahmad Ghavan, and Mohammad Mossadegh, the question of direct access of foreign diplomats to the Shah proved a thorny problem. After a successful struggle with the Shah on the issue of control of the ministry of defense, Dr. Mossadegh was urged by some of his more extremist associates to emulate the British practice and restrict the Shah's foreign diplomat contacts by requiring approval of the prime minister and the presence of the foreign minister at all audiences with the monarch.[24]

Whether this persists to date is not as important as the belief of some members of the elite that these persons are highly influential with the Shah. Thus "consultations," "suggestions," and "advice" from these sources are construed by many Iranian diplomats as serious and authoritative. The influence or "pressure" which a superpower exerts merely by making its own interest on a subject evident should not therefore be underestimated in the Iranian political context. Similarly, the pervasive influence, or perceived pervasive influence, of these states, and their penetration of Iran's political system, results in attempts by the elite, including members of the diplomatic service, not only "to build their own networks of influence domestically but also to build international ties and support." [25]

It is thus the assumption of this study that no interest groups exist on foreign policy, and that the Shah is free to formulate foreign policy decisions within a general and broad consensus, and does so. This foreign policy consensus, an aspect of Rosenau's societal variable, is characterized by emphasis on "independence," "nationalism," "development," and glorification of Iran's past. There are thus no specific interest groups concerned with specific foreign policy decisions *per se*.

Insofar as the elite, including the military, is materially rewarded and assured the possibility of personal advancement, the country's affairs are not hopelessly mismanaged. Insofar as the Shah does not depart too drastically from the general consensus, he is free to pursue

---

24 *Bakhtare-Emruz*, Teheran, July 19, 1952.
25 The quote is from Bill, *Politics of Iran*, p. 44.

policies of his own choosing. This, it must be reiterated, more accurately describes affairs at the end of the 1960's than at their beginning. It is likely to remain true for the immediate future, for the Shah
has largely managed to depoliticize foreign policy. Politics, to the
extent that it exists at all in its original sense in Iran internally, now
ceases at the water's edge.

THE IMPACT OF DOMESTIC POLITICS
ON FOREIGN POLICY

It is our contention that the roles of the foreign ministry, legislature,
and other institutions have been marginal in the formulation of
Iranian foreign policy; that there exist no parties, groups, associa-
tions, lobbies, or interest groups that are influential in this area of
decision-making; that there is no routinized or formal policy process,
with bureaucracies competing; and that there is no public debate
of alternative policies. Indeed, there is no easily identifiable, systematic source of input into foreign policy decision-making. It is recognized that the Shah is the sole and ultimate source of decisions affecting foreign policy, in all its manifestations. It was noted that the
penetration of Iran's political system and the interrelationship between domestic politics and foreign alignment have diminished in
the course of the decade, although the influence of the West, and
particularly the United States, remains pervasive in Iran's politics.
It is thus contended that in Iran, Rosenau's "individual," "role," and
"governmental" variables are to all intents and purposes the same—an
extension of the Shah's will.

The only objective internal constraints operating on the Shah's
control of foreign policy are the limitations on the country's material and manpower capabilities, and the more general foreign policy
consensus, both of which correspond to Rosenau's "societal" variable.
Our principal emphasis in this study on the operational environment
(Rosenau's "systemic" variable) and on policy outcomes is to a large
degree dictated by the absence of cumulative data on how foreign
policy decisions are made in Iran, and a reluctance to assay a psychological study of the leadership in Iran—something for which we are
not, in any case, equipped.

Nevertheless, a brief discussion of the impact of the type of decision-making system on the substance of policy is needed. In short,
we seek to answer the question: What difference does it make to the
style and *substance* of policy that decisions are made in the way they
are? It was earlier suggested that the intensity of Iran's concern with

foreign policy puts it into a particular category of small states. Iran shares with other nonindustrial states the underdevelopment of institutions, particularly bureaucracies, but differs from many in the relative insulation of foreign policy decision-making from domestic concerns or accountability.

Raymond Aron has suggested that the foreign policy of new states is largely a function of their leadership's preferences: "The diplomatic line followed by the governments of these new states depends almost exclusively on the preferences of the man (or at the very most, of the few men) in control of the majority party or the single party." [26] In many African cases this is doubtless true, and Zartman has ably documented decision-making in states possessing "institutionalized-charismatic" political leadership, in a manner strikingly analogous to the situation in Iran.[27] In several African countries, however, internal political considerations have influenced—but not necessarily determined—foreign policy. Morocco's temporary sinistristic movement in foreign policy between 1960 and 1962, and a similar movement in Ghana in 1962, are two examples. Similarly, in post-independence Nigeria domestic politics in the early 1960's naturally influenced foreign policy.[28] In nondemocratic Algeria foreign policy became not a "seductive diversion," but rather an integral part of a search for identity; Algeria's first orientation in world politics was thus an extension of its domestic experience.[29]

States where the leadership or small elite who control foreign policy is insulated from direct domestic pressures and public accountability are frequently dependent on the military, or a faction thereof, which usually works in a committee or clique. The military in these instances may have civilian front-men, but reserve for themselves the final say in foreign policy decisions (Egypt, Iraq, and Pakistan at various times fall into this category). Iran is unlike either category, in that its foreign policy is accountable neither to the populace nor

---

26 Raymond Aron, *Peace and War: A Theory of International Relations,* pp. 511–512.

27 I. William Zartman, *International Relations in the New Africa,* pp. 65–66; see also Vernon McKay (ed.), *African Diplomacy: Studies in the Determinants of Foreign Policy.*

28 For Morocco, see McKay, *African Diplomacy,* p. 39n.; Zartman, *International Relations in the New Africa,* p. 28; Doudou Thiam, *The Foreign Policy of African States,* p. XI. For Ghana, see Scott Thompson, *Ghana's Foreign Policy, 1957–1966: Diplomacy, Ideology, and the New State,* pp. 198–200; for Nigeria, see Claude S. Phillips, Jr., *The Development of Nigerian Foreign Policy,* pp. 62–87.

29 Robert Amsden Mortimer, "Foreign Policy and Its Role in Nation-Building in Algeria" (Ph.D. diss., Columbia University, 1968), pp. 2–3, 338–344, *et passim.*

to any particular group such as the military. The relative freedom of foreign policy decisions from public pressure may have a substantial impact on the substance and quality of decisions made, but it certainly affects decisional style. Several tentative hypotheses on this relationship are advanced below.[30] They are taken up again briefly in our conclusion, in the light of our findings in the intervening chapters.

1. Where foreign policy is personal, it will reflect the leader's perceptions and values and tend to be as stable as the leadership's tenure and as consistent as its views.

2. Foreign policy in this type of state will be both *less* adaptable, because the leader's prestige will be at stake, and *more* adaptable, because no need to "educate" the populace exists.

3. When controlled by one person, foreign policy will tend to project that person's temperament. It will tend to view other systems of government as "personal," and to equate personal slights with insults to the state and personal antipathy with national rivalry.

4. When the personal control of foreign policy is paralleled by domination of internal affairs, there will be the temptation to use the former to enhance the leadership's prestige internationally in order to legitimize and bolster its domestic standing.[31]

5. Given its predilection to respond to the leader's priorities, this type of system will retard the professionalization of foreign policy and discourage the development of expertise and the recruitment of talented personnel.

6. Where foreign and military policy are dominated by the same person, the normal "fire-breaks," or gaps on the continuum between pure diplomacy and pure coercion, will tend to merge, with the result that resort to the latter will come sooner than in systems where some real administrative separation is made.

7. Since there is no routinization of foreign policy-making, no

---

30 For some general hypotheses along these lines, see Wilkinson, *Comparative Foreign Relations*, pp. 78–83, 95–97, 102–112.

31 Bayne writes: "The image of a king can be enhanced domestically as well as internationally by open public notice—his personality being a symbol of the nation itself." *Persian Kingship*, p. 201. A confusion between the analytically separable interests of a leadership and that of a nation is evident here. It cannot be a scholarly assumption that what is good for the ruler is *ipso facto* good for the nation. Rather, the contention needs to be proven. Another source suggests that: "If a political group has virtually unchallenged control, it may see little need to use foreign policy to legitimize political demands it can easily fulfill." Weinstein, "The Uses of Foreign Policy in Indonesia," p. 373.

formalized foreign policy process, there will be no institutionalized feedback to facilitate and encourage a learning process by
the leadership so that future foreign policy can be adapted and
modified, and if necessary be made more congruent with "reality"
in the operational environment.

In this study our focus is on the critical aspects of Iran's foreign
policy in modern times. We attempt to illuminate its behavior as a
nonindustrial, non-Western small state which because of its contiguity
to a superpower is characterized by an intense interest in foreign
relations. We have advanced certain hypotheses concerning the impact of the mode of decision-making on foreign policy, given its
noncompetitive political system and the centralization of decision-
making powers. We have attempted to frame our data in a manner
conducive to theorizing about a certain category of small states and
to facilitating the comparison of foreign policy.

Our assumption has been that the examination of a period of recent
history need not result in a merely topical account of the recent past.
Rather, we believe that the value of a contemporary study might prove
superior to a traditional historical study, particularly given the absence of any rules regarding access to archives in Iran, and the unreliability of the documents that are likely to be preserved, in any
case.[32]

Because of Iran's relative institutional weaknesses, no detailed
analysis of the decision-making process will be attempted. Field work
on several occasions made it apparent that most of the available evidence on this issue was anecdotal in nature: useful for particular decisions, but not additive in the sense of contributing to a theory of
decision-making. Hence a general theoretical statement at the outset
would have to suffice, and our focus would be centered on the *outcome*
of decisions rather than their formulation.

In the course of our research we found that particularly after 1963–
64 there have been very few independent comments, editorials, and
analyses of foreign policy in the Iranian press, news magazines, or
books.[33] Where discussions of foreign policy occur, they are remark-

---

[32] It is also our assumption that there is a reasonable trade-off between the information obtained in interviews, which permit a contemporary study, and the
benefits of archival material, which must sacrifice any contemporary relevance. For
a discussion of participant-historians, see Arthur Schlesinger, Jr., "The Historian as
Participant."

[33] For an exception, see the criticism of the privileged position of the military
in *Tehran Journal* (editorial), Dec. 2, 1963.

ably similar in content and timing, strengthening the presumption that they, at least, reflect the government's views. The Iranian press is thus used as an indicator of the government's views on foreign relations. Parallel to this, our assumption is that the Shah has made every foreign policy decision of any moment since the late 1950's. Our references to leadership, regime, government, and policy-makers are thus essentially synonyms for His Majesty, employed to avoid repetition; but they also reflect the absence of data as to the sources from which His Majesty obtains his information.

We have approached Iran's foreign relations on two levels, the international and the regional. On the first level it is a small power, and we analyze its relations with the two superpowers (Chapters I and II) in terms of opportunities provided it by the international context; its use of tactics, levers, and arguments in its diplomacy; and the triangular relationships with the superpowers in bargaining for political support and weaponry. We note the differing perspectives of the superpowers and the small power, the specificity of power (i.e., the excess of unusable power which cannot be converted into influence), and the power of the weak. The penetration of Iran's political system by the United States in many areas, and Iran's success in obtaining America weapons, is also examined. The relationship between the small client and the giant patron, the domestic implications of Iran's alignment policy as well as the resultant complications in Iran-USSR relations, constitute other areas of inquiry. Particular emphasis is placed on the shifting configuration of international politics (the permissive context on which the small state is so vitally dependent) and an assessment of the degree of Iran's success or failure in using this context to enhance its power.

In the Middle East subsystem, Iran is a major rather than small power. Here, as throughout the study, we focus on the opportunities provided Iran's diplomacy by the international political context, and on Iran's tactics, arguments, and means of influence. Important secondary and tertiary emphases are placed on the constraints operating on Iran's diplomacy which arise from intra-Arab politics and on the degree of Iran's success in comprehending the forces at work in Arab politics. Egypt and Iraq are considered in this section; Egypt is viewed, until the late sixties, as a regional rival, Iraq as a hostile neighbor (Chapters III and IV).

More recently the regional context has shifted toward the Persian Gulf, where Iran is clearly emerging as a dominant power. The evolution of its diplomacy is examined against the background of a changing international context and in the light of its military capabilities, which have increased as the decade progressed (Chapters V and VI). With Britain's withdrawal from the region, the quest for a new security arrangement became the chief concern of both regional and extraregional powers with economic and strategic interests in the Gulf. This is considered in Chapters VII and VIII from the perspective of littoral as well as nonlittoral states. The growing competitive relationship among oil-producing countries has made oil diplomacy an integral part of Persian Gulf politics. Chapter IX investigates the scope and limitations of Iran's ability to evolve a consistent policy in this matter. In a short general conclusion, Chapter X assesses the success of Iran's diplomacy, especially in its third postwar phase since the early 1960's. A final chapter provides a postscript to the evolution of various aspects of Iran's foreign relations in the period since the completion of the bulk of this study.

Part One

THE INTERNATIONAL LEVEL

PROLOGUE

On the international level Iran is a small power contiguous to one of the superpowers. Because these attributes have determined its foreign relations with both superpowers, we should gain an understanding of their ramifications before presenting an analysis of the substance of these relations. The value of ranking states in terms of their power rests in clarifying and illuminating the behavior of states in this category in international politics or in assessing the impact of this group of states on international politics.

If the analyst takes a global or systemic view, ranking states according to gross national product, population, and other tangible indices will give a broad reading of general capability but little insight into a specific context. Hence it will not be heuristic to state behavior. Similarly, a broad ranking of states into general classifications (e.g., great, medium, small) which takes no account of geopolitical and regional environments is of little value. Small powers, it is generally agreed, have limited capabilities and usually have only regional interests. Yet clearly there are differences in the behavior of states similar in power ranking which are situated in quite different regions. (Nigeria is a great power in Africa but would look smaller bordering the U.S. or the USSR.)

Moreover, a small power on one range of issues may be a great one in other areas (e.g., Norway in maritime power, Kuwait and Libya in matters relating to international stability of currencies).

David Vital has suggested that a small state is one which has a gross national product of $300 per capita or more and a population between 10 and 15 million, or a GNP of $300 per capita or less and a population of 20 to 30 million.[1] By this definition Iran, with a GNP of approximately $675 per capita and a population of 32 million, has emerged from small-power status in the past decade; but it is doubtful whether this is of much explanatory value or will generate much in the way of fruitful theorizing about Iran's foreign policy behavior, or its security perceptions. Other scholars have emphasized economic, political, and prestige status, have sought to quantify these with appropriate indices, and have offered other figures for classifying state ranking.[2] It is not our intention to offer a definition of small states in general or to join the debate about the value of any particular definition.

Hedley Bull, in reviewing Vital's book, observed that "the question which is left in one's mind is whether, however viable the small state might be in international politics, it really represents a viable subject of study." [3] Bull's query is a pertinent one, particularly since by most criteria there are well over 100 (perhaps 120) states which can be so defined. Whether these states can be said to act differently from other states, but sufficiently like one another, to be worth theorizing about, appears dubious. One solution is to question whether there are not differences *between* the small states (industrial, nonindustrial, European, non-Western, etc.) which distinguish their behavior from others. William Paterson's comment on Vital's book makes this point succinctly: "Vital's failure to establish a class of small states obviously distinct in their external relations from other states weakens the whole book." [4] Vital's definition and analysis rests on a discussion of a truly rare and unusual class of small states which he fails to identify. In attempting to generalize Vital's prototype, the analyst is immediately faced with the problem of translation into a different geopolitical context.

Robert Rothstein has taken a more rewarding road. In rejecting objective or tangible criteria for the definition of small powers in general, he has concentrated on the subjective-psychological dimen-

---

1 David Vital, *The Inequality of States*, pp. 8, 53.

2 See Raima Väyrynen, "On the Definition and Measurement of Small Power Status," and citations therein; Jean-Luc Vellut, "Smaller States and the Problem of War and Peace: Some Consequences of the Emergence of Smaller States in Africa"; Michael Brecher, Blema Steinberg, and Janice Stein, "A Framework for Research on Foreign Policy Behavior," p. 90n.; and August Schou and Arne Olav Brundtland (eds.), *Small States in International Relations*.

3 Hedley Bull, "Force in Contemporary International Relations," p. 302.

4 William E. Paterson, "Small States in International Politics," p. 123.

sion—which results, in his view, in behavioral patterns that distinguish them from other states.

A Small Power is a state which recognizes that it cannot obtain security primarily by use of its own capabilities, and that it must rely fundamentally on the aid of other states, institutions, processes, or developments to do so; the Small Power's belief in its inability to do so must also be recognized by the other states involved in international politics.[5]

Rothstein is concerned *only* with a limited category of small powers, those that "feel they are potentially or actually threatened by the policies of the Great Powers"—that is, those states which are within an area of great-power confrontation "or which fear that confrontation will affect their interests significantly." Thus Rothstein focuses on a particular category of small powers and their security dilemma, and in this context views the unaligned state as an exception and the state involved in some form of alliance as the norm.[6] The bulk of Rothstein's empirical analysis is centered on the European small states since 1815. Like Annette Baker Fox's pioneering study of the wartime diplomacy of several European small states, *The Power of Small States* (1959), Rothstein is concerned with the behavior of the lesser units in an arena and context of rivalry and confrontation. Today Western Europe is a security community, and the foreign policy of these European small powers is conditioned by the assumption that war *within* this zone of peace is unlikely.

The singular value of the Fox-Rothstein approach to the identification of small states is that it places their foreign and security policy into a meaningful geopolitical context and distinguishes among small states by the kind of security problem they face. It distinguishes, in short, between states that are isolated or peripheral and those that are in some way involved as objects of great-power interest. Mrs. Fox has put it thus:

There are some small states which are scarcely considered at all by the great-power governments, since they are outside the arena of world politics. There are others at the focus of great-power rivalry. The remainder lie somewhere along the continuum of power between those of no concern to any great power and those of crucial importance to more than one, at least momentarily.

---

[5] Robert L. Rothstein, *Alliances and Small Powers*, pp. 27–29. For a similar definition by Annette Baker Fox, see "The Small States in the International System, 1919–1969," pp. 751–752n.
[6] See Rothstein, *Alliances and Small Powers*, pp. 4, 8, 34.

Toward the weak end of the continuum are the small states so far inside the orbit of one of the great powers that their position is seldom actively disputed. The small state in which one and only one great power is greatly interested is in a precarious position. The small states with which two or more great powers are concerned would superficially appear to be in greater danger, but the very danger provides the opportunity for its diplomacy.[7]

Apart from the international context and the dominant rivalry of the day, the state's geopolitical fatality assumes importance. As Erling Bjøl has noted: "It makes a lot of difference whether a country is an immediate neighbor of the Soviet Union, like Poland or Hungary, or whether it is at a comfortable distance from it, like Albania." [8] (Although it cannot be denied that technology can alter or modify the impact and significance of geography and terrain, it remains in many respects unalterable.) The strategic significance, as well as the implications of being small, vary for Zambia, Chad, Nicaragua, Panama, Iran, Burma, and Finland. The consequences of a failure in foreign policy for differently situated small states also varies, and this difference accounts for the greater or lesser emphases put on foreign policy by the various small states.[9]

To be useful, a study of the foreign policy of a small state should distinguish *externally* between the category of small state being examined, its strategic significance in the contemporary international system, the setting of its diplomacy (peace or war), the type of international system (multipolar, tripolar, bipolar), its geographic location, its status as an industrial or nonindustrial state (its material capability; contrast Switzerland and Iran), and the tactics and levers it employs in its diplomacy. Mrs. Fox found that in the wartime diplomacy of several European states, "at any given time, the small state's good fortune was in proportion to the number of great powers with differing demands which were interested in its actions and

---

7 Annette Baker Fox, "Small State Diplomacy," p. 344. This contention is ably documented in Mrs. Fox's book *The Power of Small States; Diplomacy in World War II.*

8 Erling Bjøl, "The Power of the Weak," p. 158; Bjøl, "The Small State in International Politics," in Schou and Brundtland (eds.), *Small States,* pp. 30–37.

9 Gustavo Lagos has suggested a typology for the foreign policy posture of underdeveloped states: (1) Countries that exercise power on a local scale with participants of equal or similar capacity; (2) those that exercise "power politics" as influence on a world scale, when the international context so allows; (3) those that aspire to become world, great, or middle powers; (4) those that renounce power politics even on a local scale (e.g., Costa Rica). Clearly 1, 2, and 3 are not mutually exclusive, and may be logical steps taken as power increases. See Lagos' *International Stratification and Underdeveloped Countries,* pp. 97–110.

able to express their interest by practical means." Vital and Rothstein agree with Mrs. Fox that great-power competition is the condition of small-power influence.[10]

The strategically significant small state is thus hyperdependent on the international environment; and because of its limited resources, it is able to influence that context only marginally. More positively, the power configuration in the international system, and the pattern of its dominant rivalries, provides the politically relevant small state with greater or lesser ability to maneuver diplomatically, to enhance its security, preserve its independence, and pursue its other values. Taking Rothstein's category of small powers in a zone of great-power confrontation, or in a zone susceptible to its effects, and recalling the small margin for error in the foreign policy of such states, it is evident that this category of small states will be distinguished by the intensity of their interest in, and the primacy of, their foreign policy.

Unlike the new states of Africa which can afford to approach foreign policy—which was for many of them a *tabula rasa*[11]— slowly, abstractly, and methodically, the small state contiguous with or in close proximity to a predatory great power, or a zone of great-power interaction, can afford no such luxury. Our focus is on the foreign policy of one such state, and is based on the following assumptions: (1) The foreign policies of the non-Western small states in general is an important and still relatively neglected area of study in international politics.[12] (2) Following Fox and Rothstein, that the diplomacy, tactics, and international behavior of a class or category of small states in a zone of great-power rivalry (which differentiates both their interest and their opportunities in foreign policy from other small states) is susceptible to comparative analysis. (3) That an

---

10 The quote is from Mrs. Fox's "Small State Diplomacy," p. 349. This critical and basic point is repeated, *ibid.*, p. 360, and developed in *The Power of Small States*, pp. 180–188, *et passim*. Rothstein too emphasizes the importance of the configuration of the international system for small-power opportunities in *Alliances and Small Powers*, p. 237, *et passim;* see also Vital, *The Inequality of States*, pp. 190–191.

11 See Claude S. Phillips, Jr., *The Development of Nigerian Foreign Policy*, pp. 4–13, *et passim*.

12 Gabriel Almond wrote in 1958: "It is perhaps as important for us today to know about the conduct and content of Turkish, Egyptian, Indonesian, and Burmese foreign policy as it is to know about that of France, Italy, and Germany." Almond, "The Comparative Study of Foreign Policy," in Roy C. Macridis (ed.), *Foreign Policy in World Politics*, 1st ed., p. 2. Macridis apparently did not share his view. In the fourth edition of this work (1972) only India, China, and Japan, of the non-Western states, are represented, all of which qualify as potential or actual great powers.

assessment of their impact singly or collectively on the international system requires more detailed case studies of the individual states' foreign policies[13]—studies which should be presented in a manner designed to facilitate theorizing.

Annette Baker Fox's study on the European small states has provided us with a useful inventory of tactics, arguments, levers, and the use of contextual opportunities employed by various industrial small states in a time of war. The degree of their success in correctly appraising the international context and maneuvering to take advantage of it has been ably documented.[14] Similarly, Ernest Stock has documented Israel's instruments of influence in its relations with the great powers, and has appraised the degree of its success. We suggest that there exists "a negative correlation between the newness of states and the rationality of their leadership." [15]

Another author, Elie Kedourie, a specialist on the Middle East, avers that: "The concepts . . . of international law and practice which have been current for centuries in the Christian West, concepts such as the concert of the powers, the comity of nations, or the sanctity of treaties, the rules of natural justice, or 'decent respect for the opinions of mankind,' are quite alien and largely unintelligible to the Middle East." [16] Unfortunately we are not told what impact this has either on the foreign relations of Middle Eastern states or on international politics in general. In the absence of detailed case studies of the foreign policies of states in the area, comments such as these are likely to remain as facile to make as they are to dismiss. Case studies leading to regional comparisons, or cross-regional comparisons between similar types of states, may yield more fruitful hypotheses for study.

Following Rothstein, we contend that the small states with interesting security dilemmas are those either situated adjacent or in close proximity to a great power, or which find themselves in an arena

---

13 Paterson has written: "What is needed now is not another general work . . . but much more intensive work on the foreign policies of individual small states, which might lead to more tenable generalizations." "Small States in International Politics," p. 123.

14 Fox, *The Power of Small States.*

15 Ernest Stock, "Israel on the Road to Sinai: A Small State in a Test of Power" (Ph.D. diss., Columbia University, 1967). Israel's tactics are outlined on pp. 137–138, 163; the quotation is from p. 224. This dissertation was published in a modified form as *Israel on the Road to Sinai, 1945–1956, with a Sequel on the Six-Day War, 1967;* Israel's tactics are outlined here on pp. 127–144.

16 Elie Kedourie, *The Chatham House Version and Other Middle Eastern Studies,* p. 11.

of great-power rivalry. Our focus is on the former class of small state. It may well be that the similar geopolitical environments of Finland, Turkey, Iran, Afghanistan, and Burma are more directly comparable than those of Iran, Iraq, and Egypt.

Certainly there are notable similarities. Burma and Afghanistan as poor, landlocked states have opted for the role of neutralist or non-aligned buffer states, deferential but correct in their attitudes toward their respective great-power neighbors. This posture has not prevented Afghanistan from maneuvering with China, or Burma from adhering to a strictly neutralist and independent line on issues of considerable importance to China.[17] Nonetheless, the 1500-mile frontier with China has profoundly influenced Burma's attitude. William Johnstone reports a Burmese politician's remark: "Back of all our public statements about 'nonalignment,' 'friendship with all countries,' 'positive neutralism,' and the like, is a constant awareness of our big and powerful neighbor to the north."[18] Johnstone observed that Burma's location contiguous to China involves "special considerations" which set it apart from other ex-colonial countries such as Ghana. He noted that Burma's limited resources had provided little inducement to foreign predators in the past, but in 1962 he was fearful and pessimistic about Burma's future, viewing Burma as nearly trapped into a "status of dependency" on China.[19] Burma has either curbed or repressed Chinese instruments of influence within its boundaries. Its ability to do this with impunity appears to be connected with its readiness to accommodate, and defer to, China's major interest—that is, China's sensitivity to the influence of other states in adjacent Burma.[20]

Deference and sensitivity toward the strategic interests of an adjoining great power is a hallmark of one type in the category of small states with which we are concerned. Burma has made a border agreement and nonaggression pact with China, under which "each contracting party undertakes not to carry out acts of aggression against the other and *not to take part in any military alliance against the other contracting party.*"[21] Like Burma, Finland, on the other end of the Eurasian land-mass, has chosen a security posture which de-

---

17 See Zubeida Hasan, "The Foreign Policy of Afghanistan," and Robert Alexander Holmes, "Chinese Foreign Policy Toward Burma and Cambodia: A Comparative Exploratory Study" (Ph.D. diss., Columbia University, 1969), pp. 237–390.

18 William C. Johnstone, *Burma's Foreign Policy: A Study in Neutralism,* p. 158.

19 *Ibid.,* pp. 276–278, 288, 294.

20 *Ibid.,* pp. 402–404.

21 *Ibid.,* p. 96.

pends more on its neighboring great power's goodwill and self-interest than on its own ability to maneuver or defend its independence. Under a treaty of friendship, cooperation, and mutual assistance, signed April 6, 1948, Finland is obligated to repel an attack from Germany, or her allies, on the Soviet Union via Finnish territory.[22] While the treaty obligates Finland to do only what any neutral is required to do, it clearly reflects an imbalance in Finland's security posture in that it sets down in an international treaty one particular set of obligations in relation to *one* great power.[23] The decision to accommodate or adapt to the interests of the neighboring great power may be coolly realistic, reflecting a reasoned understanding of historical and geographic limitations and an appraisal that the great power will be satisfied with such an accommodation and desist from pressing for satellite status.

Afghanistan, though perhaps less penetrated by the USSR, is no less dependent. Again the Soviet threat to incorporate it has never assumed great proportions, and as a buffer state it appears to satisfy Moscow's interests. The Soviet's goodwill is particularly important to this landlocked country for the transit routes it provides, and for the indirect and implicit support it would receive if its differences with Pakistan ever assumed conflict proportions.

In contrast, Turkey and Iran have not chosen deferential postures vis-à-vis the USSR. These states have not had similar historical experiences to those of Burma, Finland, and Afghanistan, and thus have not distilled similar conclusions from the past. Quite the contrary; the enfeebled Ottoman Empire was able to prolong its existence only as a result of the keen rivalry between the European great powers, and to resist their pressures by playing them off against one another. The principal and proximate threat to its existence was Russia; and the lingering "Eastern Question" of the nineteenth century, no less than the First World War, testified to the danger from that quarter.

In March 1945 the USSR denounced a 1921 treaty of friendship with Turkey and laid claim to parts of eastern Turkey (the provinces of Kars and Ardahan, which it had ceded in 1921). In August 1946 it demanded revision, by the Black Sea Powers alone, of the Montreaux Conventions of 1936 governing the Turkish Straits. Turkey joined the North Atlantic Treaty Organization in 1951, becoming a full member on February 18, 1952. Dankwart Rustow has noted

---

22 For the text of the treaty, see Anatole G. Mazour, *Finland Between East and West*, pp. 280–282.
23 For a good discussion, see Krister Wählback, "Finnish Foreign Policy: Some Comparative Perspectives," and Rolf Torngren, "The Neutrality of Finland."

that this experience gave Turkey's foreign policy great importance: "The primacy of external over internal policy can be strikingly illustrated from both the early and the more recent history of the Turkish Republic, and nothing perhaps contrasts more sharply with the situation among Turkey's Arab neighbors, where internal upheavals have time and again altered the course of foreign policy." [24] Turkey thus chose a policy of alignment with the United States over a posture of accommodation with the USSR.

Like the Ottoman Empire, nineteenth-century Persia was subject to pressure from its northern neighbor. When Britain was prepared to balance Russia, Persia's independence was secure. When Britain and Russia reached an accommodation (as in 1907), it was at the expense of Persia's sovereignty. So great was the degree of Russian and British penetration of Persia, that Iranian acceptance of the 1921 treaty giving the USSR the right to send Soviet troops into the country if a third power intervened was considered as a limitation on Russia's hitherto unregulated intrusion.[25] After the USSR exerted pressure on Iran in the post-Second World War period, the government, like its counterpart in Turkey, chose to entrust its security to alignment with a distant power rather than to rely on the limited objectives of its great-power neighbor. Unlike Afghanistan, both states possessed considerable value to the USSR—for their strategic locations, their outlets to the sea and, in the case of Iran, for its oil resources.

Thailand, like Turkey and Iran, a non-Western but not a new state, also opted for alignment with the West. Donald Neuchterlain, in an examination of three small states in alliance with the West (Thailand in SEATO, Iceland in NATO, and Australia in ANZUS), concluded that the alignment postures were the result of: (1) the failure of a previously followed neutrality policy; (2) the absence of a colonial tradition; (3) agreement between the small state and the great-power protector on the nature of the primary threat; and (4) the great power's willingness to employ its military strength to deter, or if necessary defeat, the common enemy, which is crucial to a small state's continued support for the alliance.[26] As we shall attempt to demonstrate, very similar conditions have determined the evolution of Iran's relations with both superpowers since the end of World War II.

---

24 Dankwart A. Rustow, "Foreign Policy of the Turkish Republic," p. 317.

25 See Firuz Kazemzadeh, "The West and the Middle East." For an extended discussion and citations, see Chapter II below.

26 Donald E. Neuchterlain, "Small States in Alliances: Iceland, Thailand, Australia."

Chapter I

RELATIONS WITH THE
SOVIET UNION

The Soviet Union's continued occupation and intervention during the closing phase of World War II presented a clear and present danger to Iran's sovereignty which determined foreign policy priorities. The primary objective was to liquidate the consequences of the war occupation, for the presence of Soviet troops provided it with a formidable lever of pressure that severely restricted Iranian options in foreign policy. This crisis of the survival of Iranian independence is generally considered as the genesis of the cold war and confrontation in this part of the Middle East. We begin this chapter with an analysis of those characteristics of Soviet-Iranian relations between 1944 and 1947 which radically differed from Iran's experience in the pre-1917 and post-1953 eras. These differences stemmed from both the international contexts and internal political situations.

Unlike the period at the end of the nineteenth and the early twentieth century, the international configuration of power relationships among the major interested European states had changed. The nearly equal dispersion of power among four or five European powers had now been replaced by a bipolar system. This meant that the traditional quest for a third protecting power to contain British and Russian infringements on Iranian sovereignty could no longer be undertaken. Britain had declined in power and the United States could not be considered a disinterested third power, because it was directly confronted by the other power, the USSR, with expansionist designs on Iran.

The instrumentalities to achieve foreign policy objectives had also dramatically changed. That is to say, the Soviet Union, apart from traditional or conventional leverage, had now been equipped by an effective ideological instrumentality of subversion. The tribal and ethnic diversities which surfaced with the occupation contributed to subversion, fomenting disintegrative movements.

The domestic dimension of Iranian political processes should also be mentioned. In the period from 1944 to 1947 a quasi-parliamentary system existed, under which the power to formulate and conduct foreign policy was dispersed among various factions of the ruling aristocracy. Unlike the post-1953 era, the sovereign did not exercise exclusive stewardship of the country's foreign policy. Not only the executive but the legislature was actively involved in foreign policy. To compound the matter, political parties which enjoyed a large measure of freedom invariably centered their existence on major issues of foreign policy, largely due to the ambitious and critical Soviet aims in Iran. The struggle for the preservation of Iranian independence had become the central issue on which foreign powers and their domestic supporters were compelled to take a decisive stand.

In reviewing Iran's relations with the Soviet Union against this background, the oil-Azarbayjan crisis should be examined first. Second, the evolution of these relations should be considered during the 1947–1953 period, when the struggle for consolidating Iran's sovereignty was directed toward the other traditional infringing power, Great Britain. Third, changes in the Iranian system since 1953, especially in the conduct of foreign policy and in the perception of Iran's international posture, must be investigated.

It is worth noting that several constants remained unchanged throughout this period. Geographical proximity has often been regarded as the chief determinant of Iran's policy. While this has imposed a constraint on Iranian policy-makers, it has not dictated a consistent policy stance. An analysis of the fate of 13 noncommunist states adjacent to the Soviet Union prior to World War II indicates that 5 remained independent after the war. Of these, Finland was effectively neutralized and Afghanistan retained its traditional role as buffer state. In practice, both states' policies were subject to Soviet vetoes. In answer to their security problems, the remaining three noncommunist states, Turkey, Norway, and Iran, "ditched" their traditional neutrality policy in favor of alignment with a distant power.[1]

The decision of these three to opt for alignment is perhaps not surprising. For the option, given Soviet perspectives of "friendship," ap-

---

[1] See Harold and Margaret Sprout, *The Ecological Perspective on Human Affairs*, p. 28, for a distinction between "permanent" and "occasional" allies.

pears to have been an attenuated independence subject to Soviet veto. Like mini-states elsewhere, they were not ready to compromise or limit their sovereignty for a larger state's so-called security. Under these circumstances, alignment meant alignment with a distant power in competition with the neighboring great one. As Raymond Aron has emphasized:

Alliances have a relation to the respective positions of states—the most powerful ally is less alarming if it is remote. If it is not a "permanent ally," a neighboring state easily becomes an enemy.[2]

As we will see, the first full-scale post-World War II crisis brought into play many of these external and internal factors in a dramatic and critical fashion.

THE OIL-AZARBAYJAN CRISIS

In late 1943 and early 1944 the Soviet government presented Iran with demands for an oil concession in the northern province. The demand came while the Allies were still occupying the country and at a time when foreign occupation had radically undermined the ability of the central government to cope with external pressures.[3]

The response of Iranian political groups to this demand was expressed along ideological and political lines. The leftist elements, organized in the Tudeh party and in the Freedom Front, were sympathetic. They advanced the thesis that entrenched British influence in the southern half of the country made it incumbent on Iran to accommodate the Soviet demand. This "positive equilibrium" was also couched in terms of Soviet security. Indeed, the Tudeh party used the term "security perimeter" to refer to the northern region of Iran, which was comparable to that of the British zone of influence in the south.[4]

The nationalist elements in and outside the Majlis rejected this argument as detrimental to Iran's national interest and designed to reduce the country to a vassal state. This faction advocated a concept of negative equilibrium under which there would be no new concessions to the northern neighbor but, instead, every effort to liquidate the British influence. In that way neither could use the pretext of the other's

---

2 Raymond Aron, *Peace and War: A Theory of International Relations.*

3 For a review of these, see Sepehr Zabih, *The Communist Movement in Iran,* pp. 71–107.

4 "Harime Amniyat" (security perimeter) was first used in an editorial in *Rahbar,* the organ of the Tudeh party, Nov. 17, 1944.

influence to justify infringement on Iran's sovereignty. Led by Dr. Mossadegh, this faction pushed through the Majlis a motion banning any kind of negotiation with foreigners on oil concessions as long as the occupation continued.[5]

A third posture may be attributed to the more conservative and traditional elements in the Iranian system, whose anti-Soviet policies were nourished by a prolonged hostility toward Russia, predating the emergence of the Soviet regime. For many of them the best course of action was to invoke Great Britain's treaty commitment for the defense of Iran's sovereignty.

Successive cabinets which governed Iran in this period reflected a nearly desperate effort to achieve several objectives: (1) To persuade the dominant groups in and outside the Majlis that no definitive change in Soviet relations should be made until the end of the Iranian occupation. This "procrastination" was also in line with the traditional Iranian response as a weak state toward its powerful neighbors. (2) To search for extra-regional power, including the machinery of the recently established UN, for peaceful adjudication of the Soviet-Iranian dispute. This effort, which later assumed a pro-American posture, was initially hampered by the American conviction that Britain retained a dominant position in the country and that any external support within the wartime alliance for Iran should originate from that quarter. (3) To use Iran's constitutional process, including the ratification of foreign treaty requirements and parliamentary confidence in the cabinet in power, to convince the Soviet Union of its inability to act unilaterally in matters relating to foreign relations.

The pursuance of these objectives was as much determined by the Iranian side as the Soviet. Once rebutted by the no-concession motion of the Majlis, the Soviet regime used more direct pressure by instigating separatist movements in Azarbayjan and Kurdistan.[6] Using the presence of the Red Army in these areas, Moscow took a calculated risk in pursuance of an objective which the well-organized and powerful Communist party had been unable to secure through nonviolent parliamentary means. Faced with this new crisis, various parliamentary groups opposed to the basic Soviet demand voted into power Ahmad

---

[5] Text in *Rooznamehe Rasmi* (Official Gazette of the Iranian Parliament), Session 14, II (October–November 1944), pp. 1021–1022.

[6] For an account of these two separatist movements, see Zabih, *Communist Movement*, pp. 98–122. An early Soviet version is M. S. Ivanov, *Ocherk istorii Irana*, cited in *Central Asian Review*, IV, No. 3 (1956), 312–325. Also, Pierre Rondot, "L'Union Sovietique et les confins Irano—Kurdes du Moyen—Orient," *Politique Étrangère*, X, No. 3 (1945).

Ghavam, a veteran statesman whose reputation in foreign policy dated to the constitutional movement in the early 1900's.

The new prime minister represented a consensus among nationalist and leftist groups on the need to form a cabinet with which the Soviets could negotiate. Once Ghavam's acceptability to the Soviets had been ascertained through the Tudeh parliamentary group, the crisis became the focus of intense bilateral diplomatic efforts. There were three dimensions to the formidable task that the new government faced: (1) the demand of the separatist regime in Azarbayjan and Kurdistan for the kind of autonomy which would have dismembered the Iranian territorial entity; (2) the prospect of a Soviet refusal to evacuate the northern provinces within six months of the end of the war, as agreed to under the Tripartite Treaty of 1942; (3) the potential effective paralysis of the parliamentary institution by leftist groups advocating submission to Soviet pressures.

Once the new premier was installed and the parliamentary session had ended, the third component of his task could temporarily be shelved. To cope with the other two problems, he initiated direct negotiations with the Soviets and the pursuance of Iran's complaints to the UN.[7] However, the leverage available to Iran for bringing about compliance with her requests were rather meager. Indeed, Prime minister Ghavam charted a prudent and skillful diplomatic course under which the maximum objective of securing Soviet evacuation was to be achieved, even at the cost of temporary concession on the issues of oil and Azarbayjan. Months of negotiation included a visit to Moscow and high-level talks with the Soviet authorities, and on April 4, 1946, a draft agreement embodying the above compromise was signed. Under the agreement the Soviets accepted a new deadline for complete withdrawal of the Red Army, while the Iranians accepted the formation of a joint oil company with the Soviets and a pledge to resolve the Azarbayjan problem peacefully.[8]

This compromise had several advantages for Iran: (1) a new commitment to evacuate the Red Army had been made through bilateral agreement; (2) acknowledgment was made of Soviet interest in and concern for a basically domestic Iranian problem; (3) a concession given to the Soviet side was made contingent on ratification by a parliament yet to be elected. This contingency not only made the oil

---

[7] Abdolhassein Hamzavi: *Persia and the Powers: An Account of Diplomatic Relations, 1941–1946.*

[8] Persian text in *Ettelaat,* April 5, 1946. English summary in *Washington Post,* April 6, 1946.

concession subject to an uncertain fate, but also gave the Soviets a vested interest in normalizing the domestic political situation to facilitate election of a new parliament.

To convince the Soviets of its good faith, the central government formed a coalition cabinet with the Communist membership. This in effect preempted the party as a leftist opposition to the regime. On May 9, 1946, with the fulfillment of the Soviet pledge to evacuate the country, Moscow's most important instrumentality of pressure ceased to exist. They were now left with the separatist regimes in Azarbayjan and Kurdistan, plus the recently neutralized Communist opposition in the rest of the country. On the pretext of supervising free and fair elections, the central government then sent its armies into the provinces of Azarbayjan and Kurdistan. This was a calculated risk based on two assumptions: the reluctance of the Red Army to reenter Iran in support of the separatist movement, and confidence that the Soviets would not sacrifice the chance of ratification of the oil concession by a new parliament. Indeed, the earlier experience in Gilan, in 1921, had convinced the Iranians that the Soviets preferred to pursue their diplomatic interest through government-to-government relationships, even though this required a betrayal of local Communist groups.[9] Working on these two assumptions, the government skillfully used the constitutional provisions to impress the Soviets that the new parliament could only be convened after a countrywide national election.

Similarly, although the Soviet ambassador pleaded desperately with the Shah to intercede with the prime minister in order to prevent the reentry of central government troops into Azarbayjan and Kurdistan, the Shah argued that the constitution did not empower him to do so. Proof of the validity of the Iranian assumptions did not take long. The separatist regime collapsed abruptly; and the new election produced a parliamentary majority for the prime minister which, to the surprise of very few, refused to ratify the drafted oil concession to the Soviet Union. Thus, the first crisis in postwar Soviet-Iran relations demonstrated how a small weak state could use the techniques of procrastination and reliance on constitutional prerequisites to cope with a powerful state whose authority in the area of foreign policy was unrestricted by any constitutional restraints. Indeed, as a result of this successful experience, many older statesmen urged the Shah in 1949 not to enhance his constitutional authority over the Majlis, lest in a future crisis the dispersion of responsibility in foreign policy could not be used to

---

9 Zabih, *Communist Movement,* pp. 120–122.

deflect the pressure of a major power.[10] Undoubtedly the external environment, characterized by the emerging U.S.-USSR standoff, the American nuclear monopoly, and U.S. diplomatic support, contributed to Iran's successful utilization of these techniques.

THE MOSSADEGH INTERLUDE

In the aftermath of 1947 events, the Soviets seemed resigned to the improbability of achieving credible leverage on Iran in the foreseeable future. To be sure, they did protest indications of closer ties between Iran and the Western powers. But these efforts were more of a symbolic nature than determined measures indicating a consistent effort to reintroduce their wartime influence into the country. The Mossadegh government of 1951–1953 presented an ideal condition for an activist Soviet policy in Iran, for the essence of Mossadegh's movement was a struggle against well-entrenched British political and economic influence. Its success would have meant denying to the British precisely the kind of leverage that the Soviets had sought in the northern part of the country. Mossadegh's tenure as prime minister also witnessed a reemergence of the Communist movement as a dominant force. Toward the end of that period, when the American stance changed from mild support to outright opposition to the nationalist regime, the cold-war bipolar competition further compounded the Iranian situation.

Yet the record of that period indicates considerable reluctance on the part of the Soviet Union to take advantage of these apparent objective revolutionary conditions.[11] To the extent that the Soviets were concerned, the nationalist movement was led by essentially anti-Soviet elements. The Soviet government was also suspicious of the prospect of America replacing the British oil company, and perhaps preferred a weaker British presence in proximity to their borders to the extension of the more powerful United States influence. But above all, the failure of their diplomacy in the previous crisis had a sobering effect on their foreign policy. The vain attempts of the disintegrative movement of ethnic minorities, the failure of a larger Communist movement to share in power, and the successful use of Iranian parliamentary and constitutional procedures to check Soviet goals combined to impose a cautious and rather conservative attitude on the USSR.

The nationalist regime, similarly, worked under serious handicaps.

---

10 Typical of this kind of concern was that voiced by Ahmad Ghavam in an open letter to the Shah, *Demokrate Iran*, March 11, 1949.

11 For a survey of Soviet treatment of the Mossadegh era, see *Central Asian Review*, IV, No. 4 (1956), 382–432.

There were obvious limitations to the temptation of using Soviet support in the struggle against the British. The postwar experience and the proximity of its northern neighbor ruled out effective use of the Soviet Union as a third protecting power. Additionally, the nationalist regime could not have embraced Soviet support and retained its image of strict neutrality in the cold-war disputes. Indeed when, in desperation toward the end of that era, some hints at rapprochement with the newly established post-Stalin regime were made, the nationalist government encountered very serious internal and external opposition.[12]

A further component in this regional international context was Soviet inability to offer its markets for nationalized Iranian oil products. Although local consumption of oil in the early 1950's by the communist-bloc countries precluded the import of nationalized Iranian oil, undoubtedly other than purely economic and commercial considerations prevented the Soviets from any overtures concerning oil.

In summary, the uncertainty concerning Soviet diplomacy in the last year of the Stalin regime, the fear of open confrontation with the United States, the absence of new ideological guidelines regulating international communist relations, and the inherent suspicion of all nationalist movements generated remarkable restraints on the Soviet Union during this increasingly chaotic period in postwar Iran.

POST-STALIN DEVELOPMENTS

The ascendancy of the Shah and an end to the experimental parliamentary system in 1953 coincided with the change in the Soviet leadership. Very early in this period, problems with the Soviets unresolved during the Mossadegh era, such as the issue of war debts and Iran's gold reserves, were settled. Soviet preoccupation with succession and later de-Stalinization problems did not allow for much attention to Iranian relations before 1956. By the time the Soviets were ready to promote a thaw in relations with Iran, the legacy of Stalinist policies had already driven that country to seek a Western alliance.

If Soviet defensive aims had been either to physically secure the states adjoining its southern border or to be the dominant influence therein, its failure had driven Iran into the Baghdad Pact. Whereas the threat to the integrity of Iran had previously come from foreign imperialists, Soviet postwar behavior left no doubt in the Shah's mind

---

12 A commentary hinting at this in the newspaper published by the foreign minister of the nationalist regime evoked the U.S. embassy's demand for clarification and considerable alarm in the Western press. See *Bakhtar-Emruz*, Tehran, April 4, 1953, and *Le Monde*, Paris, April 6, 1953.

where the major threat lay. "In our experience it is the new imperialism, the new totalitarian imperialism, that the world's less developed countries today have most to fear." [13]

The major issues between Iran and the Soviet Union—Iran's membership in the Baghdad Pact, 1955; the bilateral agreement with the U.S., 1959; the question of missile bases on Iranian soil, the presence of military advisors, etc.—all revolved around a decision which the Iranian leadership took to balance the great-power neighbor with a distant friendly power.

The Soviet aim throughout the 1956–1962 period had been to detach Iran from the West and persuade it to readopt its neutral policy. The *instruments* the Soviet government used in the pre-1962 and post-1962 periods have varied and have been tailored to the changing international context; and the issues, like the instruments, have varied in importance in a changing environment. For example, technological developments and the detente in the cold war virtually nullified the question of missile bases in Iran. Similarly, as Soviet policy-makers became preoccupied with events in other less stable areas on their periphery, Iran's formal pro-Western alignment became a less burning issue.

It may not be a great oversimplification to view Soviet aims in Iran as the right of veto or the right to dictate or prevent a particular foreign policy orientation. The past and future success of the Soviet Union will be determined by the international political context; for Soviet opportunism, the strength of other states, the press of other issues, and the configuration of forces in the international arena will determine events. Ceaseless vigilance in Tehran will be required. A scholar of Soviet affairs has noted:

If Iran or Turkey seeks and receives United States support in opposing Soviet demands, the pressure can be turned off. At a later time, when other countries are involved in troubles elsewhere, the Soviet Union will still be a close neighbor of Turkey and Iran.[14]

Iranian aims in this period were determined by several considerations: first among them, memories of the 1945–1953 period, when the absence of even a tacit Western commitment to Iran's security had raised questions about its capacity to survive as an independent entity.

---

13 H. I. M. Mohammed Reza Shah Pahlavi, *Mission for My Country* (hereafter cited as *Memoirs*), p. 131.

14 Philip Mosely, *The Kremlin in World Politics: Studies in Soviet Policy and Action*, p. 300.

A second consideration was the Shah's perception of the problems confronting Iran. The Allied occupation in 1942 had relegated the Iranian army to internal security functions. Throughout the war the Shah sought to increase the army's role, to obtain American advisors to buttress it, and to secure and maintain control of it himself.[15] He was aware of the need for social reform and the achievement of national unity, lest these become "pretexts" for undesirable actions.[16] Strengthening the army and assuring its control by the throne, achieving Iranian national unity, social and political reform, and redefining the role of the monarch had therefore become the postwar goals of the Iranian leadership. To accomplish them the Iranian government needed a "breathing spell," a period of internal stability and consolidation and external security. The Soviet action in Azarbayjan, in Mahabad, and in its occupied zone in northern Iran certainly promised no such interval. Rather, it suggested that Stalin had amplified the traditional Russian goal of influence to one of outright annexation, or "the conquest of Iran by the installment plan." [17]

The twin factors of Soviet wartime and postwar policy, and the international requirements of Iran and internal needs of the Shah's regime, accounted for the postwar relinquishment of Iran's traditional neutrality and a shift to the Western camp. Alignment was viewed as a prudent posture, given Soviet aims. Compared to neutrality it was also a less expensive means of arming the country and obtaining economic and military assistance.[18] Furthermore, its adoption might provide the country with a breathing spell to deal with its domestic problems.

The instruments of pressure and influence in a small state's diplomatic armory are necessarily limited. Yet a judicious use of timing and circumstances, and an understanding of the limits which external conditions set to maneuvering, can considerably stretch these apparently meager resources.[19] Relations with a friendly, geographically distant Western ally have been an important lever in relations with a hostile proximate communist "permanent enemy." Because of Soviet hostility, the Iranian leadership sought a tie with the West. This tie, in turn,

---

15 Keyvan Tabari, "Iran's Policies Towards the U.S. During the Anglo-Russian Occupation, 1941–1946" (Ph.D. diss., Columbia University, 1967), p. 20, et passim.
16 The Shah's comments were made on Nov. 6, 1943. See Foreign Relations of the United States: Diplomatic Papers, 1943, IV; the Near East and Africa, pp. 408–410.
17 Ivar Spector, The Soviet Union and the Muslim World, 1917–1956, p. 114.
18 See the Shah's comments to C. L. Sulzberger, The Last of the Giants, p. 769.
19 See Annette Baker Fox, The Power of Small States, for case studies demonstrating this for Turkey, Spain, Switzerland, Sweden, Finland, and Norway.

became an important instrument and issue in Iran's relations with the Soviet Union.

Iran's capacity to influence either of the superpowers depends on the superpower's interest in it. Undoubtedly there were Soviet security concerns about its southern border. But American interest had arisen only as a result of competition in a bipolar world. It was in a postwar context that the United States became one of the world's two superpowers, and the only democratic one. Unlike the Soviet's interest in Iran, America's concerns were not geographically determined, were unlikely to be permanent, and were not historically based. The major interest of each superpower, in Iran as elsewhere, was probably preclusive; that is, the denial of that country to the other camp. Nevertheless, it was certainly more true of the U.S. than of the USSR.

For the Shah, the thousand-mile virtually undefended border, the relative military weakness of Iran, its political fragility, and his own precarious position in Iranian politics until 1963–1964 placed certain limits on maneuverability between the giants. Because of the dissimilar geographic distance of the superpowers from Tehran, it was necessary for him to emphasize Iran's importance to Washington in order to maintain American interest in its fate.[20]

The relationship between the superpowers was another important factor in the triangular relationship. Just as the Iranian leadership could not afford to alienate its Western friends by anticipating events and repairing its relations with the USSR with concessions, neither could it afford to be too far behind a U.S.-USSR rapprochement. The fear of collusion between the superpowers at the expense of the smaller states has never been far from the Shah's mind. Therefore, relations with the USSR have never been allowed to deteriorate to a point of no return.[21]

Iran's relationships with the USSR have required the use of considerable energy to resist or deflect Soviet pressure. Iran's instruments of influence in the Soviet case have been negative; to firmly withstand Soviet pressure against the Western tie while holding out the possibility of good relations if that tie is accepted by Moscow. Since Iran's means of influence are reactive, they are difficult to document. Tactically, Soviet pressure has been deflected by a "tough" policy that has answered Soviet radio propaganda with Iranian propaganda, re-

---

[20] See the Shah's *Memoirs*, pp. 314–315, and interview in *U.S. News and World Report*, March 6, 1961, pp. 63–65.

[21] See the Shah's press conference of Nov. 28, 1959; reprinted in *Tehran Journal*, Dec. 1, 1959.

taliated in kind to a Soviet withdrawal of its ambassador, rejected Soviet protest notes by protesting Soviet interference in domestic affairs, expelled Soviet diplomats engaged in misconduct, and shrugged off the more explicit Soviet threats as "bluffs." [22]

Simultaneously the Shah has insisted on his right to determine Iran's international posture while emphasizing that Iran's ties with the West should not be considered an obstacle to good relations with the USSR. In the period between 1958 and 1962 he consistently expressed the hope that relations would improve and that rancor would give way to constructive economic cooperation.[23] While rejecting Soviet preconditions for rapprochement, the Shah and his ministers have asserted that Iran's friendship cannot be bought by aid that comes with "strings attached." [24] Nor has the Iranian leadership acquiesced to the Soviet government's attempts to determine Iranian foreign policy. "We are not intimidated," the Shah wrote,

by anybody who tries to tell us whom we should have for our friends, and we make no alliances merely for the sake of alliances or vague principles, but only in the support of our enlightened self-interest.[25]

In holding firmly to this stance, the Shah, like successive prime ministers before 1953, has used the tool of procrastination while awaiting developments elsewhere to deflect Soviet energies.

In the postwar era one period is particularly rich in the insight it yields concerning Iran-Soviet relations. From the winter of 1958 to the autumn of 1962 the Soviet government exerted various forms of pressure on the Iranian government. The principal aim was to deter Iran from signing the projected bilateral agreement with the U.S. The agreement had potential military implications for the USSR which

---

[22] For the radio propaganda, see the Shah's *Memoirs*, p. 123; on recall of ambassador as a reprisal, *Tehran Journal*, June 27 and 28, 1960, and *New York Times*, June 25, 1960; on expulsion for misconduct, *New York Times*, March 2, 1956, *Tehran Journal*, March 16, 1959, and *New York Times*, January 28, 1962; on rejection of "bluff," *Tehran Journal*, Sept. 11, 1961, and *New York Herald Tribune*, Sept. 26, 1961.

[23] See *New York Times*, July 17, 1956, Sept. 27, 1959; *Tehran Journal*, Sept. 27, 1959.

[24] See the Shah's comments, *New York Times*, Sept. 25, 1960; and Dr. Hassan Arsanjani, *Tehran Journal*, June 15, 1961.

[25] For a representative sample of Soviet propaganda directed at the throne, see Khrushchev's prediction of revolution in Iran in his interview with Walter Lippmann, *New York Herald Tribune*, April 18, 1961. This was repeated by him to Kennedy at the Vienna meeting in 1961; Theodore Sorenson, *Kennedy*, p. 615; Y. Bochkaryov, "A Shaky Throne"; and *Pravda*, Feb. 14, 1959, as translated in *Mizan Newsletter*, I, No. 3 (1959), pp. 2–3.

viewed it as affecting Soviet security and overshadowing all other issues in postwar Iran-Soviet relations. Iran viewed the pact as a necessary supplement to the Baghdad Pact for a variety of domestic and international reasons.

Iran-Soviet relations between 1958 and 1962 provided a case study of an issue separating the USSR and Iran and the means pursued by each state to obtain its ends. These means included the Soviet coordination of its instruments of pressure and inducement, and Iran's resistance to them. The period is also an interesting illustration of Iran-Soviet relationships before they were replaced by more temperate and cordial interaction. Since 1962, inducement and functional cooperation have replaced intimidation. The value both states attach to their newfound rapprochement has limited minor differences and diminished their chances of escalating and upsetting these relations.

In contrast to Iran, a wide assortment of instruments of influence are available to the Soviet government in its relations with its neighbor. From the first agreement with the United States in 1947 until the abatement of outright Soviet hostility in 1962, that government had orchestrated a variety of instruments of pressure, alternating between tones of outright stridency and friendship, with the common theme of deterring and later detaching the Iranian government from an alliance with the West. This tendency to alternate between hostility and conciliation appeared to be a hallmark of Soviet postwar policy and did little to reassure the insecure Iranian government or allay its suspicions. In an earlier example, the Soviet's annoyance with the negotiations for NATO had resulted in a series of minor incidents along the Iranian border and the closing of the Iranian consulate in Baku. Marshall Shulman has written:

Despite—or possibly because of—this thunderous orchestration of threats of civil war, sabotage, invasions, strikes, treaty cancellations, parliamentary obstruction, and international working-class solidarity, the negotiations of the North Atlantic Treaty moved steadily forward.[26]

Soviet policy has been similar in the Iranian context, alternating bluster with blandishment, offering *inter alia* economic inducements to achieve objectives that threat and hostility proved unable to attain.

The themes of Soviet propaganda in Iran between 1946 and 1950 are remarkably consistent with those of the following twelve years. Economic, political, or military agreements with the West were said to be inimical to Iran's interests. The consortium oil agreement and the

---

[26] Marshall D. Shulman, *Stalin's Foreign Policy Reappraised,* pp. 62–64.

Baghdad Pact were thus vehemently protested by Moscow.[27] It emphasized that all Iran's problems were the direct result of ties with the West. The sustained diplomatic pressure exerted by the USSR to keep Iran out of the Baghdad Pact and later to prevent the 1959 agreement embodied the use of a variety of instruments. The pressure included protest notes, assertions of Iran's "hostility" because of its agreements with the West, questions as to the legality of these agreements under the 1921 and 1927 Iran-Soviet treaties, and ambiguous and veiled threats of possible Soviet reactions.

Other means of pressure under the category of "bluster" included the fabrication of documents purporting to show CENTO's aggressive aims, border incidents which included the shooting of Iranian border guards, the shooting down of unarmed airplanes using Iranian airspace, violation of Iranian airspace, direct intervention in the Iranian political process, espionage, and attempts to sow discord between Iran and the United States. In addition, the Soviet government frequently recalled its ambassador for extended periods which coincided with a stepped-up radio and press offensive vilifying the Shah.[28] The Tudeh party had been utilized when convenient, although its usefulness had progressively diminished even before 1962.

This bluster phase of Soviet policy alternated with phases of blandishment with economic inducements during the years from 1953 to 1958. The Soviets offered to settle border and financial questions outstanding between them, including the return of eleven tons of gold, eight million dollars outstanding from a wartime debt, and minor frontier revisions. While openly hostile at Iran's accession to the Baghdad Pact in December 1955, the Soviets continued to attempt conciliation. During the Shah's visit to Moscow in June 1956 the Soviets unilaterally relinquished their rights to a seventy-year concession obtained for northern Persia. In March of the following year the Soviet government gave the Shah an Ilyushin 14 transport aircraft as a personal gift; in April they reached a new border accord with Iran, and in August offered the Iranian government unlimited credit for heavy industrial development at 2 percent interest.[29]

---

27 For typical Soviet writing in this period (1953–1959), see the comments on the Baghdad Pact: T. Korotkova, "Against Iran's Interests"; K. Ivanov and A. Vassilyev, "A Slippery and Dangerous Path."

28 For the "CENTO documents," see *New York Times,* Aug. 19, 20, and 23, 1961; *Pravda,* Aug. 19, 1961. For border incidents, Soviet overflights, and shooting of guards, see *New York Times,* April 26, 1959; *Tehran Journal,* Aug. 17, 1961.

29 See Walter Laqueur, *The Soviet Union and the Middle East,* pp. 207–208. It is interesting to note that Khrushchev lectured the People's Republic of China (when it

In this period the Soviets wove the two threads of intimidation and inducement into the single fabric of a policy patterned to fit its neighbors. Its objective was to ensure their exclusion from pacts, ties, or commitments with foreign powers, and thereby to assure Moscow's right to decide their foreign policy orientation. The Soviet's formidable variety of instruments of influence and pressure were impressive but deceptive. The very extensiveness of Soviet security interests, and the global entanglement of the communist regime, have been competing pressures on Soviet foreign policy. The order of priority for relations with Iran has not been the same as Iran's order of priority for relations with the Soviet Union. For an adjacent small state these relations have dominated its foreign policy concerns; for the Soviets these relations have been one among many.

The Iranian government has used the U.S. connection as a security umbrella while putting its domestic house in order and waiting for Soviet interests to become engaged elsewhere. Clearly this differential "span of attention" has operated to Iran's benefit. The Iranian government's firmness, international political changes, and technological innovation have allowed issues basic in the earlier period to assume a lesser significance with the passage of time.

The benefits of hindsight suggest that the exchange of notes between Iran and the USSR in September 1962 constituted a significant watershed in postwar Iran-USSR relations.[30] In these notes the Iranian government pledged not to allow any foreign missile sites to be stationed on Iranian territory. Yet it is very likely that this "turning point" occurred for reasons other than this largely symbolic pledge. This contention is supported by an examination of the issue of bases and the bilateral agreement and an assessment of political developments within Iran and changes in the external environment.

THE ISSUE OF BASES

In the mid-1950's the Soviets viewed Iran's increasing reliance on the Western states for its security as a most important and dangerous development. Particularly unwelcome were the American military advisory groups whose status was formalized in 1947. It is difficult to

---

encountered border difficulties) with the Soviet's exemplary attitude and forebearance in dealing with Iran: Edward Crankshaw, *The New Cold War: Moscow vs. Peking*, p. 108.

[30] Soviet sources regard the exchange of notes as the "turning point" in Soviet-Iran relations. See, *inter alia, Narody Azizi Afriki*, No. 2, 1968, p. 19: cited by Suleiman Tekiner, "Soviet-Iranian Relations Over the Last Half Century," p. 39.

assess the extent to which defensive or preclusive considerations dominated Soviet strategic planning at this time and the degree to which their policy was motivated by hegemonic and long-standing imperialist drives. It is sufficient to note that Stalin apparently believed that in the name of Soviet security he was entitled to make certain that only governments "friendly" to Moscow were installed along Russia's borders. Furthermore, they were to be "independent and democratic" as the Soviets understood that term.

In accordance with the Soviet view of the posture of states adjoining it, preferably the state should be under Soviet control—either directly, as with Mongolia, or indirectly, as with Eastern Europe. Only a "neutrality" or "nonalignment" sensitive to Soviet influence is acceptable—e.g., Finland and Afghanistan[31]—for this is "nonprovocative." Weak buffer states adjacent to the USSR might constitute vacuums subject to the influence of external states and are therefore dangerous to Soviet security. They may have to be liquidated, if only for preclusive reasons. Finally, any form of alliance between an adjacent state and the Soviet Union's competitors is unfriendly, provocative, and anathema. Clearly, this attitude dominated the Soviet's reaction to the foreign policy postures of Norway, Turkey, Iran, and Pakistan. Seemingly obsessed by the fear of "capitalist encirclement," the Soviets pursued toward these states a policy of bluster, menace, and threat which paradoxically brought about the very condition Moscow feared most: an alliance with the West.

Soviet reaction to the increasing pro-Western orientation of the regime since 1953 was evidenced by the flow of protest notes directed toward Tehran. When the oil consortium agreement with American and European companies was signed, Iran was accused of "straying from the path of neutrality." Rapprochement with the regional states of Turkey and Pakistan was also impermissible, and Moscow protested officially. This was followed by a further Soviet protest in late 1955 at Iran's adherence to the Baghdad Pact.[32] In each case it stressed

---

31 Soviet writings constantly hold up the Finnish and Afghan models of posture in international politics as the most friendly to the USSR. See L. Alekseyev, *Izvestiya*, Feb. 27, 1961, partially reprinted and translated in *Mizan Newsletter*, III, No. 4 (1961), p. 10; and A. Z. Arbadzhyan, "The Foreign Policy and Economic Development of Persia and Afghanistan," *Problemy Vostokovedeniya*, No. 3 (1960), translated in *Central Asian Review*, IX, No. 1 (1961), pp. 83–89.

32 The protest regarding the oil agreement may be found in Walter Laqueur, *The Soviet Union and the Middle East*, pp. 207–208, and the note protesting the regional rapprochement on p. 208. The Soviet argument in its December 1955 note was that it violated the 1921 treaty. See J. C. Hurewitz, *Diplomacy in the Near and Middle East*, Vol. II, pp. 415–421.

the danger to the USSR's security resulting from Iran's actions and, through thinly-veiled threats, the consequent danger to Iran.

Iran's increasing ties with the West were evidenced by military aid missions, oil agreements, and technical and military pacts. In the Soviet view these presaged Iran's inevitable transformation into a beachhead against the Soviet motherland. Any government pursuing such a policy was thereby guilty of an "unfriendly" act. From Tehran's viewpoint, however, Soviet hostility, overtly demonstrated since the wartime occupation, had precluded a policy of self-abnegation and trust in Moscow's peaceful intentions. The combination of Iran's exposed position and the Shah's unwillingness to subject Iran's interests and concerns to Soviet vetoes militated against any policy but prudent alliance. How best to ally with the Soviet Union's Western competitors but reassure its giant neighbor of its nonprovocative intentions constituted the major task of Iranian policymakers in the years from 1955 to 1962.

The course of Iran-Soviet relations pertaining to the question of foreign military bases on Iranian territory was illustrative of this dilemma in the pre-1962 period. Moscow's concern regarding bases in Turkey had been indicated in its December 1955 protest of the conclusion of the Baghdad Pact. Khrushchev reiterated this concern during the Shah's visit to Moscow in 1956. The Shah's defense of the Baghdad Pact emphasized its intent to strengthen "collective defense against aggression," and asserted Iran's right to defend itself. "Khrushchev," the Shah recounts,

finally agreed that Iran had no aggressive intentions against the Soviet Union, but he suggested that some big power might compel us against our will to make territory available for an attack on Russia. He intimated that perhaps we had been forced into the Baghdad Pact for that very purpose. I emphatically answered that we had joined the pact solely on our own volition and had entered it as an equal partner. . . . I said we would never allow either the pact or our territory to be used in furtherance of aggressive designs upon the Soviet Union.[33]

The visit cleared the air somewhat and was followed by a number of agreements concerning the joint Iran-Soviet frontier. The pledge was repeated the following year by the Iranian government on the occasion of a visit to Tehran by Soviet Deputy Minister Kuznetsov.[34]

---

[33] The Shah's *Memoirs*, pp. 119–120.
[34] This time particular reference was made to "atomic" bases. *New York Times*, April 20 and 21, 1957.

These pledges apparently allayed Soviet suspicions. After July 1958, when they learned that Iran was about to enter into a bilateral military assistance agreement with the United States, that pledge was no longer deemed adequate. In the course of subsequent negotiations which the Shah pursued with the USSR, the Iranian government attempted to convince Moscow that the pledge remained valid and would continue to be honored.[35] The stumbling block in these negotiations concerned the appropriate definition of a "base." According to the Shah, the Soviets sought to define a base as any facility which might conceivably have any military value, such as airports, seaports, and railroads. The Shah was not prepared to give the Soviets this much reassurance.[36] The Shah offered instead to have the term "military base" defined by international authorities and added in an appendix to any pact agreed upon. This was refused by the Soviets.

Instead, they reverted to a policy of intimidation, emphasizing that the breakdown of the discussions indicated that missiles were about to be installed on Iranian soil.[37] Policy in the period from February 1959 to September 1962 consisted of attempts to detach Iran from its Western connection by playing upon this issue of military bases. According to two press reports, Khrushchev offered the Iranian government aid and a cessation of radio propaganda in return for a promise that Iran would forbid the construction of "anti-Soviet bases." [38] There is no evidence indicating that the Iranian government had withdrawn its earlier pledge, and it must be concluded that Khrushchev again sought an open-ended definition of "bases."

---

[35] After the breakdown of the discussion with the USSR, Foreign Minister Hekmat told the Majlis: "We reminded them that for three years we had been a Pact member without making bases available to any power." *Tehran Journal*, March 7, 1959. The Shah in a press conference also confirmed that the bilateral agreement would not change the terms of the pledge: "No country has ever asked Iran for missile bases, nor would Iran concede to such a demand. . . ." *Tehran Journal*, Feb. 22, 1959.

[36] The Shah's annoyance at Soviet "great-power chauvinism" is clearly indicated when he admits that these facilities might indeed be used for military purposes, but so might the Soviet Union's. "Are the rules of the game to apply to everybody but themselves?" *Memoirs*, p. 121.

[37] A Soviet statement on March 25, 1959, was typical: "The Soviet government cannot ignore the transformation of Iranian territory into a strategic and military staging post for the imperialist powers." A. K. Lavrentyev, *Imperalistichesk aya politika S Shai i anglii v Irane* ("The Imperialist Policy of the U.S.A. and Britain in Iran"; Moscow, 1960), p. 91. Elsewhere the Soviets accused Iran of allowing the U.S. to build a missile base in the Zagros mountains. V. Fuzeyev, "In American Harness."

[38] *Christian Science Monitor*, Sept. 11, 1959; *New York Times*, Nov. 12, 1959, and Sept. 23, 1960.

Soviet policy consistently utilized every means to intimidate the regime in Iran. Thus the Soviet leadership took advantage of the May 5, 1960, U-2 incident, and ignored the Shah's prompt statement that no plane on a military mission was permitted to use Iranian airspace. Khrushchev declared that Soviet rockets would destroy all countries allowing the use of their facilities to U.S. planes engaged in intelligence.[39] To emphasize the seriousness of the U-2 incident, the Soviet government addressed an official note to Tehran accusing Iran of a "hostile act directly spearheaded against the security of the USSR" in permitting the CENTO air exercises scheduled for May 14–18 on Iranian territory, and warning of the consequences if Soviet airspace was violated.

The following year the Soviets fabricated allegedly "CENTO secret documents" which purported to confirm that Iran, Turkey, and Pakistan were bases for nuclear weapons. Propaganda stressing the "suicidal" nature of a pro-Western alignment was coordinated with these events.[40] Specific denials, such as Prime Minister Amini's statement that Iran wanted good relations with the USSR and "therefore could not allow any American military bases on Persian territory," were quoted without comment. Relations between the two states remained at an impasse on this issue until 1962.

Any attempt to assess the importance of this issue to Soviet-Iran relations must come to terms with the problem of Soviet sensitivity to foreign attack, on the one hand, and Iranian determination to maintain its independence on the other. It must balance legitimate Soviet security concerns at that time against the Iranian government's determination not to have its independence violated through excessive deference to this concern.

Available evidence supports the contention that the "issue" became a pretext by which the Soviet Union sought to pressure Iran away from any type of Western connection disapproved of by Moscow. No distinction was made in Moscow between the policies of Turkey, Iran, and Pakistan, despite the fact that Turkey allowed atomic weapons on its soil and both it and Pakistan permitted the United States to use its airbases for U-2 missions. Nor did the Soviets attempt to define *precisely* what sort of eventuality concerned them most. On the contrary,

---

39 The Shah's statement was made in Sweden; *Tehran Journal,* May 8, 1960. Khrushchev's threats were carried by the *New York Times,* May 9, 1960.

40 Text of note on "CENTO" exercises in *New York Times,* May 15, 1960; the contents of the "CENTO documents" were reported in *Pravda,* Aug. 19, 1961. For representative propaganda, see K. H. Gregoryan, "Iran: Servitors of U.S. Aggression," and L. Admanov and L. Teplov, "CENTO: After the Tehran Session."

their terms were as vague and general in negotiations as they were deliberately blurred in the literature. The separable concepts of military assistance, military acquisition, foreign advisors, foreign military bases, military equipment, and foreign missile bases were consistently equated in Soviet literature, and all considered equally "unfriendly." [41]

According to Khrushchev, Soviet concern was rooted in the fear that the United States might use Iranian territory for nuclear weapons, even against the Iranian government's wishes and despite any pledge to the contrary. This concern would appear to have been unrealistic, for the Soviet policy-makers were well aware of the different significance Washington attached to NATO member Turkey and CENTO member Iran. It is unlikely that the Soviet government would have credited the United States with the intent to place nuclear weapons in the unstable Iran of 1959–1961 and thereby risk their possible capture by elements hostile to the United States. It was also unlikely that the United States would station missiles in a country in which it had not been willing to even indirectly underwrite the security of the regime. Finally, in the absence of a significant Iranian airforce, the Soviet Union had virtual freedom to violate Iran's airspace. Soviet intelligence could certainly have known whether missile bases existed or were under construction, and could accurately have estimated whether they were planned.

The significance of the issue of foreign missile bases in Iran-Soviet relations has been greatly exaggerated. This is partially explained by the Soviet's consistent use of the term as a symbol rather than a physical entity. The importance the Soviets attached to the international posture adopted by adjacent states has been noted, as has the "provocative" nature of an alliance by an adjacent state with a state competitive or antagonistic toward the USSR. This concern has manifested itself in an attempt to exercise a veto over certain developments in bordering states and, in the case of Iran, to undo its Western connections. To this end the definition of "bases" was left open-ended. At the same time consistent Soviet harassment of the regime, alternated with inducement, was intended to give the beleagured Iranian regime every psychological incentive to "normalize" relations with its powerful neighbor—on Soviet terms.

On the Iranian side, a foreign alliance and a military aid agreement with the United States were deemed prudent, and Soviet conditions to neutralize Iran were viewed as too high a price to pay for Soviet good-

---

[41] Typical of this approach is the article by Observer in *Izvestiya*, April 21, 1962, quoted in *Mizan Newsletter*, IV, No. 6 (1962), 11.

will. At the same time the Shah attempted to convince the Soviets that Iranian security need not mean Soviet insecurity; that Iran's Western ties could be reconciled with normal relations with the USSR.

While constituting a legitimate security concern, the issue of foreign missile bases was more often used as a synonym for an Iranian foreign policy posture with which the Soviet leaders were unhappy. That issue was a lever for Moscow to utilize when expedient, to pressure the government in Tehran, and as a catchphrase to condemn Iran's departure from neutrality. The utility of this issue from 1956 to 1962 is a most convincing reason for the USSR's refusal to formally accept Iran's specific reassurances regarding a missile base. The Soviet acceptance in September 1962 of Iran's pledge "not to permit rocket bases of any sort on its soil" was in fact an acceptance of a pledge with which it had been dissatisfied for the past six years. More significantly, it was an admission that Moscow no longer sought the *formal* detachment of Iran from its Western commitments.[42]

THE 1959 BILATERAL AGREEMENT
AND ITS AFTERMATH

The events of 1958 in Lebanon and Iraq had been very disquieting to the Shah. His anxiety was additionally compounded by U.S. failure to formally enter the Baghdad Pact and provide what Tehran considered "adequate" aid, or to underwrite the regime by guaranteeing it from subversion, indirect aggression, and domestic agitation. In pressing Washington for a bilateral agreement, the Shah sought as firm and as wide-ranging a commitment as possible. The Soviets, on the other hand, were concerned about an agreement's effects on the crumbling structure of the Baghdad Pact. The regularization of Tehran-Washington relations by this instrument was viewed as a threat which would solidify Iran's pro-Western orientation and give Washington access to Iranian territory. The proposed agreement would thus sharply reverse the deterioration of the regional alliance.

The bilateral-agreement episode in Iranian relations with the U.S. and the USSR was a situation in which the interests of each state in the triangular relationship were involved, and it provides an instructive example of how each utilized its instruments of influence. In the

---

[42] The Iranian note is printed in full in *Pravda*, Sept. 16, 1962, and translated in *Mizan Newsletter*, IV, No. 9 (October, 1962), 19. See also K. Ivanovsky, *Pravda*, Sept. 17, 1962, "Important Step on Path to Improving Relations Between the USSR and Iran"; complete text in *Current Digest*, XIV, No. 37 (October 10, 1962), 16–17.

following analysis no attempt is made to chronicle all events or to reconcile apparent differences in the published evidence.[43] The focus is on instrumentalities.

When the Soviets learned of the proposed bilateral agreement in 1958, they protested to Tehran, by pointing out that this pact would be a violation of Article 3 of the Iran-Soviet 1927 treaty and hostile to the USSR. The Iranian answer denied the existence of a new pact, deplored Soviet interference, and stressed Iran's defensive foreign policy orientation. The Soviet supplementary memorandum which followed on December 28, 1958, took much the same line.[44] An authoritative article by "Observer" in *Pravda*, December 6 hinted that the USSR might send troops into Iran if the pact was signed. A month later this stick was followed by the carrot in the form of an offer "to make efforts" to improve relations.[45] Negotiations led by Deputy Foreign Minister Semenov in Tehran subsequently broke down and Iran-Soviet relations plummeted to their nadir. The Soviet foreign ministry blamed the Iranian government for the breakdown, and a press and radio propaganda campaign began immediately thereafter, synchronized with border incidents, accusations, and protest notes.

The propaganda attempted to distinguish the Shah's regime from the Iranian people, to underline the harm caused Iran by continued ties with the West, and to emphasize neutrality as the only correct international posture for Iran.[46] The message that this was the only safe course for Iran to adopt was accentuated in an incident that occurred three months after the breakdown of talks. Iran had protested

---

[43] The Iranian version of the events is found in the Shah's *Memoirs*, pp. 121–124; the Shah's interview with C. L. Sulzberger, July 17, 1961, in *Last of the Giants*, p. 769, and Foreign Minister Hekmat's report to the Majlis in *Ettelaat*, Feb. 15, 1959. The Soviet version is found in A. Irandoust, "Restoring the Truth." The main differences in the two versions concern: (1) which side took the initiative—each maintains the other did—and (2) what were Soviet conditions for an Iran-Soviet pact? The Soviet version is that Iran's membership in CENTO was accepted and not an issue. The Iranian version is that the Soviet price for the annulment of Articles 5 and 6 of the 1921 treaty and a nonaggression pact was the virtual severance of all ties with the West.

[44] The text is in *Pravda*, Nov. 1, 1959. The Iranian reply is in *Ettelaat*, Nov. 8, 1958. See also V. Viktorov, "A Harmful Policy." The text of the supplementary memorandum is in *Pravda*, Jan. 17, 1959.

[45] For the Pravda article, see *New York Times*, Dec. 7, 1958. During the period November 1958–January 1959, three issues of *New Times* carried articles denouncing the projected pact, alleging it harmed Soviet security. See *New Times*, Nos. 4 and 5 (1958 and 1959).

[46] For a representative sample of this line of argument see V. Viktorov, "Why Evil Times Have Fallen"; Y. Bochkaryov, "A Shaky Throne"; and V. Mayevskiy, "Independence Sold," in *Pravda*, Aug. 26, 1959.

Moscow's violation of her airspace by an attack on an unarmed Iranian plane. The Soviet government rejected that protest by pointing out that Iran's policy of permitting "foreign aircraft belonging to third powers" to fly over Iranian territory near the Soviet Union was "provocative" and a "hostile act." [47] So hostile did the Soviet press and radio offensive become in the aftermath of the 1959 episode that the Iranian government reportedly considered severing diplomatic relations with Moscow, and sought diplomatic support from its CENTO allies.[48]

The Soviet Union did not concentrate solely on intimidation. During the discussions in Tehran it also offered massive economic aid. In the Shah's words: "They told us that the aid given to India and other countries would be nothing compared to what they would give us." [49] On his return from Moscow after a nine-month absence from Tehran, the Soviet ambassador publicly expressed his hope for improved relations between the two governments and delivered a message to the Shah offering technical economic assistance. This was subsequently elaborated upon by an offer of an 85 percent Iranian and 15 percent Soviet profit split in a joint oil project in northern Iran, conditional upon there being no anti-USSR bases allowed in Iran. Other, similar offers were made the next year. The Shah's reply was still the same: while desiring good relations with the USSR, he was ". . . not prepared to buy friendship at any price." [50] From these proposals it would appear that Soviet rapprochement conditions continued to include the weakening of Iran's links with the West.

The orchestration of intimidation and inducement did not achieve for the Soviet Union its principal aims: neutralization of Iran and severing Iranian military ties with the U.S. In analyzing the danger posed by the Iran-U.S. bilateral agreement, Moscow had emphasized its strategically provocative nature to Soviet security. Yet simultaneously, Soviet propaganda emphasized that the alleged domestic function of the agreement was to obtain U.S. "police support" for the regime. Sometimes the activities of U.S. military advisors in Iran were said to "directly contradict the assurances of Iran's leaders that they want to maintain neighborly relations with the Soviet Union." At other times Iran was castigated for its relationship with the Western oil

---

47 Soviet May 2 and May 31, 1959, notes are found in *Pravda*, June 4, 1959.
48 See the report in *The Times* (London), April 30, 1959, and *UN General Assembly, Official Records*, XVI, 1011 Plenary Meeting, Friday, Sept. 22, 1961, p. 35.
49 Interview with the Shah, *U.S. News and World Report*, March 6, 1961, pp. 63–65.
50 See *New York Times*, Sept. 27, Nov. 9, and Nov. 12, 1959, and Sept. 23 and 25, 1960.

companies.[51] The Iranian government may perhaps be forgiven for its inability to operationally define what the Soviet Union considered "nonprovocative," short of a defenseless nonaligned Iran dependent on Moscow for both arms and a market for its oil.

Moscow apparently did not attempt to establish priorities in its relations with Iran. Judging from Soviet propaganda, the presence of American advisors, the acquisition of American arms, an agreement with Western oil companies, a rapprochement with other regional states, and the conclusion of any agreements not first cleared with Moscow were equally unfriendly acts. Privately the Soviet government probably discriminated between the unacceptability of these actions. Yet the Shah's evidence that the Soviets sought a practical veto over any development of road, rail, sea, and air facilities suggested that this was not the case.

The Soviet policy of extracting harsh preconditions prior to the normalization of relations with its weaker southern neighbor was self-defeating. By relying principally on intimidation, it only drove Iran closer to Moscow's competitor and confirmed Tehran's belief that non-alignment for a state bordering the USSR involved too high a risk.

The Iranian government's serious misgivings about the adequacy of the United States' commitments, coupled with Soviet interest in preventing the completion of the contemplated bilateral agreement, set the scene for dynamic interaction between Iran and the USSR. Talks were undertaken with the Soviet Union concerning the establishment of a new kind of relationship. It is impossible to determine whether the Shah deliberately entered these discussions intending to exploit them by brinksmanship and thereby improve his bargaining position with the U.S.[52] It is quite possible that the talks took place because of a joint desire to change the existing state of relations. The Shah, feeling

---

[51] For documentation of these points in the order presented in the text: "Observer" article, *Pravda*, Dec. 6, 1958; L. Alexeyev, "U.S. Military Mission in Iran and Iranian National Interests," p. 113; and F. Alterov, "The Oil Consortium—Neo-Colonialism in Action."

[52] For the Soviet's comment on the Shah's "brinkmanship," see *New York Times* Feb. 16, 1959. The Shah had intimated that he used the Russians as a lever on the U.S.: "In its initial form, the (U.S.) draft proposal was meaningless. We were so fed up that we turned a listening ear to Russian proposals for a nonaggression pact. . . . Finally Moscow proposed that Iran could remain in CENTO but would still sign a fifty-year nonaggression pact with the Soviet Union instead of the bilateral pact you were then offering. . . . We told your government, and President Eisenhower wrote begging me not to accept the Russian proposal. . . . But the United States then sent us a more explicit draft. . . ." Quoted in Sulzberger, *The Last of the Giants*, p. 770.

harassed by the USSR and let down by Washington, may have entered
into serious discussions hoping to reach an understanding with Moscow.
The Soviets, seeking to gain by negotiation and inducement what they
had hitherto failed to obtain by intimidation, likewise had reason to
enter into discussions.

The negotiations failed *principally* because of the stiff Soviet conditions by which Moscow offered to annul the essentially academic de-
bating points of Articles 5 and 6 of the 1921 treaty, in exchange for a
long-term nonaggression treaty with Iran and Iran's severance of all
meaningful ties with the West. Certainly the Shah's second thoughts
and allied pressures also contributed to this failure.

Undeniably the Iranian government utilized its parallel discussions
with both governments as a means of enhancing its bargaining power in
the serious discussions it sought. When the Soviet price appeared too
high, the talks were stretched out rather than immediately terminated.
With hindsight it would have been unlikely that the Shah would
cavalierly use the Russians to obtain a more explicit U.S. draft and
so have damned future relations with Moscow. In any event, there is
little doubt that the Shah felt insecure about his relationship with the
United States, that he was aware of the genuine domestic costs to his
own position regarding the Western tie, and that he found little in
the American commitment not already available to some genuinely
nonaligned states.

The possibility of neutralizing the opposition, ending Soviet harassment of the regime, and receiving an equal amount of aid from the
Soviets seems to have encouraged him to seriously consider the Soviet
terms for a rapprochement. Nonetheless, the very nature of the talks
rings somewhat false. The Iranians were not particularly concerned
about the academic and disputed issue of the interpretation of Articles
5 and 6 of the 1921 treaty and Article 3 of the 1927 treaty.[53] Although
the Soviets had periodically used them for propaganda purposes, any
implications of direct Soviet military intervention in Iran were coun-
tered by the West. Rather, the more immediate Iranian concern was
to maintain an effective and viable security posture while dealing with

---

[53] The text of these treaties may be found in Hurewitz, *Diplomacy*, pp. 90–95,
154–156. The Iranian view is that the subsequent exchange of letters limited the
reference in Articles 5 and 6 solely to "Czarist revolutionary elements." The Soviet
government has insisted that the treaty refers to *any* hostile element. Similarly, regarding the scope of Article 3 of the 1927 treaty, the Soviets have insisted on their
right to interpret which agreements are directed at them. Subsequent to the 1959
discussions, the Iranian government denounced Articles 5 and 6 of the 1921 treaty—
New York Times, March 3, 1959; *Tehran Journal*, March 3, 4, and 5, 1959—and were
in turn denounced for this action—*Pravda*, March 15, 1959.

pressing and long overdue internal economic and social problems. Confronted with the Hobson's choice of continued Soviet truculence[54] if he retained Iran's Western ties, or complete *reliance* on Soviet goodwill and Iranian military *impotence,* the Shah chose the embrace of the distant "devil" rather than the potentially stiffling bear-hug of the neighboring giant.

According to the Shah's version, the upshot of the episode was a "more explicit" U.S. draft. Yet it is likely that Iran's moderate success in maneuvering between the superpowers had been accomplished more out of genuine weakness and indecision than of calculated shrewdness and skill. Little had been accomplished in resolving Iran's security dilemma by inadvertently antagonizing the Soviets. Similarly, the Soviet refusal to provide any clear and reasonable alternative to the vacillating Iranian policy-makers during their reassessment had been a mistake. It had also been a reflection of Soviet heavy-handed diplomacy.

THE 1962 RAPPROCHEMENT: THE IRANIAN POLITICAL SETTING

Just as the decision to abandon Iran's traditional neutrality policy had been motivated by internal and external considerations, the move toward rapprochement was also prompted by these requirements.[55] At least since the fall of Dr. Mossadegh, the domestic opposition had closely linked the survival of the regime to American support. By the early 1960's American support for the regime had willy-nilly become inextricably entwined with its support for Iran's international status quo. Consequently, those elements which opposed the regime for any reason also tended to be hostile toward the U.S. If the Tudeh party is viewed in the light of a negative protest movement, its hostility to the regime, quite apart from any ideological or political underpinnings with Moscow, would predispose its members to oppose the U.S. tie. As has been pointed out in another study:

One offshoot of this negative protest in Iran has been the attitude towards major foreign powers which is directly connected with their support or opposi-

---

[54] The choice given Iran was clearly described by M. Ivanov, "Which Road Will Iran Take?" in *Mirovaya Ekonomika I Mezhdunarodnyye Otnosheniya* (February, 1959), condensed and translated in *Mizan Newsletter,* I, No. 3 (1959), 4; to wit: Either Iran will seek a policy of "neutrality and cooperation with peace-loving states" or it will participate in military blocs against the USSR.

[55] Keyvan Tabari, in "Iran's Policies Towards the U.S.," depicts the range of foreign policy postures existing: the Shah and Ghavam favoring a U.S. alignment to balance Great Britain and the USSR, and Mossadegh seeking "negative equilibrium," while the Anglophiles preferred a "perpetual inclination" toward Great Britain, and the Communists favored a similar orientation toward the Soviet Union.

tion to the Iranian regime. The closer the identification of the regime with a foreign power, the more intense the hostility has been toward that power; the more pronounced the hostility of a foreign power to the regime, the more frequent, however vague, the support for it.[56]

The Shah might thus be motivated to enjoy good relations with both superpowers as a means of neutralizing external support for his internal opponents.

It should be emphasized that quite apart from the regime's indefatigable opponents, a sentiment nearly approximating a mystical belief in the efficacy of a policy of neutrality has long existed in Iran. The belief is that neutrality is at all times and in all contexts a viable security policy. Its corollary is that Iran's problems are due to the involvement of foreign powers rather than vice versa. A tie with one foreign state, therefore, would undermine the "true nationalism" of the regime, for its suggested dependence.[57]

This was the consistent line of the Tudeh party starting in 1956. By 1960, at the Seventh Plenum of the Iranian Communist party, the Tudeh was prepared to support any government *inter alia* which withdrew from all military pacts. In the period of domestic political fluidity of 1960–1962 when the two political creations of the regime were feuding, the desire for achievement of this goal prompted the Tudeh to support the National Front.[58]

Internal opposition to continued reliance on one power, as both an organized and a general sentiment, was an important parameter in the Shah's thinking. Between 1960 and 1962, when Iranian politics experimented with a controlled two-party system, several figures who favored improved ties with Moscow were appointed. The dismissal of Prime Minister Manouchehr Eghbal, who was vehemently disliked in Moscow, had an international connotation. His replacement, Sharif Imami, immediately vowed to seek better ties with the USSR.[59]

Thereafter Soviet propaganda attacks declined, and whether by cause or coincidence, Soviet Ambassador Pegov returned to Iran. Sharif Imami then accepted an invitation to visit Moscow, but the trip never materialized. He was replaced in June 1961 by Ali Amini, a

---

56 Zabih, *The Communist Movement in Iran*, p. 247.

57 See the Shah's spirited defense of his "positive nationalism" in his *Memoirs*, pp. 124–127, 297. See also Richard W. Cottam, *Nationalism in Iran*, pp. 310–311, and L. P. Elwell-Sutton, "Nationalism and Neutralism in Iran."

58 Zabih, *Communist Movement*, p. 226.

59 *New York Times*, Aug. 31, 1960.

man the Soviets and others considered an "American appointee." [60]
Yet even now, hopeful indications for those who favored neutralism
were the inclusion in the new cabinet of Noureddin Alamouti, a former
communist, and Ghomali Farivar, a previous leader of the Iran party.[61]
Moscow welcomed the replacement of Amini by Assadollah Alam in
July 1962, and that government was in power in September when the
notes containing Iran's pledge were exchanged.

Yet it cannot be said that internal political developments in Iran
played a decisive role in the Shah's attempts for a rapprochement with
the Soviet Union. The Shah was aware of the sentiment favoring a
balanced policy and indicated his readiness to tolerate the possibility
of better Soviet ties. This movement to the center was reinforced by
the state of his relations with Washington.

The new Kennedy administration had not been giving the Shah's
regime the support he desired. Even under the previous administration
the Shah had had great difficulty in obtaining a commitment that
justified the political costs he had incurred through reliance on the
U.S. But the new administration appeared to encourage the Shah to
reconsider his excessive dependence on Washington. Its encouragement
of rapid social reforms, its backing of an activist prime minister, and
finally its termination of defense support underscored their differences
in perspective. The Shah's disquiet with the state of Iran-U.S. relations combined with his awareness of its political costs provided a
further incentive to normalize relations with the USSR.

However, this discomfort did not run so deep as to encourage the
monarch to sever his defense ties with the U.S. Whatever differences
existed between Tehran and Washington were overshadowd by the
common objective of maintaining Iranian independence through Irano-
American military links. Instead, the Shah sought again, as he had done
repeatedly and unsuccessfully since 1956, to convince the Soviet government that his policy of good relations with the West need not be an
obstacle to good relations with Moscow.[62]

The Shah was to find new incentives in the early 1960's to repair
those ties, in an opportunity to "steal his opponents' clothes while they
were bathing," and neutralize the issue of rapprochement with the
Soviets, while simultaneously asserting his independence from the

---

[60] See, for example, *International Affairs* (Moscow), No. 8 (September, 1961), pp. 114–115.

[61] "Notes of the Month: Crisis in Iran," *The World Today*, XVII, No. 6 (1961), pp. 227–229.

[62] *New York Times*, Sept. 25, 1960, and July 24, 1958.

U.S.[63] Finally, the international context was such that he might do this without jeopardizing Iran's security. Nonetheless, it was the Soviet government's terms, its preconditions for rapprochement, that remained the principal factor around which rapprochement would founder or flourish.

THE INTERNATIONAL CONTEXT: THE SINO-SOVIET DISPUTE

By the early 1960's a number of developments had emerged which facilitated Soviet rethinking of its policy toward Iran, and hence the process of rapprochement between them. These changes in the international system had considerably altered the larger context within which Iran-Soviet relations were situated, and on which they were dependent. The most important factors included the emergence of a serious Sino-Soviet dispute, the impact of affluence on Soviet revolutionary goals, the muting of the cold war, the fragmentation of the two blocs clustered around two poles, and finally, new technological developments.

Surfacing of a serious dispute within what earlier had appeared to be a doctrinal monolith had led to a seemingly irreconcilable schism by 1962. Stemming from primarily political differences, the rivalry involved the utilization of communist doctrine and dogma. The Shah, like General de Gaulle, perceptively forecast the emerging differences in the communist bloc. He had noted in 1960 that the differences between the USSR and a nuclear China would reach such an intensity that ". . . the Russians will gradually be driven to an understanding with the noncommunist powers." He predicted that "warm friendship with the Russians will then become possible." [64]

The Shah's perception of Soviet preoccupation with its Chinese neighbor, particularly on their joint border areas, has conditioned his attitude toward increased ties and cooperation. The Shah's belief that this preoccupation elsewhere makes the Soviets require a quiet southern border region, as well as economic and practical considerations, have encouraged him to engage Iran in functional cooperation with the Soviet Union. Evidently Iranian foreign policy toward the USSR is based on the anti-balance of power premise—e.g., Soviet problems

---

[63] Karim Sanjabi, a leader of the National Front, told Harrison Salisbury in 1961: "If the National Front comes to power, we will adopt an independent national foreign policy which might range to either side as the interests of the country would dictate." *New York Times*, Nov. 6, 1961. The phrase "independent national (foreign) policy" officially supplanted "positive nationalism" shortly thereafter as an expression of the foreign policy of Iran under His Majesty.

[64] *Memoirs*, pp. 315–316.

elsewhere will prevent Moscow from taking advantage of increasing trade ties between the countries and encourage it to promote stability on its southern flank.

These considerations made it easier for Iran to engage in a stepped-up economic relationship with the USSR. More importantly, the events of the past decade have confirmed the shift in Soviet priorities which stemmed from its differences with Peking and did in fact lead to a reassessment of its policy toward Iran.[65]

In addition to Soviet preoccupation with the neighboring Chinese doctrinal heresy, a new popular Western view of the Soviet Union had emerged. This view envisaged the imminent emergence of a conservative Soviet Union, blessed with industrial plenty and more responsive to consumer demands. Confronted with similar pressures as its superpower "enemy brother," the United States, the Soviet economic and political system would "converge" with the American.[66]

The implication of this "fat-man" theory for Soviet foreign policy would be the acceptance of the doctrine of "peaceful coexistence" as the first indication of this developing conservatism. This popular and simplistic view was based on an irrefutable premise: the Soviet Union as a mighty industrial superpower was subject to responsibilities and pressures which tended to "derevolutionize" its original heady goals. This was evidenced by the Soviet government's participation in summit conferences in 1960 as well as the de facto acceptance by each superpower of the other's area of predominance. In 1960 the Shah's view of the evolutionary erosion of the Soviet Union's "revolutionary" goals was evident when he wrote: "In the best sense the Russians are year by year becoming more conservative." [67]

However, there was always the possibility that this evolutionary trend toward similarity, if not convergence, might lead to collusion between the superpowers at the expense of their smaller clients. Apprehension about this possibility encouraged the Iranian leadership to mend its fences with the USSR before such a superpower rapprochement "left it in the lurch." By the mid-1960's talk in Washington about "bridge-building" surely gave the Iranian government an incentive to hedge its bets against superpower collusion by pursuing its own parallel designs with its neighbor.

---

[65] For a general discussion of the impact of the Sino-Soviet rift, see Adam Ulam, *Expansion and Coexistence: The History of Soviet Foreign Policy, 1917–1967*, p. 678.

[66] For a sophisticated discussion rejecting "convergence," see Zbigniew Brzezinski and Samuel P. Huntington, *Political Power: USA/USSR*, pp. 409 *et seq.*

[67] *Memoirs*, p. 316.

Iranian statesmen were aware that international circumstances as much as their own wartime statecraft had originally involved the United States in Iran's fate. The configuration of political forces in the international arena in the postwar era, the existence of the two superpower "enemies by position" and ideological competitors, had brought about a bipolar system. Mossadegh clearly recognized the importance of these factors to Iran's fate when he interrupted the director of the Point IV program's humanitarian explanation by saying, "If it weren't for our neighbors at the north, you would not be here." [68] However, by the early 1960's the bipolar system appeared to be giving way to a new political configuration.

By 1962 waning of the cold-war intensity had given rise to what has been called a "limited adversary" relationship between the two superpowers. Each was confronted with problems involving the management of its block. In the West, Charles de Gaulle's foreign policy symbolized the loosening of the blocs. He found he could assert France's interests and achieve a limited independence without sacrificing the security of the nuclear umbrella. The Shah of Iran knew and greatly admired Charles de Gaulle. This respect was returned, for de Gaulle chose Iran as the first country to visit in October 1963 in his attempt to reestablish French influence in the Middle East. On that visit he emphasized the similarities in the two countries' foreign policies. Charles de Gaulle was both a model for the Shah to emulate and a potential third-power balance—a trusted friend who might diminish Iran's reliance on the rigid bipolar balance.[69] Significantly, France could help diversify Iran's arms suppliers, as it had done in the case of the Arab-Israeli dispute.

The example de Gaulle set was of a resourceful statesman taking advantage of the international context to maneuver France into a position of prominence, pursuing her national interests through "grandeur" and in so doing maintaining good relations with both blocs. France's potential role as third power is succinctly stated by de Gaulle:

The vast Empire of Iran, bordering on Russia, was constantly exposed to the encroachments of the Anglo-Saxons, and was anxious to find support from other quarters. The Shah was therefore prepared to offer France a preferential position in business, education, and mineral search. Appreciating the wisdom

---

68 William R. Warne, *Mission for Peace* p. 26.

69 For comments on the visit, see *Le Monde* (Paris), Oct. 22, 1963. For the Shah's comments on his relationship with de Gaulle, see Bayne, *Persian Kingship in Transition,* and see De Gaulle's *Memoirs of Hope: Renewal and Endeavor,* pp. 261, 264–265, for his wartime comments on the Shah.

of this course, France developed a cooperative relationship with Iran which was to grow apace.[70]

After his rapprochement with the USSR, the Shah's reaction to the changing international context included the pursuance of Iran's self-interest in an independent national policy. This involved "bridge-building" with Iran's communist neighbor and its socialist allies in Eastern Europe, and included a diversification of foreign policy interests. A Regional Cooperative Development was established, trade ties with Eastern Europe were extended, and a more active regional role was undertaken. None of this involved the renunciation of Western ties or a diminution in the importance of the U.S. tie for either ultimate defense, weaponry, or diplomatic support. It was, rather, that the *urgency* of the need for that tie diminished. This diminished need partially resulted from the rapprochement with the USSR and was in turn a function of the international context which allowed Iran to play a more "independent" role.

For Iran-Soviet relations, then, the loosening of the blocs originating in detente had two implications. For Iran the detente raised the possibility of a rapprochement with the USSR, costing nothing in security, and holding out the possibility of a more "independent" future role. For the Soviets the detente was paralleled by problems of the scope and pace of liberalization in Eastern Europe as well as the Chinese challenge, and raised the possibility of a settlement in the bordering states which might provide it both security and a breathing spell. This possibility was enhanced by the progress in technology.

Developments in technology facilitated the removal of what had ostensibly been the principal Soviet bone of contention with the Iranian government, namely, the issue of foreign bases in Iran. The chief fear of Moscow regarding Ankara, where it was realized, and Iran, where it was not, was that these governments might allow atomic weapons or missiles to be stationed on their territory, adjacent to the Soviet Union. Since the delicate central strategic balance between 1949 and 1962 depended on the air arm of the U.S. and the USSR, any peripheral bases gained by the other superpower gave it an advantage in surprise attack capability and constituted a real danger.

The natural apprehension felt by Moscow, surrounded as it was by U.S. nuclear manned bombers in Europe, was that the U.S. advantage in

---

70 De Gaulle, *Memoirs of Hope*, p. 265. Bayne, *Persian Kingship*, p. 213, rightly emphasizes France's "third-friend" role fitting into a "traditional mode" in Iran's foreign policy.

warning time might be too tempting to ignore. Iranian assurances to the contrary were not considered an adequate guarantee against the possibility that Tehran might follow Ankara's example. The supstantial replacement of manned bombers by medium-range ballistic missiles such as "Jupiter" and "Thor" did nothing to alleviate Moscow's anxiety in the 1957 period. These unhardened liquid-fueled missiles, susceptible to a "first strike" attack and provocative in their implied "first strike" posture, were later replaced by hardened solid-fueled intercontinental ballistic missiles, and by 1962 had become obsolete.[71] Given their range, these newer missiles did not require bases along the periphery of the antagonist superpower. The growth of sea-based missiles such as Polaris in 1963 further diminished the importance of these bases. No doubt the political atmosphere of detente, and the removal by new technology of one of the principal Soviet fears regarding Iran, facilitated the Soviet acceptance of Iran's pledges concerning missiles.

The September 1962 Iran-Soviet rapprochement occurred for a numbem of reasons relating to international and internal Iranian factors. On the Iranian side the Shah sought to normalize relations with the USSR, for he sensed an international environment propitious for security and maneuver, and an opportunity to escape an excessive dependence on the United States. At the same time the obvious practical benefits of normalization and the opportunity to neutralize the issue of his foreign policy among his domestic opponents were not overlooked. Increased ties with an increasingly conservative and preoccupied USSR were not to be feared, while a rapprochement was useful in anticipating any possible superpower collusion. However, the price the Shah was prepared to pay did not include the severance of ties with the West or the subjugation of Iranian foreign policy to a Soviet veto.

From the Soviet perspective there was no need to insist on the preconditions previously required. Normalization of relations with that border state might bring security to its frontiers while it dealt with other more pressing problems in Asia. Particularly since technology had overtaken the issue of "missile bases" in Iran, it might be wise to attempt to obtain by inducement a *de facto* neutral on its borders rather than insist through intimidation on a *de jure* neutral. In the final analysis the 1962 rapprochement occurred because the Soviet

---

[71] By the autumn of 1962, if not earlier, the Jupiter missiles in Turkey and Italy were known to have been obsolescent. See Sorenson, *Kennedy,* pp. 285, 785n., and William Kauffmann, *The McNamara Strategy,* pp. 213–214. See also Albert Wohlstetter, "On the Value of Overseas Bases."

government accepted a long-offered pledge from the Iranian government.

THE SECOND ERA: SINCE 1962

The second era of Iran-Soviet relations since the 1962 rapprochement is more complex and variegated than the earlier period. The evolving international system has provided the setting within which these relations have developed and has conditioned the limits of the rapprochement. Political developments both within the region and internationally have facilitated the detente by providing a hospitable external environment. Internal developments, the launching of the "White Revolution," the consolidation of his domestic position, and Iran's rapid economic growth, which has averaged 10 percent annually from 1965 to 1970, have allowed the Shah to take advantage of external conditions and pursue a more "independent" foreign policy.[72]

In emphasizing the external environment which provided the Iranian leadership with a context more amenable to maneuvering, the dependence of the small state's role on the environment and forces essentially beyond its control must be stressed. A number of developments in the course of this period have confirmed the wisdom of moving toward normal relations with the USSR. Of foremost importance had been the dropping of Soviet conditions that Iran become neutral in return for "normal" relations. In temporarily giving up this condition, the Soviet leadership had not necessarily lost hope of attaining the same goal in a different way; nevertheless, in seeking friendly relations with Iran they also sought secure borders.[73]

Since 1962 events elsewhere have consumed a great deal of Soviet energy. Normalized ties with Iran provided the Soviets with both the security in the proximity of their borders and flexibility in coping with problems elsewhere. Economic considerations probably played a minor role in the deepening of Iran-Soviet trade relations, and these were entered into primarily for political reasons. However, it is also true that in such areas of Iran-Soviet cooperation as oil and gas, the USSR stood to benefit as much as Iran by the acquisition of cheap energy and its ready transportation to the Soviet Central Asian Republics.

---

[72] For figures on economic growth, see Jahangir Amuzegar and M. Ali Fekrat, *Iran: Economic Development Under Dualistic Conditions*, p. 113.

[73] After his trip to Moscow in the same year, the Shah told E. A. Bayne that the Soviets "do not want war, but need peace, just as Iran does, to develop." *Persian Kingship*, p. 217.

In mending his fences with the USSR, the Shah had not renounced his agreements with the West. American involvement and overextension in Vietnam had, by 1970, led Washington to a reassessment of its role in world affairs. The possibility of American retrenchment or neo-isolation, plus the differences already evident between his perspective and Washington's concerning regional affairs, clearly encouraged the Shah to rely as little as possible on the United States. The thaw in the cold war and the decline in the imminent security problem posed by the USSR gave Tehran added incentive to cooperate in trade matters and joint border ventures.

As the Soviet Union ceased to threaten Iran, other security questions hitherto overshadowed came to the forefront. The threat of Arab nationalism, particularly as pursued by Nasser's Egypt, was of special importance to the Shah. Although improved relations with the USSR could not be utilized to deal with this question, they did serve a useful function later on. However, it is unlikely that this possibility was already envisaged in Tehran. At the same time, the potential functions of the rapprochement were seen rather as (1) the intrinsic value of improved relations and possible practical benefits likely to follow; (2) the internal function of mending fences with Moscow in terms of Iranian domestic politics; and (3) the potential maneuverability it would give Tehran, its possible leverage and symbolic lessening of dependence on the United States. Clearly, the "unintended consequences" of improved relations with the USSR have benefited Iran's diplomacy in regional politics.

REGIONAL POLITICS

The Soviet government's attitude in regional affairs had usually been opposed to the Iranian position. The Soviets had found a regional ally in Nasser's Egypt to oppose the Baghdad Pact, and had continued to criticize its successor, CENTO, throughout the 1960's. Moreover, in the era of hostility toward Iran the Soviet government had taken the opposing side in regional quarrels and had tried to involve regional states in its own differences with Iran. For example, in Iran's dispute with Iraq in 1959, Moscow radio accused Iran of deliberately aggravating its quarrels with Iraq when world tensions were being relaxed, and in the following year when Iran-UAR diplomatic relations were severed, the Soviet Union took the Egyptian side.[74] Similarly, in the Soviet dispute

---

[74] *Ettelaat*, Dec. 5, 1958; and a commentary on "The Position of the Kurds in Iran," wherein it is alleged that U.S. and Iranian policies "are bound . . . to transform Iranian Kurdistan into a bridgehead for destructive activities against the

with Iran regarding the 1959 bilateral agreement, the attention of the Iraqi ambassador to Cairo had been drawn to the dangers to Iraq's security allegedly resulting from the conclusion of a U.S.-Iranian agreement.

A cursory glance at regional affairs indicates little similarity or congruity between Iran-Soviet interests from 1962 to 1967. In 1963, during the perennial dispute between the Iraqi government and the Kurdish minority, the Soviet Union warned Iran, Turkey, and Syria against any aid to the anti-communist Iraqi government in its "genocidal" war against the Kurds. Iran's continued membership in CENTO has also been important to the Soviets, although the interests of rapprochement have inclined them to neglect it. In the early period of rapprochement the pact's military exercises had provided an opportunity to protest its aggressive designs, but by the latter part of the decade the pact was being ridiculed and its alleged unpopularity in Pakistan and Turkey was instead communicated to Iran.[75] It is unlikely that Moscow welcomed the emergence of the Regional Cooperation for Development organization in 1964, but it has not publicly criticized it.

In 1969, in answer to a question whether there were any strains between CENTO or the RCD and the Soviet Union, the Shah replied:

Our relations are based on mutual respect. We are not asking them what they are doing in the Warsaw pact. So why should they ask us what we are doing in other places?[76]

In the light of this attitude, the USSR has not openly pressed this issue.

The most important regional question for Iran between 1963 and 1967 was the Soviet Union's direct opposition to Iran in its staunch backing of Nasser. Soviet-Egyptian interests overlapped at first, since they shared an opposition to Western-inspired regional pacts and an antipathy for the U.S. brand of imperialism. After considerable hesitancy the Soviet government adopted Egypt as its principal protegé and client, underwriting Nasser's regional excursions, including the lengthy, costly, and ultimately unsuccessful Yemen campaign. The Shah's concern for Iranian security in the light of Egypt's activism in

---

young Iraqi Republic," in *BBC Summary of World Broadcasts*, Part I; USSR, Second Series, No. 11 (April 27, 1959), pp. SU/11/A4/1–2.

75 For the Soviet (and its Arab clients') protest of military exercises, see *New York Times*, April 8, 1964, and Viktor Kudryavtsev, "Repairs Won't Help," *Pravda*, May 29, 1969.

76 Press conference in New Delhi, *Keyhan International*, Jan. 5, 1969.

the Arabian peninsula was expressed in the Islamic alliance, and was rapidly denounced by the Soviet government. This "alliance" was in fact a diplomatic entente between the monarchical states of Sa'udi Arabia, Jordan, Morocco, and Iran which were opposed to Nasser's activism. The Soviet Union denounced the project as sponsored by imperialism and backed by reactionaries, and supported Nasser's threats to enter into armed struggle against "reactionary-imperialist alliances." [77]

Soviet support for Nasser and opposition to Iran was not merely verbal. In the Yemen war the Soviet Union provided Nasser and the republicans with airplanes and pilots, while Iran provided the royalists with training and light material. Yet despite this difference, the proxy-war did not hinder the development of Iran-Soviet relations. Nevertheless, it underlined the limits of rapprochement with the USSR as far as regional politics were concerned, and underscored the opportunism of the Soviet regime. Moreover, it demonstrated the importance of self-defense for the Iranian government in the absence of a status-quo northern neighbor and the presence of the regionally ineffective CENTO.

Events in the Middle East since 1967 have altered the regional balance of power. The basic weakness of Egypt, its defeat in the war with Israel, and the subsequent departure of Egyptian troops from the Arabian peninsula ended the threat of an Egyptian hegemony on the southern shore of the Persian Gulf. At the same time, continued political stability in Iran, a booming economy, and increased defense outlays, combined with the announcement of Britain's departure from the Persian Gulf by 1971, altered the scenario in the Gulf. The Soviet government's perception of the changed situation is well illustrated by the new policy of watchful waiting it has adopted toward the subregion. It is also noteworthy that the Iranian government has become aware of the possibilities inherent in the situation for the neutralization of Soviet support for its opponents in the area.

Since 1967 there have been a number of disputes in Gulf politics between Iran and the Arab states. The Shatt al-'Arab question with Iraq, the ownership of the Bahrayn Islands, the question of the Union of Arab Emirates, and the disposition of the islands of Abu Musa and the Greater and Lesser Tumbs, which have been disputed by Iran on the one hand and the Shaykhdoms of Sharjah and Ras al-Khaymah on the other, are all cases in point.

---

[77] G. Savid, "Alliance Against Progress," and G. Sterkina, "Behind the Screen of the Islamic Pact."

The Soviet Union has avoided taking sides in these disputes. Admittedly this is not surprising in the case of Iran's disputes with the Emirates or Bahrayn, for they are not considered paragons of progressivism, but it is remarkable in the instance of Iran's disputes with Iraq. Iraq, though chronically politically unstable, has been one of the largest recipients of Soviet aid in the Arab world, ranking third after Egypt and Algeria.[78] Its ideological preferences and nonaligned posture have generally been more compatible with Soviet thought than with Iran's. Nevertheless, throughout the dispute between Iran and Iraq concerning the Shatt al-'Arab in particular and the future of the Gulf in general, the Soviet Union has remained prudent. In contrast to its behavior in 1959, the Soviet government has merely expressed regret over the dispute and published factual reports, neither allocating blame nor indicating a preference for either side. There are even some indications that it may have played a moderating role in 1971 in restraining Baghdad from aggravating the situation.[79]

Similarly, in the dispute over Iran's claim to Bahrayn, the Soviet government's stance has been cautious. While originally backing Iran's claims in the dispute with Great Britain, the Soviet Union has not commented on the subject since the mid-1950's. By 1968 the continuation of the claim had become an obstacle to Iran-Arab cooperation in Gulf affairs and it necessitated Iran's opposition to a federation or union which included that archipelago. The Arab states rejected the Iranian claim with varying degrees of intensity, and this claim became a source of tension with even the normally friendly states of Sa'udi Arabia and Kuwait. In addition, Cairo, Baghdad, and Riyadh strongly backed the proposed federation. In this situation the Soviet government neither supported nor rejected Iran's claim to Bahrayn. Indeed, a map published in *New Times* in February 1968 showed Bahrayn's ownership as "(Brit. Iran)".[80] Nor was the Soviet government a supporter of the federation of Shaykhly states. The one unequivocal and safe Soviet action in Gulf politics was designed to alienate none of the regional states, but criticized the British for "pretending" to leave the Gulf.[81]

The Iranian government at this time deliberately went out of its

---

[78] Marshall Goldman, *Soviet Foreign Aid*, p. 149.

[79] For Soviet comments on the 1969 differences, see *Izvestiya* April 23, 1969; *Pravda*, April 24 and 26, 1969, in *Mizan*, Supplement A, IV, No. 3 (May/June, 1969), 7. For a hint of the Soviet's restraining role, see *New York Times*, Jan. 30, 1972.

[80] See Dimitry Volsky, "On the Persian Gulf," p. 14.

[81] For a succinct account of Soviet problems finding a policy in this period, see "The USSR and the Persian Gulf," *Mizan*, X, No. 2 (March/April, 1968) 51–59.

way to neutralize potential Soviet opposition to its Gulf policy. There is some indication that this had become an intentional policy, as relations between the states continued to improve and were paralleled in the economic field. An example of such an attempt to neutralize Soviet policy is offorded by the question of the federation in 1968. At this time the USSR had taken no firm position on the federation. The Iranian government, however, was opposed to it and hence was ranged against the Arab states, "progressive" and "reactionary" in Soviet parlance. Undoubtedly the Shah felt isolated regionally and pressured domestically to maintain the claim to Bahrayn. The Soviet position on the federation at this moment of vulnerability was thus a minor test-case of its attitude toward Iran.

Lest the Soviets failed to understand, the Shah emphasized his position when he laid the foundation for the Isfahan steel mill just two weeks before Prime Minister Kosygin was due to visit Iran. "I warn even our present friends that if they ignore Iran's interests in any respect, especially in the Persian Gulf, they should expect from Iran treatment befitting their attitude." [82] The result, according to one report, was that Kosygin endorsed Iran's rejection of the federation.[83] What is certain is that the Soviet leadership did not then embarrass the Iranian government in its regional relations. It has also not taken the opportunities to isolate Iran or win credit with the Arab states indiscriminately.

While there are many reasons for Soviet reluctance to back Iraq since 1969, including Iran's refusal to support Soviet-backed peace initiatives in the Middle East conflict, it is remarkable that Soviet policy in the Arab-Israel zone has not carried over to the post-1969 Gulf region. Despite ample opportunities for creating divisions, the Soviets have been cautious. In the absence of a coherent Soviet Gulf policy, it is still too early to judge what their position would be in a serious Arab-Iran split. Nevertheless, the effective neutralization of the USSR in regional disputes affecting Iran since 1967 is impressive. This neutrality no doubt stems from the new value the USSR attaches to its relations with Iran.

INTERNAL BENEFITS

A useful side benefit resulting from the improvement in Iran-USSR relations concerned the impact of this rapprochement on dissidence in

---

82 The Shah's comments at Isfahan, mimeo. in Persian (Foreign Ministry transcript), March 13, 1968.
83 *New York Times*, April 6, 1968.

Iran's political process. Unlike the effect of the rapprochement on regional politics, the impact on domestic politics was probably recognized by Iran's leadership in 1962. The movement toward reconciliation substantially decreased the type and frequency of Soviet attacks on the regime, and criticism of the Shah and the monarchy has virtually disappeared. Since these improved relations roughly coincided with the launching of the "White Revolution," Soviet commentators have found much to praise in Iran. The pledge concerning "rocket bases" was itself called "an important step," and Khrushchev noted its value in a speech to the Supreme Soviet.[84]

The land-reform project was viewed with cautious optimism as a blow to feudalism, and opposition to it was denounced as "reactionary." The increased ties between the states were reflected in visits exchanged by important and lesser luminaries and reported in Soviet press accounts during the remainder of the decade. Parallel to the economic projects, there was evidenced a new interest in Iran and its culture.[85]

With the improvement of relations between the Soviets and Iran, the Tudeh party found itself increasingly undercut. While communist parties have not been an important instrument in Soviet policy in the postwar Middle East, the sacrifice of the Tudeh party on the altar of Soviet national interests is interesting. Not only did the party lose an important mentor, but the Soviet Union had gone so far as to return to Iran some Tudeh refugees from the pre-1953 period.[86] By 1967, due in part to the Soviet-Iran detente, the Tudeh party split into a faction representing Peking and another representing Moscow. By 1970 Maoism may thus have replaced the traditional Soviet brand of communism among the regime's most adamant opponents engaged in a "protest" movement. This may not have been due so much to any ideological purity, but rather was a result of its failure to come to an accommodation with the regime.[87] The regime's 1971 recognition of the People's Republic of China as the "sole" government in China was

---

84 K. Ivanovsky, "Important Step on the Path to Improving Relations Between the USSR and Iran," *Pravda*, Sept. 17, 1962, in *Current Digest*, XIV, No. 37 (Oct. 10, 1962), 16–17; and Khrushchev's report on the international situation at a session of the USSR Supreme Soviet, *Pravda*, Dec. 13, and *Izvestiya*, Dec. 12, 1962; in *Current Digest*, XIV, No. 52 (Jan. 23, 1963), 8.

85 See, *inter alia*, V. Medvedev, "Iran's Land Reform"; K. Ivanovsky, "A Good Start" and "Blow at Feudalism." For indications of an interest in Iran in general, see Stella Mazurenko, "Tehran Summer"; and "Recent Soviet Writing on Persia," *Mizan*, VI, No. 7 (July/August, 1964) 11–15.

86 Zabih, *Communist Movement*, pp. 240–242.

87 See "World Strength of Communist Party Organizations," *U.S. Dept. of State, Bureau of Intelligence and Research*, Pub. 8239, 19th Annual Report, p. 104.

no doubt partially inspired by the domestic considerations involved in "neutralizing" another source of potential support for the regime's opponents.

Improved Iran-Soviet relations in the period from 1962 to 1970 have served as a deterrent upon Soviet attacks on the regime, have undercut the resources of its domestic opponents, and since 1967 have been an important consideration in neutralizing potential Soviet support for Iran's rivals in regional politics.[88]

This is not to imply that the rapprochement has had no effect on Iran's foreign policy. On the contrary, considerations arising from a desire to offend neither of the superpowers have acted as a new parameter in postwar Iranian foreign policy. Hence the Iranian position on Vietnam has been vague, and its support of the Arab position regarding the territories acquired by Israel has no doubt partially been conditioned by Soviet sensitivity. It may also have been Soviet encouragement of Tehran that brought about the reestablishment of diplomatic relations with Egypt in 1970. While it has tempered Iranian foreign policy, the rapprochement may also have encouraged ill-considered attempts to "please" the Soviet Union. For example, the Iranian government has supported a nuclear free zone, a project understandably close to the Soviet heart but of largely undetermined impact on Iran's long-range security interests.[89]

RELATIONS WITH THE SUPERPOWERS AND AN
"INDEPENDENT NATIONAL POLICY"

The transformations in international politics combined with the political stability and economic vitality of Iran in the latter part of the 1960's have changed the character of Iran's relations with the superpowers. The primary importance of relations with the U.S. and the USSR and the need for maintaining a balance between them certainly remains. But the sense of overriding urgency has evaporated. Balance is now sought to compensate for the alignment with the West, and good relations with both superpowers are valued as much for the freedom to maneuver as for security reasons. Iran's stability and economic growth in a troubled and turbulent region have in turn given the superpowers a new perspective. Khrushchev's predictions of revolution have

---

88 For neutralization of opposition resulting from the rapprochement, see Hélène Carrière D'Encausse, "L'Iran en Quête d'un Equilibre," p. 234; and Arnold Hottinger, "Consolidated Regime in Iran."

89 The text of the joint communiqués referring to this may be found in *Pravda*, July 29, 1967. The Iranian foreign minister's reference to it is in the UN's general debate in document A/PV 1940 (Sept. 27, 1971) p. 62.

not been borne out, nor have the forecasts or prophecies of American social scientists been any more accurate. For the Soviet Union, Iran has become an important factor on its borders and in the Gulf region. For the United States, the value of a stable and friendly Iran has not diminished with the detente in the cold war nor the change in relationship from client to "equal" ally.

The change in the character of Iran's relations with the superpowers from pawn, supplicant, and client to a stable regional state has also increased the Iranian government's leverage on Moscow and Washington. Iran has been able to use its new relationship with the superpowers, and Moscow in particular, to achieve some of its own ends.

The 1959 discussions with the Soviet government were primarily a defensive move rather than a conscious manipulation of risks to pressure the United States. Iran's improved bargaining position, however, has since permitted the conscious employment of the same tactic as a lever on Washintgon.

In 1966 the Shah attempted to obtain a ground-to-air missile network for the Persian Gulf—the oil-refinery area of Abadan in particular. In the face of American hesitancy and procrastination, he let it be known that he was considering the possibility of purchasing this network in Moscow. Presumably the intention was to demonstrate Iran's alternative sources of supply. Since the arms were to be purchased, this may also have been a means of improving the credit terms Washington might offer. However, Moscow was concerned that this network might possibly be used against Egypt and was therefore hesitant in providing it. The U.S. subsequently agreed to provide the arms requested, both directly and through its NATO ally, the United Kingdom.[90]

In contrast to the aftermath of the 1959 discussions, when the Soviet Union accused Iran of brinksmanship, the Shah took no chances .He subsequently decided to buy 110 million dollars of nonsensitive military transport equipment from the USSR anyway, primarily to demonstrate his independence and forestall any ill will. He remarked to Bayne: "I could not withdraw altogether now. . . . It would be the same as saying to them and to the world that I am an American puppet. I am not." [91]

The same tactic of pressuring the U.S. government by airing the possibility of obtaining arms from Moscow was repeated prior to the Shah's visit to Washington in 1969. Presumably it was a credible threat, in the light of the 1966 purchase. It should be emphasized that this

90 See *New York Times,* July 14 and Sept. 19, 1966.
91 Bayne, *Persian Kingship,* p. 224.

tactic was employed to pressure Washington to sell the type and quantity of arms he thought Iran needed, rather than those arms Washington deemed adequate or suitable. Its success depended on both the acquiescence of the Soviets, who reportedly offered Iran arms on favorable terms in 1965, and on Washington's continued interest in remaining Iran's principle arms supplier.[92] For while the diversification of the source of arms supplies was in itself symbolic and welcome, the Shah did not intend to replace his dependence on American manpower and material with reliance on Moscow. Sympathetic American understanding of Iran's relationship with the USSR was thus necessary to keep this tactic from backfiring.

Moscow and Washington have either tolerated or welcomed this relationship and have found there are advantages in a strong stable Iran acting as a buffer in the region. Both superpowers have discovered, however, that the price of maintaining this buffer may be "a measure of support for Iran's political interests in the region." [93] The Iranian government, in turn, has been careful not to identify too strongly with either superpower, but to maintain friendly relations with both. This policy of equilibrium is illustrated by the Iranian reaction to the invasion of Czechoslovakia. While he formally condemned the Soviet action in August 1968, the Shah refused to cancel or postpone his scheduled visit to Moscow in the following month—despite requests from both Great Britain and President Johnson of the United States.[94]

The changed international environment has given the Iranian government not only more maneuverability between the superpowers and a relatively new importance, but also more opportunity to actively pursue its own interests in world politics. The increased travel to and from Iran by the Shah and foreign statesmen since 1962 has contributed to a diversification of Iran's trade and diplomatic ties. For the regime the amplification of these ties has served the useful domestic function of symbolizing the assertion of Iran's independence from the superpowers.[95] Nevertheless, since 1972 this "independent national policy" has been a reactive one built primarily on appearance and has been negative in the sense that its goal has been to escape the control of the superpowers.

---

[92] The Shah hinted at the need for a small state to catch the eye and attention of a superpower; *ibid.*, p. 224.

[93] Leonard Binder, "Factors Influencing Iran's International Role," p. 36.

[94] Bayne recounts that the American and British ambassadors in Tehran, later the state department, and finally the White House joined in efforts to talk the Shah out of the visit. "A Heritage from Xerxes," p. 5.

[95] For the Shah's expression of Iran's independent national policy, as a reorientation of foreign policy, see *Keyhan International*, Aug. 19, 1965.

Iran-Soviet trade and commercial relations have vastly intensified from 1962 to 1970 and have paralleled their improved political relations. From the Iranian standpoint, practical cooperation has been desirable both in itself and for its political benefits, for "normalization" has diversified Iran's sources of aid and contributed to its development. For the Soviets, the aid and trade relationship has impressed the Iranian government with the benefits of the practical alternative of neutralism and the peaceful nature of Soviet intentions. In concluding commercial agreements with Iran, the Soviet government has obtained a "presence" in that country which it had been denied since the Second World War.[96]

Seen in the total context of Soviet foreign policy, aid toward Iran after 1964 reflects Moscow's increased political emphasis on the Asian countries along its borders. From 1965 to 1968 Iran received more than one-fifth of the total Soviet economic aid committed to Afro-Asia, and Iran, Afghanistan, and Pakistan together accounted for one-third of that total. In 1967 three-quarters of Soviet development assistance went to the Middle East, and most of it consisted of a 200 million dollar loan to Turkey. In 1968 the combined credits of 178 million dollars to Iran and 127 million dollars to Afghanistan accounted for over 99 percent of the total Soviet assistance.

A similar increase in trade relations and practical cooperation between the border states and the Soviet Union has been evident since the September 1962 watershed in their relations.[97] In July 1963 an agreement was reached on the building of a hydroelectric project on the frontier river of Aras near Atrak, and it began operation in 1971. There have also been joint construction of twelve grain silos, dredging the Caspian Sea, and cooperation in fish-breeding reservoirs. The Soviet government also provided a loan of 36 million dollars at an interest rate of 3.6 percent.[98] This was followed on the occasion of Brezhnev's visit to Tehran in November by a transit agreement whereby Soviet goods received favorable rates in their movement to the Persian Gulf and Iranian goods received similar treatment in their transit to Europe. Trade relations and the timing of their development became very

---

[96] Wynfred Joshua and Stephen P. Gibert, *Arms for the Third World: Soviet Military Aid Diplomacy*, pp. 50 and 20 *et seq*. The authors define this pattern as a policy of "intrusion."

[97] See R. A. Yellon, "Shifts in Soviet Policy toward Developing Areas," in Raymond Duncan (ed.), *Soviet Policy in Developing Countries*, pp. 279–280; Joshua and Gibert, *Arms for the Third World*, p. 132. For more general studies, see Walter Laqueur, *The Struggle for the Middle East: the Soviet Union in the Mediterranean*, pp. 1–42; and Arnold Klieman, *Soviet Russia and the Middle East*, p. 47 *et seq*.

[98] *Tehran Journal*, June 29 and July 29, 1963.

much a function of relations between the states, and it appears that the Soviet government sought an opportunity in the ripening relationship to make a grand breakthrough in financing a major aid project.[99]

The present Shah, and his father before him, had long desired a steel mill in Iran. Western firms, particularly West German and American companies, had not been enthusiastic on purely practical and economic grounds, and the possible site of the project had been much debated. The Shah, on the other hand, wanted the steel mill as much for immediate political and prestige purposes as for the long-range economic benefits. The Soviets sensed the opportunity and were not slow to hint at their readiness to help. As early as July 1963 on a visit to Iran, Vasily Alekseevich Sergeev, an undersecretary of the Soviet ministry of economy, had pointed out the benefits of a steel mill and offered Soviet aid in its construction, alluding at the same time to Soviet aid in the construction of the Indian Bhilai steel mill. Similar hints were dropped by Soviet Ambassador Gregory Zietsev some six months later, but he denied that the construction of the steel mill had been discussed by the Iranian and Soviet governments.[100] The cabinet of Hassanali Mansur, which took office in March 1964, continued to pursue the possibilities of the project, but as late as the following March there was no hint that aid in the project would come from other than Western sources.

However, as a result of the Shah's visit to Moscow in the summer of 1965 an arrangement was worked out whereby an iron and steel complex in Isfahan, a machine factory plant, and a gas pipeline to Soviet territory were to be built with Soviet assistance. The iron and steel mill was to have a capacity of 500,000 to 600,000 tons per annum, and started operation according to plan in 1970.

In exchange for this and other aid, Iran was to repay the USSR in natural gas and certain agricultural and industrial goods.[101] Perhaps to maintain a political balance in these matters, the Iranian government obtained 200 million dollars of credits from private British, French, and West German companies to finance its branch of the gas pipeline to the Soviet border. This pipeline was inaugurated and started operation in October 1970 when the Shah and President Podgorny met at the border town of Astara.

Under the agreement Iran was to supply the USSR with seven

[99] Marshall Goldman has noted that the Soviets tend to stress basic industrial projects and "have a knack for the spectacular." *Soviet Foreign Aid*, p. 189. See also John S. Reshetar, Jr., "The Soviet Union and the Neutralist World."

[100] *Tehran Journal*, July 30, 1963, and Jan. 16, 1964.

[101] See *The Economist*, Jan. 4, 1966; *Pravda*, Jan. 14, 1966.

billion cubic meters of gas annually beginning in 1970 and to increase the amount to ten billion between 1976 and 1985, when the situation will be renewed. The estimated $650 million cost of building the pipelines, which were to be supplied by Soviet creditors, has reportedly been revised upward. By 1972 close to $632 million was spent on the main trunk line. Various other costs for such ancillary projects as a gas refinery complex on the pipeline route were met by loans from sources other than the USSR.

In the aftermath of the oil crisis of 1973–1974 serious thought has been given to extending the project beyond Soviet-Iranian borders in order to deliver gas supplies to such West European industrial countries as Germany by various transshipment methods.[102]

Soviet terms in both the construction of the steel mill and the offer of arms were very attractive, and significantly, the Soviet government had taken the initiative.[102] The timing of the 1965–1966 offers and agreements are also significant, for it was in 1965 that the U.S. government declared Iran a "developed" country and began to "phase out" economic and military aid. In stepping into this gap, the Soviet government has not hesitated to emphasize the benefits accruing to Iran from barter arrangements with the USSR. For a country like Iran with a chronic balance-of-payments deficit, an annual debt-servicing obligation equal to 12 percent of its vital foreign-exchange receipts has obvious advantages. Soviet propaganda has also stressed the employment the projects will bring and extolled the unique benefits of cooperation in trade with the USSR.[103]

The expanding rate of trade between Iran and the USSR in the past decade is also remarkable. Soviet exports to Iran have increased tenfold in that period. Iran is only outranked by Egypt as a market in that region of the world and constitutes a market two and a half times as large as Iraq. At the same time, by 1970 the Soviet Union had become Iran's largest customer for non-oil exports. And more importantly, it was the only one of Iran's major trading partners with which trade was nearly balanced.[104]

Joint cooperation in trade and practical endeavors has done much

102 Jane Perry Clark Carey, "Iran and Control of Its Oil Resources," *Political Science Quarterly*, Vol. 89, No. 1, March 1974, pp. 169–170. See interview with the Shah, *New York Times*, Feb. 21, 1967.

103 For the question of foreign exchange, see Amuzegar and Fekrat, *Iran*, p. 49 and 49n.; and Julien Bharier, *Economic Development of Iran, 1900–1970*, pp. 114–115, 120, *et passim*. For a representative sample of Soviet comments about benefits of trade for Iran, see I. Shatalov, "Iran 1347," p. 77.

104 For unofficial documentation, see: "The Soviet Stake in the Middle East," *Middle East Economic Digest*, XIV, No. 35 (Aug. 28, 1970), 1010; and Bharier, *Economic Development*, p. 113.

to dispel the distrust lingering from the cold war period. There are both practical and political incentives for this continued cooperation. For the Soviet government, it holds out the possibility of the continued supply of cheap accessible fuel for its central Asian republics, and the provision of conveniently located energy supplies, in the event that the USSR needs to import oil. An obvious potential for expanding the relationship will be realized if the project for a "42" oil pipeline from Bushehr in southern Iran to Astara comes to fruition. Another potential area of oil cooperation is in the Caspian region, where the lure of inexpensive Middle Eastern oil may encourage the Soviet government to use its own oil supplies for political and foreign-exchange purposes.

From the Iranian viewpoint the commercial and trade relationship is based on an important premise relating to politics. The Shah's belief is that the nature of the trade ties will eventually transform the character of Iran-Soviet relations. That is, by introducing an element of planned dependence on the Iranian economy and especially Iranian oil supplies, the Soviet government will be constrained to preserve good relations with the Iranian government. In due course, so the thinking runs this functional cooperation will "socialize" the Soviets into a civilized attitude.

While this is obviously an oversimplification, it is indicative of a train of thought of the Iranian leadership. It believes that there would be little for the Soviets to gain and a great deal to lose both regionally with the Arab oil-producing states and Iran and, globally, with the United States, Japan, and Western Europe, if the USSR attempted to divert, deny, or withhold Middle Eastern oil from its present markets. It is unlikely that the Shah believes that the Soviet government will be "socialized" purely through functional cooperation. Rather, he believes that the economic element, the dependence of the USSR on imported oil, the desire for secure frontiers, its commitments and preoccupations elsewhere, and the desire not to revive NATO and the cold war, or to antagonize the region, will adequately deter the Soviets from aggressive designs on Iran or any other Gulf oil-producing state in the near future.[105]

While the Soviet Union has undoubtedly become enmeshed into a limited form of dependence on trade relations with Iran, the reverse is true to a far greater extent. As noted earlier, the Soviet government

---

[105] For Soviet energy needs and an excellent brief assessment of Soviet aims, see Robert E. Hunter, "The Soviet Dilemma in the Middle East. Part II: Oil and the Persian Gulf," esp. pp. 1–12; and Peter R. Odell, *Oil and World Power*, pp. 166–170.

has historically used economic and trade relations with Iran for political ends. The need for caution against self-delusion and extravagant ethnocentricism as to the importance of Iran in Soviet trade or political calculations must therefore be stressed. At the present time and in the existing international context, trade with the USSR has undoubtedly benefited Iran. Moscow has even vocally backed the Iranian government's periodic requests for increased revenues from the Western oil companies, and the results of its own agreements in December 1967 and July 1969 in neighboring Iraq may indirectly have aided Iran's negotiating position in 1969.[106]

While he has attempted to "socialize" the great power to the north, the Shah has not dispensed with his tie with the West. Whether or not the Shah truly meant the comment he made in Moscow in 1965 that "if a state could choose its neighbors itself, we would choose you," there is little doubt that Soviet policy has changed radically for the better since the start of the decade. Yet it would not be prudent to assume that Soviet long-run aims have changed. The aim of neutralizing Iran, *de facto,* through its detachment from the West, is now merely pursued by different tactics and instruments. President Podgorny's statement in Iran in March 1970 that "Iran is now strong enough to pick her friends" is, perhaps, indicative of an attempt to win Iran to neutrality through flattery rather than through intimidation.[107]

THE INTERNATIONAL CONTEXT

In the early part of the decade Soviet policy sought minimally and defensively to deny, reduce, or preclude Western influence in the Middle East. By the latter part, however, it had sought and achieved a more positive position of influence in the area. This is perhaps best symbolized by the 1971 treaties of friendship with Egypt and India, its tangible foothold in the Arab world, and the reality of a Soviet naval presence in the Indian Ocean. While the opportunities afforded the USSR by the international political environment may remain the key to assessing Soviet intentions, it is indisputable that by early 1972 there had been an enormous increase in Soviet capabilities in naval and airlift power and in the globalization of its regional reach.

However, against the Soviet diplomatic successes in the 1967 Middle

---

106 See Hunter, "Soviet Dilemma," pp. 11–12; and L. Skuratov, "Oil Consortium Against Iran," D. Kasatkin, "Assault on Oil Monopolies," and R. Andreasyav, "New Aspects of Middle East Countries' Oil Policy."

107 The Shah's comment, made to the Soviet public on June 21, 1965, in Moscow, is quoted in *Mizan,* VII, No. 1 (July/August, 1965), 21–22. Podgorny's statement is reported in *Kayhan International,* March 3, 1970.

East and 1971 India-Pakistan wars, her problems elsewhere must be recognized.

Whether to give priority to dealing with the Western or the Chinese adversary, and how to allocate resources between the needs of this two-front external struggle and needs of domestic consumption and development.[108]

A Soviet presence, if not predominance, is likely to remain a fact in the Middle East, but in the present period of diplomatic fluidity it is difficult to envisage the precise form this presence will assume. Vague Soviet hints about "an Asian security system" have been aired, but little concrete action has so far emerged.

For Iranian statesmen the concept of a Soviet-sponsored regional security system under its tutelage is anathema. For it would obviously replace the rough equilibrium the regime has sought to establish between the superpowers. Although this equilibrium is disproportionately weighted in favor of the U.S. in order to balance the geographic proximity of the USSR, it has nevertheless become temporarily satisfactory to all three states. At any time this balance can be jeopardized by a change in the Soviet role in South Asia, particularly if it is not counterbalanced. In the event of increased Soviet influence in both India and the Arab-Israel zone, and an American policy of disentanglement, a reassessment of the practicality of equilibrium would most probably have to be made.

In the face of Soviet predominance, the Iranian leadership might then be encouraged to trim its sails and to "tack" with the dominant power of the continent. It should not be inferred from the preceding sections that the Soviet government values its relations with Iran enough to remain impartial in any issue affecting Iran. Any issue sufficiently important to the USSR will witness Soviet involvement commensurate with that importance, whatever the effects on Iran-Soviet relations. Soviet behavior in December 1971 during the Indo-Pakistan dispute, and specifically its readiness to risk these relations by troop movements on Iran's borders, should it attempt to aid Pakistan, again underscore both the opportunism of the USSR and the limited impact a small state can have in effecting a superpower's calculations.[109] It is therefore appropriate to conclude this chapter by outlining the areas of potential stress in Iran's relations with the Soviet Union.

The most important of these in the foreseeable future relates to the

---

[108] Richard Lowenthal, "Continuity and Change in Soviet Foreign Policy," p. 4. See also Marshall D. Shulman, "The Future of Soviet–American Competition."
[109] See *New York Times*, Nov. 30, 1971.

difficulties of reconciling the multi-lateral Soviet-Middle East interests with that of the bilateral ties between Moscow and Tehran. Soviet multilateral interests in the region are an outgrowth of its globalism, and at times have sharply conflicted with its interests in maintaining its detente with Iran. Just as the latter's increased interest in regional political development has occasionally conflicted with Soviet Middle Eastern policies, both states are conscious of these difficulties, as was indicated in recent events. In April 1972 when a Soviet-Iraq friendship treaty was signed without the prior knowledge of the Iranian government, the displeasure of the Shah prompted Soviet efforts to allay Iran's misgivings. Ultimately another summit visit occurred, which produced a Treaty of Cooperation between the two.[110]

The prospect of another blow to the territorial integrity of Pakistan through Soviet-Indian support of Pakhtunistan is another source of anxiety for Iran. Remembering a similar threat to its sovereignty in the early postwar period and the reputed counsel of Soviet authorities to grant local autonomy to Pakhtunistan within the context of a Pakistan nation state the Iranian government has shown considerable unease toward Soviet-Indian and Soviet-Afghani cooperation.[111] Indeed, a sense of isolationism characterized the Iranian attitude in 1972–73 when some journalists used the term Moscow-Baghdad-New Delhi axis, embracing Iran on three sides. Reaction to this concern was partially responsible for the renewed interest in resurrecting the CENTO treaty in the summer of 1973.

Overemphasis on a security alliance with the West involves risks of endangering the detente with the Soviets—risks the government seems determined to avoid. Therefore the annual visit of the Shah to Washington in July 1973 was conveniently balanced by the Iranian prime minister's visit to Moscow the following month.[112] As long as the two superpowers retain global interests and as long as Iran pursues a dynamic and active regional foreign policy, these stresses are likely to continue.

---

[110] *Keyhan,* Tehran, Oct. 29, 1972.
[111] *Iran Tribune,* Tehran, February, 1973.
[112] See communiqué on the visit in *Ettelaat,* Tehran, Aug. 12, 1973.

Chapter II

RELATIONS WITH THE
UNITED STATES

The primary area of concern in a study of Iran-U.S. relations is the vast apparent disparity in power and leverage between the two nations, and the necessarily divergent perspectives between a superpower with global interest and commitments[1] and a small state primarily concerned with external security and internal stability. These differences in capacities and interests are reflected in the size of military establishments and bureaucracies serving their foreign relations activities, and in the differing priorities attached to particular events by the partners. The differences in emphasis and priority emanating from disparities in power and divergent perspective have been lucidly evoked by Arnold Wolfers in his description of the coalition leader as the hub of a wheel joined to its allies on the rim of spokes.

The build-in tension "inevitable" in such a situation is that the "coalition leader whose strategy must be guided by global considerations will find it difficult to satisfy both the ally, who, in a particular case is on the firing line and those allies who happen to be remote from it." [2] While for the United States the primary danger to international peace and security has been the communist great powers, many

---

[1] A former U.S. Ambassador to NATO has described the pressures of international commitments succinctly: "The United States belongs to 53 international organizations, and attended 633 international conferences in the twelve months ending in mid-1965. . . . For the twenty-four months ending in mid-1965, we went to more conferences than the U.S. government attended in its entire national history from 1789 to 1943." Harlan Cleveland, *The Obligations of Power: American Diplomacy in the Search for Peace,* p. 57.

[2] Arnold Wolfers, *Discord and Collaboration: Essays on International Politics,* pp. 210–211.

of her allies have been absorbed by more immediate threats, both internal and regional, which may have been only vaguely related to communism.[3]

An analysis of Iran-U.S. relations should start with a reference to the reactive nature of the American stance toward Iran and the third-power emphasis in Iranian policy toward the U.S. In this sense the inception of American postwar policy toward Iran was determined above all by actions designed to counter the policies of the other super-power, Russia. Similarly, Iran's policy was conditioned by the geo-political distance and disinterest of the United States and the evolving cold war confrontation between the two superpowers. Several factors in the immediate postwar era contributed to a certain degree of ambivalence in Iranian policy toward the U.S.:

(1) The wartime alliance had fostered the impression that interest in Soviet-American postwar cooperation would prevail over support for Iran's struggle against the Soviet Union. There was general belief also in America's return to isolationism, which was reinforced by the speedy withdrawal of the American expeditionary forces from Iran before British and Soviet withdrawal. (2) The Iranian ruling groups generally believed in the ascendancy of Great Britain in the postwar era, which was reinforced by American policies in a number of other critical regional cases, notably the initial British intervention in Greece. (3) American economic and commercial interests were not of a nature which could form leverage for seeking deeper U.S. involvement in Iran. Therefore the Iranian objective of reliance on the U.S. as a disinterested and distant power had certain limitations. That is to say, these very characteristics which suited the U.S. role as a third power worked against a positive response to Iranian demands. Also, in the cold war between the two superpowers, Iranian interests became entangled in global and strategic considerations which were not always compatible with the concept of third-power protection.

Nevertheless, as noted earlier, the Soviet diplomatic offensive prompted a series of American responses beginning in 1945. While most historians agree that Soviet involvement in Azarbayjan Kurdistan marked the start of the cold war and the superpower confrontation which began in the early fifties, a different interpretation has more recently been placed on this episode.

The new school of revisionist interpretation of the genesis of the cold war holds that American economic imperialism was the real "fluid stream" striving to fill "every nook and cranny available to it in

---

[3] *Ibid.*, p. 215.

the basin of world power." [4] As proof of this assertion, these New Left historians refer to the dispatch of Patrick Hurley and Herbert Hoover, Jr., to Iran in September 1944, to secure oil concessions there before Soviet demands were made for them. To these historians, the Soviet intervention was basically defensive. One writes, "To the Russians it seemed only fair that they be allowed to participate in the exploitation of Iranian oil, all the more so since the terms they wanted were less favorable than those enjoyed by the Anglo-American oil companies." [5]

Further, the revisionists contend that both separatist regimes enjoyed genuine popular support in those provinces and were a response to the utter disaffection with the corrupt central government. Finally, the delicate and skillful UN-supported initiative to compel Soviet evacuation of northern Iran is dismissed as resulting from normal bilateral diplomatic negotiations.[6]

This type of interpretation is closely allied to the Iranian Tudeh party's "public stance." Namely, the historically accurate account of the chronological order of U.S. and Soviet demands for oil concessions, the unpopularity of the central government in these provinces, and the final but delayed departure of the Red Army are all presented as legitimate and defensive Soviet responses. This type of analysis, amounting to advocacy of a "positive balance" between powerful interventionist neighbors, ignores the fact that when the central regime refused the U.S. demand for oil concessions, the U.S. did not use the presence of its armed forces to compel compliance with its request as did the Russians. It ignores the similarly strong xenophobic nationalism which at the end of 1946 turned the tide against Soviet-backed separatist regimes. And furthermore, it ignores the fact that those "normal" diplomatic negotiations between Tehran and Moscow involved wresting a draft agreement for oil plus a patently "interventionist" pledge from Iran to settle the Azarbayjan problems peacefully and "with due regard for the legitimate grievances of their inhabitants." [7]

Obviously the gradual entrenchment of American interest in Iran after 1953 makes this retrospective analysis somewhat plausible. What

---

[4] For a discussion of the background of Iran-U.S. relations, see Abraham Yesselson, *United States-Persian Diplomatic Relations, 1883–1921;* Justus D. Doenecke, "Iran's Role in Cold War Revisionism," p. 97.

[5] Stephen E. Ambrose, *Rise to Globalism: American Foreign Policy, 1938–1970,* p. 131.

[6] Gabriel Kolko, *The World and the United States Foreign Policy,* Vol. II, *The Limits of Power, 1945–1954;* pp. 240–241. For a balanced view on this matter consult Gary R. Hess, "The Iranian Crisis of 1945–1946 and the Cold War." *Political Science Quarterly,* Vol. 89, No. 1, March 1974, pp. 117–146.

[7] See Chapter I above.

would have developed had the Soviets succeeded in their early postwar diplomacy in Iran, on the other hand, remains conjecture. Nonetheless, the American stance in this crisis, followed by the 1947 agreement for military aid and training, the extension of the Point Four program in 1950, and a measure of sympathetic toleration of the nationalist regime in its initial phase were all indicative of a gradual emergence of Iranian-American relations as the dominant concern for Iranian policy-makers.

The fall of the Mossadegh regime, preceded by expressions of American concern about a possible communist takeover and the reported CIA intervention in the overthrow of that regime, have been extensively reported elsewhere.[8] The significance of these events is that: (1) for a majority of Iranians the fall of Mossadegh meant the end of an era and the beginning of a new one in which Iran abandoned its efforts at remaining out of the cold war and now became very much enmeshed in it; (2) it meant an end to the postwar parliamentary multiparty system in which the formulation and conduct of foreign policy were not the exclusive responsibility of the Shah; (3) the American takeover of nearly 40 percent of the former British petroleum operation in Iran meant that American economic and commercial interests had begun to be entrenched in the country. For the Iranian authorities this meant that the distant power had now become an interested one and therefore likely to act as a protective power.

It is against this brief background that by 1955 the Shah, finding common ground between his conception of Iranian security and that of the Republican administration in Washington, decided on alignment with the Western powers in the form of the now defunct Baghdad Pact. It should be noted that resistance to the proposed alignment was not confined to nationalist neutralist elements. As a matter of fact, General Fazlollah Zahedi, who succeeded Mossadegh as prime minister in August 1953, had to be replaced at least in part for his opposition to the Baghdad Pact. It was left to Hussein Ala, Zahedi's successor, to officiate over Iran's adherence to the pact.

With his assumption of supreme and exclusive control of Iran's foreign policy, the Shah was provided an opportunity to air his views in opposition to those who had long cherished a stance of neutrality for the country. He expressed the belief that since that traditional neutrality policy had failed in World War II, it would be prudent for an exposed small state to seek protection in alliance.[9] The threat to

---

8 Richard W. Cottam, *Nationalism in Iran*, and others.
9 See the Shah's speech to the Foreign Press Association, London, reprinted in the *New York Times*, May 9, 1959.

Iranian security by the Soviet Union, the divisions within the Iranian polity, and the strength of the Tudeh party, as well as the precarious position of the young monarch, encouraged the Iranian leadership to tie its fortunes to a strong and distant power.

This the Iranian government attempted to do by joining the Baghdad Pact in 1955. However, it soon became clear that United States support of the Pact would not be followed by formal adherence to it. Although the United States had mobilized the "Northern Tier" states, joining its creature could have entailed excessive costs such as the risk of alienating important neutrals like India and Egypt, and domestic political problems involved in ratifying a treaty which involved an enemy of Israel. The U.S. therefore, held a weak "associate" membership which only temporarily satisfied the Iranian government.

Despite these equivocations the initial attitude of the United States toward Iran's adherence to the pact was another example of controversial historical interpretations which some of the revisionist historians of the cold war era cherish. To Secretary of State John Foster Dulles has been attributed a consistent and zealous intent to complete a circle of pro-Western defense pacts around Russia.[9a] Several recent accounts of U.S.-Iranian interaction concerning the Baghdad Pact show Dulles's role to be quite different from the stereotype of self-righteous moralist bent on forcing a reluctant Iran to join the pact.

Norman B. Hannah, who served in the Bureau of Near Eastern and African Affairs of the State Department during part of Mr. Dulles's tenure, has given an illuminating account of U.S.-Iranian contacts in the fall of 1955.[9b] He relates that the Secretary was quite concerned about the Soviet adverse reaction to Iran's adherence to the pact. According to him, on October 29, 1955, an urgent message had come from United States Ambassador Chapin in Tehran indicating Iran's unequivocal intention to join the pact and asking the department's views in response to a public announcement of Iran's decision.

The bureau drafted a reply for the Ambassador to deliver, saying in essence that joining the pact was for Iran to decide. The United States was not a member of the pact, had no intention of joining, and its economic and military assistance programs would not be affected by Iran's adherence to the pact. The draft reply stressed that while the U.S. would not urge Iran to join, it would avoid discouraging her

---

[9a] Townsend Hoopes, *The Devil and John Foster Dulles*, Boston: Atlantic/Little Brown, 1973.

[9b] *Foreign Affairs*, Vol. 52, No. 3, April 1974, pp. 646–650.

from taking an action which she might feel would strengthen her regional position during the critical post-Mossadegh period. The bureau was cognizant of Iran's need for external stability and felt that the U.S. should not deter her from joining the pact if it enhanced Iran's sense of security, "the more so since, by the very act of deterring her, we would acquire an obligation to provide the security which she sought in the Baghdad Pact."

Dulles's reaction to the draft reply was negative. Hannah quotes him: "I understand that at some stage Iran might want to participate in a regional defense system, but not now. It's too soon after their troubles. Are they even able to assume the obligations of mutual security commitments? But, the main point is that we are having a Big-Four foreign ministers' meeting in Geneva in a few weeks . . . the meeting to follow the summit conference which the President attended. . . . Iran's joining the Baghdad Pact may anger the Russians. They'll say it is a threat to them . . . they'll say we put the Iranians up to it. It risks souring the Big-Four meeting. I think we ought to tell the Iranians frankly and suggest they take no action now." After consulting Secretary of Defense Charles Wilson, the Chairman of the Joint Chiefs of Staff, Admiral Radford, and the Director of the CIA, Allen Dulles, the secretary drafted a cable to the embassy in Tehran to advise against adherence to the pact at that time because of the proximity of the Four Power meeting.

The bureau reaffirmed its reservations about this advice, arguing that it would cause a corrosive suspicion of Iran at a critical time in its political development. Dulles in turn disagreed with the bureau's assessment of the precarious internal situation of Iran and pointed out that he was asking only a delay, not nonadherence to the pact. However, he saw the bureau's point and ordered a redrafting of his instruction to the ambassador, which read in part, "Nevertheless, after taking the foregoing [Dulles's admonition against joining] into account, if, in your judgment, our refusal to give a favorable public reaction to their decision to enter the alliance with their neighbors would seriously risk setting in motion an irreversible downward spiral in the effectiveness and prospects of the government, also inhibiting its ability to join the pact at some later date, then in line with the following (our proposed message), you may say that we will comment favorably if and when the Iranian government decides to announce its adherence to the Baghdad Pact."

The upshot of this whole episode was that the Iranian government did not budge from its determination to join. The secretary's apprehension about the impact of this decision on the Big-Power conference proved unwarranted. As Hannah has noted, this account also showed Secretary Dulles to be an effective and pragmatic statesman, not bound by an incurable pactamania, which his critics so indiscriminately attribute to him.

The events of 1958, the disturbances in Jordan and Lebanon and the regicide and revolution in Baghdad, soon demonstrated the inadequacies of the Baghdad Pact, and more specifically, from the monarch's viewpoint, its inability to guarantee the regimes themselves. Never fully satisfied with the vagueness of that pact,[10] the Shah now sought a more tangible U.S. commitment to the security of the country and his regime. The American reaction to the post-Suez war Soviet penetration of the Arab Middle East was formalized in the Eisenhower Doctrine, which promised aid if a country was directly attacked by a communist-controlled nation. This also did not go far enough for the Shah because the doctrine could not be decisively evoked in the 1958 crisis in Lebanon and Jordan.

He urged the U.S. to enter a bilateral pact with Iran and requested more military and economic aid to finance an increase of two divisions in the army.[11] Unlike Pakistan and Turkey, Iran was not a member of any other pact and consequently had no formal commitment from the United States. This source of insecurity to Iranian policy-makers was little dispelled by the eventual compromise in which the U.S. concluded identically-worded Executive Agreements with Iran, Turkey, and Pakistan as a substitute for formal adherence to the Baghdad Pact.[12]

Alliances are traditionally recognized as having certain functions such as: (1) the aggregation of power or fragmentation of an opposing bloc; (2) the facilitation of inter-allied control of restraint of any ally; (3) the promotion of international order by the delineation of opposing sides; (4) the provision of internal security for one or both

---

[10] In 1955 Iran had urged that the headquarters of the Baghdad Pact be switched from Ankara to Tehran and be given a unified military command like NATO. See *New York Times,* Jan. 31, 1955.

[11] *New York Times,* Feb. 12, 1959.

[12] It bears emphasis that while NATO fully protected Turkey, and SEATO Article IV(i) gave Pakistan a "legally binding commitment to take appropriate action in the event of aggression by means of armed attack in the treaty area," Article I of the bilateral agreements envisaged such appropriate action as may be subsequently agreed. See "U.S. Security Agreements and Commitments Abroad, Greece and Turkey," Hearing before the Senate Subcommittee on U.S. Security Agreements and Commitments Abroad of the Committee on Foreign Relations, 91st Cong., 2nd Sess., Part 7 (June 9 and 11, 1970), pp. 1855–1860.

allies.[13] For Iran, increased identification with the U.S. provided certain potential benefits as well as certain costs. In summary they are: *Benefits:* increased external security; (implied) enhanced internal security; regional non-isolation through association with non-Arab states. *Costs:* alienation of domestic political elements; aggravation of relations with the USSR; annoyance of "nonaligned" nations.

For the United States the bilateral agreements represented the limit of its commitment to the erstwhile Baghdad Pact, now CENTO, and provided the formal link necessary for the integration of the NATO and SEATO pacts. The main aims of the Iranian regime were to gain some assurance of American protection, to obtain modern weaponry, and by this partnership to increase its leverage on the U.S. for additional support and aid.[14]

The other possibilities theoretically open to Iran in regard to the cold war were limited and not without cost. These were: (1) a posture of self-abnegation or dependence on its great power neighbor, on the Finland or Burma model; (2) armed neutrality on the Sweden or Switzerland model; (3) a buffer-state posture on the Afghanistan pattern, implying both dependence on the great-power neighbor and non-alignment. "Armed neutrality" was hardly a practical course and neither options 1 nor 3 could have appealed to the Iranian leadership. Both options implied excessive dependence on the goodwill of the neighboring Soviet Union and promised less security or independence than a truncated or attenuated precarious existence as an independent unit. Their implications for the institution of the monarchy, as well as the possibilities of aid, were hardly encouraging to Iranian policymakers.

The decision to align Iran with the West in the cold war had definite costs; it implied a loss of prestige and status and, in psychological terms, constituted a "serious derogation of independence." While ideally alignments were to be avoided, Iran's security did not appear to permit this. As Rothstein has noted: "Nonalignment is viable for a

---

[13] See Robert E. Osgood, *Alliances and American Foreign Policy*, pp. 21–22; George Liska, *Alliances and the Third World*, pp. 23–25; Robert Rothstein, *Alliances and Small Powers* (hereafter cited as *Small Powers*), pp. 46–47; and Raymond Aron's discussion in *Peace and War: A Theory of International Relations*, pp. 506 *et seq.*

[14] See John C. Campbell, *Defense of the Middle East: Problems of American Policy*, pp. 59–60. Whether the decision to take sides was the "best" means to exert pressure to obtain armaments and aid depends on the situation of the country. For military aid received by Iran, see below. For a lively discussion of an alternative approach in a different context, as exemplified by Nasser's Egypt, see Miles Copeland, *The Game of Nations: The Amorality of Power Politics.*

Small Power only so long as it is not threatened by a Great Power;
once directly threatened it is difficult to avoid alignment with another
Great Power." [15]

Internally, too, the decision had costs. For despite the failure of
neutrality, the socially conscious segment of Iranian society abhorred
the departure from traditional policy and preferred the international
posture of nonalignment. Nonetheless, the Shah pursued a policy
of alignment and risked the inevitable domestic reaction—i.e., comparisons with the corrupt Qajar regime's capitulations, allegations
of "baggage-train nationalism," aggravation of relations with both
the Soviet Union and the Tudeh party, and alienation of such self-
proclaimed neutrals as Nasser's Egypt. The closer ties seemed essential
and, paradoxically, the 1959 bilateral pact is both an indication that
the Shah felt sufficiently strong to handle the resultant criticism and
exposed enough to require further buttressing.

In retrospect it is easy to see that the decision was a tactical one
based on an assessment of both the international system and the
domestic requirements of the monarchy. It allowed the Shah a breathing spell and an opportunity to broaden his base of support by pursuing social reform, while maintaining a modicum of external security. Furthermore, the nature of the relationship with the United
States was unrestricted and allowed for a silent demise or alteration
in emphasis within a changed political context. It gave the Iranian
government a "moral" lever on the U.S. to extract aid, and a political
lever on the Soviet Union in bargaining to dismantle or de-emphasize
that tie.[16]

The use of a tie with a superpower to extract favors and aid is
examined in detail below. A crucial dimension has often been overlooked by "realists" in Iran who have argued that an explicit tie with
the U.S. is unnecessary because the U.S. would come to the aid of
Iran, when it is in its interests, without such a tie; and not come to her

---

[15] Robert L. Rothstein, "Alignment, Nonalignment, and Small Powers, 1945–
1965," pp. 404–405, 416, and *Small Powers*, p. 34. Liska makes the same point about
the cost to status of alliance in an anti-colonialist age: George Liska, *Nations in
Alliance: The Limits of Independence*, pp. 37–39; see also pp. 125–126. Also consult Donald E. Neuchterlain, "Small States in Alliances: Iceland, Thailand, and
Australia."

[16] On the latter point, Robert Keohane speaks of an "Al Capone" alliance: an
unequal alliance between a small power and a contiguous imperialistic Great Power
"in which remaining a faithful ally protects one not against the mythical outside
threat but rather against the great-power ally itself." The alliance thus serves as a
form of "protection-money" in gangland terms. Robert O. Keohane, "Lilliputians'
Dilemmas: Small States in International Politics," p. 302.

aid when it is not in her interests, despite the existence of a tie. The policy-making machinery of the U.S. is susceptible to the appeal of the "loyal ally," and the dynamics of most commitments and ties are a great deal more humdrum and less apocalyptic than the ultimate commitment of troops and combat.

In the give and take of discussion on military grants, loans, and credit sales, it can have done Tehran little harm to point to its commitment to the West, to emphasize the costs involved to Iran in this commitment, and to suggest that this sort of loyalty should not go unnoticed or unrewarded.

PERSPECTIVES ON INTERNATIONAL AFFAIRS

Within the different perspectives and responsibilities each partner brought to the 1959 commitment, an unresolved tension remained. Although the bilateral and Baghdad pacts had been costly internally and regionally, the Iranians believe that their benefits should outweigh their costs. Charlton Ogburn, Jr., has put this difference in perspective in reference to the Baghdad Pact:

Those who had 'stood up and been counted' on the side of the United States in the contests that mattered most to it naturally expected that the United States would also stand up and be counted on their side.

He suggests that the Iranian regime expected the U.S. to support the "monarchy against any settling elements." [17] This difference in perspective between the U.S. and Iran on the regional functions of the tie has been amply corroborated both by Iranian sources and by the reaction of the Pact's regional states to the Cyprus and Kashmir disputes.[18] The U.S., however, was not merely concerned with its allies and partners in regional pacts. Given the global competition for power and prestige between the U.S. and the Soviet Union, the uncommitted nations and certain key nonaligned states such as India, Egypt, Ghana, and Yugoslavia, appeared to the aligned countries to have assumed an importance to Washington's thinking that often overshadowed that of the committed states.[19]

In short, in a bipolar world, the competition for the "third world"

---

[17] Charlton Ogburn, Jr., "Divide and Rule in the Middle East," p. 38.

[18] For the Shah's reaction, see E. A. Bayne, *Persian Kingship in Transition*. For differences in perspective among regional states, see the memoirs of a former Iranian ambassador to both Turkey and Pakistan: Hassan Arfa, *Under Five Shahs*.

[19] For an analysis of Iran's changing attitude toward nonalignment, see S. Zabih, "Change and Continuity in Iran's Foreign Policy in Modern Times."

assumed a zero-sum character, in which a gain for one side was viewed
as a loss for the other. As a result, the distinction between an ally and
a neutral or nonaligned state became blurred.[20] From the perspective
of the committed states like Iran it appeared that these nonaligned
states shared all the benefits of an alliance (security, aid) and none of
the costs (the stigma of loss of independence, loss of independence in
UN voting, domestic political repercussions).

The Shah repeatedly pointed out that aid to Iran was a trickle in
comparison to aid to some nonaligned countries. Similar criticism had
been voiced by Ayub Khan, who publicly asked, "Is there any percentage in being an American ally?"[21]

The Iranian perspective differed from that of the U.S. not only on
questions of aid. In security matters the regional perspective was frequently of paramount importance. Thus the Kennedy administration's
rapid recognition of the revolution in Yemen was viewed by Iran as a
poor way to discourage Nasser's designs in the Arabian peninsula. Iran
felt that regional considerations were important and should not be
sacrificed to the U.S. global perspective, and it persisted in interpreting
the alliance in regional terms. Although the differences in perspective
between the U.S. and Iran on Nasser's behavior in the Arabian peninsula did not lead to a breach between Tehran and Washington, the
potential remained until 1967. The Shah's support of his regional
partners, his aid to the Yemeni Royalist forces, and his statement in
the wake of the 1965 India-Pakistan war that "now we know that the
United States would not come to aid us if we are attacked"[22] reflected
a fear and skepticism about the real value of the U.S. commitment.

In this connection it should be noted that what might appear from
the Western perspective as an ideal or paradigmatic settlement of an
area dispute between East and West, may appear from the perspective
of a small state as an ominous if not absolute "sellout."[23] Lack of

---

20 See Henry Kissinger, "Coalition Diplomacy in A Nuclear Age," in Linda B.
Miller (ed.), *Dynamics of World Politics: Studies in the Resolution of Conflict,* p. 48.
It should be noted that the key nonaligned states were not strategically exposed. The
case of Afghanistan, which adopted a posture of buffer state, has a historical dimension.

21 *New York Herald Tribune,* July 14, 1961; see also Ayub Khan, "The Pakistan-
American Alliance: Stresses and Strains."

22 Bayne, *Persian Kingship,* p. 220.

23 For the Shah's view of the Laos settlement, see *U.S. News and World Report,*
March 6, 1961, p. 65, wherein he says: "We certainly do not want any deals made
between the United States and the Soviet Union whereby our country would be
'neutralized.' . . . We hope you in the United States don't forget who your friends
are."

empathy for the superpower's perspective is paralleled by an equal blindness on the part of the superpower for the problems of states in their regional settings. Certainly it is instructive to note that superpower needs normally take precedence in foreign policy over allied states' interests. The evolving dialogue between Washington and Peking and the Nixon doctrine has given America's Southeast Asian partners of Thailand and the Philippines every incentive to accentuate their own independence.

For the small power, the decision to align may be taken for overwhelming security reasons. The alignment may prove its value in providing external security and economic and military aid in exchange for a limited sacrifice of complete autonomy in international relations. Nevertheless, the danger remains for the small power that global considerations may bring together the great power with which it is aligned and the one who threatens its security. This resultant rapprochement may then take place at the expense of its interests.

For this reason, despite the existence of a "permanent enemy" in the North, the Iranian government has been hesitant to rely totally on the U.S. Historical experiences with Britain and Russia in the early twentieth century have molded this attitude. Similarly, Iran has recognized the failure of the "third country" strategy (whether in the shape of France or Germany) to alter the simple fact that small powers' friendships exercise little attraction for a large power if it is at the expense of a large power's friendship.[24] Alignment thus becomes a tactical principle to be used when absolutely necessary but in such a way as to not constitute a provocation to the "permanent enemy." Neutrality, rather than nonalignment, is a credible posture only when the state is sufficiently strong to enforce it. At that stage of Iranian development, it was considered a chimera.

IRANIAN POLITICS: THE AMINI EPISODE

It has been observed that the U.S. did not intend to underwrite the particular Iranian regime so much as to give a minimum amount of security against external threats. However, the Iranian government may have viewed the relationship in terms of support for the regime. The problems from the U.S. perspective appeared to be posed in a vicious circle: while desiring strong and secure governments to combat the

---

[24] For a discussion of Persian attempts to interest Germany in playing a third-power role, see Bradford E. Martin, *German-Persian Diplomatic Relations, 1873–1912.*

threat of communism, the U.S. did not wish to back "undemocratic" unpopular oligarchic regimes. Yet regimes of the latter type, while often effective in bringing at least short-term stability, were unenthusiastic about broadening their bases of support.

This dilemma had been observed in the 1950's: "The strategic purpose of the Mutual Security Program to reinforce the existing governments collides with the program's aims in the realm of economic and technical assistance, which call for fundamental economic and social reforms." [25] The moral and operational dilemma for U.S. policymakers appears to have been resolved on an *ad hoc* and individual country basis. In the case of Iran the distinctions between the U.S. commitment to the country's security rather than to the regime have been rather tenuous. The reason is that in building up both the state and its government against internal and external enemies, as conceived by the U.S., the regime has been built up against all its enemies, however it chose to define them.[26] What the U.S. might perceive as a legitimate opposition party in the country might not be so viewed by the Iranian government.

Whatever the aim of U.S. policy-makers with regard to the internal politics of countries with which the U.S. was associated, its impact on the domestic politics of these nations cannot be doubted. Apart from the difficulty of distinguishing aid to a particular state and aid to the regime or government in charge of that state, the very association between the two governments in the form of the 1959 pact had domestic implications. In the intangible but nonetheless real perception of Iranian opposition groups, U.S. ties negotiated by a particular regime suggested American support for that regime. The U.S. thus appeared to wield a veto on political developments within certain countries,[27] and possessed an immense importance in the internal as well as external politics of Iran in the early sixties.

The Shah has denied that the bilateral pact was to strengthen his

---

25 J. C. Hurewitz, *Middle East Dilemmas: The Background of U.S. Policy*, pp. 254–255.

26 Walter Lippmann, writing just prior to the bilateral pact, noted that "The problem of Iranian security . . . is essentially an internal problem. . . . The principal purpose of (U.S.) support of Iran is . . . to uphold the Shah's government, which is aligned with us." *New York Herald Tribune*, Dec. 15, 1959.

27 Two students of Turkey's foreign policy have written that in the view of the opposition to the Menderes regime, "the provision for American armed assistance in case of 'indirect aggression' was nothing less than a U.S. commitment to intervene on behalf of the Menderes regime in the event of an attempted coup." A. H. Ulman and R. H. Dekmejian, "Changing Patterns in Turkish Foreign Policy, 1959–1967," p. 773.

position internally, although it was reported that during negotiations for the pact that he asked for "blanket assurances against aggression from any source, communist or not." [28] Nevertheless in early 1960 he was in a precarious position. Having witnessed a revolution in Iraq and a coup in Turkey, he must have felt profoundly dependent on U.S. friendship.

This dependence was multifaceted, and embraced not only external security functions but also economic support and military grants, the building of the security organization and support for the monarch. Although in the Shah's view this was not the best possible arrangement, the 1959 pact nevertheless formalized a U.S. commitment of sorts to Iran. In 1958 the U.S. and Iranian governments had agreed on an appropriate force level for the Iranian army. The U.S. had agreed to provide economic support for the budget to finance the resultant expansion, given the Iranian government's inability to cover the expenses. The 1958 force-level agreements, the 1959 pact, and the flow of American military and economic grants to Iran reflected U.S. interest in the Iranian situation. It also gave the U.S. government an added incentive to ensure that these funds were well spent and that wise policies were adopted, a matter of particular concern since American aid operations had been sharply criticized in Congress in the 1950's.[29]

Early in 1960 there was some question as to whether U.S. aid ought to be made conditional, and particularly whether that government should subsidize a potentially wealthy country whose government was not acting decisively in instituting tax and other reforms to remedy its continued inflation.[30] If these considerations represented one view in Washington, in Tehran it must have looked different. Taxing the wealthy or instituting reforms created powerful enemies which the Shah could ill afford. What made good economic sense in Washington had great political costs for their architect in Tehran. This disparity in

---

[28] Interview in *U.S. News and World Report,* March 23, 1959, p. 55; *Tehran Journal,* Feb. 18, 1959. It must be stressed that whatever the intentions, "if internal conditions are unstable and the regime is threatened, aid will be more directly internal security aid than may be the case in other instances." George Liska, *The New Statecraft,* p. 140.

[29] "United States AID Operations in Iran," Hearings before an H. R. Subcommittee of the Committee on Government Operations," 84th Cong., 2nd Sess., May 2, 31, June 1, 6, 8, 9, 12, 13, 19, 25, 26, 27, 29, and July 16, 1956.

[30] See the *Report of the Staff Survey Team of the Subcommittee for the Review of Military Assistance to Korea, Thailand, and Iran* (Washington, D.C.: GPO, 1960); and *Report of the Staff Survey Team of the Subcommittee for the Review of Mutual Security Programs on Economic Assistance to Korea, Thailand and Iran,* with Subcommittee recommendations (Washington, D.C.: GPO, 1960).

perspective has been a constant theme in Washington-Tehran relations, particularly with regard to Iranian internal political developments.

One example demonstrates the way the immense U.S. influence in
Tehran could be wielded. The opposition to the Shah's regime believed
that he survived only because he was backed by Washington. They also
believed that Washington was capable of directing policy in Tehran,
particularly in using U.S. power, influence, and leverage to "pressure"
the regime into reforms and curb corruption.[31] Although it is not altogether clear, apparently in late 1959 after Eisenhower's visit to
Tehran, Washington had concluded that given the Shah's weak base, it
would be prudent to take out insurance by cultivating contacts with
opposition groups. This was regarded as "normal practice" by Washington, but the Shah demonstrated little enthusiasm for it. From his
vantage point it must have looked dangerously like a self-fulfilling
prophecy, i.e., carte blanche for opposition groups which would em-
bolden them to undermine his position.[32] Whether the U.S. government had such intentions or was merely hedging its bets or putting
pressure on the Shah to move faster in reforms, it cannot be doubted
that its orientation to the developing areas altered with the incoming
administration.

Under John Kennedy, American policy toward the third world was
based on two premises: that internal politics of these countries would
be more influential than superpower inducements in determining their
international posture; and that in the future, leaders undertaking
large-scale redistribution of wealth and political authority would be the
most stable. As one student of American foreign policy notes: "The
conclusion drawn for U.S. foreign policy was that the United States
would lose influence in these nations, and over their ultimate choice of
friends and benefactors in the international system, unless we identified
ourselves with those social and political forces demanding greater social
justice." [33]

Among the third-world countries, Iran was of particular concern in

---

[31] See *New York Times*, Jan. 29, 1960, and July 23, 1961 (section VI).

[32] Some scholars saw American policy in Iran as misguided, and argued for support of the new middle class. See, for example, Manfred Halpern, "Perspectives on
U.S. Policy: Iran." One of the Shah's most powerful arguments for American support at this time was presumably his identification of American interests with his
own, and emphasis on the dangerous alternatives to continued rule by himself.

[33] Seyom Brown, *The Faces of Power: Constancy and Change in United States
Foreign Policy from Truman to Johnson*, pp. 369–370.

the early Kennedy years. During the dramatic summit meeting with Khrushchev at Vienna in June 1961, the Soviet leader referred to the potential for revolutionary upheaval in Iran as a critical issue in Soviet-American relations. According to Khrushchev, Iran was a typically unstable Western-aligned country, about to experience a revolutionary upheaval. Although the Soviet Union would not in any way be involved, its mere proximity to Iran would lead the United States to blame Moscow for such a course of events, and thus damage Soviet-American relations. Walter Rostow, one of Kennedy's foreign policy advisors, has related that Khrushchev depicted such a gloomy scenario of impending upheaval in Iran that when Kennedy returned to the United States he requested a full report on the Iranian condition, to ascertain the accuracy of the Soviet prognosis.[34]

Partly as a result of that experience, the new administration became keenly interested in Iran's internal situation. Although Khrushchev's remarks were made at a low point in Iran-Soviet relations, and therefore hardly disinterested, Kennedy felt that no genuine coexistence with the Soviets could be achieved if countries on the periphery of the Soviet Union and aligned with the United States harbored the seeds of deep-rooted socio-political unrest.

This conclusion was translated into policy in several ways. One method was to use foreign aid to stabilize, speed, or influence change in the recipient country. In Iran, the admittedly fragmentary and circumstantial evidence suggests that U.S. policy was quite direct in seeking reform.[35] The appointment in May 1961 of Ali Amini, a former ambassador to the U.S. and a friend of Kennedy's, to the post of premier was significant. Amini was an outspoken advocate of reforms, and he appeared to be appointed after American "advice" rather than to be the Shah's own choice. Bayne quotes American Ambassador Julius Holmes as remarking to him that "Amini's government represents a last chance for Iran," and concludes that it seems clear that Amini was an "American nominee, at least after the fact." [36]

Early in the period of Amini's premiership, significant differences between both the Shah and Amini, and the Shah and Washington, surfaced; and these were intimately related to the question of perspective.

---

34 Personal interview, March 12, 1973, Austin, Texas.

35 Edward Mason, speaking from personal experience in Iran, is skeptical about the leverage that the granting of foreign aid gave the U.S. He stresses the "sensitive . . . political situation." Mason, *Foreign Aid and Foreign Policy*, pp. 23–24.

36 Bayne, *Persian Kingship*, pp. 191–192, 194.

Briefly, while Washington wanted land reform, an anti-corruption drive, and the institution of taxation, it also wished to preserve at least a semblance of democracy. However, if parliament was sitting, these measures would not be passed. Once convinced of this, the U.S. accepted the need for functioning without a parliament, although it urged the Shah not to take power openly.[37]

This advice can be interpreted in two ways: either the U.S. was interested in protecting the monarchy from the criticisms and the social forces the reforms would unleash, or it intended to build up the institution of prime minister under Ali Amini. While American policy-makers may not have seen these intentions as mutually exclusive, it seems unlikely that the implications of a strong premiership in Iran were lost on the Shah.

In a modernizing monarchy, alternative centers of power were anathema to the Shah, and a strong premiership implied a dispensable throne. In this connection the Shah was reportedly much concerned with how American newspapers identified the author of the Iranian reforms, and was irked by references to "Amini's reforms" rather than the "Shah's reforms."

The Kennedy administration appears to have viewed affairs in Iran from a global vantage point, with little concern for the domestic political implications. From Washington, reforms in Iran seemed to be indicated, so a "strong man" was suggested and reforms initiated. For the Shah, the issue of authorship of these reforms was critical if the monarchy was to survive; it was important that the reforms create neither a new center of competing power nor alienate those segments of society on which the monarchy depended. It was precisely in this area that the Shah clashed with Amini, for Amini's attempt to pare down the military struck at one of the foundations of the regime.[38]

Since the Shah had alienated the landlords without having yet won the support of the peasantry, he could ill afford to remove one of his principal sources of support. The American government pressured Amini and the Shah on the issues of austerity, anti-corruption, and reform, but finally in 1962 relaxed the policy of pressure and reverted to a more detached stance regarding internal Iranian developments.

---

[37] See *ibid.*, p. 192, and Cuyler Young, "Iran in Continuing Crisis," esp. pp. 288–289.

[38] See the *Washington Post*, July 21, 1961 (editorial); *New York Times*, July 20, 1962. See also Samuel Huntington's brilliant discussion of modernizing monarchs, *Political Order and Changing Societies;* in this connection, esp. p. 189.

The Shah was later to single out 1961–62 as the "worst period" of American interference, when it tried to "impose your type of regime on other people." [39] One can only speculate on U.S. motives in non-pursuance of an activist social engineering policy in Iran. No doubt it was due partly to the very success of the reforms, partly to the Shah's astuteness, and partly to the pressure of other issues.

MILITARY EQUIPMENT

The Shah's decision to align Iran with the U.S. was partly to obtain the material aid likely to ensue from such a tie. While American military missions had provided economic aid to Iran in the 1950's, only in the 1960's did that materiel assume significant proportions. This donor-recipient relationship in military aid consisted of two phases: 1960–1965 and 1965–1970. In this as in other areas of Iran-U.S. relations, differences in the perspectives and influence of the two nations are notable. These differences concern the size and function of the army, the amount of material needed, and the forms the assistance should take.

In this relationship U.S. policy-makers exercised the leverage of their donor position to achieve their goals, while Iranian policy-makers utilized changes in the international system to achieve their aims. The transition from U.S. grants and budgetary support to credit sales coincides approximately with the two phases and also saw a change in the Iran-U.S. relationship. This together with other events altered the instruments of leverage and transformed the relationship from one of patron-client to near equality. The question of military force levels, the amount of expenditure on the military, and the question of "retiring" corrupt senior officers in a topheavy officer corps all have domestic political implications.

In 1959 the Shah had backed Iran's alignment policy as a cheap method of providing security and had defended Iran's expenditure on armaments as small in comparison to that of Iraq or Switzerland.[40] At this time the Iranian monarchy was fully dependent on the U.S. for arms and external security and vulnerable to internal political discontent. Given the nature of American aid and its dependence on annual congressional review and its moods, the Shah appears to have

---

[39] Interview in *U.S. News and World Report,* Jan. 27, 1969, p. 49.
[40] *Tehran Journal,* press conference, Sept. 30, 1959.

been unwilling to reduce the military. From Washington's perspective, the military was too large and the outlays to the armed forces excessive, wasteful, and damaging to the economy.[41]

These differences in emphasis and in perspective have decreased in the course of the decade. In the early period from 1959 to 1964 the Shah felt doubly vulnerable. He was engaged in social reforms which threatened to upset and change society, while simultaneously he was faced with the uncertainty of full U.S. backing. In addition he was regionally isolated by the USSR. The U.S., in turn, actively involved in Iranian affairs while pressuring the Shah into reforms, counseled a cutback in the size of the military. A one-third reduction of the Iranian armed forces and their modernization was agreed to in 1961 by the Shah, once he was assured of American support on a five-year basis.[42]

The American government's use of its aid relationship to restrain Iran's arms acquisitions has been amply documented in congressional hearings.[43] From that testimony it appears that annual or biannual discussions have been held on arms sales and grants. There were "understandings" or "agreements" arrived at between the U.S. executive branch and its Iranian counterparts in 1958, 1961, 1962, 1964, 1965, 1966, and 1969. Generally the American position has been that arms purchases should not be on a scale to weaken the economy and that supply of equipment should be geared to the growth of the recipient's economy. However, the American executive branch of government has been ready to make "understandings" as to the amount of equipment it would grant or sell *over a number of years.*[44]

The shift from grant to credit sales parallels the growing vitality of the Iranian economy and the increased involvement of the U.S. in Southeast Asia. By the end of the decade the Iranian-U.S. relation-

---

[41] See, for example, Eisenhower's speech to the Majlis in which he says military strength alone cannot ensure security. *New York Times,* Dec. 15, 1959.

[42] Hearings before the H. R. Committee on Foreign Affairs on the Foreign Assistance Act of 1963, 88th Cong., 1st Sess., April 30, 1963, pp. 397, 423. See also Hearings before the H. R. Committee on Foreign Affairs on the Foreign Assistance Act of 1964, 88th Cong., 2nd Sess., 1964 (remarks of Robert MacNamara to Senator Aiken), p. 517.

[43] See, *inter alia,* Hearings before the H. R. Committee on Foreign Affairs on the Foreign Assistance Act of 1967, 90th Cong., 1st Sess., 1967, p. 118; Hearings before the Senate Committee on Foreign Relations on the Foreign Military Sales Act of 1968, 90th Cong., 2nd Sess., 1968 (remarks of Paul Warnke, assistant secretary of defense for international security affairs), pp. 109, 116.

[44] Hearings before the H. R. Committee on Foreign Affairs on the Foreign Assistance Act of 1965, 89th Cong., 1st Sess., 1965 (remarks by Brig. Gen. Eugene L. Strickland, U.S. Air Force director, Near East and South East region, office of assistant secretary of defense for international security affairs), p. 743.

ship had been completely transformed. Now Iran *bought* most of her arms from the U.S., although she received credit financing. The post-Nixon-doctrine U.S., seeing Iran as a force for peace in the region, no longer discouraged her arms acquisition.

FIRST PHASE, 1960–1965

In 1961–62 the U.S. viewed with disfavor the Iranian government's outlays for the military, its perennial budgetary deficit, and its failure to undertake economic and social reforms. As noted earlier, the Amini period ended with the premier's inability to reduce the army or guarantee U.S. aid. In 1962 the U.S. cut its "supporting assistance," reportedly on the advice of Ambassador Julius Holmes, and pressured the Shah to undertake reforms.[45] As a result of the multi-year agreement of 1961, which gave the Shah some insurance vis-à-vis the armed forces, the military was reduced by one-third over a period of years.

By 1964 Washington decided that the Iranian government's oil revenues permitted it to purchase some of its military requirements, and therefore grant military assistance was phased out and credit sales substituted. As a result of this Memorandum of Understanding of July 4, 1964, Iran was expected to buy most of her requirements for cash, while the U.S. government agreed to assure and facilitate credit arrangements for these purchases.[46] The Majlis then passed a bill authorizing the government to obtain a $200 million credit from American banks to be guaranteed by the U.S. government over a five-year period. It bore an interest rate of 5 percent and was repayable over a ten-year period.[47]

SECOND PHASE, 1965–1970

A number of factors have changed the Iranian-U.S. relationship since 1965. These may be summarized as the emerging U.S.-Soviet

---

45 See the *New York Times*, Aug. 26 and 30 (editorial), 1962; and *Report of a Study of U.S. Foreign Aid in Ten Middle Eastern and African Countries,* submitted by Sen. Ernest Gruening, Subcommittee on Reorganization and International Organizations of the Senate Committee of Government Operations, 88th Cong., 1st Sess., Oct. 1, 1963, pp. 23–24.

46 Hearings before the Committee on Foreign Relations on the Foreign Assistance Act of 1966, 89th Cong., 2nd Sess., 1966 (remarks by General P. Adams, commander-in-chief, U.S. strike command), p. 460; and Hearings before the H. R. Committee on Foreign Affairs on the Foreign Assistance Act of 1967, 90th Cong., 1st Sess., 1967, p. 114. The phasing out of grants was to be gradual. In 1964 military aid was 100 percent grant; during the period 1965–1967, it was a blend of grant and cash and credit purchases. By fiscal year 1969, it was overwhelmingly cash and credit purchase. See Harold Watkins, "Neutral Iran Will Add F-40's to Strengthen Air Defense," p. 50.

47 *Tehran Journal,* Oct. 26, 1964.

detente and the talk in Washington of "bridge building"; the increased involvement in and preoccupation of the U.S. with Southeast Asia; the failure of the U.S. to act in the 1965 Indo-Pakistan war; the increasing vitality of the Iranian economy; and the fear of Nasser's Egypt. The Shah's visit to Moscow in 1965 and his cordial reception crystallized the desire of the Iranian leadership to repair its relationship with its superpower neighbor. Not only would this be a wise policy with respect to a possible superpower rapprochement, but it also made good sense practically and was welcomed domestically. In addition, it might provide leverage on the U.S. and serve to show the government's displeasure with the shift to arms sales. At the same time it could diversify the sources of Iran's arms supplies. Moreover, it would serve a symbolic role as an assertion of independence.

The Iran-U.S. military-aid relationship has fluctuated widely in the changing international context of 1965–1970. It is significant that Iranian policymakers have obtained much of what they had requested, insofar as available information shows what was actually requested.[48] This success is due partly to the changing international context and its effect on U.S.-Iranian relations and partly to the persuasive advocacy by Iranian officials in Washington and effective maneuvering by Tehran, the latter two having been greatly facilitated by the sympathy and receptivity of the American policy-making machinery. In addition, both the perspective of Washington and the leverage available to it have changed. The second phase of this relationship can be analyzed in terms of developments before and after 1968.

The 1965–1968 period, covered by the 1964 Memorandum of Understanding, is characterized by the initiation of an "independent national policy" in Iran's foreign relations. In 1967 this cultivation of ties with the Eastern bloc and the USSR resulted in a barter deal between Tehran and Moscow in which Iran was supplied with over $100 million worth of military vehicles. In the United States, foreign policy was increasingly preoccupied with Vietnam. In congressional quarters the growing skepticism concerning the course of that policy and the candor of the President with Congress in foreign affairs was translated into fresh scrutiny of executive actions by the passage of the Foreign Military Sales Act in 1968.

This Act terminated the "revolving fund" by which the President had bypassed annual congressional authorization; it specified a ten-

---

[48] For figures on U.S. military aid, see Appendix.

year ceiling for credit arrangements; and, most importantly, it prohibited the granting of direct credits by the Export-Import bank for military purposes by less developed countries. Due to the difficulties of obtaining commercial bank loans, in effect it limited military credit for "less developed countries" to funds authorized and appropriated by Congress to the department of defense.[49] This legislation was disturbing to the Iranian government because it threatened to upset Iran's "agreements" on credit with the executive branch. The problems raised by the passage of the act were circumvented by the termination of U.S. economic assistance to Iran in 1967 on the grounds that it was no longer a "less developed country." As a result of this change in status, it was eligible for financing by the Export-Import bank.

Since 1968 the relationship can best be characterized as one of equality and harmony of interests. This period will be analyzed in terms of Iran's perspective and leverage.

DIFFERING PERSPECTIVES

Significant differences in perspective existed between Washington and Tehran concerning the function and aim of the bilateral pact. The Shah viewed the alliance in terms of security, i.e., domestic and regional threats, while the U.S. refused to interpret the pact in regional terms and therefore did not back either side in the 1965 Indo-Pakistan hostilities. Thereafter, when it appeared to Tehran that the United States had done little to undo the effects of the war or discourage a *fait accompli,* there was added incentive to build large deterrent forces.

Another difference in perception of regional threats was evident in Washington and Tehran's reactions to the Yemen war. The Kennedy administration, cognizant of Nasser's importance in Middle East politics and to global interests, quickly recognized the Republic of Yemen.[50] Iran, in contrast, trained and supplied Royalist troops to fight Nasser. Iranian policy-makers, aware of a small state's minimal margin for error, viewed the potential threat of other states in terms of capability rather than intent. Naturally they preferred the prudent policy of over-armament to underarmament.

It is not surprising that interpretations of regional threats by Tehran

---

49 Hearings before the Senate Committee on Foreign Relations on the Foreign Military Sales Act of 1968, 90th Cong., 2nd Sess., 1968.

50 Nadav Safran, *From War to War: The Arab-Israeli Confrontation, 1948–1967,* p. 133.

and Washington should differ. They viewed events from divergent geographical perspectives, and the cost of "failure" or error varied considerably for each state. For Iran it might mean survival; for the U.S. it might be a marginal loss. Naturally from these divergent outlooks conclusions differed as to the armaments required. The U.S. sought constantly to "restrain" Iran in its purchases and in the size of its military establishment. Similarly, Iranians sought to impress upon U.S. officials the dangers of weakness. The gulf between the two views is well illustrated by Chester Bowles' description of his discussion with the Shah in Tehran in late 1961.

When I asked him what defense problems particularly concerned him, he came up with some surprising answers in the following order: first, Nasser and Egypt (which is a thousand miles away); second, the Afghans, who, he said, might be backed by Russian Uzbeks dressed in Afghan uniforms; and third, the Iraqi. The Soviets, he said, were primarily *our* problem.[51]

A similar difference in view was apparent in 1965–66. Iranian policy-makers were fearful of the introduction of supersonic aircraft and long-range surface-to-air missiles in the UAR and Iraq, and pressed Washington for equivalent weapons.[52] The Americans, however, not only deemphasized Nasser's danger to Iran but began to "phase out" grant military aid and substitute credit sales.[53]

American policy-makers, beset by numerous global problems and ties, tended to view armaments and military establishments in a practical and functional manner, particularly if Washington was paying the bill. Weapons were necessary for fighting an enemy. If there were no plausible enemy, less weapons would be needed. From Tehran's viewpoint weapons also had a ceremonial and symbolic dimension. Thus, regardless of the actual warlike intentions of Baghdad or Cairo policy-makers, they owned modern weaponry which Tehran did not. This was as psychologically aggravating as it was potentially dangerous militarily. Furthermore, it is possible that U.S. policy-makers were

---

[51] Chester Bowles, *Promises to Keep: My Years in Public Life, 1941–1965*, p. 370.

[52] According to the Stockholm International Peace Research Institute, *Yearbook of World Armaments and Disarmament, 1968–1969*, pp. 47–48, supersonic aircraft were received by the UAR in 1962, Iraq in 1963, and Iran in 1965. Similarly, the UAR and Iraq obtained long-range surface-to-air missiles in 1963, and Iran only in 1965.

[53] See remarks by Lt.-Gen. Mohammed Khatemi, commander of the imperial Iranian air force, deploring this shift to sales, in Watkins, "Neutral Iran Will Add F-4D's," p. 54.

aware of the Shah's dependence on the military but tended to under-
rate power of that domestic pressure group.[54]

In sum, with dissimilar perspectives and stakes involved, policy-
makers in Tehran and Washington viewed regional threats differently.
These differences were not insurmountable and were primarily "in the
nature of things." Most could be narrowed by arguments and persuasive advocacy. Where they could not, each side could resort to levers
and instruments of pressure to convince its partner.

The 1959 tie between Iran and the U.S. gave Iranian policy-makers
a "moral lever" whereby they could hope to favorably influence U.S.
attitudes and policies. Persuasive advocacy, astute diplomacy, and
knowledge of the U.S. political system are indispensable weapons to a
small power in a partnership with a large one. Day-to-day diplomacy
in this type of relationship does not depend solely on articulate presen-
tation, moral suasion, and persuasive advocacy. The accurate perception of the other's interests is also required to convince its policy-
makers that the interests of both states are compatible, if not identical.

There can only be speculation about the types of arguments advanced in private bilateral negotiating sessions. Nevertheless, there is
some circumstantial evidence for the types of arguments advanced by
Iran. A reconstruction of these possible arguments may shed light on
this facet of Iran-U.S. relations.

The most dynamic and fluid period of the Iran-U.S. relations which
concerned military equipment is in the 1967–1969 period. The Senate,
in particular, was critical of U.S. involvement in Asia and the far-
flung security commitments. It scrutinized both arms sales policy and
the executive branch's tendency to keep large and significant areas of
policy hidden from congressional review. The Foreign Military Sales
Act ended much of the power that had been the domain of the
executive branch. This mood and the termination of credit sales
financing to less developed countries by the Export-Import bank may
have raised misgivings in Tehran that the 1964 five-year agreement
would not be extended.

The Shah visited the United States in June 1968 and reportedly
sought to buy 600 million dollars in U.S. arms over six years, that is,
to obtain another long-term "commitment." The administration formally granted him 100 million dollars for the next year, with the

---

[54] One observer writes "The pressure for expansion was almost wholly domestic,
since the external threats to Iranian security, for the time being at least, were contained." J. C. Hurewitz, *Middle-East Politics: The Military Dimension*, p. 293.

remainder of the request subject to annual review. The communiqué reflected Iran's concern for sustaining "an adequate defense force," and "the President expressed the desire of the United States to continue co-operating with Iran to this end." [55] The U.S. offer was by no means a rebuff. It represented an acceleration of purchases in which under the 1964 arms agreement Iran had been purchasing weapons at the annual rate of 50 million dollars. Nevertheless, it is unclear whether the method of financing the sales was especially favorable to Iran, for it appears to have been at prevailing commercial rates.

In the Iranian view of international politics, its government could point to a loyal friendship to the United States, its refusal to condemn the U.S. in Vietnam, its support on major issues in the United Nations, and its general pro-Western orientation. Since 1967 the value of this friendship to the U.S. had risen, for the war in the Middle East had underscored the relative stability of Iran and its moderation in interna-tional politics. In addition, in late 1969, the Iranian government could have pointed out a number of trends in Middle East politics neces-sitating further Iranian armaments. Some of the following arguments may have been used: (1) Given the general instability in the area Iran was "a force for peace." (2) The danger of the *fait accompli* in international politics had underscored in 1967, as in 1965, the necessity for arms as a deterrence. (3) The January 1968 British announcement of its intended withdrawal from the Persian Gulf had immense security implications, and (4) not the least of these were the Soviet Union's aims, as witnessed by the visit of its warships to Umm al-Qasr in Iraq in May 1968. (5) The militancy of neighboring Iraq, as evidenced by the Shatt al-'Arab crisis of January 1969, could also have been cited.[56] Iranian diplomats may also have pointed to their own exemplary be-havior in dropping the claim to Bahrayn and constructing an informal entente with Sa'udi Arabia and Kuwait.

The Shah made an inspired if unsuccessful attempt to convince the Nixon administration that America's need for oil imports and the Iranian government's desire for U.S. arms on favorable terms could be met by means beneficial to the U.S. balance of payments. That could

---

[55] For text of communiqué on June 12, 1968, see *Department of State Bulletin,* Vol. 59, No. 1514 (July 1, 1968), p. 15. It appears that in 1968 "assurances" were given, or an "understanding" reached, that Iran would receive credit assistance of approximately 500 million dollars over the next five years for the acquisition of more Phantom aircraft.

[56] Arguments 3, 4, and 5 are known to have been stressed by Iranian officials. See *New York Times,* Oct. 14, 1969.

be accomplished by having the U.S. designate an Iranian oil quota of 100 million dollars annually in exchange for a guarantee that this money would be spent on U.S. arms. During his visit to the U.S. the Shah made this argument quite explicit. He met members of the Senate Foreign Relations Committee in Washington and appeared on television to explain it. He argued that Iran wanted the means to protect herself without relying on others; that Iran now had to buy its arms in the world market; that Iran knew and trusted the U.S. and its equipment; and that the U.S. already relied on imported oil. In exchange for an oil quota, the Iranian government would guarantee that "every cent" of the income Iran realized on U.S. oil sales would be spent in America. This argument shrewdly linked the U.S. need for overseas oil, her troubled balance of payments position, and Iran's need for armaments with backing for the recently espoused "Nixon doctrine."

What we need (the Shah said) is to have enough means to be able to take care of any situation that might arise in our region alone, because my views are that it is unfair and becoming impractical that every nation when in trouble will just send a wire to Washington. 'Please come to our help.' First of all, I don't know if you can do it anymore. Secondly, it could become very embarrassing. Thirdly, that could lead to a confrontation with another big power.[57]

The argument blended the Nixon doctrine and the danger of super-power confrontation with the necessity for sufficiently arming regional states. Although the Shah's argument for an oil quota was not accepted, the need for increased military grants and sales as a corollary to the Nixon doctrine has been recognized by the U.S. government.[58] It is thus particularly instructive to note the changes in the method of financing.

To fulfill U.S. obligations under the 1964 Memorandum of Understanding, grant aid of approximately 26 million dollars was given to Iran in 1969. Thereafter grant aid assistance was restricted to training

---

[57] See transcript of "Meet the Press," NBC, Sunday, Oct. 26, 1969, Vol. 13, No. 41, p. 3. The Shah's call for the exclusion of nonlittoral powers from the Gulf antedated Nixon's statement on Guam. See *New York Times*, March 25, 1969.

[58] The defense department's written answer to Sen. Fulbright's question, "Do you expect total arms exports by the United States to expand as the Nixon doctrine is implemented?" read thus: "The growing use of credit-assisted sales of military equipment, as well as increased MAP, seems clearly indicated for the immediate future." Hearings before the Senate Foreign Relations Committee on the Foreign Military Sales Act Amendment of 1970 and 1971, 91st Cong., 2nd Sess., May 11, 1970, p. 54.

and military assistance on the order of 500,000 dollars a year.[59] Since 1968 Iran has been buying arms from the U.S. at the rate of 100 million dollars a year. Clearly, that grant assistance has been a negligible proportion of the total since 1969. Credit assistance in sales, however, has been assured by the U.S. government on a large scale. For fiscal years 1968 and 1969, Congress authorized 100 million dollars of credits under the Foreign Military Sales Act. Since 1970 this source of credit has been replaced by the Export-Import bank. According to one well-researched report appearing on July 25, 1971:

In the last five years Washington has provided credits for $220 million worth of Iranian aircraft purchases in the United States.

The Iranian government is currently negotiating for $140 million more in 1971 credits from the Export-Import bank to pay for 32 new model Phantoms.[60]

The Export-Import bank provides half of the required funds directly and guarantees private bank loans for the other half. It is rare for this bank to finance sales of military equipment. This financing is a symbol of the transformation of the American perspective regarding the size and quality of armed forces necessary for Iran.

This, together with the unpublicized nature of American involvement in Iran's defense build up, suggests that the "restraint" role of the U.S. may have given way to a desire for disentanglement, the development of friendly regional centers of power which determine for themselves "how much is enough." While this may be financially less costly to the U.S., it is unclear whether the new and vast expenditures on military equipment can be borne by the Iranian economy without detriment to development.[61]

Since the Iranian government now buys its military equipment, government officials have sought new ways of supplementing the annual oil revenue to meet the expenditures. In January 1971 successful negotiations were completed with the international oil companies for a fixed increase in revenue for five years. This deal reportedly is to bring the Iranian government 3,600 million dollars over five years (1971–1976), i.e., an increase of 415 million dollars per annum. The

---

[59] See Hearings before the H. R. Committee on Foreign Affairs on the Foreign Assistance Act of 1968, 90th Cong., 2nd Sess., 1968 (remarks by Gen. Conway), pp. 793, 787.

[60] See *New York Times*, July 25, 1971. For fiscal year 1971, the Export-Import bank financed a loan of 120 million dollars. See *Secretary of State's Report to Congress*, pp. 89, 344.

[61] See Appendix I.

Iranian budget presented in February 1971 indicated that the whole of this increased revenue was to be alloted to military expenditure.[62]

While being "concerned" about excessive expenditure on military equipment, the U.S. position on this issue has clearly changed in the past decade. Iran is considered a friendly regional state and the U.S. wishes to encourage these in "self-help." Iran's increased and additional oil revenues can support additional expenditures on armaments. Furthermore, Iran is a sovereign state whose policy-makers' views are bound to differ from U.S. perspectives. Finally, as the Iran-U.S. relationship has become more equitable, U.S. "leverage" has diminished.

The traditionally accepted material indices of "power" such as size of population, geography, GNP, literacy rate, steel and coal production are of more value to students of international politics when qualified as to "power for what." It is generally accepted today that "power" is a relational concept relative both within a context and the end for which it is used. It is a paradox of the present international system that while the relative traditional elements of power of small states have actually declined, their status, prestige, and influence have increased since the First World War.[63]

This increased importance of the small state has not necessarily led to increased influence in the small-great power relationship or in the international system. This is partly due to the proliferation of new states, as well as the need for shrewd knowledge of the machinery of that government which is the object of influence. As Annette Fox notes: "The capacity for the small states to speak up in the international system has grown remarkably since 1919, but the possibility of being heard has not increased at the same rate." [64]

In a friendly relationship with a superpower, the instruments of persuasion available to small states' leaders are primarily persuasive advocacy, appeals to common interest, and perhaps the use of "moral" levers. The superpower object of these appeals and pressures must be interested in the small state which is attempting to influence it. In the Iranian case the U.S. has had an interest in that nation's security since 1945, and the continuation of interest has posed no problem to the Iranian government. Differences between the two countries have been minor and generally settled by discussion. Where discussions have failed, instruments of leverage have been mobilized and sanctions implied simultaneously with protracted discussion. A brief inventory

---

[62] *Keyhan International,* Feb. 20 and 27, 1971.
[63] Rothstein, *Small Powers,* pp. 3, 267.
[64] Fox, "The Small States in the International System, 1919–1969," pp. 762, 764.

of the "levers" utilized by the Iranian government is suggestive of the types of power available to some small states.

One of the sources of aggravation to the Iranian government in the early 1960's was the level of aid. From the perspective of Tehran it appeared that the costs in political aggravation of alignment were not compensated for by aid. The continued heavy flow of aid to nonaligned states which had paid none of the costs of commitment was thus especially galling. The Shah condemned this in his memoirs, and two prime ministers specifically referred to the lack of American aid as reason for their resignations.[65]

The Iranian government has relied primarily on moral suasion or leverage by playing the loyal ally. But it has not been averse to implied threats. In an interview with Harrison Salisbury in November 1961 the Shah said that if Iran did not obtain the aid it needed from her friends, "What a gain for communism." Two days later the Iranian prime minister stressed that to make Iran a showplace for noncommunist life, "much depends on our getting assistance from our American friends." [66]

Iranian policy-makers have also stressed their loyalty to the U.S.; Amini pointed out that "Iran is America's only sincere friend in this part of the world." At the same time prominent Iranian politicians have implied a cost-benefit approach to Iran's international posture. In 1959 Senator Jamal Imami indicated his shock at the level of aid for Iran:

I found Iran at the bottom of a long list of countries receiving United States assistance whereas nations who flirt with the opposing camp get ten times as much American support and assistance as Iran.[67]

The "power of the weak" can be the power of persistence, the power to concentrate on one issue, and the power to procrastinate. Another form of power sometimes possessed by small states or their leaders is the "power" to be a nuisance, i.e., the power to disturb the status quo, or to damage the interest of the superpower. The power often requires the readiness by small states' leaders to threaten to inflict a wound on oneself, or one's country, unless certain conditions are met.

Of course, success requires the positive interest of the blackmailed

---

[65] See the Shah's *Memoirs*, p. 312 *et seq*. Prime Minister Ali Amini specified that it was only a "friendly complaint," *New York Times*, July 19 and 20, 1962; Prime Minister Assadollah Alam, *New York Times*, March 8 and 11, 1964.

[66] See *New York Times*, Nov. 5, 1961; *Tehran Journal*, Nov. 7, 1961.

[67] *Tehran Journal*, Feb. 1, 1959.

power in avoiding the threatened step and the readiness of the small states' leaders to make credible its implementation. As Raymond Aron has noted, the sign that a region of the world is becoming a theater or a stake of the cold war is the reversal of the ordinary relationship between the strong and the weak.

'Help me or I will succumb to communism' is how the argument runs, endlessly repeated in various forms by which the so-called pro-Western leaders ask the help of the superpower. 'What you refuse me I will obtain from the other side.'

This "power" also comes from the margin of superiority given to the slightly and conveniently "irrational" partner in a game of competitive risk-taking. In this respect it is analagous to Schelling's concept of "the power to blow one's brains out on somebody else's new suit." [68]

The Shah allegedly threatened to abdicate in a period when he felt he was not obtaining the U.S. support he deserved. He was quoted as saying during a visit to Washington, "Let me tell you quite bluntly that this king-business has given me personally nothing but headaches." [69] If this is a correct interpretation of the statement, it exemplifies the "power of the weak" in which the weak capitalizes on his weakness.

The effectiveness of this tactic in a state's basic international posture will depend on both its credibility and the concern of the state which is being threatened. This tactic was used in 1959 to elicit a stronger U.S. commitment to Iran's security and again in 1966 for a specific arms request. The Shah's visit to the USSR in 1965 had demonstrated the improvement of relations between the two countries. Furthermore, the political stability and economic vitality in Iran paralleled the international detente which had made the cold-war issue less urgent. Threatening to "change sides," while still effective in drawing attention to oneself, did not carry the same implications as it did in 1959. By 1966 Washington probably recognized that a "normalization" of relations between Tehran and Moscow was a logical and perhaps inevitable development. In Tehran the fence-mending with the USSR was considered important both for its intrinsic and domestic benefits,

---

[68] Aron, *Peace and War*, pp. 383–394; Thomas C. Schelling, *The Strategy of Conflict*, p. 127, *et passim*.

[69] See *New York Times*, April 14, 1962; *Tehran Journal*, April 14, 1962. Both Howard Wriggins and Richard Cottam view the statement as a threat to abdicate. See Wriggins, "Political Outcomes of Foreign Assistance; Influence, Involvement or Intervention," p. 222; and Cottam, *Competitive Interference and Twentieth Century Diplomacy*.

i.e., in the neutralization of anti-regime leftist groups and in the assertion of a role in international politics independent of the United States.

In Iran a shift in the leverage available to the U.S. had occurred between 1960 and 1966. The Shah was stronger domestically, the economy was more vital, and relations with the USSR had improved. U.S. supporting assistance had been terminated in 1962, grant aid was being phased out, and economic aid was to be ended in November 1967. Finally, the U.S. government was involved in Southeast Asia and susceptible to the "nuisance" that could be caused by a determined irate partner. When confronted with a solid front on specific issues, the U.S. either might be unable to successfully pressure the Iranian government or, alternatively, might even be successfully pressured itself.

The very fact of partnership between independent states required less blunt instruments of pressure than might be the case in an antagonistic relationship. Differences between the two governments on the proper allocation of resources between military and economic projects could seldom be settled through blunt instruments. As the late John McNaughton, assistant secretary of defense on ISA (International Security Assistance), remarked in reference to Iran, "There is obviously a limit to the influence we can bring to bear on them." [70]

As regards Iranian leverage on the U.S., there were at least two variables: (1) The USSR must be ready to accept Iranian requests. If Iran were to threaten the U.S. with movement to the USSR, either in its posture, as in 1959, or for a particular weapons-system, such as the SAM-2 in 1966, the USSR must be interested in such a development. While the USSR was interested in 1959, in 1966 it was unwilling to supply the missiles requested. (2) The threat to "go to the other side" has both diminishing returns and credibility, as it relates to minor issues. With repetition it may no longer be credible to either of the states. Furthermore, for a small state bordering a large state or superpower, security may not lie in maintaining equally good relations with the proximate and distant superpowers. Indeed, to ameliorate the effects of an asymmetrical geographical situation, security may rest in the cultivation of stronger ties with the distant superpower. Geography may set definite parameters on the threat to normalize relations or go to the other side. Thus Egypt might be able to threaten this normalization with more credibility than Iran.

---

[70] Hearings before the Senate Select Committee on Disarmament of the Committee on Foreign Relations, March 2, 1967.

The Shah's hint of discussions with the Soviet Union for military equipment that the U.S. would not supply effectively elicited a U.S. counter-offer to modernize Iranian air defense forces. Presumably this was an improvement in the terms originally offered.[71]

However, in the sensitive field of sophisticated weapons systems, the limitations of the threat to go to the other side were quite apparent. One reliable American report notes that: "Iran talked about getting the Soviet SA-2 surface-to-air missiles, and we said, 'If you buy them, you get no F-4's.'" [72] The U.S. was sensitive about the introduction of Soviet technicians and instructors necessary for the use of the missiles, the security implications thereby raised for the modern F-4's performance, and the possibilities of espionage. In reacting sharply, the U.S. government showed its concern for the security of its most modern weapons systems and served notice on the limits to Iranian maneuvering. The negative reaction of the Soviet Union additionally served to undercut this ploy.

The U.S. government's counter-offer demonstrated its sensitivity to maneuvering and the value it attached to maintaining its predominant political influence in Iran. The belief that its influence came partly from its arms-supplier status was translated into policy by "preemptive selling"—i.e., in order to forestall sales or grants of military equipment by the Soviet Union, it sold the arms requested.[73] On the other hand, the Iranian government had initiated arms talks with the USSR and was unwilling to antagonize that government by breaking off the discussions.

Consequently an agreement was announced in February 1967 whereby the USSR would supply Iran with nearly 110 million dollars worth of nonsophisticated military vehicles. This agreement did not make the Iranian armed forces dependent on Soviet spare parts, nor, did it require Soviet technicians. It served the function of nominally diversifying the sources of Iran's arms supplies and thereby so constituted a limited assertion of Iranian independence. It is unclear

---

71 Watkins, "Neutral Iran Will Add F-40's," p. 54.

72 *Ibid.*

73 See, in particular, Hearings before Senate Subcommittee on Near Eastern and South Asian Affairs of the Committee on Foreign Relations on "Arms Sales to Near East and South Asian Countries," 90th Cong., 1st Sess., March 14, April 13, 20, 25, and June 22, 1967, pp. 5–6, 51, 99–100, *et passim.* For a trenchant criticism of U.S. arms policies, see "Arms Sales and Foreign Policy," a staff study for the Senate Committee on Foreign Relations, 91st Cong., 1st Sess., 1965 (Washington, D.C.: GPO, 1965).

whether it brought pressure on the United States to supply the arms the Iranian government had requested.[74] Ultimately, susceptibility to this form of pressure depends on the belief that U.S. interests are better served by supplying friendly states with arms they are determined to obtain.

In day-to-day diplomacy, great powers have a wider panoply of instruments with which to register their displeasure, while small states are relatively powerless. Since they give no economic aid, they cannot terminate it. Economic boycotts are likely to be most damaging to the small state, and the severance of diplomatic relations is likely to hamper its own diplomacy.

However, the small state can register its displeasure in voting in the United Nations.[75] It seems likely that the Iranian leadership's displeasure with the U.S. 1964 decision to sell arms rather than to give them away encouraged the Iranian government to indicate its displeasure in that manner. The Shah and his spokesmen repeatedly reiterated that the destiny of Iran is determined in Tehran.[76] The 1965 and 1966 General Assemblies were the first occasions that the Iranian government abstained on the Albanian resolution backing Peking's representation in the UN and on the U.S.-supported resolution declaring this an "important" question. In light of the international context in Southeast Asia at that time, probably the U.S. did not pressure the Iranian government to back its resolution. Although in 1967 a partial reversal was effected when the Iranian delegation voted for the American-backed resolution, it continued to abstain on the Albanian draft. In a limited fashion the Iranian government had indicated its displeasure.

THE POLICY PROCESS IN THE UNITED STATES

To influence the United States, the Iranian government has had to argue persuasively and exercise what leverage is available. In addition,

---

74 The U.S. decision to sell F-4 aircraft to Iran was conveyed to the government of Iran on July 20, 1966. The barter transaction with the Soviet Union was announced by the prime minister of Iran on Feb. 19, 1967. U.S. Defense department statement in *Arms Sales to Near East and South Asia*, p. 100. One source suggests that the Iranian government has since used this agreement as a leverage on the U.S. SIPRI, *Yearbook*, 1968–69, p. 54.

75 For a catalogue of actions taken by the Turkish government after its annoyance with the U.S. over Cyprus, see Ulman and Dekmejian, "Changing Patterns in Turkish Foreign Policy."

76 See also General Khatemi's statement in Watkins, "Neutral Iran Will Add F-40's."

it must understand the dynamics of the U.S. political system and adapt its arguments to it. An agreement with the executive branch of government could be rendered useless if rejected or stymied by the legislative branch. In this section the focus will be on those segments of the American internal political machinery responsible for decisions affecting foreign policy. Three areas are of particular concern: (1) relations between the executive and congressional branches of government; (2) the role of Congress, attentive publics, and interest groups; (3) relevant agencies in the executive branch.

Executive-congressional relations cover both the arguments put forward by the state and defense departments and tactics employed by them with Congress.

The state and defense departments have justified military grants or sales to Iran with various reasons. These have ranged from the Shah's "unique peaceful revolution," and the "reformist" nature of his program, which widened the power base, to an emphasis on the link between these reforms and the U.S. support which made them possible. This latter point was made most explicitly by Assistant Secretary of State Lucius D. Battle:

The success the Shah has achieved has been phenomenal and has aroused the envy of others who would prefer to see what the Shah calls his "White Revolution" change color. Our economic assistance, now shifting from grant to credit sales, has assisted Iran in maintaining the security and stability which are prerequisites for economic and social development.[77]

U.S. self-interest has also been emphasized in terms of the loyalty of Iran in the UN or in crises of particular concern to the U.S. Similarly, the buildup of these "forward defense countries" has been stressed as of benefit to the U.S. defense, for they constitute the "cheapest U.S. defense dollars" spent and relieve the U.S. of both expenses and manpower "which we would otherwise have to assume." [78] Grants and sales also have been advocated for the influence they would give the U.S. in Iran. The convergence of U.S.-Iranian interests in the Persian Gulf has also been noted.[79]

---

[77] Hearings before the H. R. Committee on Foreign Affairs on the Foreign Assistance Act of 1968, 90th Cong., 2nd Sess., 1968 (remarks by Lucius D. Battle, assistant secretary of state for Near Eastern and South Asian affairs), p. 251. Robert MacNamara stressed the same point in Hearings before the H. R. Committee on Foreign Affairs on the Foreign Assistance Act of 1964, 88th Cong., 2nd Sess., 1964, pp. 88, 114.

[78] Hearings before the H. R. Committee on Foreign Affairs on the Foreign Assistance Act of 1964, 88th Cong., 2nd Sess., 1964 (remarks by MacNamara), p. 87.

[79] Hearings before the Senate Committee on Foreign Relations on the Foreign

The executive branch, whether or not wittingly, has indirectly presented Congress with *fait accompli*. Agreements, understandings, and assurances arrived at between U.S.-Iran negotiators on aid levels or financing of sales, while carrrying no legal weight, constitute undertakings by the executive branch subject to congressional approval. The annual hearings hint at agreements *inter alia* in 1958, 1962, 1964, 1966, and 1968. These tend to be presented to Congress as accomplished facts, the substance of which are not debatable. For example, in the 1967 hearings before a congressional subcommittee it was learned that only after it was divulged by the press did Congress learn of the sale of F-4 Phantom jets to Iran. The relevant agencies in the executive branch which made the agreement in August 1966 intended to inform Congress about it some six to nine months thereafter, when it was necessary to appear before it for additional appropriations.[80]

Another method used until 1967 to bypass Congress and congressional power over appropriations was the practice of financing so-called "X-country" loans for arms sales by the Export-Import bank. These were then guaranteed by the department of defense. By this method and the so-called "revolving fund" which used military credit sales Congress authorized for other purposes, the defense department could "multiply congressional appropriations into programs of military credit sales which were many times larger than the appropriations." [81]

Congressional strong reaction to these tactics was expressed in the 1968 Foreign Military Sales Act which terminated the "revolving fund" and prohibited the financing of military sales by the Export-Import bank to any underdeveloped country. In the future the U.S. government source of military credit for less developed countries became the funds authorized and appropriated annually by Congress to the defense department. There had been no U.S. government definition of "less developed country" applicable to all agencies. Thus for AID's purposes Iran might remain a "less developed country," while the Export-Import bank does not consider Iran a "less developed country" and hence it is eligible for continued financing.

Military Sales Act of 1968, 90th Cong., 2nd Sess., 1968 (remarks by Paul Warnke), pp. 12, 24.

80 See Sen. Symington's comments in Hearings before Subcommittee on Near Eastern and South Asian Affairs of Committee on Foreign Relations, 90th Cong., 1st Sess., 1967, pp. 13–14, 62–63, 79, *et passim*.

81 Hearings before the Senate Committee on Foreign Relations on the Foreign Military Sales Act of 1968, 90th Cong., 2nd Sess., 1968, pp. 1–7.

In 1970 Congress amended the Foreign Military Sales Act and cut credit financing. The following year it disclosed the allocation of military aid for individual countries. And despite the President's known objections, the House has attempted to cut aid to Pakistan and Greece.[82] The attitude of Congress to military aid requests had become increasingly more important and problematic.

There is no core of ethnically interested U.S. public concerned with Iran. Unlike the Jews, Italians, Greeks, and Poles, there are few votes at stake in any particular issue affecting Iran. Unlike the UAR, Iranian aid requests do not suffer with Jewish voters because of enmity with Israel or from competition with the Southern bloc because of cotton production. However, there is the petroleum industry with vast investments in the Persian Gulf region, which can be expected to mobilize its lobbies in support of Iranian interests.

In the absence of pressure from their constituencies, most congressmen and senators have chosen their own orientation on Iranian affairs. Given their lack of knowledge of Iranian affairs and interests in them, more often than not congressional subcommittees have tended to be swayed by executive arguments or influenced by "image." Given the pressure of competing and more urgent issues, it is the rare congressman who has been particularly interested in Iranian affairs. This has been more true of the House than the Senate.

While opponents of the Shah's regime have gained inexpensive coverage by organizing protests during the Shah's visits to Washington, by writing letters to editors, and buying advertising space in newspapers, they have been unable to spark widespread interest in Iranian affairs or distaste for the regime. Both in editorials and the selection of new items covered, the *New York Times, Washington Post,* and *Christian Science Monitor* have generally been well disposed to the regime.[83]

Public relations firms such as Ramesh Sanghvi's have been hired to enhance the reformist image of the Shah, to increase interested American awareness of Iran, to support economic aid, and to promote tourism. Today the importance of "image" in influencing the U.S. has

---

[82] For figures on foreign military sales during the period 1965–1971, see a statement by Undersecretary John N. Irwin in "New Approaches to International Security Assistance," reprinted in *Department of State Bulletin 44,* No. 1662, Feb. 22, 1971, p. 226.

[83] For a criticism of the press in this regard, see Cottam, *Competitive Interference,* p. 176 *et seq.,* and p. 194.

informed the monarch's actions.[84] The additional leverage of "benevolent" leader that may obtain through a "good image" might also be as significant a dimension in interpersonal relations between heads of state as is "prestige" in international relations. Finally, one might cite the activities of the Iranian embassy in Washington, which attempts to maintain good relations with key congressmen and keep open channels of communication, which may be useful in preventing a critic of the regime today from becoming a perennial critic. Nonetheless, the Iranian government's interaction with the executive branch of the U.S. government has been the principal arena in which policy has been forged and requests accepted and acted upon or pigeonholed.

Policy is debated in the state department as in an "adversary" system. In contrast to the Arab states which may have to contend with the Israel desk, Turkey with the Greek desk, Pakistan with the India desk, Iran has no longstanding adversaries friendly to the U.S. An increase in Iran's military equipment thus does not *ipso facto* bring down criticism from other desks. The state department has generally been less sympathetic to arguments about the militancy of the "radical" Arab states and the dangers they pose to Iran than Tehran might have hoped.

But since 1964 this has not been translated into any significant denial of arms to Iran. The basic fact that a strong Iran would serve U.S. interests and the limitations of an alliance in dictating a sovereign partner state's security requirements have ameliorated many differences in emphases between the two. Furthermore, sales for influence and leverage and preemptive selling have gained state department support, while the defense department has normally concurred in arms sales on technical grounds, such as the need for missiles to defend oil installations in southern Iran, or a new generation of jet planes to offset neighbors' acquisitions.

Undoubtedly the large number of Iranian military officers and pilots trained in the U.S. and exposed to Western ideas have been welcome in the department of defense.[85] More recently, the defense department

---

84 Opponents of the regime have formed, *inter alia,* "United Patriots for Justice," which is a registered lobbyist organization which engaged in "political activities" in 1965–1969.

85 Figures vary: Watkins, "Neutral Iran Will Add F-40's," quotes a figure of 1,825 Iranian air force personnel trained in the U.S. between 1950 and 1967, p. 62. Maj.–Gen. Ekhardt, Commander of the U.S. Military Advisory Group in Iran (MAAG), put the figure at 4,500; *Tehran Journal,* March 4, 1964. "Military Assistance and Foreign Military Sales Facts," Defense Department ISA Booklet, March, 1971, on p. 15 gives the figure of 8,597 between 1950 and 1970.

is said to have encouraged the Nixon administration to sell arms at commercial credit rates to countries such as Iran, which are capable of absorbing the costs.

The U.S. ambassador in Iran coordinates sales activities, but the impact of his role varies according to the strength of his convictions and persuasive ability, the esteem of his colleagues, his "access" to senior U.S. officials, and his relationship with the Shah. In the past decade three U.S. ambassadors have been assigned to Tehran, Julius Holmes (1960–1965), Armin Meyer (1966–1969) and Douglas MacArthur III (1969–1972). The latter two are known to be particularly sympathetic to the Shah's domestic efforts and to Iranian arms requests. They have argued their case vigorously and persuasively.[86]

The institutional structure in the executive branch has not always permitted other agencies the opportunity to discuss each arms request. The process of policy review normally allows for the views of the departments of state, defense, treasury, and AID to be heard. The arms control and disarmament agency and the bureau of the budget may also be involved. The former is seldom a major participant in review processes relating to specific countries, and was not consulted on the decision to sell Phantom planes (F-4's) to Iran.[87]

The review of a request focuses *inter alia* on military legitimacy, the recipient's ability to pay and the potential effect on the peace and stability in the area. Frequently the secretary of defense and the President actively involve themselves in the final decision. Given the Shah's interest in these matters, this is probably the case with Iranian requests.[88] The presence of the defense and state departments on the one hand, and the treasury department and AID on the other, is aimed at reviewing both the military-diplomatic and the economic aspects of a particular request. The latter two departments are said to be particularly influential in terms of the credit arrived at for a given sale, although this matter is also the subject of interagency discussion.

It should be noted that despite AID's objection on economic grounds to the scope of the programs and U.S. commitment to Iran in 1966, it was unable to prevent the agreement. This may be partially explained

---

86 For a discussion of the role of the ambassador in Iran-U.S. relations in an earlier period, see Richard Cottam, "The U.S., Iran, and the Cold War."

87 For the strengthening of the role of the U.S. state department in the policy process since 1968, see John N. Irwin II, "New Approaches to International Security Assistance," *Department of State Bulletin 44*, No. 1652 (Feb. 22, 1971), p. 224 *et seq.*

88 In 1968 Paul Warnke referred to discussions with Iran "at the high levels of government," Hearings before the H. R. Committee on Foreign Affairs on the Foreign Military Sales Act of 1968, 90th Cong., 2nd Sess., 1968, p. 45.

by the series of "understandings" arrived at between U.S. and Iranian officials from 1958 to 1968. These became quite complicated and made the donorship of grant and provision of credit an ongoing process not easily interrupted.

Furthermore, it is likely that changes in a number of factors since 1966 have undermined arguments against credit to Iran. Iran's economic upsurge since the middle of the decade, the increased revenue from expansion of oil production and better terms, and the massive increase in revenues negotiated for a five-year term in January 1971 would seem to undercut objections to increased expenditure on armaments. In addition, the termination of U.S. grant aid, except for a military advisory group and the Peace Corps, has undercut U.S. leverage, while the espousal of the Nixon Doctrine and the building up of friendly regional states has given increased momentum to those bureaucratic elements who would argue for a well-armed Iran.

The Shah of Iran has managed to maintain an excellent personal relationship with two Democratic and one Republican presidents. If anything, the monarch appears to be on better terms with Richard Nixon than with his predecessors.[89] This may be partly due to a more equitable relationship between the two countries compared to the earlier period of U.S. "social engineering" and interference in Iranian affairs, and Iranian dependence on U.S. largesse. Iran's "independent national policy" has brought self-respect to the Iranian leadership no less than to its people, without obscuring the common interests of both states.

The United States has welcomed Iranian independence because it means that the U.S. is no longer automatically blamed for everything that occurs in Iran. While the U.S. was involved in Vietnam, the Shah carefully eschewed any self-serving criticism. U.S. policy-makers, preoccupied with pressing matters in other parts of the globe and within their own society, have appreciated the fact that a visit from the Shah has not meant more problems. Instead, the vitality of Iran underlined in American policy-makers' eyes an area of success in foreign policy. The belief in the convergence if not the identity of Iran-U.S. interests in the Middle East and the Persian Gulf has been given concrete application by U.S. support of Iranian policy in the Gulf.

---

89 For a warm exchange between the Shah and President Nixon, see *Department of State Bulletin 61* (Nov. 10, 1969), pp. 356–400.

APPENDIX

Several trends are clear from tables 1, 2, and 3: (1) The change from grants to sales accelerated in 1964. (2) Military expenditures increased, even as aid declined. (3) An increasing percentage of the GNP has been spent on defense. The percentage of the GNP in defense nearly doubled from 1964 to 1971; yet this masks the fact that the *size* of the GNP was also growing at a very rapid rate. Hence defense expenditure nearly quadrupled in a decade. (4) Expenditures in millions of dollars indicate roughly the amounts of money involved. The sets of figures for current versus constant prices show the magnitudes of real expenditure involved, allowing for inflation and devaluation. (5) Figures are unreliable, and to be taken as approximations.

While Iranian sources are rarely comprehensive, the following table corroborates increased resources devoted to defense.[90]

Yearly Expenditures (in billions of rials)

1347 (1968–1969)	36.5
1348 (1969–1970)	47.7
1349 (1970–1971)	58.4
1350 (1971–1972) (estimated)	78.6
1351 (1972–1973) (projected)	100.9

In 1970 the Shah observed that Iran's rate of economic growth of 8 to 10 percent a year "has been achieved despite an allocation of between 5 and 7 percent of our gross national product to defense (which I consider not to be adequate but simply what we can afford)." [91] An economist has recently expressed doubts as to the country's ability to continue this rate of growth into the 1970's. He observes that there has recently been an increase in inflation, and a substantial and growing deficit in the balance of payments. In addition, he foresees as "inevitable" a growing proportion of military expenditure in the national budget. He observes that defense and security services accounted for 40 percent of ordinary budgeted expenditure in 1970.[92]

---

[90] "Report of the Prime Minister on the State of the Iranian Economy, 1347–1348, and Government Programmes for the Year 1351" (Tehran: Central Bureau of the Budget: Plan Organization, 1972), pp. 74, 78–79.

[91] "Address of the Shahanshah Aryamehr and Reports by the Prime Minister and the Plan Organization Managing Director at the Historic Session on Plan Organization, Dec. 29, 1970" (Tehran: offset press, Imperial Government of Iran), p. 13.

[92] Amuzegar and Fekrat, *Iran: Economic Development Under Dualistic Conditions*, pp. 104–134.

Table 1

IRANIAN MANPOWER AND MILITARY CAPABILITY

	1960	1961	1962	1963	1964	1965	1966	1967	1968	1969	1970	1971	1972
Population (in millions)	21.2	22.1	22.8	23.4	23.9	24.5	25.5	26.3	27.1	27.9	28.7	30.5	31.7
Force Levels													
1. ISS		210,000	208,000	208,000	208,000	180,000	180,000	180,000	221,000	221,000	161,000	191,000	
2. ACDA				208,000	208,000	206,000	225,000	225,000	225,000		238,000		250,000
Estimates of Military Expenditures (in millions, U.S. dollars)													
1. ISS	166	147.6	125	170	195	217	255	480	495	594	779	1,023	1,915
2. ACDA			186	191	233	227	322	440	553	648	833		
3. SIPRI (current figures in Iranian currency, million rials)	13,857	14,137	14,170	14,469	16,523	20,941	23,850	31,075	39,750	47,300	55,700	64,819	133,050
(constant price figures in millions, U.S. dollars, 1960 prices/1960 exchange rates)	182.9	181.0	180.1	183.0	201.2	250.11	285.0	366.3	465.7	536.9	619.5	686.7	

Military Expenditures (as percentage of GNP)										
1. ISS	4.4	4.1	3.9	4.1	3.8	3.9	4.9	5.6	5.0	7.1	8.5
2. ACDA	4.1			4.6	3.8	5.0	5.9	6.9	7.1	8.2	

Sources: Institute for Strategic Studies, "The Military Balance," annual, 1960–1970 (London: ISS). U.S. Arms Control and Disarmament Agency, "World Military Expenditures," annual, 1966–1971 (Washington: ACDA). Stockholm International Peace Research Institute, "World Armaments and Disarmaments Yearbook," 1972 (New York: Humanities Press, 1972), pp. 86–89. (Compare with figures in *ibid.*, 1970, pp. 270–273.)

Table 2

IRANIAN MILITARY EXPENDITURES COMPARED TO MILITARY ASSISTANCE*

Year	Military Grant Aid	Military Expenditures
	(in millions, U.S. dollars, at 1960 prices/1960 exchange rates)	
1960	67.4	182.9
1961	46.1	181.0
1962	50.0	181.0
1963	48.1	183.0
1964	38.7	201.2
1965	43.0	252.0
1966	37.5	338.7
1967	35.5	409.9
1968	(17.1)	433.7
1969	...	581.3
1970	...	772.0
1971	...	1,230
1972	...	2,000
1973	...	2,010

Sources: SIPRI, "Yearbook," 1969–70, pp. 284–285. "The Military Balance," annual, 1973. (London, IISS)
* I.e., Western powers grant aid.
Discrepancies between figures here and those of the ISS and ACDA, and within these agencies from year to year, is accounted for by the difficulty of obtaining accurate figures; the differences in estimates (current prices, constant prices, or a particular base year); and problems of currency devaluation. A *rough indication* of the relationship between grant aid and expenditures; and between military expenditures, population growth, and expenditure per capita is possible, however.
For a good discussion of Iran's arms purchases see SIPRI, *The Arms Trade with the Third World*, pp. 574–579.
The value of Soviet arms aid between 1967–1970, which are *not* grants, is estimated at roughly 290 million dollars. See testimony of Bernard Lewis in Hearings before the Subcommittee on National Security and International Operations, Senate Committee on Government Operations, March 17, 1971, p. 100.

Figures recently cited in the Iranian press are also significant: in the March 1970–March 1971 budget, defense expenditure was reported to have risen by 222 million dollars, to 772 million dollars.[93]

In March 1971–March 1972, defense expenditures were calculated at one billion dollars, an increase of 30 percent.[94]

In the March 1972–March 1973 budget, defense expenditures rose by 23 percent over the previous year.[95]

---

[93] *Tehran Journal*, Feb. 9, 1970. See also *New York Times*, Feb. 9, 1970.

[94] *Keyhan International*, Feb. 27, 1971. The Shah corroborated the billion-dollar figure in an interview with some Norwegian journalists, *Ettelaat* (air ed.), Aug. 1, 1971. *Keyhan International*, March 6, 1971, reported that the same rate of increase of 30 percent was envisaged for the next five years.

[95] See *Keyhan International* (weekly ed.), Feb. 5, 1972, and "Text of Address

Table 3

BREAKDOWN OF U.S. MILITARY AID TO IRAN INTO GRANTS AND SALES

Fiscal Year	Grants (in millions, U.S. dollars)	Sales (credit) (in millions, U.S. dollars)
1960	89.1	
1961	49.2	
1962	33.3	total 1.2
1963	66.0	
1964	27.3	
1965	49.9	12.9
1966	41.2	52.2
1967	41.1	38.9
1968	38.7	56.7
1969	50.9	99.2
1970	15.2	189.7
1971	6.6	114.2
Cumulative Grants, 1960–1971: $423.4 million		
Cumulative Sales, 1965–1971: $563.8 million		

Source: Based on calculations of figures found in "Military Assistance Facts" (Washington: Office of the Assistant Secretary of Defense, International Security Affairs), May 1966, May 1967, March 1968, May 1969, March 1970, March 1971, and April 1972.

Finally, in October–November 1972 the government requested and obtained authorization for an *additional* expenditure of 700 million dollars for defense.[96]

Delivered by Prime Minister Amir Abbas Hoveyda to the Majlis in Presenting the 1351 (1972–1973) National Budget" (Tehran, Jan. 25, 1972), p. 38.
[96] *Keyhan International* (weekly ed.), Oct. 28, 1972, Nov. 18, 1972.

Part Two

THE REGIONAL LEVEL

PROLOGUE

On the regional level, especially in the last decade, Iran has become a major if not dominant power. The elevation of Iran's regional significance has taken place in the changing context of interaction between the international system and the Middle Eastern subsystem. An analysis of Iran's regional foreign relations necessitates understanding the nature and evolution of this context.

The postwar international system was a novel one not only for the proliferation of new national actors with different value systems entering an expanded global system but also for the transformations associated with decolonization, the appearance of a universal actor (the United Nations), and the emergence of thermonuclear weapons—weapons which are capable of having systemic consequences. This last fact has ruled out large-scale wars except as ultimate threats, and at the same time has complicated and emphasized the control of limited violence because of the fear of escalation and the unsuitability of nuclear weapons for local conflicts. It has thus altered traditional security calculations for both great and small powers.[1]

The rigid bipolar pattern of world politics characterized by the dominance of Soviet-American rivalry in 1945–1962 gradually gave way to a looser fragmented system, still bipolar on the nuclear arms level, but multi-polar politically. If Soviet-American rivalry dominated the 1950's, the overlapping interests of *les grands frères* became more conspicuous in the 1960's. The dissipation of the dominant tensions of the

---

[1] That is, a great deal of today's power is unusable, and much of it cannot be translated into influence. See Rothstein, *Small Powers*, p. 239.

cold war has resulted in the decentralization of issues in international politics, the weakening of alliance systems, and the surfacing of regional issues which have assumed a new salience.

The international context provided the small states with a propitious environment within which to maneuver: (1) superpower rivalry has given small states the opportunity to use their enhanced value to pursue their own objectives; (2) the assumption of the diminished likelihood of nuclear war has raised the importance of regional or local conflicts insofar as their escalation might result in systemic conflict; (3) mutual deterrence has obstructed great-power intervention, and as a result the smaller states in their subsystems are freer to act.[2] Thus if the rivalry of the superpowers in the 1950's was manifested in a preclusive interest in the third world to prevent the other's occupation or control of the target state, by the 1960's the rules of the game had been sufficiently codified to virtually rule out the open use of force in these areas. The emergence of regional and local issues, the recognition by the superpowers of a limited-adversary relationship in addition to the increased importance of other issues (e.g., North-South questions), all contributed to and reflected the fragmentation of the earlier dominant issue.[3] This in turn was reflected in a change in the kinds of relations certain small states now had with the superpowers, e.g., Cuba, Rumania, and Iran. To the extent that states like Iran were useful to the U.S. as symbolic allies and anticommunist bases in the 1950's, they were now valuable in the 1960's for their stability and dependability. If Iran viewed the U.S. as a protector and patron in the earlier part of the decade, it now looked upon it as a friendly power and an important source of foreign investment.

The regional setting of a state (its "geographic-historical" zone, in Aron's phrase) constitutes a context and provides a parameter for the international behavior of that state. This is readily seen by comparing the range of foreign policy choices available to the nations of Africa

---

2 For a discussion of these points see, respectively: Fox; "The Small States in the International System, 1919–1969," p. 756; Rothstein, *Small Powers*, pp. 237–250; Stock, *Israel on the Road to Sinai*, p. 83.

3 Jorge I. Dominquez writes: "More countries are center powers than ever before, though they are largely centers of local subsystems. . . . The structure of the international system has been transformed through a process of fragmentation of the linkages of the center to the peripheries. . . . There is still a global system for a variety of purposes. But global fragmentation has become a dominant and accelerating trend. . . . The scope and domain of the global system have narrowed." Dominquez, "Mice That Do Not Roar: Some Aspects of International Politics in the World's Peripheries," pp. 207–208.

with those of Central America, and the latter with the states adjacent to the USSR or China. Geopolitical fatalities do not, of course, determine a state's orientation or its foreign policy. Choice is involved. Iran's posture to the USSR differs from that of Afghanistan; and Thailand's vis-à-vis China differs from that of Burma.

The concept of a regional or subordinate system reminds us that within the global system, subsystems may exist in a concrete rather than merely theoretical way. Common history, proximity in geography, and perhaps similar religion, culture, and language, may thus help distinguish the states of a particular area and underscore that their area of principal interaction is in their geographic-historical zone. The limited power of most states is an important factor serving to restrict their interests to their immediate region. And the region is often characterized by concentration on a single dominant issue which has serious subsystemic (but not global) consequences.[4]

These subsystems can be, and frequently are, discontinuous from the global system (though penetrated in a few issue areas), serving as the centers of various cross-pressures in international politics. While in early 1970 there was a war in Southeast Asia, peace on the Indian subcontinent and Arabian peninsula, and intermittent conflict in the eastern Mediterranean, by 1973 there was relative peace in all these zones— including, in the Indian subcontinent, a peace which was the aftermath of a rapid war. The prevalence of armed conflict in many areas of the world since 1945 suggests that the international system may be more durable than it might superficially appear.[5]

Regional subsystems may be characterized not only by their relative autonomy, the dominance of specific issues, and the limited power of their actors, but also by varied opportunities they afford the small state to maneuver for security. The Western European zone of peace is an integrated system which renders maneuvering unnecessary, while the hierarchical Eastern European system makes it difficult, but essential, for the small state which is bent on preserving its diplomatic freedom. The small state in a peripheral subsystem dominated by one powerful state clearly has less opportunity to improve its situation (e.g., Zambia in Southern Africa).[6]

---

4 See Oran Young, "Political Discontinuities in the International System." Young argues that subsystems in the international system differ significantly from one another in terms of both actors and issues.

5 On this point, see Fox, "The Small States in the International System," p. 758.

6 Clearly a state can be a member of two regional subsystems at the same time, e.g., Egypt in the Middle East and Africa. For the constraints and choices of

It is not our intention to prove the existence of a regional subsystem in the Middle East.[7] In the interest of parsimony we merely advance the contention that the area bounded by Pakistan in the east and Turkey and Egypt in the west comprises a subsystem, for our purposes, in the period 1960–1971. In this system there have been essentially two issues of major regional importance: (1) the attitude toward the USSR, imperialism, decolonization, and alignment; and (2) the attitude toward Israel. The states contiguous or in close proximity with the USSR— Turkey, Iran, and Pakistan—chose to align with the Western bloc in the period when their leadership perceived their security threatened. The Arab states, in general, feared the Western brand of imperialism (or colonialism in North Africa), which they had experienced, more than its more distant communist variant. Toward Israel the non-Arab states adopted a half-hearted but not belligerent attitude, while their Arab neighbors viewed this question as the dominant regional issue of the postwar world.

The differences between the Northern Tier zone and the Arab-Israel zone, corresponding after 1958 with the non-Arab/Arab states, is not of course a sharp one. There exist overlapping interests between Iran and Turkey and some of the Arab states (Jordan and Sa'udi Arabia, for example), and profound differences between the Arab states (e.g., Sa'udi Arabia and Iraq). Nevertheless, within the Middle East subsystem there is a gap between those involved in the Arab-Israel conflict militarily, politically, or economically, and those not thus involved. Consequently there are what may be called local systems within the regional subsystems insulated by the weakness of some of the regional states (or their distraction and commitment elsewhere), which form pockets of local autonomy. The Persian Gulf is arguably one such local system. The concept is not an essential one, but to the extent that it conveys the image of a relatively autonomous area of the Middle East insulated from the Arab-Israel zone, it will suffice.

To sum up: The changing international context, from one of confrontation and hostility to limited cooperation between the superpowers, has not decreased Iran's security or maneuverability. No longer valuable to the U.S. as a base, it is now an asset as a stable

---

Eastern European states, see William Zimmerman, "Hierarchical Regional Systems and the Politics of System Boundaries." For a peripheral subsystem, see Larry W. Bowman, "The Subordinate State System of Southern Africa."

[7] See especially Leonard Binder, "The Middle East as a Subordinate International System"; Louis J. Cantori and Stephen L. Spiegel (eds.), *The International Politics of Regions: A Comparative Approach;* and Michael Brecher *et al.,* "A Framework for Research on Foreign Policy Behavior," p. 83.

dependable friend. No longer a weak state on its southern border, Iran is increasingly viewed as an important regional power by Moscow. The inability and reluctance of either superpower, for a variety of reasons, to intervene in the subsystems of the world has given regional states increasing latitude to achieve their own objectives in these areas. The opportunity to do so, however, is limited by the type of regional subsystem in which the state is located. While the small state is unable to affect or change the international context on which it is dependent, its ability to successfully forecast or anticipate such changes and to work with them to enhance its own security—in short, to use its diplomatic acumen and skills—can make a great deal of difference. The examination of Iran's relations with the superpowers and its assessment of the changing international context shows the degree to which its leadership has been realistic in its perceptions and evaluations, and the success or failure of its policies based on its projections.

The study of Iran's regional relations will demonstrate the degree to which logical consequences from these perceptions have been drawn in determining the substance of these relations. Our choice of Egypt and Iraq as states with which Iran's regional relations have been centered is based on the premise that in the past decade the Iranian leadership's (perceived) principal security concern, apart from the Soviet Union, has been with Nasser's Egypt in particular, and the concept of Arab nationalism of the "radical" variety, in general. Relations with bordering Iraq and distant and influential Egypt serve as starting points and contrasts, in a study of Iran's foreign relations in the region.

The coverage of the Persian Gulf subregion is based on the premise that beginning in the early 1970's this area has become a new zone of conflict for regional as well as extra-regional powers.

In this part, too, we will eschew a chronological and comprehensive narrative in favor of an analysis of those salient features of interplay between states which illustrate tactics and instruments of influence used to pursue foreign policy objectives.

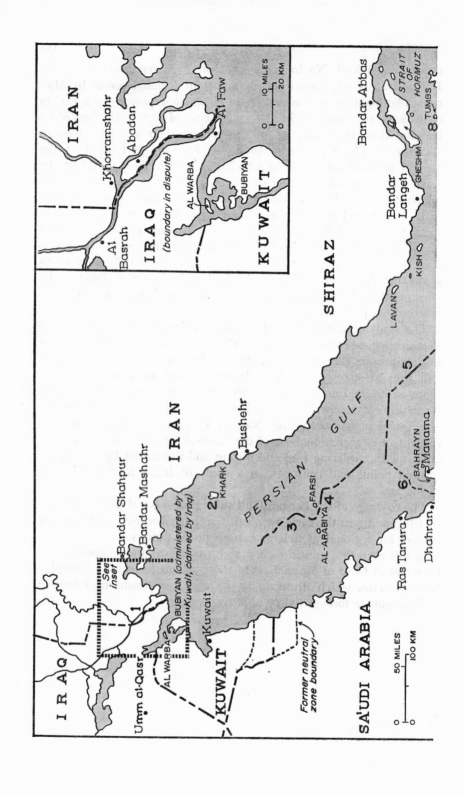

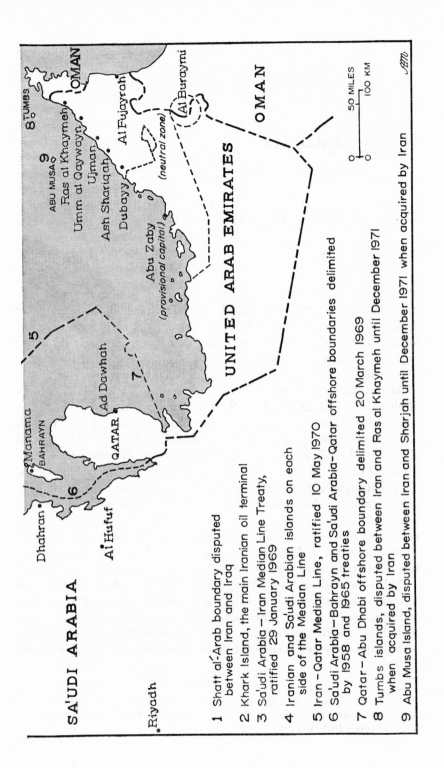

SA'UDI ARABIA

Riyadh•

Dhahran•

Al Hufuf•

•Manama
BAHRAYN

QATAR
Ad Dawhah•

6

5

7

Abu Zaby
(provisional capital)

UNITED ARAB EMIRATES

OMAN

(neutral zone)

Al Buraymi

Al Fujayrah•

Dubayy•
Ash Shariqah•
Umm al Qaywayn•
Ras al Khaymeh•
ABU MUSA 9
Ujman•

8 TUMBS

OMAN

0   50 MILES

0   100 KM

1 Shatt al-Arab boundary disputed
   between Iran and Iraq

2 Khark Island, the main Iranian oil terminal

3 Sa'udi Arabia–Iran Median Line Treaty,
   ratified 29 January 1969

4 Iranian and Sa'udi Arabian islands on each
   side of the Median Line

5 Iran–Qatar Median Line, ratified 10 May 1970

6 Sa'udi Arabia–Bahrayn and Sa'udi Arabia–Qatar offshore boundaries delimited
   by 1958 and 1965 treaties

7 Qatar–Abu Dhabi offshore boundary delimited 20 March 1969

8 Tumbs islands, disputed between Iran and Ras al Khaymeh until December 1971
   when acquired by Iran

9 Abu Musa Island, disputed between Iran and Sharjah until December 1971 when acquired by Iran

Chapter III

RELATIONS WITH EGYPT

Prior to the Egyptian Revolution in July 1952, Iranian-Egyptian relations had been rather uneventful. The simultaneous involvement of both countries in an anti-British struggle in the early 1950's created certain bonds of affinity between the two states, although no active support for each other could be mustered, in view of their preoccupation with this struggle against a major Western power.

At the end of 1951, when the Iranian nationalist leader Dr. Mossadegh paid a visit to Mosstafa Nahaspasha, his counterpart in Egypt, some negotiations for the coordination of their foreign policy vis-à-vis Great Britain took place.[1] The basic differences between the Egyptian dispute with Britain and the Anglo-Iranian oil dispute over nationalization of the oil industry, as well as the inherent instability of the Egyptian regime, precluded any concrete action. However, their common element of Anglophobic nationalism was reinforced by another bond in July 1952. This new phenomenon was the anti-monarchical sentiment that in that month brought about the downfall of King Farugh in Egypt and the victory of the Mossadegh forces in a critical test of strength with the Shah.[2]

This time again the staggering foreign problems faced by both the Egyptians and the Iranian nationalist regimes did not permit their coordination of policies. Thus the objective conditions for cooperation and alliance were overshadowed by the preoccupation of each country with issues closer to home—the Suez bases and the Israeli question

---

1 See *Ettelaat*, Dec. 10, 1951.

2 For a detailed analysis of this issue see, *inter alia*, *Times* (London), July 17–23, 1952. For an example of anti-monarchical editorials in the Iranian press, see *Bakhtar-Emruz*, Tehran, July 24–25, 1952.

for Egypt, and the oil dilemma and relations with the West and the Soviet Union for Iran.

It was only after the 1954 British-Egyptian agreement that Iranian attention was drawn to Egypt. Indeed, one of the chief causes of misgiving with the Nasser regime was Iranian unhappiness over its exclusion from regional countries whose invasion by extra-regional, presumably Russian, forces would have justified the re-entry of British troops into the Suez bases under the 1954 treaty.[3]

From this time the two states moved progressively away from each other in terms of their conception of external and internal sources of threat to their security. The divergence of their views obviously was strengthened by the avowed anti-monarchical outlook in Cairo, as opposed to the very opposite which characterized the Iranian regime with the fall of Mossadegh in 1953.

As we have seen in other chapters, each of the two states sought and secured an external protective power, the choice of which determined its regional policies. Thus, the choice of the Baghdad Pact for Iran and the pro-Soviet nonalignment for Egypt meant that the international bipolarization would have concrete regional consequences. Iran would emphasize Egyptian "opening of the Middle East to the Soviets" to pressure the Western powers to deny the Egyptians any measure of support; while the Egyptians would point to the Baghdad Pact and closer U.S.-Iranian ties to encourage the Soviets in their anti-Iranian posture. It was precisely this kind of pressure and influence which played a role in the American withdrawal of the Aswan Dam offer.[4]

THE NASSER ERA

It has only been under Nasser that Egypt has become a source of concern for Iranian diplomats. Situated in different zones geopolitically, the two states' foreign policy emphases serve as sharp contrasts. While the Shah's principal fears were Soviet imperialism and subversion, Nasser's were Western imperialism, Western bases, and divisive Western-sponsored pacts. While the Shah welcomed the Baghdad Pact and the Eisenhower Doctrine, to Nasser they were anathema. While the Shah received and later bought his arms from Washington, Nasser did his shopping in Moscow.

In addition to these background differences and the issue of Israel,

---

3 See, *inter alia, Keyhan,* Sept. 12, 1954.
4 Bayne, *Persian Kingship,* pp. 221–222.

by 1961 the additional factor of "ideology" was added. This stemmed primarily from the conclusions that Nasser drew regarding the role played by the "reactionary" classes in allegedly wrecking the union with Syria, and the policy implications he derived therefrom—to wit, the necessity of destroying this class if Arab unions were to be successful and Arab unity achieved. In Egypt's foreign relations this involved a more hostile stance toward all "reactionary" Arab states that might stand in the way of unity. Iran, as a regional state bordering eastern Arabia, came to be included in this context, for it adjoined what was already referred to as the "Arab gulf" and the "occupied south" (i.e. southern Arabia).

It should be noted that there remained a great imbalance in the two regional states' foreign relations. Nasser sought an activist role, involving himself in African affairs of the Congo and Biafra as well as Middle Eastern affairs of Israel, inter-Arab disputes such as Yemen, and nonaligned conferences and summits. Throughout the decade the Egyptian government, active in many diverse fields, overextended, and subject to powerful competing issues, gave perhaps less emphasis to relations with Iran than did the latter state to its regional rival. Throughout the decade Egypt was thus subject to powerful pressures competing for its time and energy, pressures which did not intrude on the Iranian government. The latter, having made its peace with the USSR, pursued its regional foreign policy in its own "backyard," with a single-minded emphasis on the Egyptian threat which bordered on the obsessive.

The rupture in diplomatic relations between the Egyptian and Iranian governments in July 1960 was a symptom of much more basic differences between them than could be diagnosed before that date. As the decade progressed, these differences intensified so that the original reason for the severance of relations, Israel, became one facet in a multi-faceted rivalry between the two regional states.

Particularly after the Suez invasion in 1956, Nasser found himself thrust into the vortex of Arab politics in the role of a leader. In becoming the spokesman for Arab nationalism, Nasser's Egypt extended the horizons of traditional Egyptian diplomacy. Hereafter the Egyptian government, as an Arab government, considered itself to have a legitimate interest in events in the entire Arab world, in the oft-repeated phrase "from the Atlantic Ocean to the Arab Gulf." And it eagerly set about attempting to influence and effect the course of politics in eastern Arabia. It did this by emphasizing its opposition to the British imperial presence in the "occupied south" and by stressing the dangers of imperialism, particularly of the Western variety, and its collusion with Zionism. According to this analysis, membership in Western-sponsored pacts, the presence of British or American bases, and the British "protection" of the shaykhdoms of the Gulf were harmful to Arab interests and examples of imperialism-Zionism colluding to impede Arab unity.

The Arab shaykhdoms of the Persian Gulf were one particular focus of Nasserite propaganda, and by 1960 this was already an un-settling phenomenon for the Iranian government, which found itself opposed to what it considered Nasserite meddling in the region. Nasser's encouragement of a Kurdish rebellion had elicited an Iranian note of protest in 1958,[5] and Egypt's hostility to the Baghdad Pact, of which Iran was a member, and the Eisenhower Doctrine, which was supported by Iran, its alleged interference in Lebanon and its support for, and encouragement of, revolution in Baghdad, were viewed with deep apprehension by the Iranian government. Yet the preoccupation of the government with Soviet aims, possible subver-sion, and domestic instability, displaced any Iranian reaction to Egypt's policies. Indeed there is no mention of Nasser's Egypt in the Shah's memoirs, published in 1960, although one may speculate on the in-fluence of the concept of "positive neutralism" on that of "positive nationalism", which is mentioned.

The Shah's failure to indicate any interest in Egypt in 1960 is probably indicative of Iran's preoccupation with the cold war at that time. However, the decline of the cold war in the course of the decade allowed the Iranian leadership more time and energy to devote to its regional concerns and even to stress their primacy in its foreign policy. This shift in priorities regarding the security threats by mid-decade is perhaps best illustrated by a newspaper article which indicated that an American airlift exercise in Iran in January 1965 for CENTO was interpreted by Iranians as a signal of U.S. ability to aid them against Nasser's Egypt rather than the USSR.[6] To understand why Nasser's Egypt was viewed by the Iranian government as its principal security threat from 1962 to 1967, we must first examine Nasser's stated aims and the Shah's interpretation of them.

The Shah's view of Nasser's aims and intentions in eastern Arabia and the Persian Gulf, as much as Egypt's capabilities and actual ac-tivities, decisively influenced the evolution of Iran-Egypt relations in this period. Nasser's activities in the Middle East, and his opposition both to Western pacts and monarchical regimes, were certainly im-

---

5 For text, see *Ettelaat*, June 4, 1958.
6 *New York Times*, Jan. 31, 1965.

portant considerations coloring the perception of the Iranian leadership.

Yet it was Nasser's reaction to the revolution in Yemen, his support
for the republican elements, which took the form of a 50,000-man
army, and his continued propaganda in the Gulf region which particularly worried the Shah. He feared that a dynamic but poor republican Arab state might bring about a (forced) unity with the far
richer Gulf shaykhdoms under the pretext of Arab unity, but in
actuality with the neo-colonialist intention of exploiting their mineral resources for its own ends. Even without such an economic interpretation of Egyptian interest in the Gulf region, the Iranian government may well have deemed it prudent to be anxious about any
Arab unity scheme which might confront it with a strong, rich, unified, and perhaps revolutionary neighbor. This latent opposition to
any proximate Arab unity scheme might thus become manifest when
it was seen that the would-be unifier was Gamal 'Abd al-Nasser. The
Shah's view of Nasser was not a sympathetic one.[7]

If the Shah was unsympathetic to Egypt's security concerns and the
historical roots of Nasser's Arab nationalism, which were often expressed in opposition to Western imperialism and in hyperbolic rhe-
toric, Nasser was equally insensitive to the reasons for the Shah's
choice of alignment as a security posture. Paradoxically, both of these
regional states' leaders seemed to pursue similar long-run goals. The
struggle against the captivity of small nations for the Shah was akin
to Nasser's efforts to secure the right to "decide individual questions
of international politics on their merits, and not in accordance with
whether or not they fitted into one or another of the Great Powers'
schemes of things." [8]

What separated them was the choice of means. The Shah opted for
alignment, while Nasser partly chose and partly was chosen, after
adopting nonalignment. In taking strong positions on the Baghdad
Pact, the independence of Algeria, the Congo, the Algerian-Morocco
border conflict, Palestine, the future of Yemen, the "occupied south"
and the "Arab Gulf" Nasser believed that he was expressing Egypt's
view of nonalignment and its sense of nationhood. But in Tehran,
Nasser's interest in the Gulf region was not viewed as legitimate, na-

---

[7] See Bayne, *Persian Kingship*, p. 209. This analogy is pervasive in the Shah's
allusion to Nasser, and was echoed by the daily press; see, for example, *Ettelaat*,
Nov. 11, 1964.

[8] The quote is from Copeland, *The Game of Nations*, p. 143.

tural, or even acceptable, particularly since Egypt was a non-littoral state.

Finally, there arose between the two states an "ideological" difference. This was accentuated by, if indeed it did not grow from, the secession of Syria from the UAR and its prompt recognition by Iran. Nasser drew the conclusion that the breakup was the work of a certain class in Syria. Henceforth, he would pay particular attention to the types of regime and the existence of the reactionary classes within them which must be destroyed before union could again be attempted. After the secession, in Malcolm Kerr's words, Egypt "assumed the stance of the militant revolutionary, uncompromisingly dedicated to the overthrow of all its conservative neighbors." [9]

In this ideological scheme the Iranian regime and such conservative Arab monarchies as Sa'udi Arabia were relegated to the status of class enemies of the Arab revolution. However, ideological differences played basically a symbolic role in Egypt-Iran relations. It was the Yemen adventure which polarized the two states in a bitter confrontation.

The danger of Nasser's activity in Yemen lay not in a direct attack on the oil fields of the Arabian peninsula or an invasion of the Gulf shaykhdoms but rather on the tremors of instability his presence might cause in the region, and possibly on the inadvertent expansion of the conflict.[10] The Shah's government viewed Nasser's involvement in the Arabian peninsula as "imperialist and expansionist" and responded to it as a military threat.[11]

EGYPTIAN TACTICS, 1960–1967

It is perhaps natural that Egypt should pursue and seek to emphasize the line that Iran's differences were with the Arab world in general. In transforming differences between the two states and amplifying them into an Arab-Iranian dispute, it could polarize the conflict and thus pressure hesitant or more moderate Arab states to toe the Arab line and isolate Iran. This is precisely the fairly successful tactic

---

9 See Malcolm Kerr, *The Arab Cold War: Gamal 'Abd al-Nasser and His Rivals, 1958–1970*, p. 25. See also J. C. Hurewitz, "Regional and International Politics in the Middle East," in Georgiana G. Stevens (ed.), *The United States and the Middle East*, p. 96.

10 Consult John Badeau's discussion of the Yemen conflict, *The American Approach to the Arab World*, p. 133. See also Robert Stephens, *Nasser: A Political Biography*, pp. 378–431.

11 The phrase is the Shah's; see *The Times* (London), Dec. 8, 1964.

which was adopted by the Egyptian government during these seven years. By 1964 it had accused Iran of interference in Lebanon's elections and had exerted pressure on it to declare the Iranian ambassador *persona non grata* for making certain comments on Nasser's foreign policy.[12]

Not to be outdone in any competition with Egypt to prove its Arab credentials, the Syrian government had provoked a similar break with the Iranian government. In November 1965 it referred to the Iranian province of Khuzistan as "Arabistan" which, it alleged, was part of the "Arab homeland," although it later denied that there had been any intention to harm relations between the states.[13]

An alternative tactic used to a lesser extent was to use the Muslim ties of the states as a means of influence to pressure Iran and Turkey on their relations with Israel. More specifically, Nasser used these religious bonds to amplify his dispute with the Shah by having the Rector of Al-Azhar, Shaykh Mahmud Shaltut cable the Shah in 1960 about his relations with Israel, and later in 1963 to request that religious dignitaries arrested in uprisings against the Shah's reform program be set free.[14]

The success of the tactic of polarization depended largely on the state of Egypt's relations with other Arab states and the presence of an overriding issue in relations between Arab and Iranian. The issues of the Persian Gulf and Israel provided potentially overriding issues which might well have polarized Arab and Iranian, had not the ever present centrifugal forces of the Arab world existed.

At the time of the severance of relations with Iran in July 1960, Nasser accused the Shah of selling himself to imperialism and Zionism, "at a cheap price." In Nasser's view Zionism, imperialism and "reaction" were manifestly related. "The battle with Zionism is also a battle with imperialism, imperialistic stooges, and the reactionary elements." [15]

From 1960 to 1967 an acrimonious propaganda debate raged between Cairo and Tehran, in print and on the airwaves. Radio Cairo took up Nasser's theme and emphasized that the Shah was "reac-

---

12 See *Christian Science Monitor*, Aug. 4, 1964.

13 *New York Times*, Nov. 11, 1965, and *Chronology of Arab Politics*, III, No. 4 (October–December, 1965), 415.

14 See *Middle East Record*, I (Tel Aviv: Israel Oriental Society, 1960), p. 219, and *Chronology of Arab Politics*, I, No. 2 (April–June, 1963), 170.

15 Address by President Gamal 'Abd al-Nasser at the Arab Socialist Union in Celebration of the Anniversary of Unity Day, Cairo, Feb. 22, 1966 (Cairo: National Publication House), p. 27.

tionary," "corrupt," and unpopular and that he was using his alliance with the West to support an army on which he was dependent. The army's function was merely that of putting down coups, it alleged, and internal disorders in Iran were gleefully depicted as the onset of a coup, while the Shah's reform program was scorned.

The Egyptian government pursued this line when the Shah and King Faysal of Sa'udi Arabia in December 1965 called for an Islamic Conference which was intended to bypass the Arab League institutions dominated by Nasser. While not opposing Islamic cooperation in principle, Nasser believed that the proposal was a Western-inspired means of diluting his influence. In February 1966 he pointed out that Egypt had never opposed cooperation among Muslim states "as long as it is for God and for Islam and not in the interests of America and Britain. . . . No one can believe that the Shah of Iran and Bourguiba will combat atheism and spread the teaching of Islam." [16]

In this important speech he dealt lengthily with relations with Iran and the origins of the reactionary Islamic "Pact," as he labeled it, which he traced to the first Western-sponsored pacts in the 1950's.

The main concern of the Egyptian government, however, was to undermine the Iranian government's position with the shaykhdoms of the Gulf. Aware of the absence of strong bonds between the "protected" mini-states and Tehran, the Egyptian tactic was to attempt to exploit their fear of Iran's intentions and to underline the "anti-Arab" character of Iranian aims by linking them with Zionism and imperialism. In this campaign the Egyptian government had the powerful instrument of its ubiquitous radio stations at its disposal, as well as such organizations as the Arab League. In addition, it had an important audience—an emerging middle class which was politically aware even if it was not yet politically articulate, in the larger states of Bahrayn and Kuwait.

By undermining Iran's (embryonic) relations with these states, the Egyptian government served two purposes, for it could at one and the same time pose as the potential savior of these states while regionally isolating the Iranian government. In thus polarizing Iranian and Arab in the Gulf into two camps, Egypt could assume the leadership of the Arab camp. Among the several tactics used, the labeling of the Persian Gulf as the "Arab" Gulf and the province of Khuzistan as "Arabistan" stand out, in the way they disturbed and infuriated

---

16 *Ibid.*, pp. 3–40.

the Iranian government. These tactics were "successful" in that the
endemic instability in Iraq and Syria encouraged a more-Arab-than-
thou stridency in these matters which appeared to give the Arab
side of the Gulf more unity than it in fact possessed. The tactic exerted
considerable pressure on the shaykhdoms, however, and caught them
in a crossfire between the requirements of a policy of prudent cordiality with a large neighboring monarchy and vocal lip-service to
the "Arabism" of the Gulf in the manner dictated by their persuasive
Arab brethren.

The theme constantly emphasized by Cairo was the similarity (explicitly stated) of the Iranian and Israeli states, their alleged collusion,
the analogies between Iranian immigration to the Gulf states and
the Zionists' earlier immigration to Palestine. This posed, it was alleged,
a threat to the "Arabism" of the Gulf, and it was being abetted by the
British in much the same way as it (allegedly) was in Palestine. The
ultimate result would be, it was suggested, a new Israel set up in the
Arab east. Radio Cairo's "Arabian Gulf program," beamed to the
Gulf states, thus sought to discourage any Arab-Iranian interaction
in the area, and therefore painted even minor issues as part of a
masterplan. Illegal Iranian immigration to the Gulf Arab states, long
a fact of life and a two-way traffic, was particularly singled out. As
one journalist noted in 1964, "Many wild tales are told in the Arab
world about Iranian incursions in the Gulf area. Sheikhdoms are
urged by Cairo and the Arab League to put an end to it." [17] A commission of the Arab League was sent to the Gulf region to study
Iranian activities in the area, but found little enthusiasm for Cairo's
attempts to alienate the shaykhdoms from Iran and little support for
Cairo's charges.

If Nasser was unable to obtain the shaykhdoms' active support for
his attempts to isolate Iran, he was able to utilize Iran's differences
with Iraq. In a joint communiqué issued in May 1965, a few months
after Iran and Iraq had clashed on the Kurdish question, both governments referred to this question:

Attempts are now being made to efface and expunge the Arabism of the Arab
Gulf districts and to change their national character by opening the door to
foreign immigration in order that the original Arab inhabitants of these
districts should become strangers in their homes. All these conspiracies aim at
creating a new 'Israel' to ensure the interests of imperialism in this area.[18]

---

17 *Christian Science Monitor*, Dec. 15, 1964.
18 Communiqué of the Iraqi-UAR Unified Political Command on its First Session,
held in Cairo May 19–May 25, 1965. *Egyptian Gazette*, May 26, 1965, quoted in
Arab Political Documents, 1965, pp. 217–219.

And Nasser himself alluded to this immigration threat several times the same year.

This issue was emphasized until the following year, when the question of the Islamic Conference replaced it as the focus of interest, and in turn was replaced by the deterioration of relations on the Israeli front. This did not mean that the matter was dropped. On the contrary, Iran's differences with other Arab states continued to be brought into and mixed with its alleged plans in the Gulf area. As late as May 26, 1967, a few days before the six-day war, Cairo Radio was still warning about Iran's intentions: "Colonialism is plotting against the Arabism of the Arabian Gulf and trying to assassinate the Arabism of the Gulf."

IRANIAN TACTICS, 1960–1967

The Iranian government's first priority in dealing with Nasser was to avoid any semblance of criticism of the Arab world in general by differentiating Nasser's activities from those of the rest of the Arab world. In the course of the next few years Iran emphasized that Nasser was a "minion of communism," that he forbade the exercise of freedom of speech, that the UAR remained scientifically backward, and that a "new" class dominated Egyptian society while the worker and the peasant lived on black bread. In addition, Nasser's pretensions to democracy and justice were ridiculed.

In seeking to prevent the polarization sought by the Egyptian government, the Iranian government labored under certain constraints which precluded its taking full advantage of the ever-present factionalism in the Arab world. The foremost constraint was the fact that while the Nasserites and Ba'thists were often in conflict, they agreed on emnity toward Iran and the "reactionary" camp. Thus while locked in opposition to one another for most of the period 1960–1967, they still both backed the republican elements in Yemen and opposed King Faysal and the Shah. This fact limited the ability of the Iranian government to effectively utilize the hostility between the Nasserites and Ba'thists to counter any polarization between Iranian and Arab, and gave the Iranian government only the peripheral opportunity to attempt to exacerbate or prolong the hostility between these factions, without being able to utilize it productively.

A secondary constraint stemmed from the nature of the relationship between the monarchial and republican elements in the Arab world. While Iran was able to temporarily ally itself with the kindred regimes of kings Hussein, Hassan, and Faisal, the nature of Nasser's appeal, and the press of other issues in the Arab world, always threatened to undercut this limited cooperation. In the final analysis the Arab world gravitated around Nasser in times of trouble and was responsive to its own problems, internal and external. As Malcolm Kerr has noted: "The Saudi and Jordanian monarchs were habitually poised to grasp at Egyptian overtures as a kind of security blanket" as much as were the Ba'th who sought to "boost their own legitimacy and self-confidence." [19] (Parenthetically it should be noted that the cross-pressures of Arab politics prevented states such as Lebanon and Kuwait from taking sides.)

A final constraint stemmed from conditions of the Iranian government's own doing. In fighting Nasser's attempts to divide Arab and Iranian, the government was handicapped by its own inability to contain its conflicts and concentrate on Nasser's Egypt. In the years from 1960 to 1971 Iran's relations with Iraq were almost permanently poor; relations with Lebanon were twice endangered—in 1966 the ambassador was recalled and in 1969 relations were severed; relations with Syria were poor from 1965 to 1971; and there was even a "tiff" with Sa'udi Arabia in 1968. The potential dividends of playing off one hostile Arab state against another cannot be said to have been fully realized by the Iranian government. And it would appear that by 1967 the absence of any sharp division between Arab and Iranian had little to do with Iranian policy and was more the result of perennial intra-Arab differences.

However, the Iranian government did attempt to exacerbate differences between Nasser and his rivals in order to forestall any Arab unity under Nasser's auspices. It did this by emphasizing Nasser's expansionism and his quest for hegemony, which it was said was due to domestic poverty and bankruptcy.[20] It also sought to emphasize Nasser's ambitions and to appeal to the individual nationalism of the Arab states. Typical of this trend is a report in March 1963 when Iraq-Syrian-Egyptian unity appeared to be a possibility:

Discussions with young officers and Syrian and Iraqi nationalists reveal that Colonel Abd al-Nasser is desperately trying to reestablish his absolute leadership over nations such as the Syrian and Iraqi nations as President of the United Arab Republic.

. . . Syrian and Iraqi Arabs are seeking unity and fraternity with all Arab nations, including the Egyptian people, but under no circumstances are prepared to accept Colonel Gamal Abd al-Nasser's dictatorship and despotism.[21]

---

19 Kerr, *The Arab Cold War*, p. 156.
20 This was a persistent theme in editorials; see, for example, *Ettelaat* for December 1964 and January 1965.
21 *Ettelaat* (editorial), June 22, 1963; *ibid.* (editorial), March 5, 1965.

In addition to encouraging fragmentation and factionalism in the leftist or "radical" camp of Syria, Iraq, and Egypt, the Iranian government also sought positive cooperation with the more like-minded Arab states who were equally at odds with Nasser. The Shah cultivated relatively strong ties with the monarchies of King Hussein of Jordan, King Hassan of Morocco, and King Faisal of Sa'udi Arabia, as well as President Bourguiba of the republic of Tunisia.[22] The Shah joined King Faysal in the December 1965 call for a conference of Islamic states which was intended to bypass Nasser's domination of the Arab League and strengthened Faisal's position as the keeper of the Holy Shrines. Both states in a joint communiqué also condemned outside interference in the affairs of Yemen.[23] Iran, Jordan, and Sa'udi Arabia also provided assistance to the royalist cause in Yemen against the republicans supported by Nasser. The Iranian government emphasized, after Faisal's accession to the Sa'udi throne, the practical alternative he offered to all moderate Arabs.

The Iranian government was particularly sensitive to Nasser's attempts to polarize Arab and Iranian in the Gulf into two camps, often by utilizing sympathetic newspapers in Kuwait or Lebanon to make his points for him. It thus attempted to ensure that the vicissitudes of its relations with Egypt did not affect its embryonic relations with the Gulf states or the other Arab states, and that its criticisms of Nasser and his claims to Khuzistan and the Persian Gulf were not interpreted as Iranian hostility to the Arabs in general.

Officials and newspapers were thus at pains to point out that their criticisms were directed at Nasser's subversion only: "The Iranian people do not mistake Nasser's ambitions for the aspirations of the Arab people and believe that Nasser and the Arab nations have two separate accounts." [24] In 1964 the theme of Nasser's divisiveness was brought up by Premier Hassanali Mansur. In May, while addressing the Senate, he pointed out that there had recently been propaganda attacks and threats of aggression against Iran. Although these had been reflected in Arab journals and publications, he was sure that they did not convey the opinions of the Arabs as a group but rather that of "one single ambitious and avaricious individual." [25]

22 These relations were cemented by exchanges of visits in the period 1964–1966, the Shah traveling twice to Morocco in that period, with Bourguiba, Hussein, and Faisal visiting Tehran in 1965.

23 Text of the joint Iranian-Saudi communiqué of Dec. 13, 1965, may be found in Persian in Elamiehaye Moshtarek 1349, pp. 33–34; in Arab Political Documents, 1965, p. 449.

24 Sedaye Mardom, June 24, 1965.

25 See the report of the speech in Tehran Journal, May 3, 1964.

The Iranian government's desire to discriminate in its attacks was both a logical policy by which to avoid the polarization Nasser sought and to counteract more extremist proposals suggested by some sources in Iran. In December 1964 in a speech to the Senate the prime minister indicated his concern lest relations with other Arab states suffer as a result of harsh exchanges between Iran and Egypt.[26] Particularly troublesome were the charges of illegal immigration by Iranians to the Gulf states for colonizing purposes. Iranian replies pointed out that the Gulf had two shores, one Iranian, one Arab, and that Iran had no claim to the Arab side. As far as immigration was concerned, there had always been a two-way traffic, with Arabs coming to live in Iran and Iranians going to live with the Arabs.[27]

To strengthen Iran's ties with the Arab states against Nasser, the Iranian government had recourse to emphasis on the common Islamic heritage of the two states. This line was pursued not only through constant reiteration in newspapers, and through the call for an Islamic conference with King Faysal, but also as a weapon of propaganda against Egypt's activities in Yemen and its support for Greece in its dispute with Turkey over Cyprus. In December 1964 the Shah made his first public reference to Nasser by name when speaking at a religious ceremony. He charged him with "spending one million dollars a day for the killing of Muslims in Yemen and secretly sending arms to the Cyprus government for the massacre of Turkish Muslims in Cyprus."[28]

YEMEN AND THE GULF

The Iranian government believed that Nasser's intervention in the Yemen civil war in 1962 reflected his intention to establish a foothold on the Arabian peninsula in order to eventually penetrate the rich Gulf shaykhdoms. According to this view, Nasser was motivated by the neo-colonialist aim of obtaining the mineral resources of the area, and the pretext of Arab unity was merely a cloak to obscure this aim.

The Iranian reaction to Nasser's Yemen activities thus reflected Tehran's apprehension about the region's susceptibility to conflagra-

---

26 *Tehran Journal*, Dec. 29, 1964; see also *Ettelaat* (editorial), Dec. 1964.

27 This reply was carried by *Keyhan* on Jan. 13, 1965.

28 *The Times* (London), Dec. 4, 1964. For a full text of this and other speeches made by the Shah in 1964 and 1965, see *Orient* (Paris), First Trimester, No. 37 (1966), pp. 175–238.

tion should Nasser be allowed to strike the revolutionary spark. The traditional insulation of the Gulf states, their archaic political structures, and the rapid influx of oil wealth into the region, combined with immigration and an increased interest in the region by non-Gulf Arab states, undoubtedly augured a politically volatile future for the area. This likelihood was enhanced by the impending withdrawal of the British troops as Britain contracted the last of its imperial commitments in the region. This withdrawal had been first heralded by Kuwait's independence in 1961, and its likelihood was underscored by the events to follow that independence. Between 1961 and 1967 it was apparent to most observers that it was only a question of time before the British ultimately withdrew totally. Nasser's activities in the peninsula were intended to accelerate their departure from South Arabia—and probably succeeded. The aftermath of the British withdrawal from Aden in 1967 and the establishment of the People's Republic of South Yemen was precisely the sort of outcome that the Iranian government dreaded would be repeated in the Gulf's politics.

The Iranian government's view of its differences with Egypt in Yemen was thus a trial run, or rehearsal, for what might occur closer to its territory in the future. The geographic distance from Yemen to the Gulf was foreshortened in this perspective, and Yemen took on a significance and resonance quite separate from its own intrinsic value. Similarly, Nasser's difficulties in Yemen, the failure of a campaign lasting five years involving 50 to 70,000 troops and hundreds of millions of dollars, were dismissed by the Iranian side as any indication of Nasser's capability to launch an attack on Iran.

In its analysis Iran appears to have concluded that Nasser posed a military threat to the region and possibly even the threat of direct invasion. Its reaction was to coordinate support for the royalists in Yemen with the Sa'udi and Jordanian governments and to formally denounce Nasser's action in Yemen as "an act of aggression." The foreign ministry reported that "Iran is opposed to Egypt's present aggressive foreign policy." [29]

The Shah also took his case to the West, and the United States in particular, to convince them of Nasser's danger in the area. He argued that it was the Egyptians who opened the Middle East to the Russians and that aid to Nasser should be suspended. The Shah viewed Western aid to Nasser as capitulation to blackmail, and believed that the West neglected its allies in favor of troublemakers. The Shah

---

[29] The phrase is the Shah's. *Tehran Journal,* March 9, 1965. Also *Ravabete Khareji-e Iran dar Sale 1346,* pp. 44–45.

made this point in Washington and repeated it in December 1964 in an interview with West German journalists:

We have no intention of opening a consulate general in East Berlin, or of recognizing that regime in any form . . . But we are amazed when (West Germany) gives more aid to a state like Egypt, which does nothing but stir up trouble in our part of the world, than it does to us.[30]

The Shah argued that Egypt's threat in the Gulf and its armaments acquisition necessitated an equal buildup of the Iranian armed forces for defensive purposes, and he made this point in Washington in June 1964 and repeated it in the CENTO meetings of 1964 and 1965. He also believed that the United States' Middle East policy encouraged Nasser in his adventures.[31] In December 1966 he referred to Egypt as "imperialist and expansionist" and pointed out that its arms purchases and foreign policy "are today diametrically opposed to Iran's fundamental interests in the Persian Gulf and in parts of south Iran."

Since the United States government did not share his estimate of Nasser's military threat and had also begun to "phase out" grants of military weapons to Iran, the Shah determined to independently replenish his armed forces. After an almost incidental arms agreement with the USSR in February 1967, the shift in Iranian security priorities was dramatically illustrated by the report that the army stations in northern Iran would be shifted from the Russian border to the Persian Gulf to "counter the increasing UAR threat." [32]

THE INTERNAL DIMENSION

The rivalry with Egypt had its domestic side. Since the differences between the governments were at least theoretically partly ideological and supposedly concerned different methods of modernization, this element of the rivalry was never far distant in their exchanges. On several occasions the Shah voiced his belief that Nasser was hostile toward Iran because of his jealousy of the reforms the Shah had launched in Iran and because of Nasser's own domestic reform failures, which the Shah belittled.[33]

---

30 *Tehran Journal*, Dec. 9, 1964; see also *ibid*. (editorial), Feb. 28, 1968, and Jan. 30, 1965.

31 *New York Times*, April 29, 1964; *Christian Science Monitor*, June 5, 1964. See also Badeau, *The American Approach*, p. 102.

32 *Tehran Journal*, Feb. 20, 1967.

33 See the Shah's comments reported in *The Times* (London), June 12, 1963, and March 9, 1965, and the *Tehran Journal*, March 8, 1965.

The Egyptian-inspired claims to Khuzistan and the Persian Gulf as Arab property were deeply resented by Iranian nationalists, and the government has consistently objected to any such references in international gatherings. The Iranian Central Bank is representative of all Iranian institutions in refusing to deal with or accept any documents which include the phrase "Arabian Gulf."

The Egyptian government, however, was accused of more than merely propaganda attacks on Iran. It was accused of backing those elements in Iran hostile to the Shah's "White Revolution" and of organizing espionage rings and financing riots in June 1963. The Chief of the State Security Service (SAVAK) reported that there were very strong indications that Nasser was behind the riots, while Prime Minister Alam blamed an "unnamed foreign country" for the disorders, and the Shah charged a "Moslem Middle-Eastern power" with responsibility. Without actually naming Nasser, he did assert that Nasser's type of government was subversive and deceitful.[34]

The following year sixteen Iranians were charged with conspiracy to instigate an uprising in Khuzistan, having allegedly established contact with Arabs in Basrah, Iraq. In response to the mounting Arab claim to Khuzistan, Iranian Prime Minister Mansur declared that "Iran will stand by her territorial rights in the Persian Gulf. She has no aggressive ambitions but will never allow aggression against Iranian soil." [35]

It seems plausible that the constant accusations of Egyptian interference in Iranian internal affairs were designed to serve several purposes. In the first place they made it easier and more palatable to explain the domestic resistance encountered in the Shah's reform program. Secondly, they diverted attention from the domestic difficulties in the country by focusing on the new threat to the nation, the "wolf at the door" which might hopefully provide a new unity. This would explain the orchestration of anti-Nasser sentiment which could be accurately characterized as a campaign. Thirdly, an exaggeration of the Egyptian threat justified the Iranian government's decision to seek additional arms and increase spending on the military.

Now that the USSR was manifestly no longer a threat, it was convenient for the government to point to the threat posed by Nasser to justify its increasing defense expenditures. Thus as one newspaper headline trumpeted, "Nasser forces military loan," and reported three

---

34 *The Times* (London), June 7, 1963; *Tehran Journal*, June 8, 10, and 16, 1963; *Ettelaat* (editorial), June 16, 1963; *New York Times*, June 6, 1963.
35 *The Times* (London), April 23, 1964.

months later, "His Imperial Majesty the Shahanshah yesterday said that Iran no longer faces any real threat of aggression from the Soviet Union. The danger today comes from Egypt." [36]

THE QUESTION OF ISRAEL, 1960–1967

Of major importance in Iran's relations with Egypt has been the question of the scope and nature of Iran-Israel relations. Given its extreme importance to Egypt, particularly since June 1967, it is useful to contrast how this issue has been handled in Iran-Egypt relations in the two periods, 1960–1967 and 1967–1971. The issue is particularly important in relations between the two states insofar as it illustrates, particularly in the earlier period, an issue which could be used by Egypt or any other Arab state to generalize a dispute between itself and Iran into an Arab-Iran dispute.

Given the nature of Arab sensitivities to the question of Israel, Iran's relationship with Israel could be adduced as evidence of Iran's Zionism, its collusion with "imperialism." Her anti-Arab policy, and her alleged immigration plans in the Gulf could be compared to the Zionist immigration to Palestine. In counteracting this tendency to polarize the conflict, the Iranian government has benefited from intra-Arab factionalism and disputes, both within the "radical" camp and between the "radical" and "conservative" segments of the Arab family.

It was the question of Iran's relations with Israel that ostensibly, at the beginning of the decade, caused the ten-year rupture in relations between Iran and Egypt. Iran had extended *de facto* recognition to Israel in 1950 and had set up a consulate in that country. Subsequently, in 1952, the consul-general was recalled due to budgetary considerations. On July 24, 1960, the Shah of Iran, in answer to a question at a press conference, routinely affirmed that *de facto* recognition had been granted. Whether as a result of a misunderstanding, or more likely due to the basic differences in orientations between the states outlined above, President Nasser chose to interpret this statement as indicating a departure in Iran's relations with Israel and as formal (*de jure*) recognition. Despite Iranian clarifications, Nasser attacked the Shah by name, and severed diplomatic relations with Iran on July 26.

The deeper causes of the Iran-Egypt rupture were already evident,

---

[36] *Tehran Journal*, Oct. 26, 27, 1964.

and apart from the differing outlooks of the two regimes toward the cold war and a security posture and modernization, the dispute widened in this period to embrace the question of the Egyptian role in Eastern Arabia and the Persian Gulf. Yet the question of Israel has not been of minor consequence in Iran's relations with Egypt (or the Arab world in general), for it has undoubtedly exacerbated other differences and deeply affected the Arab's perception of Iran and, as it were, psychologically conditioned their view of Iran's role in Middle East politics. Nevertheless, the Arab world has been no more united on the question of Iran's relations with Israel than it has on any other major issue. This inability to present a solid front was evident from the outset. When Nasser called upon all the Arab states to sever ties with Iran as a result of her relations with Israel, Iraq's President Qasim, though at that time at odds with Iran over the Shatt 'al-Arab, nevertheless deemed his competition with Nasser more important and urged moderation in the Arab League. Similarly, Iran was the beneficiary of Nasser's enmity with Faisal, Hussein, and Bourguiba, and in a reverse pattern in the 1969–1971 period, of his hostility toward the Iraqi Ba'th. In the former case, rapprochement was possible in the short-lived Islamic entente; while in the latter, Nasser's rivalry with the Ba'th, paralleling Iran's similar antipathy toward that regime, has allowed a reconciliation between Tehran and Cairo.

After 1960, Iran's relations with Israel took on a new dimension, facilitated by the severance of relations with Egypt and the consequent decline in Arab leverage to encourage restraint, and stimulated by a common apprehension of Nasser's Middle East goals, the two non-Arab states provided each other with useful regional counterweights to their common (potential) enemy. Despite the fact that the Iranian government still felt unable to extend Israel the *de jure* recognition she sought, relations intensified in the period 1960–1967. Apart from Israel's reported aid in setting up the state security organization (SAVAK), cooperation ranged from Israeli aid in the agricultural field, to air-links, trade, including the sale of oil, and military training. Of the latter area, Bayne writing in 1968 informs us:

It began with quiet ties between intelligence services, and retains this mutual security interest even to the point where the Iranian command once informally suggested that Israel train Persian paratroopers . . . and in the fact that every general officer in the Shah's army has visited Israel and hundreds of junior officers have undergone some aspects of Israeli training.[37]

---

37 Bayne, *Persian Kingship,* p. 212. The cooperation was also based on political considerations, such as the potential expertise Israeli agriculturists might provide

Politically this relationship, based on the view that the-enemy-of-my-enemy-is-my-friend, gave each state a useful regional counterweight in its differences with Egypt. Israel lost thereby the almost complete regional isolation resulting from its differences with the Arab states, and Iran gained an unpublicized but nonetheless real source of technical knowledge and a small market for her oil. Israel's interest in preventing Arab unity overlapped with Iran's, and both states were reported to have cooperated in funneling arms via Iran to the Kurdish minority in its dispute with the central Iraq government.[38]

In addition, there is a great deal of respect in the Iranian leadership for Israel's achievements, developmental and military. Bayne illustrates this by reporting "Although a meeting between the Shah and such Israeli leaders as David Ben-Gurion would be difficult to arrange, because it would have to be private and unpublicized, His Majesty has several times expressed to me the hope that it might be done." [39] Whatever the motivation for this type of meeting, the knowledge that two of his enemies might coordinate activity against him was unsettling for Nasser. In a detailed statement about relations with Iran made in 1966, Nasser with the benefit of hindsight pointed out the reasons for his severance of ties.

The Shah declared at a press conference that his country recognized Israel. And so, a country said to be an Islamic member of the Baghdad Pact opened all opportunities of activity to Israel and helped it to work against the Arab homeland.

Actually Iran became in recent years a base for Israel threatening the Arab countries. In 1961 an Israeli paper called *Kol-Aaam* reported the conclusion of a secret agreement between Iran and Israel and said that the agreement was signed at Tehran airport by Ben-Gurion who was on his way to Burma. That report was published on December 6, 1961. . . .

The stopover in Tehran was preplanned and talks were held between Ben-Gurion and the prime minister of Iran. The two sides studied the role of Israel in the defensive systems of the countries of CENTO. They also affirmed the importance of reinforcing the economic, political, and military cooperation between the two countries.[40]

Iran in agricultural development, which gave rise to a project in Qazvin, as well as technical aid to Iran's fledgling farm cooperatives. See Peter Avery, *Modern Iran*, p. 492.

38 See Leonard Binder's cryptic, unsubstantiated comment in "Factors Influencing Iran's International Role," p. 39.

39 Bayne, *Persian Kingship*, p. 212.

40 Nasser's Address on Anniversary of Unity Day, Feb. 22, 1966, pp. 26–27.

Almost equally important from the Arab point of view was Iran's commercial relationship with Israel.[41] In Arab eyes, Israel was the creation of Western imperialism and the base for its activity in the Middle East. This interpretation of the identity of aims between Zionism and Western imperialism was given added weight by the tripartite Suez invasion of 1956. Thus Nasser was able in 1960 to generalize his differences with Iran regarding Israel into a dispute affecting the Arab world as a whole, and he had in the Arab League a ready-made forum in which to make this point.

In July 1960 a statement by the Secretariat of the Arab League was forwarded to the Arab states' foreign ministers' meeting. It was stated herein that relations between Egypt and Iran had deteriorated after the Suez conflict when the USSR had stopped oil supplies to Israel and Iran had sent eight million tons of petrol to Eilat. Some of this oil was subsequently used by Israel (it was asserted) to supply Western countries and hence circumvent the Suez Canal.[42] The Arab League meeting of 1960 did not achieve agreement on the severance of its members' relations with Iran, but it did threaten to extend an economic boycott to Iran.[43] The conference of Arab oil experts in Kuwait in November of that year recommended that Arab governments contact Iran to prevent Iranian oil being supplied to Israel.[44]

In February 1963 delegates of seven Arab states at the Palestine experts' conference in Cairo recommended that the Arab states reconsider their relations with Iran in the light of its cooperation with Israel. In December 1964 the Arab states through the Arab League Economic Council decided "to exert further efforts to stop the flow of Iranian oil to Israel." [45]

For the Arab states the economic boycott of Israel had great moral psychological significance, in that it reflected their refusal to accept Israel's existence as a state and, in the absence of practical alternative political-military means, to effectively register their antagonism towards that state. Although not espousing an Arab variant of the Hallstein Doctrine, the Arab states considered economic and political inter-

---

41 Iran's trade with Israel is heavily unbalanced, with Iran exporting far less than she imports. Although trade has increased in the past decade, it is still not of great importance to Iran. However, it is notable that Iran imports more from Israel than from any other Middle Eastern state. Between 1960 and 1969, imports increased from 147 to 817 million rials, while exports jumped from 12.5 to 72.5 million rials. Echo of Iran, *Iran Almanac*, 1970, p. 361.

42 *Ha'aretz*, July 28, 1960, cited in *Middle East Record*, I (1960), pp. 307–308.

43 Robert W. MacDonald, *The League of Arab States*, p. 121.

44 *Ha'aretz*, Dec. 4, 1960, cited in *Middle East Record*, I (1960), p. 307–308.

45 *Christian Science Monitor*, Aug. 4, and Dec. 14, 1964.

course with Israel an unfriendly act, particularly if the party so en-
gaging was a regional Muslim state. Trade with Israel and any recognition of that state constituted a denial of the Arab case in Palestine
and hence a direct rejection of the Arab cause.

Although no formal attempts were made by the Iranian government to distinguish between its *de facto* recognition and commercial
ties with Israel and the justice of the situation in Palestine, we must
assume that this is implicit in mere extension of *de facto* recognition,
which implies no moral judgment but an acceptance of a reality.
And the Iranian government has acted as if they were separable, by
stressing that questions of politics and trade should be distinguished,
and has taken a purely pragmatic view of the latter.[46] In this view,
oil is the nation's most important resource and should be wisely utilized
for the development of the country.

The government has taken a similar position regarding oil embargoes applied to Rhodesia and South Africa, arguing that unless
embargoes are 100 percent effective, Iran will not forego this source
of income. In the case of an embargo of oil to Israel, it must not be
overlooked that Israel is the only industrial state in the region and
the sale of oil is necessary to finance needed imports. Finally, it should
be noted that Iran and several Arab states are competitors in the
export of oil, and that these Arab states demonstrated little sensitivity to Iran's plight in its nationalization crisis, and in several cases
secured long-term increases in production as a direct result of Iran's
forced cutback in production at that time.

A further argument made by the Iranian government is that it cannot control the flow of oil through the Consortium, and that in any
case, since oil can be trans-shipped many times, its ultimate destina-
tion cannot always be precisely determinable.

The relationship between Iran's oil exports to Israel and the Arab-
Israel dispute was clearly illustrated in May 1967. It has generally
been overlooked that one reason why Abd 'al-Nasser took the step of
announcing a blockade of the Gulf of Aqaba had to do with the flow
of oil from Iran to Israel's port of Eilat. At this time Nasser was
particularly critical of the trend of diplomatic cooperation among
the Arab monarchical states and Iran and Tunisia under the banner
of an Islamic Conference. Iran's trade with Israel provided a useful

---

46 For example, Premier Hassanali Mansur's comment, "Oil is business, not
politics," *Tehran Journal*, Sept. 30, 1964; and the Shah's reply in an interview: "We
always separate the question of trade from politics," in NBC's "Meet the Press," Oct.
26, 1969; see also *Ettelaat* (air ed.), June 4, 1970.

brush with which to paint the proposed conference as Zionist inspired. It demonstrated once again the capacity of one of the Arab states to generalize a dispute and by invoking a particular symbol to place its opponents on the defensive. Thus in attacking the Islamic "alliance," much was made of Iran's commercial relations with Israel. Nasser's speech on May 23 at the UAR Advanced Air Headquarters exemplifies this:

I would like the Islamic Alliance to serve the Palestine question in only one way—by preventing the supply of oil to Israel. The oil which now reaches Israel, which reaches Eilat, comes from Iran. Who then is supplying Israel with oil? The Islamic alliance—Iran, an Islamic alliance state. Such is the Islamic alliance. It is an imperialist alliance, and this means it sides with Zionism, because Zionism is the main ally of imperialism.[47]

On the same day the Egyptian government called upon Jordan and Sa'udi Arabia to inform Iran that oil could no longer be shipped to Israel through the Gulf of Aqaba as a result of the announced blockade.[48]

As a result of the ascendancy and dominance of the Arab-Israel dispute, the divisions within the Arab world were temporarily submerged. Just as King Hussein had had to make his peace with Abd 'al-Nasser earlier, so too did the Sa'udis at least verbally rally around the flag. The Sa'udi government denied any knowledge of Iran's commercial relations with Israel and affirmed its absolute support for the UAR stand in closing the Gulf of Aqaba to Israeli navigation and to ships carrying strategic material, including oil.[49]

The Egyptian government, however, was not prepared to let the opportunity of making its point slip by. The undersecretary of the Egyptian foreign ministry, Dr. Muhammad Hassan al-Zayyat, put forward the following evidence to substantiate the Egyptian charge that Iran supplied 80 percent of Israel's oil requirements. (1) A Sa'udi government memorandum submitted to the Arab League on May 1, 1961, which stated that the National Iranian Oil Company had the right to conclude marketing contracts on behalf of the Iranian government and supplying Israel with oil. (2) The Arab ambassadors in Tehran, including the Sa'udi ambassador, repeatedly contacted the Iranian government in 1964 and 1965, regarding the sale of oil to Israel in

47 Cairo Home Service, in Arabic, May 23, 1967; on BBC, May 24, 1967.
48 New York Times, May 24, 1967; The Times (London), May 24, 1967.
49 Al-Ahram (Cairo), May 31, 1967.

accordance with a decision issued following meetings between Arab oil experts and the Boycott of Israel Office. (3) Finally, Dr. al-Zayyat noted that the oil which reaches Israel is delivered to Eilat via the "Arabian" Gulf which means it originated from the Arab states or Iran. "It is unreasonable to assume that this oil is being received from the Arab states. Therefore, it is established that all the oil which Israel receives comes from Iran." [50] The same statement noted that Israel imported more than three million tons of oil a year from Iran, accounting for about 80 percent of its total requirements of about four million tons of crude oil.

Since the war, the Arab states at the Arab oil conference held in Cairo in 1968 have warned the oil companies against sending Iranian oil through Israeli pipelines. All the Arab states have pledged to use the Suez-Alexandria pipeline rather than the Eilat-Ascalon Israeli pipeline, but Iran has to date made no such commitment nor has it undertaken to obtain such a commitment from the Consortium.[51] However, the improvement in relations with Egypt since 1967, and especially 1970, has increased the possibility of cooperation in this field between Tehran and Cairo. Any joint ventures, however, would perhaps have to await a settlement of the dispute with Israel.

If the Iranian government has been unwilling to forego commercial relations with Israel out of respect for Arab sensibilities, it has nevertheless affirmed the rights of the Palestinians. In numerous resolutions in the United Nations it has supported their right to a choice between compensation or repatriation into Palestine-Israel. Until 1967 this was as far as the Iranian government would commit itself on the Arab side, and this position was reflected in the communiqués issued after King Faysal's visit to Iran in December 1965 and President Abd 'al-Rahman Arif's visit in March 1967. It was again reaffirmed in an official Iranian government statement on the eve of the war in 1967.[52] The war, however, forged a new political situation in the Middle East and in response to this, Iran's policy towards Israel was modified.

---

[50] Text of UAR Foreign Ministry statement on Iranian oil in Cairo Home Service, in Arabic, May 31, 1967; on BBC, June 2, 1967.

[51] *Iran Almanac,* Oct. 24, 1968; *Middle East Economic Digest* (London), XII, No. 42 (Oct. 18, 1968), 1025–1030.

[52] Text of Iran-Sa'udi communiqué in English may be found in *Arab Political Documents,* 1965, p. 449, and in Persian in *Elamiehaye Moshtarek 1349,* pp. 33–34. English text of Iran-Iraq communiqué (excerpts) in *Iran Almanac,* 1967, pp. 249–251; see also *The Times* (London), March 20, 1967. Persian text in *Elamiehaye Moshtarek 1349,* pp. 83–87.

IRAN-EGYPT RELATIONS SINCE 1967

The war of June 1967 was a turning point in Iran's relations with Egypt. Although it was not immediately obvious to either state, Nasser's defeat and the withdrawal of Egyptian troops from Yemen by the end of that year contributed to a totally new political situation.

In the first place, the Egyptian government's energies were hereafter almost exclusively devoted to its dispute with Israel. The quest for the return of its occupied territories and the problems of leadership of the Arab world radically changed Egyptian priorities. Iran was a beneficiary of the war, in that Egypt was hereafter deeply involved and committed on a different front, while its military capabilities were also substantially diminished. Egyptian "intentions" in eastern Arabia were in due course scaled down to reflect its political priorities and its diminished capabilities in that theater.

Iran was also a beneficiary of the war economically, for by increasing oil production during the short-lived Arab oil embargo after the war, she regained her former position as the largest oil producer in the region. Another factor slowly appreciated by the Iranian leadership was the essentially moderate role that Abd 'al-Nasser was playing in intra-Arab politics. Yet if this last realization came to Iranian policy-makers, it did so slowly.

The Iranian government immediately after the 1967 Arab-Israel war took the position that Israel's occupation of Arab lands, for whatever purpose, was contrary to the United Nations Charter and was therefore illegal and unacceptable. It has since that date urged Israel's speedy withdrawal, vehemently protested the annexation of Jerusalem, and affirmed the rights of the Palestinians to repatriation or compensation. It has also provided humanitarian relief aid through its Red Cross organization. The Shah took the opportunity in the aftermath of the war to affirm publicly for the first time that Israel had a right to nationhood while criticizing, nevertheless, its June conquests.[53] The Iranian government did not, however, actively seek a reconciliation with Egypt immediately.

Up until June 1967 the official Iranian stance on any resumption of diplomatic relations with Egypt had been firm and explicit. Since Egypt had terminated the relations, a resumption of ties was contingent on the following: The Egyptian government must (1) under-

---

[53] *New York Times,* Sept. 14, 1967.

take a pledge of non-interference in the Gulf region; (2) take the initiative to restore the severed ties; and (3) "apologize" for its past behavior in any way deemed appropriate in order to create a climate favorable for a reconciliation.

After the war these conditions were softened. The Iranian government dropped the requirements of an apology and a formal statement of non-interference in Gulf politics, while continuing to insist that Cairo take the initiative in the resumption of ties.[54] However, the Iranian government continued to attach extreme importance to the Gulf region and exhibit sensitivity to developments there, particularly in the light of Britain's withdrawal from southern Arabia in 1967. It was therefore inclined to judge the utility of a restoration of ties with Egypt on the basis of the attitude Nasser showed to Iran's interests in the Gulf. With the Egyptian government, in turn, recognizing the need for maximum support for its position on its area of primary interest (i.e., its dispute with Israel), the stage was set for a *quid pro quo*. Before this could materialize, there remained several issues in the Gulf to be settled—the disposition of Bahrayn, the future of the Arab shaykhdoms union, and the Iran-Iraq disputes of 1969–1971.

On all these questions the reconciliation of Iran and Egypt may have foundered but for the sensitivity that each state displayed for the other's interests. The Iranian government, while not going further than the position sketched above on the question of Israel, nonetheless played a more prominent, vocal, and active part in its support for the Arab cause. Aware that Israel's value as a political counterweight to Egypt had diminished as a result of Egypt's defeat and its own increasing economic vitality, and perhaps unsettled by the accelerated intrusion of the USSR into the region politically as a consequence of the Egyptian defeat, the Iranian government downplayed its relations with Israel.[55]

The Egyptian leadership, cognizant of the role of intra-Arab forces in unleashing a war for which it had been unprepared, adopted hereafter a policy more focused on Egypt's own interests, thereby becoming less a hostage to pressures on its right or left. Nasser thus became a "moderate" in his search for peace with Israel, accepting the United

---

54 See *Ravabet Khareji-e Iran dar Sale 1347*, p. 5; *Ravabet Khareji-e Iran dar Sale 1348*, p. 72.

55 "There is also some apprehension that Israel's desirable role as a cooperative regional military power might easily change into that of an expansionist proximate one." Sepehr Zabih, "Iran's International Posture: De Facto Nonalignment Within a Pro-Western Alliance," *Middle East Journal* (Summer, 1970), pp. 317–318.

Nations' Security Council Resolution 242 (November 22, 1967), and later the Rogers ceasefire plan of June 1970, while these were rejected by Syria, Iraq, and Algeria. Nasser's "moderate" character was enhanced by the overthrow of the moderate Taher Yahya regime in Iraq by a rightist Ba'thist regime which, in confronting the Iranian government in the Gulf's politics, underlined for Tehran the fact that its principal opponent was situated much closer to home than Cairo. With the passage of time, Tehran and Cairo found they had a common antagonist in the new regime in Baghdad which attempted to undermine both Nasser's diplomatic approach to a settlement with Israel and Iran's relations with the Gulf Arab states.

In contrast to the earlier period examined above, the Egyptian government became markedly reluctant to insult the Iranian government or to take the several opportunities offered by the issues to polarize Arab and Iranian in the Gulf, by stressing the threat posed by Iran. Yet it was not easy after the activist tendencies of the last decade in the region for the Egyptian government to reverse itself overnight. The Iranian government's endorsement of Britain's withdrawal from the Gulf *after* the British decision was announced overlapped the Egyptian government's similar view. But its claim to Bahrayn, which temporarily unsettled its relations with Sa'udi Arabia from March through June 1968, and its consequent attitude toward the Arab shaykhdoms' embryonic federation, were diametrically opposed to Arab interests.

The Egyptian government's response was circumspect: it still stressed the dangers posed to the "Arabism" of the Gulf by imperialism and foreign immigration, but it eschewed direct criticism of Iran or personal insult to the Shah. It did nevertheless support the proposed federation of Arab shaykhdoms which the Iranian government opposed, but not in such a way as to exacerbate Iran-Arab relations in the Gulf.[56] Although reportedly relinquishing the role of protector of Arab interests in the Persian Gulf to Sa'udi Arabia, the Egyptian government moved slowly to extricate itself from a major role in Gulf politics.[57] The Iranian government, which consistently after January 1968 reiterated the theme that Gulf affairs should be determined by Gulf littoral states found this welcome. For although Egyptian troops had been withdrawn from Yemen in the autumn of 1967 and Egypt

---

[56] See for example *Al-Ahram*, Cairo, Feb. 28, 1968.

[57] For reports indicating that Egypt had given Saudi Arabia carte blanche in the Gulf, see *The Times* (London), Feb. 5, 1968; *Christian Science Monitor*, March 16, 1968.

remained preoccupied with Israel, the Egyptian government retained considerable power to influence Gulf politics and a considerable nuisance capacity, which was reflected in the Iranian government's continued sensitivity to Egypt's policy.

There is some evidence that consideration was given in Tehran and Cairo to a resumption of ties in 1968, which was reflected by a premature (and erroneous) disclosure by *Al-Ahram* in June that diplomatic relations were about to be restored.[58] The rapprochement between Iran and Sa'udi Arabia in June, cemented by the Shah's visit to that country in October 1968 and his declaration in January 1969 (in New Delhi) of the Iranian acceptance of a plebiscite to determine Bahrayn's status, removed any remaining obstacles impeding a restoration of ties. This reconciliation was given an added fillip by the impartial and factual tone adopted by the Egyptian press in Iran's dispute with Iraq in early 1969 (in contrast to the vehemence shown by, say, Syria). [59]

This impartiality was not overlooked in Tehran, and presumably served to emphasize to Iranian policy-makers that Iran-Egypt relations had entered a new era. Politically neither state had any major interest in conflict after July 1968, while it was increasingly apparent to both states that the other could be diplomatically helpful in their respective areas of major concern, i.e., for Iran the Gulf, and for Egypt, Israel. The liquidation of Iran's claim to Bahrayn and Egypt's activity in the Gulf further removed any impediments to a rapprochement. Finally, the coup is Baghdad in July 1968 and Iraq's subsequent activities in opposition to Nasser's approach to a settlement with Israel, and Iran's policies in the Gulf, found Tehran and Cairo on the same side in opposition to an Arab state. In May 1970 the Shah commented in a press conference upon the changed Egyptian attitude toward Iran, and the following month special envoys were exchanged by the two states to examine the resumption of diplomatic relations. At the end of August, full diplomatic relations were restored between Iran and Egypt.[60]

Abd 'al-Nasser's death the following month occurred before ambassadors had been exchanged, but the Iranian government paid its respects by calling for three days of mourning and dispatching a delegation headed by Prime Minister Amir Abbas Hoveyda to the funeral.

---

58 *Al-Ahram*, June 13, 1968; *The Times* (London) June 14, 1968.
59 For contrast, Cairo Home Service, in Arabic, April 22, 1969, and Damascus "Voice of the Arabian Peninsula," in Arabic, April 29, 1969; on BBC, April 22, 1969.
60 *Iran Tribune*, May 1970, p. 9.

The restoration of diplomatic relations was generally welcomed in the region, including the Soviet Union, and the only dissenting voice came from Baghdad.[61] Just as the Ba'thist regime in Iraq had opposed the Rogers peace initiative earlier that year, it opposed Cairo's policy of compromise and reconciliation in the Gulf. The Egyptian and Iranian governments, in turn, had attacked the Iraq government before the formal restoration of ties, using similar and in one case identical arguments.[62]

Prime Minister Hoveyda's visit to Cairo for Nasser's funeral, and the warmth evident on both sides, suggested an acceptance by each government of the terms of the new relationship. On the Egyptian side it was clear that this involved non-interference in Gulf politics. On his return from Cairo, the Iranian prime minister told reporters that on the Persian Gulf, Iran's views were clear. Iran wanted the future of the region determined by the littoral states alone, and he was glad that the Egyptian government thought along similar lines.[63] The Egyptian government subsequently studiously eschewed any criticism of Iran's claims to Abu Musa and the Tumb islands by pointing out that peaceful settlement was possible. A year later, when Iranian troops were poised to occupy the islands, the Egyptian government again urged moderation in the Arab world. It reportedly argued that these islands were not important enough for the Arabs to be concerned about them, and emphasized that the primary issue confronting the Arab world was that of Israel.[64]

Following the Iranian seizure of the islands the Egyptian government, though doubtless embarrassed, did not support Iraqi suggestions in the Arab League Council to terminate relations with Iran, nor did it participate in the discussions and attacks on the Iranian action in the Security Council.[65]

61 For Soviet approval of the reconciliation, Moscow Radio in Persian to Iran, Aug. 24, 1970; for Iraq's comments, 'Al-Thawrah's' condemnation of UAR policy, Sept. 6, 1970, and 'Al Jumhuriyah,' Iraqi News Agency, Aug. 24, 1970.

62 For Cairo's comment, paralleling Tehran's, that the Iraq regime had fabricated the Shatt al-'Arab dispute to escape its responsibilities vis-à-vis Israel: Cairo, on BBC, Aug. 17, 1970.

63 Keyhan International (weekly), Oct. 10, 1970.

64 See New York Times, Aug. 16, November 7, 1971.

65 For Egypt's moderate reaction, see Ettelaat (air ed.), Dec. 2, 1970. The quid pro quo nature of the Iran-Egypt reconciliation is illustrated by the seizure of the islands which, when the issue was brought to the Security Council, coincided with the beginning of the Indo-Pakistan hostilities and the Egyptian government's attempts to moblize diplomatic support against Israel in the UN. Concentration on the complaint against Iran would have weakened and slowed down Egypt's search for allies against Israel in the diplomacy at the UN.

To underline the transformation in Egyptian policy toward Iran, it must be noted that six Arab states including two non-Gulf states— Libya, Algeria, Kuwait, Iraq, the Union of Arab Amirates, and South Yemen—participated in the UN debates to protect Arab interests and doubtless to outshine the other states in their "Arabness." The refusal of the Egyptian government to allow these pressures to jeopardize its relations with Iran or undermine its own concentration on the "question of the Middle East" debate in the UN testifies to its new and primary concern for its own interests.

On the other side, the Iranian government now became more sensitive to Egyptian interests. It condemned Israel's bombing of Egyptian civilian facilities in early 1970 and it expressed the opinion in March 1971 that it was now up to Israel to respond positively to Gunnar Jarring's suggestions, while praising the Egyptian response as positive and helpful.[66]

Bilateral activity between the two states accelerated, and ambassadors were exchanged in January 1971. On April 10 Egyptian Foreign Minister Mahmoud Riyad made a weeklong visit to Iran, which included a four-hour audience with the Shah. This visit was returned by Iranian Foreign Minister, Ardeshir Zahedi on May 10–14—the first visits at this level between the states in 21 years.[67]

Trade and other delegations have been exchanged, trade and air links restored, and a cultural agreement signed, and there has been discussion of possible cooperation in oil activities. The Iranian press had devoted more intensive coverage to affairs in Egypt and has prominently displayed favorable Egyptian comments about Iran.[68]

In October 1971 President Sadat, who is fluent in Persian, stopped over in Tehran and met the Shah *en route* to Moscow. One result of the intensive activity and rapprochement between the states has been the definite change in Iran's posture regarding the Arab-Israel dispute. While it had taken a position midway between the parties to the dispute until 1967, since the war it has ceased to claim any neutrality. In a recent press conference the Shah underlined this by re-

---

[66] See *Ettelaat* (air ed.), March 4 and 6, 1971, editorial entitled "Israel errs," and *Keyhan International* (weekly), March 13, 1971. Iran's stand was praised by Egypt; *ibid.*, March 20, 1971.

[67] For details of Iran-Egypt relations since August 1970, see *Ravabet-e Khareji-e Iran dar Sale 1349*, pp. 93–99. For Iranian press comments on the visits, see *Ettelaat* (air ed.), April 6–8, 1971.

[68] See, for example, Massudi's reports from Cairo, a series entitled "Life Near the Banks of the Nile." *Ettelaat*, June 13, 1971, *et. seq.* For Egyptian comments reported, see *Ettelaat*, Nov. 28 and 29 and Dec. 2, 1970, and May 18, 1971. Egyptian criticism of Iraq was also noted: *Ettelaat* (air ed.), July 10, 1971.

jecting the possibility of being a mediator, since that would require neutrality. Iran, he said, was not neutral, and he took the position that the occupied territory must be returned.[69]

For the time being, Iran-Egypt relations are on a firm foundation. As a result of the 1967 war and its own increasing strength in the region, the Iranian government is less sensitive and vulnerable to Arab hostility. In addition, its need for Israel as a tacit regional ally has diminished, and by acknowledging the Arab cause more vocally it has been able to "cash in" on this by utilizing its diplomatic support for Egypt as a *quid pro quo* in exchange for which Egypt does not unsettle, or take advantage of, Iran's relations with the Gulf's Arab states. Egypt's moderate attitude has been particularly valuable to Iran in 1968–1971, at a time when Iranian claims and policies have been vocally resisted by Iraq and Syria and, more distantly, Algeria and Libya.

Whether this *quid pro quo* will prove temporary and evanescent with the flux of international politics, or serve as a cement in the relations between the states, it is still difficult to discern. But it appears that in either case, Iran's newfound strength in the Gulf will preclude a return to the 1960–1967 scenario. Similarly, it appears that the Egyptian government (unless it succumbs to the pressures of intra-Arab politics and once again seeks a leadership role with no regard to its own interests) is unlikely to resume an active role as in the earlier period in Gulf politics. Neither state, in fact, has a conflict of interest important enough to it, or intractable enough, to interfere with the cordiality of the present relationship. Provided Iran pursues a moderate policy toward the Arab shaykhdoms, and Egypt retains its freedom from the cross-pressures of Arab politics, relations need not be jeopardized.

While a theoretical case may be made for Iran's security concerns regarding Arab unity and Arab nationalism, it appears from the international politics of the region in the past two decades that this concern will remain as latent as the goal is chimerical. Unlike Israel, Iran has no "permanent" issue between itself and its Arab neighbors. Insofar as issues arise between Iran and the Arab states, they are more likely to be issues effecting its immediate neighbor Iraq, rather than Egypt.

---

[69] See *Keyhan International* (weekly), Jan. 29, 1972.

Chapter IV

IRAN-IRAQ RELATIONS

Unlike its relations with Egypt, Iran's relations with Iraq have not improved in the course of the decade. If relations with the former state took place, in Rosenau's terms, in Iran's "regional environment," its interaction with Iraq has occurred in its "contiguous environment."[1] In the course of the decade the interaction between Iran and Iraq and the sources of tension between them have been similar to the relations of many newer states and areas subject to past European imperialism. This is particularly true as regards their boundary dispute.[2] But the degree of volatility of Iraqi politics is unusual even in the developing third world and has had its impact on Iraq's foreign policy.

In addition, regional or intra-Arab forces have been another constraint on Iraqi foreign policy insofar as its leadership has considered it important to prove its Arab credentials in a way harmful to a purely local Iraqi national interest. Perhaps reflecting their status as leaders of a new nation-state, the Iraq governments have indeed been in search of a role in the overlapping Arab-Muslim worlds, a role which has been divisively shaped by the ideological predisposition of the leadership that has happened to seize power. The constant interplay of domestic political factionalism on regional foreign policy, and the reverse, has made Iraqi foreign policy unusually susceptible and even hostage to these two endemically unstable areas—Iraqi politics, and regional Arab politics.

Iran has had no such problem in that decade. Its internal politics,

---

[1] See James N. Rosenau, *The Scientific Study of Foreign Policy*, pp. 307–338.
[2] For a brief discussion of contemporary boundary disputes, see Evan Luard (ed.), *The International Regulation of Frontier Disputes*.

in marked contrast to that of its western Arab neighbor, have been remarkably stable, subject to neither the whim nor the caprice of the latest coup, and characterized by pragmatism. In Iran the formulation and implementation of foreign policy have been under the direct control of the monarch.

In this chapter, relations between these states have been separated into two chronological periods, July 1958 to December 1968 and January 1969 to December 1971—i.e., from the Qasim revolution to the British announcement of their intended withdrawal from the Gulf, and from that date until their actual departure. Within these periods we have focused on the salient issues between the states: the Shatt al-'Arab, the Kurdish question, and the shaping of Gulf politics. Two features in Iran-Iraq relations are emphasized: the constant tendency for differences in one area to spill over or to encompass the entire range of relations between the states, and the increased tendency of Iran to take a harder line in its relations with Iraq.

THE SHATT AL-'ARAB QUESTION

The July 1958 revolution in Iraq was greeted in Tehran with considerable dismay.[3] It was a setback for both the Baghdad Pact and the cause of monarchy in the region. Abd' al-Karim Qasim's early moderation was welcomed nonetheless and his regime speedily recognized. Nothing disturbed the tranquility of relations between the governments until November, when the Iraqi government advanced its claim to twelve miles of territorial waters. The Iranian response was to expand its own claim of three miles to match that of its neighbor.[4] The following March, Qasim formally terminated Iraq's connection with the Baghdad Pact (which hereafter became known as the Central Treaty Organization, or CENTO). In Tehran the decision was not any less painful for having been expected, for it opened a wide breech in the regional security system at a time when Iran-USSR relations were particularly poor.

The manifest fluidity, if not stability, of politics in post-revolutionary Iraq, and the role of the communists in that country, were further cause for Iran's disquiet. But these misgivings were not allowed to generate a premature hostile attitude toward Iraq. Thus, for ex-

---

[3] Peter Avery reports that the 1958 revolution "caused grave consternation in the Iranian Cabinet." *Modern Iran*, p. 479.

[4] This was done by an amendment to the 1934 Territorial Waters Act adopted in April 1959. For texts of both, see *Iran Almanac*, 1971, pp. 661–662.

ample, the Iranian government raised no objections to the sale of British arms to the Qasim regime, in part to avert that state's excessive reliance on Soviet arms.[5]

FIRST PHASE, 1959–1960

The eruption of the dispute with Iraq in December 1959–January 1960 changed the situation, and the issue of the Shatt al-'Arab waterway became a central issue in the relations between the two states. It should be noted that this question had never been fully resolved since the conclusion of the July 1937 treaty. That treaty, in Articles 4 and 5, envisaged a subsequent agreement by the two states on a joint commission for delimitation and demarcation of their joint frontier, and the joint administration of the waterway. In April 1949 the Iranian government, through its embassy in Baghdad, proposed to the Iraqi government a draft agreement on the joint administration of the waterway.[6] Fifteen months later the Iraqi government replied with a counterproposal, that the commission be limited to consultative rather than executive authority. No progress was made in narrowing the two positions, and the Iraqi government continued to use the fees and dues obtained from Iran's use of the waterway for its own purposes from 1937 to 1959.

After the conclusion of the Baghdad Pact, the Iranian government in a note (September 1, 1957) had outlined its position on the issues and suggested the appointment of a Swedish arbitrator to facilitate the resolution of the differences. Subsequent discussions between the prime ministers of the two states, in Karachi in the same year, had appeared to result in agreement in principle on the appointment of a joint committee to draft a proposal for the administration of the Shatt al-'Arab.

Discussions continued with the new Iraq regime during the UN General Assembly session in New York, and several notes were exchanged during October–November 1958. The new regime in Baghdad, like its predecessor, was unenthusiastic about a meeting. It privately argued that Iraqi public opinion was not yet ready for a settle-

---

[5] See Humphrey Trevelyan, *The Middle East in Revolution*, p. 154; and *New York Times*, May 12, 1959.

[6] The subsequent discussion of the political exchanges prior to 1960 is taken from "Some Facts Concerning the Dispute Between Iran and Iraq Over the Shatt al-'Arab" (Tehran: Ministry of Foreign Affairs, May, 1969); and "The Shatt al-'Arab: The Boundary Line Between Iran and Iraq" (London: Imperial Iranian Embassy). For the geography of the dispute, see Alexander Melamid, "The Shatt al-'Arab Boundary Dispute."

ment of the dispute. In any event, relations with the new Iraqi regime deteriorated in 1959 when Iraqi authorities interfered with Iranian ships and ships belonging to the Iranian Pan-American Oil Company (IPAC), occasioning the exchange of several harsh notes.

It was against this diplomatic background that the Shah in a press conference on November 28, 1959, expressed his dissatisfaction with the new Iraqi regime.

"In the past we had agreements with Iraq on the Shatt al-'Arab which were never respected by Iraq. . . . Naturally a river which forms the boundary between two nations cannot be used exclusively by one side only. . . . We cannot accept the imperialistic policy of Iraq in this respect. We hope, however, that the government will accept our friendship, adopt a good neighborly policy, and not only try to settle all outstanding differences but also make it possible for the two nations to maintain the best possible relations as two good neighbors. . . ." [7]

Abd' al-Karim Qasim reacted to the comment by asserting Iraq's claim to the entire waterway, including the three-mile stretch of water opposite the port of Abadan ceded to Iran in 1937.[8] The verbal exchanges then gave way to practical measures: Iraq expelled a number of Iranian nationals and imposed employment restrictions on others, while the Iranian Majlis condemned Qasim. Both sides exchanged propaganda, alerted their armed forces, and fortified their frontier. However, it was clear from their statements that neither government was prepared for or expected the confrontation to lead to actual hostilities or a state of conflict.

The Iranian reaction to the claim is noteworthy: while preparing militarily for a conflict, it appears to have had serious doubts about its capabilities. Thus, the Shah has written:

Iraq has only about a quarter of our population and a fifth of our land area, yet her air force is more powerful than ours. It includes many of the latest jet fighters that easily outperform our earlier American ones, and unlike us, she also possesses modern jet bombers. Moreover, Iraq's armed forces as a whole are better equipped than ours.[9]

Therefore, its reaction in the form of asserting its claim to half the Shatt al-'Arab under the 1937 treaty was fairly mild.

---

[7] "Press Conferences of His Imperial Majesty Mohammad Reza Shah Pahlavi of Iran" (Tehran: Keyhan Press, 1960), pp. 49–50.

[8] Text in "Some Facts Concerning the Dispute Between Iran and Iraq," pp. 58–59. See also Uriel Dann, *Iraq Under Qassem: A Political History, 1958–1963*, p. 264.

[9] *Memoirs*, pp. 313–314.

The 1959–60 episode also revealed the tendency for a dispute between the states in one area of their relations to be rapidly expanded to encompass the whole gamut of their relations. For example, the conditions of Iranian-born nationals residing in Iraq, as well as that of itinerant Iranian Shi'a pilgrims, were exacerbated and hampered by various Iraqi restrictions in this period of strained relations.

Neither state in this period made a determined effort to insulate one area of rivalry from the overall relations, or to contain specific differences, lest they adversely effect other important areas of their relations. Thus in the 1959 dispute Qasim not only refused to implement the 1937 treaty, but claimed the entire waterway and some Iranian territory, Khuzistan, including the port of Khorramshahr, for good measure.[10]

The actual dispute subsided by mid-January 1960. The Iranian government still controlled the three-mile strip of water opposite the Abadan refinery, and the Iraqi government still controlled the Basrah port authority. No joint committees had been formed, and Iranian grievances regarding Iraq's failure to provide for joint administration of the Shatt al-'Arab remained, if anything, more profound than ever.

SECOND PHASE, 1961

Another chapter in the Iran-Iraq dispute over the Shatt al-'Arab during the Qasim regime occurred in the following year. Between January and December of 1960 relations had steadily improved, particularly after July 1960 when the Shah and Qasim found themselves with a common regional rival, Nasser. Tehran and Baghdad resumed diplomatic discussions on their differences.

The Iranian government focused on the continued exclusive Iraqi administration of the joint waterway, despite the 1937 treaty provision for its joint administration. It also charged that navigation dues collected by that authority had been illegally used by the Iraqi government for projects other than those stipulated, i.e., the maintenance and improvement of the waterway. The aim of the Iranian government now was to come to some sort of agreement which ensured that Iranians handled the conduct of port operations in Abadan and in Iranian ports and waters.

---

10 See *Tehran Journal*, Dec. 18, 1959. The Iraqi newspaper *'Al-Thawrah*, a strong supporter of Qasim, demanded a plebiscite under United Nations auspices in the Iranian province of Khuzistan which, it said, was known to Arabs as "Arabistan," because the majority of the population is Arab.

The Iraqi government responded by claiming that the Iranian Oil Consortium had earlier signed an agreement with the Basrah Port Authority; hence whatever rights Iran had, they had in effect been waived, and Iraq was therefore unwilling to discuss the matter further.

At this point, on August 23, 1960, Iran instructed all navigation agencies in Khorramshahr to make use of the port officials of Iran as of August 27, 1960. However, in response to the threat of legal action by the Basrah port authority and a request for time by the Iraqi foreign ministry, the Iranian government relented and postponed this deadline. In October Iran indicated optimism about breaking the stalemate, and in January 1961 bilateral discussion for drafting new rules regulating passenger transit between the two countries were held.[11]

Yet the gulf separating the two states on the question of the Shatt al-'Arab remained as wide as ever. Dissatisfied with the progress of its discussions with Iraq, the Iranian government on February 16, 1961, issued a ruling under which vessels entering Iranian waters or ports would henceforth be guided by Iranian pilots rather than Iraqi pilots from the Basrah port authority. The latter reacted by calling an immediate strike and refusing to handle ships either bound for or leaving Abadan. Since such ships had to pass through some forty miles of Iraqi territorial waters on the way up or down the Shatt al-'Arab between its mouth and Abadan, a jam ensued in the waterway. Within four days eleven tankers and one cargo ship were idle in the river, and by the end of the month the refinery tanks in Abadan had been filled up and refining was cut down to the insignificant amount used locally. The blockage in the port of Abadan and the subsequent cutback in operations at the refinery did not mean that Iranian oil exports were paralyzed, because two-thirds of Iranian oil was exported crude, and Abadan was used for the export of refined oil. It was nonetheless a costly disagreement for Iran. Due to the dispute, Abadan refined 60 percent less oil in March 1961 than in the previous March, and Iran lost a total of some 30 million dollars.[12]

Intensive diplomatic activity followed the onset of this dispute. The Iraqi government refused to compromise, and the Iranian government was unwilling to violate Iraq's territorial waters. On the Iraqi side there was no pressing need for dispatch, for by procrastination it could expect in time to obtain a reversion to the *status quo*

---

11 *Tehran Journal*, Nov. 9, 1960, and Jan. 10, 1961.
12 "Some Facts Concerning the Dispute," pp. 55–56.

ante. Predictably, on April 23, 1961, the Iranian government agreed to return to the *status quo ante* pending the outcome of bilateral negotiations. Owing to continued disagreements, these discussions failed to materialize.[13]

OTHER ISSUES IN IRAN-IRAQ RELATIONS, 1961–1968

Between 1961 and 1968 there was no new incident involving the Shatt al-'Arab, although a number of secondary differences persisted. Some of these resurfaced in the wake of Qasim's demise in February 1963. In April the new regime made public its intention to build a 12-inch oil pipeline from Khaneghain on the Iraq-Iran border to Baghdad. The oil reserves of both Khaneghain, on the Iraq side of the border, and Nafte-Shah and Khaneh, on the Iranian side, were fed by a common subterranean source. The Iraq action signaled a decision to maximally increase its exploitation of these geographically joint reserves. Both this issue of the oil fields astride the Iran-Iraq border, and differences on the limits of the two states' territorial waters in the Persian Gulf were taken up in negotiations in late July 1963, when the Iraq minister of petroleum, Dr. Abd al-Aziz Wattari, visited Tehran.[14]

Regarding the latter issue, Iraq claimed that in opening up an offshore area of 40,000 kilometers in the Gulf, Iran had infringed on Iraq's territorial waters. But it was clear that the two states' differences on the Shatt al-'Arab border severely complicated agreement on the division of territorial waters at its mouth in the Gulf.

Agreement was reached on the joint exploitation of oil resources in the border field, the specific volume which each state could extract annually was laid down, and inspection by each country of the other's operations was provided for. The two states could only reach agreement "in principle" on the joint exploitation of the disputed waters in the Gulf, and the details were left for a subsequent meeting.[15]

The apparent political success of the discussions reflected and reinforced the improvement of Iran-Iraq relations. The Iraqi government of February–November 1963 included a strong Ba'thist contingent which, though doctrinally opposed to the Iranian monarchy, shared

---

13 See *Tehran Journal,* April 24, 1961, and *Middle East Record,* II (1961). It was the Iranian intention to settle the dispute by a treaty duly ratified by the legislatures of both states. See: "Some Facts Concerning the Dispute," p. 62.

14 *Tehran Journal,* April 16, May 2, June 15, and July 17, 1963.

15 *The Times* (London), Aug. 6, 1963.

with the Iranian leadership a rivalry with Nasser. This appears to have been the chief reason for the improvement of relations which even survived the ouster of the Ba'thist faction in November 1963.

On February 25, 1964, an Iraqi delegation led by the Foreign Minister Sobhi Abd 'al Hamid and the Minister of State Abd 'al-Razaq Mohiuddin arrived in Tehran. The week-long visit was to clarify the issues between the states as well as to serve a "good-will" function, but the vagueness of the final communiqué indicated little substantive progress on any of the contentious issues.[16]

In the meantime the feud between Iran and Egypt was reaching its zenith. It will be recalled that a favorite Egyptian tactic in its relations with the Iranian government was to attempt to range against it all the Arab states of the region by invoking the threat to the region's Arabism. Iraq's shift toward a pro-Egyptian orientation after the November 1963 anti-Ba'thist coup now caused Tehran considerable concern and complicated the two states' relations. In addition to Iran, both the Shi'a and Kurdish communities in Iraq opposed the Nasser-inspired pan-Arab unity contemplated by the Iraq-Egypt military union of March 26, 1964.

This identify of interest between Iran and the Iraqi Kurds and Shi'a aroused the Iraqi authorities' suspicions that Iran was actively encouraging the Shi'a-Sunni, Arab-Kurd division within its borders. In response they revived Iraq and Arab claims to Khuzistan (or "Arabistan" as they called it), causing a further deterioration in relations.[17] As it became clear that the Abd al-Salam 'Arif regime was not headed for union with Egypt, relations improved.

Once Abd 'al-Rahman Bazzaz consolidated his position as Iraqi prime minister, the chances of detente appeared even brighter. Yet while Iran and Kuwait had agreed to study the question of territorial waters and the continental shelf in June 1965, and Iran and Sa'udi Arabia reached a tentative agreement in December 1965 and subsequently modified in October 1968, no progress was made on this issue. With Iraq the issue was, of course, complicated by the intractable dispute over the rights of the two states in the Shatt al-'Arab.

Apart from the Shatt al-'Arab boundary dispute and the related frontier question of the Khaneghain-Khaneh-Nafte-Shah oil field, and the continental shelf-territorial waters, there were other issues between the states, such as the status and treatment of large numbers of Irani-

---

16 For a critical editorial by *Ettelaat*, probably inspired by the Iranian government, see *Tehran Journal*, March 5, 1964.
17 See *The Times* (London), May 15, 1964.

ans who had long lived in Iraq without giving up their Iranian citizenship.

All the above issues were taken up by the two parties during the visit of the Iranian foreign minister, Abbas Aram, to Baghdad in December 1966, and again when President Abd 'al-Rahman Arif visited Tehran in March 1967. But progress on the key substantive issues lagged far behind the "atmospherics" of relations between the states.[18] The improvement in relations was translated into only marginal agreements. The basic differences between the two states remained and outlasted the subsequent visit to Tehran of Prime Minister Tahir Yahya in June 1968 and the overthrow of the Arif regime by a Ba'thist junta the following month.[19]

This continued impasse may be attributed to two basic factors: (1) the genuine desire not to give away what is viewed as Iraq's by treaty; (2) assuming desire for a compromise settlement, a major constraint on Iraq's leadership is imposed by the divided nature of that leadership, the temptation to excel in proving one's Arab credentials, and the need to avoid alienation of the more extremist members of the military junta of the day. Thus the issue of bilateral interstate relations has become enmeshed in the network of the multilateral inter-Arab as well as intra-Arab relations.

THE KURDISH QUESTION

Since World War II the question of Kurdistan has played a significant role in Iraqi-Iranian relations. In the early postwar era the Soviet-sponsored separatist movement in Kurdistan was actively aided and abetted by Kurdish elements across the frontier in Iraq. Mullah Mostafa Barzani, who had crossed back into Iraq with the downfall of the Kurdish insurrection in Mahabad, was in turn driven out of Iraq in the winter of 1947 by a joint Iraqi-British military operation. Barzani's group, however, eluded the Iranian army in Kurdistan and Azarbayjan and drove some 800 miles through Iranian territory across the Arasi river to their Soviet sanctuary.

Up to the July 1958 revolution in Iraq, the Kurdish separatist movement remained fairly dormant in both Iran and Iraq. In Iraq a sys-

---

[18] For the text of the joint communiqué issued at the conclusion of the Arif visit, see the Iranian foreign ministry publication, *Elameihaye Moshtarek* (Tehran, 1971), pp. 83–87.

[19] For a discussion of Iran-Iraq relations from March 1967 to March 1968, see *Ravabet-e Khareji-e Iran dar Sale 1346* (Tehran, 1969), pp. 26–30.

tematic military and political purification literally resolved the Kurdish problem as an indigenous phenomenon, though its potentials for
revival through Soviet-communist agitation were never ignored in
either country.

During the 1960's the Kurdish revolt against the central government of Iraq became the critical issue in the two states' relations. As
Iraq's neighbor, and a country with numerous Kurds itself, Iran
has been involved indirectly since the start of the differences between the Kurds and republican Iraq.

In 1959, for instance, an Iraqi officer, Colonel Barnarny, had accused Iran and Turkey of sponsoring a minor revolt among the Kurds.
Many Iraqi Kurds had in fact at that time taken refuge in Iran, and
had done so again in December 1961 when the Kurdish revolt intensified and negotiations with Qasim's regime had broken down. In the
following year, while prosecuting the war against the Kurds, Iraqi
planes had strafed several Turkish border villages and in so doing
lost one aircraft to Turkish groundfire.[20]

The Soviet government, too, was at least indirectly involved. Well
aware of the anti-CENTO potential of the Kurdish revolt, it supported
the Kurds. Despite the 1962 detente with Iran, the Soviet government in July 1963 had even accused Iran, Turkey, Iraq, and Syria
of planning military activities in northern Iraq.[21] Although Iranian
Kurds had joined with Syrian and Iraqi Kurds in fighting Iraqi
forces in the summer of 1961, it is doubtful that this reflected a decision by the Iranian government to intervene, given its other preoccupations and its own fear of Barzani's communist orientation.[22]
The support by the Iranian Kurds of their Iraqi counterparts more
likely reflected a genuine identification with, and sympathy for, the
Iraqi Kurdish movement.

Ironically, it was during the moderate civilian tenure of Abd al-
Rahman Bazzaz that the Kurdish question assumed significance in
Iran-Iraq relations. In the prosecution of the war against the Kurds,
Iraqi troops had already on several occasions violated the frontiers
and airspace of neighboring Iran and Turkey. Prime Minister Bazzaz
responded to the deterioration in relations by: (1) seeking to employ

20 See *New York Times,* May 6, 1959, Aug. 16–21, 1961, and Sept. 17, 1961.

21 *New York Times,* July 10, 1963.

22 Derk Kinnane, *The Kurds and Kurdistan,* p. 64. Also see Hassan Arfa, *The
Kurds,* p. 105; and Darius Homayoun, "The Same Old Iraqi Line," in *Tehran Jour-
nal,* June 18, 1963. In general, see Lettie M. Wenner, "Arab-Kurdish Rivalries in
Iraq"; Dana Adams Schmidt, "Recent Developments in the Kurdish War"; and
David Adamson, *The Kurdish War.*

King Faysal of Sa'udi Arabia, who enjoyed good relations with the Shah, as a mediator; (2) mobilizing diplomatic support in the Arab League to deter an Iranian attack; and (3) agreeing to discuss the issues separating the states.[23] Agreement was subsequently reached by the two states on three points: (1) the withdrawal of Iranian troops from the border area; (2) the termination of mutual recriminations and propaganda campaigns; (3) the formation of joint committees to discuss the issues separating the states.

Like other facets of relations between the states, the Kurdish question was an issue which assumed greater or lesser significance according to the temperature of overall relations between Tehran and Baghdad. More secure domestically and on better terms with the USSR, the Shah had recently consolidated a regional role by participating in the founding of the non-Arab RCD and, with King Faysal, in an Islamic Unity front. The wide range of differences with Iraq, and especially that state's refusal to revise the 1937 treaty on the Shatt al-'Arab as well as the memory of the events of 1959 and 1961, must surely have rankled the Iranian leadership.

The Iraq-Kurdish war presented Iran with an opportunity which it would have been unable to take up earlier in the decade. In 1961–62 aiding the Kurdish revolt would have been unthinkable, for Barzani was considered a communist and a potential Iraqi tool against Iran. Reportedly, Iranian authorities had even discussed possible cooperation with the Ba'thist Iraq regime of February–November 1963 in operations *against* the Kurds.[24] Be that as it may, by 1965 Iran's new strength, and its frustration over the continued friction with Iraq over a number of issues, permitted Iran a reassessment of its attitude toward the Kurdish uprising.

In early January 1966 there were reports of an agreement between Iranian Premier Amir Abbas Huvayda and Mostafa Barzani for supplying the Kurds with arms and advisors. Other reports indicated that Iran also acted as a conduit of arms shipped to the Kurds from Israel.[25]

---

23 *New York Times*, Jan. 1 and 8, 1966, and *The Times* (London), Jan. 1, 1966. The most the Arab countries would promise was contained in the Syrian reply: "The Syrian Arab Republic, realizing that such a situation threatens the security of the entire area . . . supports Iraq . . . in its efforts to settle this dispute in a friendly and peaceful way." See *Chronology of Arab Politics*, IV, No. 1 (January–March, 1966), p. 65.

24 See Ahmed Tarokh, "The Shatt al'Arab: The Dividing Line," in *Tehran Journal*, Feb. 24, 1965, who quotes "reliable sources" in Baghdad.

25 Lecture by Talcott Seelye of the U.S. state department at Columbia University, May 13, 1970.

The short-run arguments in favor of Iran's decision to support the Kurds are not difficult to trace. The Kurds, like the Iraqi Shi'a, opposed any move by the Iraqi government toward an Arab union; their attitude thus coincided with Iran's. Secondly, the Kurdish war, by weakening the Iraqi government and by preoccupying it, reduced its military and political capacity to effectively deal with other issues. Bayne's observation that Iran's air force planes were inferior to those of the Iraqi air force in the winter of 1965 perhaps understates the degree to which these planes fulfilled an internal function—for approximately three of the five divisions of the Iraqi army, and much of its air force, were involved in the internal war with the Kurds between 1961 and 1966.[26] Finally, the Iranian leadership appears to have concluded that the Aryan Kurdish population in Iran, as one group in a multi-national nation-state, was relatively well integrated and posed no danger as a potential fifth column within Iran's own borders.[27]

The Bazzaz government sought a settlement with Iran partly to further its goal of good relations with its neighbors and partly as a first step to a settlement with the Kurds. But the terms of Bazzaz's twelve-point settlement with the Kurds in June 1966, leading to a ceasefire in July, did not survive their author's period as premier. They were never implemented by Bazzaz's successors, and as a result a *de facto* Kurdish revolutionary council continued to control a large section of Iraqi Kurdistan. The Kurdish insurgency also subsided and remained quiescent in the remainder of Abd 'al-Rahman Arif's presidency. That issue, as far as Iran-Iraq relations were concerned, receded into the background between 1966 and 1968.

The "Arabistan" Question, 1969–1971

The new Ba'thist government of July 1968, perhaps even more so than its predecessors, was constrained by domestic and foreign forces to define its priorities. Externally it had to define its orientation in relations with Iran and Israel. Domestically it was faced with con-

---

26 See Bayne, *Persian Kingship*, p. 222; and Nadav Safran, *From War to War*, p. 179.

27 Contrast T. Cuyler Young's observations on the Kurds in Iran in the earlier 1950's with the Shah's apparent confidence today. See T. Cuyler Young, "The National and International Relations of Iran," in T. Cuyler Young (ed.), *Near Eastern Culture and Society*, p. 201; and the Shah's comments in *Nashriyeh-e Akhbar va Asnad: Az Farvardin ta Shahrivar* (Tehran, 1971), pp. 229, 237. For a new view of Barzani as a "pragmatic conservative," see "The Kurds: A Long Line," *Iran Tribune*, May 2, 1969, p. 15.

tinued Kurdish unrest. To resolve the former, in the autumn of
1969 it launched a new military offensive.[28] But in April a more serious dispute with Iran over the Shatt al-'Arab prompted the Iraqi
leaders to seek peace with the rebellious Kurds. Secret negotiations
held in Beirut ended in an agreement on March 11, 1970, on a
fifteen-point formula which *inter alia* gave the Kurds amnesty, recognized Kurdish as an official language, promised them a Kurdish vice-
president and proportional representation in the revolutionary command council, cabinet, civil service, and the armed forces.[29]

The Iraqi motive for the settlement is not difficult to discern; another prolonged war with the Kurds promised to further weaken
an already divided polity and expose the state to serious weakness in
its dispute with Iran.[30] In addition, the regime, despite its past doc-
trinaire opposition to other nationalisms besides Arab nationalism,
having alienated virtually every other significant group in Iraq, now
needed the Kurds as a source of political support domestically. Finally,
given the serious nature of the dispute with Iran in the border area
and potentially in the Gulf, a settlement with the Kurds held forth
the promise not only of a breathing spell for the Iraqi army and the
opportunity for a freer hand in the south, but also the possibility of
turning the Kurdish sword back against Iran.

Iran's reaction to the agreement was mixed. While Tehran publicly hailed it, the above implications were not lost on the government. A further cause for concern was the ambiguity concerning the
extent of Soviet involvement in the agreement. Hitherto Iranian support for the Kurds had been an inexpensive policy to pursue. Dana
Adams Schmidt expressed the triangular relationship succinctly: "The
more bitter the dispute over the Shatt, the more the Iranians allow
arms and ammunition to slip over their border to the guerrillas of
General Mustafa al-Barzani, the Kurdish leader, and the more the
Iraqis vow to suppress the Kurds." [31]

---

28 See *New York Times,* March 30 and Sept. 12, 1969.

29 For good discussions of the March 11, 1970, agreement, see "Iraq's Kurds—Autonomy at Last," in *Le Monde* (weekly selection), March 18, 1970. The agreement was
preceded by a general amnesty in January; see Edouard Saab, "Iraq—Peace in the
North and a Bloodbath in Baghdad," in *Le Monde* (weekly selection), Jan. 28, 1970.
See also Jean-Pierre Viennot, "Le Malheur d'une Nation sans Etat," *Le Monde Dip-
lomatique,* April, 1970; *New York Times,* May 19, 21, and 24, 1969 and March 12, 13,
and 15, 1970.

30 The Iraq interior minister formally announced in February 1970 that because of
differences with Iran and the Kurds, Iraq was not ready for war with Israel. See
Ettelaat (air ed.), February, 1970.

31 *New York Times,* May 19, 1969. The Iraqis alleged that Iranian units sometimes

But the March 1970 agreement between the Kurds and Iraq signaled the change in Baghdad's priorities and somewhat neutralized an Iranian instrument of pressure on Iraq. Although Iraq had made vague claims to "Arabistan" in the past, it had done so only spasmodically and even half-heartedly. But Baghdad now took the initiative. During the April 1969 Shatt al-'Arab dispute, the Iraqi Deputy Premier and Interior Minister Salih Mahdi Ammash observed that

Iraq has never seriously differed with Iran over the Shatt al-'Arab; it is Iraqi territory.

The difference should have been over Arabistan, which is Iraqi territory annexed to Iran during the foreign mandate and which is called Ahvaz against the will of the Iraqi people.[32]

In May and June this theme was reiterated by Baghdad radio and combined with reports from "Occupied Arabistan," allegations of Iranian brutality against Arabs, accounts of meetings of the "Arabistan Liberation Front" which was poised to start a revolution, etc.

Whether the Iranian government will again utilize the Kurds in its rivalry with Iraq will depend on the eventual fate of the March 1970 agreement and the future course of Iran-Iraq relations. The steady deterioration of relations between the states from 1968–1971, including numerous border incidents and subversion makes it all the more likely that in the event of renewed Iraq-Kurd hostilities, Iranian support will be substantial and perhaps even overt.[33]

THE LATEST PERIOD

The apparent removal of the Kurdish question from the forefront of Iraqi-Iranian relations and the British announcement of their intended military withdrawal from the Gulf by December 1971 combined to redirect attention to the perennial Shatt al-'Arab dispute.

Since the Iran-Iraq confrontations earlier in the decade, much had changed. Iran was now a more powerful state militarily, with a stable government and on good relations with both superpowers as well as most of its neighbors. The Iraqi regime, on the other hand, had few

---

actually fought on the side of the Kurds, see *The Times* (London), July 15, 1969. Barzani denied this: "To say that we have been helped by the Soviet Union or any other power is nonsense." *Newsweek*, Dec. 7, 1970, p. 41.

32 Beirut Radio News Service, in Arabic, April 22, 1969.

33 The Iranian Foreign Minister Abbas Khalatbari was quoted by *Combat* (Paris), Dec. 8, 1971, as saying that Iran could aid the Iraqi Kurds militarily "if open conflict started" with government forces. See "Chronology," *Middle East Journal*, XXVI, No. 2 (Spring, 1972), 168.

regional friends and numerous regional rivals, a paper nonalignment which barely concealed its pro-Soviet orientation, and a chronically unstable revolutionary "condition." The change in both the stakes and the context was reflected in the intensified rivalry between Iran and Iraq from 1968 to 1971. Paradoxically, the new Iraqi regime had started with a conciliatory stance toward Iran. As a matter of fact, bilateral discussions to resolve all outstanding problems between the two states had taken place in Baghdad in mid-February 1969.

The abrupt breakdown of these talks, however, indicated the lack of any substantive progress on the issues separating the two. The intensity of the breakdown can be accounted for chiefly by reference to two phenomena unrelated to the two states' unwillingness, inability, or ignorance of compromise: the increased importance each attached to the *stakes* of the dispute, and the changed regional *context*.

The British announcement of its plan to withdraw from the Persian Gulf both heralded and accelerated the movement of new political forces in the Persian Gulf region. The dynamics of Iran-Iraq relations in the period from January 1968 to December 1971 are thus fundamentally based on the wider issues of the future of the Gulf, the political evolution or revolution of the shaykhdoms, and the respective roles of the two northern Gulf states in Gulf politics.

Whatever reservations it may have had about the timeliness of the British announcement, once it was publicly made Iran opposed any attempts by the British Conservative party or Gulf shaykhdoms to extend the announced deadline, or reverse the decision. As a result, both the Iraqi and Iranian government were agreed after January 1968 on the need for establishment of an indigenous security system after the British departure.

But even under the Arif regime, it did not appear that Iran and Iraq would be able to cooperate constructively on this question. The orientation of the two regimes in international politics differed, and regionally they had taken opposing sides in the Yemen war. In addition, monarchical Iran feared that Iraq could be counted upon to support the revolutionary movements in the southern Arabian peninsula and the People's Republic of South Yemen (PRSY).

There was also the Iranian claim to Bahrayn, which complicated Gulf politics by necessitating Iranian opposition to the proposed Union of Arab Emirates lest Bahrayn be included in that union. Finally, there was the temptation for the Iraqi regime to utilize Iran's claim and opposition to the union to isolate it in Gulf politics. By posing as the "Arab" protector of the small shaykhdoms, Iraq could at once enhance its own influence and isolate and exclude an ideologically distasteful non-Arab state and rival from an active and effective Gulf role.

These temptations proved too alluring for the new Ba'thist regime. Like their predecessors, the Ba'thists adopted a two-track policy: on the surface they sought to improve relations with Iran through contact, while at the same time they tacitly opposed Iran's evolving Gulf policy. A fierce war of nerves over such familiar issues as Iranian immigration to the shaykhdoms, the Arab versus Persian character of the Gulf, and the still unresolved Bahrayn issue was launched once again. The differences on the Shatt al-'Arab at that time assumed an even greater and symbolic importance, for they heralded the start of a serious rivalry between the states both on their borders and in the small shaykhdoms to the south.

THE SHATT AL-'ARAB AND ITS AFTERMATH

The April 1969 Shatt al'-Arab confrontation was the third time within a decade that the question of rights in the waterway figured prominently in Iran-Iraq relations. It was also the most important incident in Iran-Iraq relations in the period under consideration, for it symbolized a new and much wider rivalry between the two.

The immediate antecedents of the breakdown and the course of the April 1969 incident need not concern us here. The superficial improvement of relations had appeared jeopardized by the failure of the Iran-Iraq delegations to reach preliminary agreement in their discussions in Baghdad. The essence of the impasse was the wide gap in their respective stances. Iran wanted a new treaty based on accepted "principles of international law," which it believed included the concept of a *thalweg* or median line in the division of waterways. The Iraqis insisted that the 1937 treaty, in which the border was on the Iranian bank of the river, should be the basis for negotiations.

According to the official Iranian version, the principal cause of the April 1969 confrontation was the Iraqi government's behavior on April 15,[34] when the deputy foreign minister of Iraq summoned the Iranian ambassador to the foreign ministry and pointed out that since the Iraqi government considered the waterway Iraqi territory, it would require in the future that all ships flying the Iranian flag lower

---

[34] For reconstruction of events, see *Ravabet-e Khareji-e Iran dar Sale*, 1348, pp. 34–41, and *ibid.*, 1349, pp. 49–57.

their flags in the waterway, and that all Iranian nationals on board ships transiting Iraqi water disembark.

The Iranian response to what it viewed as an "ultimatum" was as rapid as it was firm. On April 19 the 1937 treaty was formally denounced in the Iranian Senate and declared abrogated as a result of Iraq's failure to abide by its provisions. This time the Iranian government, more sure of its capacity to deal with Iraq, moved swiftly to change the existing situation on the waterway. It placed its naval and air forces in the Gulf on full alert, and advised Baghdad that attempts at interference with Iranian shipping would result in conflict. To show its capability and resolve, it provided Iranian or Iran-bound shipping with military escort.[35]

In the face of the rapid and firm Iranian response, the Iraqi government backed down and made no attempt to enforce its threat, and the situation today remains much as it was prior to the crisis. Iranian *de facto* use of the waterway, with its flag flying and its nationals transiting Iraqi territorial waters, continues.

Prior to an analysis of the tactics employed by the two states from January 1970 to December 1971, we will sketch the salient features of their relations in the period remaining before the British departure.

If possible, Iran-Iraq relations in these two years went from bad to worse. The only interlude in this period of unrelieved hostility occurred between December 1970 and July 1971. During this period, both states halted their press and radio propaganda attacks while the oil-producing states closed ranks and found common cause in the Organization of Petroleum Exporting Countries (OPEC) to successfully pressure the Western oil companies for higher royalties.

This overlap of mutual interest and its successful insulation from the domain of high politics were nonetheless shortlived. The Iranian claim to three islands in the Gulf was resisted by the Iraqi government, and in July 1971 the propaganda truce ended. The two states had by this time created a chasm of such width between them that this limited cooperation assumed only marginal significance in their overall relations.[36]

---

35 For contemporary Western press accounts of the incident, see *The Times* (London), April 21, 22, 23, 24, 1969; *New York Times*, April 20, 23, 25, 26, 1969; *The Economist*, April 26, 1969, pp. 32–33; and *Le Figaro*, April 21, 1969. For official Persian sources, see *Ravabet-e Khareji-e Iran dar Sale*, 1349, pp. 49–57.

36 For one such report, see *Keyhan International* (weekly), Feb. 20, 1971. Cooperation in even a functionally autonomous area of mutual interest appears unlikely to

In two respects 1970 was an eventful year in Iran-Iraq relations and Gulf politics. The settlement, however temporary it may prove, by the Ba'thists of the Kurdish question in March 1970 gave them a freer hand with which to pursue a more active Gulf role. Similarly, the Iran-Bahrayn settlement through the auspices of the United Nations ended one of the principal impediments to Iran's Gulf diplomacy. These settlements allowed both states to concentrate their energies on wooing the small Gulf shaykhdoms and on maneuvering to weaken each other's position.

The dispute over the Iranian claim to three Gulf islands was the latest manifestation of their rivalry. But when Iraqi diplomacy was unable to arouse the other Arab states to form a solid anti-Iranian front over this dispute, the frustrated Iraqi government resorted to a by-now-familiar technique. In October it began the systematic process of expelling Iranian residents, which by the end of December involved approximately 30,000 people.[37] Finally, in answer to the Iranian occupation of the disputed islands at the end of November, the Iraqi government severed diplomatic relations with Iran and also with Britain for acting in "collusion" with Tehran and failing to act on its treaty obligations to prevent the invasion.

TACTICS AND ARGUMENTS EMPLOYED IN IRAN-IRAQ RIVALRY

The rivalry of the two states for predominant and perhaps exclusive influence in Gulf politics has been played out with the Gulf states as the audience and the judge. Before analyzing their tactics, instruments, and arguments, we must emphasize the differing and asymmetric aims of Iran and Iraq in the Gulf.

The Iranian government had not yet formulated a positive policy for the Gulf. Its primary aim was to ensure the security of the region and the unhindered passage of maritime traffic. It decided that the

---

recur in the immediate future. The intensity of the political rivalry has "spilled back" and politicized the area of oil cooperation. Thus in June 1972 the Shah, believing it was no longer in Iran's interest to present a solid front in backing the Iraq oil nationalization in OPEC, served notice that Iran would assure the West of a continued oil supply. In breaking the unanimity on which the strength of OPEC depends, he undermined the impact of Iraq's nationalization. See *The Times* (London), June 29, 1972; *New York Times,* June 26 and 27, 1972.

[37] The official Iranian figure for expellees between October 1971 and March 1972 is 44,941. See *Ravabet-e Khareji-e Iran dar Sale,* 1351, p. 72. Later Western sources place the figure closer to 60,000. See *New York Times,* January 1, 5, 9, and 31, 1972.

best means to achieve this end was to exclude nonlittoral states from any security arrangement and to seek cooperation with and between the Gulf states themselves. Its principal motivation, and the motor force driving it into cooperation with the Gulf states, was thus a preclusive aim: to prevent and deny their takeover by hostile non-Gulf states and to shore them up against disruptive local or domestic forces.

The Iraqi government's aim in the Gulf, at its maximum, can in contrast be viewed as a positive one: to seek to extend revolutionary movements to the Gulf and to encourage or sponsor such organizations as the Bahrayn Liberation Front and the Popular Front for the Liberation of the Occupied Gulf (based in Aden). At its minimum the aim became preclusive: to deny Iran the opportunity to cooperate with the Gulf Arab states.

In addition to the potential use of the dissident Kurds against Iran, the new Ba'thist government in Iraq sought to aid and abet the Iranian dissidents as a new instrument of pressure. The Baghdad government thus gave Teymur Bakhtiar, a discredited former Iranian state security chief, diplomatic status and a political sanctuary, facilitated his cooperation with other militant Iranian dissidents (such as the Communist Reza Radmanesh) in planning attacks on Iran, and used him in their hostile radio broadcasts beamed to Iran. The Iraqi government also reportedly encouraged and aided Iranian subversives in their guerrilla activities against the Iranian regime.[38]

In Gulf politics Iraq resorted to a number of tactics and arguments that resemble those used by Cairo in its propaganda war with Tehran in the mid-sixties. This was especially evident in its attempts to practice a diplomacy of polarization between Arab and Iranian, to isolate the Iranian government, and to make full use of the number of Arab states in the region, a natural and convenient constituency in regional politics on which Iran, as a non-Arab state, could not draw.

Like its Cairo counterpart, however, it found that though indubitable the rhetorical appeal of "Arabism" did not recommend itself as an all-embracing platform cutting across other Gulf issues as a guide to concerted action. Notable among these other issues were

---

[38] See *Ravabet-e Khareji-e Iran dar Sale,* 1349, p. 53; *Ettelaat* (air ed.), March 7, April 25 (editorial), Dec. 12, and Dec. 13, 1970 (editorial); *Ayandegan,* Sept. 22, and Dec. 23, 24, 28, and 29, 1970. See also *Ettelaat,* Aug. 23, 1971; and *Keyhan International* (weekly), Jan. 2, 1971. Iraqi attempts had little appeal to Iranians, in part because of Bakhtiar's great unpopularity. *The Times* (London), July 7, 1969.

the questions of Iraq's motives and the apprehension of the other Arab littoral states that there would be no one to guard the Iraqi guardian should they enter into closer cooperation in defense affairs with the Baghdad regime or entrust to it the formulation of a common Gulf policy. Thus Iraq, while enjoying with the other Gulf Arab states the (theoretical) advantage of its Arab nationality, has been handicapped in its relations with them by the caution and skepticism with which they have viewed its "revolutionary" regime and by its predecessors' claim to Kuwait. Basically, Iraq had resorted to three types of techniques in its competitive rivalry with Iran in the Gulf: (1) it has sought to undermine Iran by *accusations* regarding its intentions; (2) it has *pressured* all the Arab states, including those bordering the Gulf, to support its positions on Gulf issues; and (3) it has appealed to all the Arab states in the name of the Gulf's "Arabism" to work together against Iran.

The Iranian government has concentrated much of its energies on trying to discredit the Iraqi Ba'thist regime in the eyes of the Gulf Arab states. Its diplomacy has sought to accentuate those areas in which its aspirations coincide with those of its neighbors. The primary overlap of aims in the Gulf has been the interest shared by Iran and the shaykhdoms in ensuring local tranquility after the British withdrawal. The active pace of Iranian diplomacy seen in the Gulf since 1968 has been geared to spreading the recognition of this identity of interest in the traditional polities that comprise the Gulf's southern littoral. Iran has tried to project the image of a "natural protector" of the shaykhdoms in a potentially turbulent Gulf. As the only regional state possessing a significant military and naval capability, its aspiration to play the role of protector should be understood as protection from Iraq in the first instance, and secondarily from revolutionary movements in the Gulf, whether these were sponsored by a Gulf or non-Gulf state.

It was notable that the Iranian press picked up and pursued this theme of Iran's role as the natural protector of the Gulf states after the phrase was used in a French news-magazine, *L'Express*.[39] The same image was reflected in an article sympathetic to Iran published in a Beirut newspaper, *Al-Hayat*. Commenting on the shaykhs' attitudes, it observed:

---

[39] For the original article, see *L'Express*, No. 979, April 13–19, 1970, p. 25. For Iranian press commentary on this theme, see *Ettelaat* (air ed.), April 13, 14 (editorial), and 17, 1970.

The rulers realize what "the danger of Red infiltration" means, and how it threatens to dominate the whole Gulf. Furthermore, the Gulf rulers seem to have confidence in the attitude of Iran.[40]

While seeking to buttress the image of a benevolent and satisfied elder brother, the Iranian government sought to portray Iraq as a rapacious black sheep in the Gulf family. Frequent accusations of its sponsorship of subversion in Iran were made and much publicity was given to Iraqi defectors who criticized the Baghdad regime's unpopularity and decadence.[41] The Iraqi government was depicted as an anti-religious regime pursuing an anti-Arab policy and deeply involved in subversion and agitation in the region. Its anti-Arab policy was evidenced, it was alleged, by its failure to aid the Arab cause against Israel, and its connections with unnamed outside powers, which was said to account for its belligerency in the Gulf.[42]

To lend credence to these accusations and to pursue its own brand of polarization among the Arab states, a favorite Iranian tactic was to harp on Iraq's feuds with other Arab states. Iraq's declaration in February 1970 that as a result of its dispute with Iran, and the Kurdish problem, it was unable to confront Israel, was thus sarcastically reported by Iranian newspapers.[43]

But it was Iraq's differences with Egypt which were of most interest to Iran, for it was Nasser and Egypt's policies which could determine the failure or success of the united Arab front sought by Iraq. Baghdad's generally belligerent attitude lent considerable support to this objective. In trying to convince the Arab world of the dangers to the "Arabism" of the Gulf and the seriousness of the issues which it equated with that of Palestine, the Iraqi government sought general Arab approval both for its leadership and championing of the Arab cause in the Gulf and their acceptance of its subsequent inability to contribute to the Israeli front.

The implications of the Iraqi tactics were not lost on the Egyptian leadership; in exchange for championing the Arab cause in the Gulf, the Iraqi government would obtain a free hand in Gulf politics while at the same time being exempted from any need to contribute to the Arab cause against Israel. The Egyptian leaders showed little en-

---

40 *Al-Hayat* (Beirut), May 25, 1970, quoted in *Record of the Arab World*, p. 3200.

41 For Iranian accusations of subversion see in particular *Keyhan International* (weekly), Jan. 2, 1971.

42 This is illustrated in *Ettelaat* (air ed.) editorials of Aug. 8, and Oct. 18 and 19, 1970; *Ettelaat*, July 16, 1970; *Keyhan International* (weekly) editorials of June 2, 1970, and Nov. 6, 1971; *Peygham-e Imruz*, July 28, 1970.

43 *Ettelaat*, Feb. 21, 1970.

thusiasm toward such a scheme. After all, in exchange for this potential springboard to Arab leadership and rivalry with Egypt, the one card the Iraqi government held, that of curbing its attacks on Egypt's search for a diplomatic solution in its conflict with Israel, was not very tempting.[44]

If Iranian diplomacy in some measure neutralized Egypt as a potential supporter of Iraq, it should not be supposed that Iraq's failure to create a solid anti-Iranian Arab front was also due to Iranian statecraft. To be sure, Iranian diplomacy was active but it was not necessarily well guided or effective. No sooner had Tehran dropped its claim to Bahrayn than it activated its claim to the islands of Abu Musa and the Greater and Lesser Tumbs, giving the shaykhdoms new pause about Iranian intentions.

The attempt by the Iranian government in March–July 1970 to seek a formal defense grouping with Sa'udi Arabia and Kuwait seemed predicated both on a misreading of its inter-Arab implications and a failure to adequately assess its utility to Iran. Nor could Iranian intentions, however well phrased, be considered any more trustworthy than Iraq's. Iran's attempts to bypass the Iraqi regime to create a defense system with Sa'udi Arabia and Kuwait were bound to fail, if only because such moves were blatantly divisive of the Arab states of the Gulf, evoking on Iraq's part the July 1970 Al-Bakr proposal for an Arab defense organization—a suggestion equally doomed to failure for its similar inability to appreciate the smaller states' reluctance to become entangled in Iraqi-Iranian disputes.

Just as it used its rivalry with Egypt earlier in the decade to mobilize public opinion and a sense of nationalism, and to increase defense expenditure, so has the Iranian government used its later dispute with Iraq. The Iraqi representative's statements in the United Nations in 1969 and 1970, implying that Iran was an alien in the Gulf, were particularly singled out. In February the Iranian Foreign Minister explained the increase in Iran's defense budget thus: "We have no alternative but to resort to defense measures when the Iraqi delegate to the UN claims that Iran is an alien power in the Persian Gulf." [45] The Shah himself alluded to the same remarks more than a year after they were originally made.[46]

---

[44] For two fine discussions of Iraq-Egypt relations which have the ring of authenticity and are corroborated by other sources and subsequent events, see *Keyhan International*, Aug. 10 and 12, 1970.

[45] Quoted on Tehran Home Service, in Persian, Feb. 23, 1970.

[46] See the text of the Shah's speech, *Keyhan International* (weekly), Oct. 10, 1970.

SUMMARY

Iran-Iraq relations in the years from 1959 to 1971 have been almost uniformly poor. No progress has been made on the resolution of the differences between the states that revolve around their mutual frontier, the Shatt al-'Arab, the oil fields straddling the border, the continental shelf, and the rights and responsibilities of the two states toward Iranians residing in or visiting Iraq on pilgrimages. Although the climate of relations improved in the premiership of Dr. Abd al-Rahman Bazzaz—i.e., during the Presidency of the second Arif—no substantive progress was made on these issues. It was noted that the Iranian government did not differentiate the character of the Bazzaz government from other Iraqi governments, and it was suggested that domestic politics and inter-Arab politics have been an important constraint hindering and at times precluding the possibility of Iraqi compromise with Iran. It was also observed that the Iranian government's reaction to the various crises and confrontations between the states has undergone a modification reflecting its increased power and changing priorities in foreign affairs. Thus, from being on the defensive in 1959 and succumbing to Iraqi pressure in 1961, it has since 1965 seized the initiative. It has utilized the Kurds as a lever against Iraq and taken a hard line on the Shatt al-'Arab since 1969. The tendency for differences between the states in one area to spread and cover other areas in their relations was noted.

It was emphasized that the announcement of the impending British withdrawal from the Gulf amplified the stakes of the differences between Iran and Iraq on the Shatt al-'Arab and lent their rivalry on the waterway a symbolic dimension. The rivalry was now transformed into a question of which state was to achieve hegemony in the Gulf, and has spread into competitive relations in all spheres. This period was characterized by the complete deterioration of relations until they were severed in December 1971 by Iraq. Finally, it was concluded that Iraq's failure to mobilize the Gulf Arab states against Iran was due chiefly to its own inept diplomacy and only marginally due to Iranian statecraft.

Chapter V

IRAN AND THE PERSIAN GULF, 1958–1967

Although never a maritime power, Iran in the past made brief and short-lived attempts to build, purchase, and maintain a navy. Nader Shah in 1748, Nasser-ud-din Shah in 1885, and Reza Shah in 1932 all built or purchased small numbers of ships. There were however two principal impediments to the development of Iran's navy and indeed that of the south: Iran's preoccupation with Russia in the nineteenth century, and the degree of government control and internal cohesion necessary to impose its authority on the provinces—which fluctuated between periods of semi-autonomy and periods of subservience to the central government. In addition, Britain's presence and its interdict on naval warfare, while applying in theory only to the trucial principalities, in practice extended to all Gulf states. The lack of an Iranian navy, which reflected rather than caused its vulnerability, left the government powerless to resist foreign naval pressure. Starting with the Dutch attack on Qishm island in the 17th century, and continuing with Britain's occupation of Kharg island (1838–1842, 1852–1857) and Britain's periodic naval pressure, *inter alia,* in 1885, 1932, and 1951, Iran remained exposed to states possessing superior naval power. In addition Iran's possessions in the Gulf varied with the size and effectiveness of her fleet; in the eighteenth century at various times the islands of Qishm, Kharg, and Bahrayn were lost, while at other times these islands were regained and to them were added Muscat and Oman. The possession of even a small fleet enabled the central government to enforce its writ in the south, to the extent of preventing smuggling and arms traffic and protecting its territories from the depredations of local pirates. Iran's present interest in the Gulf and in a navy cannot thus be divorced from its historical experience.

EFFECTS OF BRITISH PRESENCE IN THE GULF

The British presence had psychological consequences for Iranian attitudes towards the Gulf, and emphasized the country's weakness, vulnerability, and dependence, but not all of the effects of the British hegemony in the Gulf were equally deleterious. The British presence and the establishment of a system of quasi-protectorates on the Arabian littoral brought peace and security to the region. It brought peace to the often warring Arab tribal principalities on the southern shore, and between the latter and Iran, by freezing territorial disputes, and it brought security for the local states vis-à-vis non-Gulf states. It insulated the Arab shaykhdoms from the political vicissitudes of the outside world by orienting them eastwards towards India. It thus isolated them from the tremors of politics in the Arab west until approximately the 1956 Suez episode.

While prohibiting Iranian expansion in the Gulf, the British by virtue of their dominant presence in the Gulf also brought Iran a measure of security (particularly in the postwar world of 1945 to 1971) by allowing Iran to concentrate its energies inward and northward. In this period Britain's military presence, balanced by a United States economic and political presence, by guaranteeing Iran's security in the south gave the Iranian government a valuable breathing-space to attend to more pressing issues, without diluting and scattering its limited resources in the south. In this postwar world it was perhaps natural that a new Iran-Great Britain relationship should emerge. No longer totally dependent on Britain, the Iranian government came to perceive the advantages of a British presence in the Gulf. Sir William Luce, a senior British official in the Gulf, noted this: "To the Shah, with his fear of the spread of Nasserism eastwards, the British presence in the Gulf has been an important factor for the security of his country." [1]

The overlap in Iran-Great Britain interests, which lies beyond the

---

[1] Sir William Luce was governor of Aden from 1956 to 1960, political resident in the Gulf from 1961 to 1966, and Britain's special representative in the Gulf, with the task of easing the problems involved in Britain's departure, in 1970–71. The quote is from his "Britain in the Gulf; Mistaken Timing over Aden," p. 279.

scope of this work,[2] is best glimpsed in the similar attitude both states adopted towards Nasser and the Yemen war (as contrasted with that adopted by the United States). Nonetheless, it was clear after Britain's departure from India and Palestine in the 1940's, and her accelerated imperial disengagement in the two subsequent decades, that her days in the Gulf were numbered. Thus as Iran's resources increased in the mid-1960's and the security of her northern border seemed more assured, she devoted an increased proportion of her energies to the south. The British government's announcement in February 1966 of its intention to withdraw from the crown colony of Aden by the end of the following year served to confirm the impression that its departure was imminent. The way in which this departure was conducted—that is, Britain's withdrawal from the Aden base without providing a defense treaty for the South Arabian Federation—may well have undermined the confidence of the Gulf's rulers in Britain's role as protector.[3]

THE EVOLUTION OF IRANIAN INTERESTS IN THE GULF

Starting with the Suez incident of 1956, the wall of British protection around the Gulf states began to crumble. Interest in politics and Arab unity and news of developments elsewhere in the Arab world, fostered by Cairo's radio programs, grew apace. The revolution in Iraq in 1958, Tehran's rift with Cairo in 1960, and the Kuwait incident of 1961 all drew Iran's interest towards the Gulf.[4]

The Gulf has been intimately linked with Persian nationalist and cultural mythology, and its symbolic dimension in Iranians' perceptions of Persia's past greatness and historical heritage should not be minimized. The tenacity with which the Iranian government clung to its claims in the Gulf, and its sensitivity to correct use of its name, reflect this jealousy of past history as well as the internal political aspect of questions affecting the Gulf. The Iranian leadership, doubt-

---

[2] There is a great deal of literature available on Britain and the Persian Gulf, 1945–1971, mostly in the form of British newspaper articles, periodicals, and memoirs.

[3] See Sir William Luce's "Aden's Shadow Over the Gulf," *Daily Telegraph* (London), April 12, 1966.

[4] For example, Egypt's break with Iran in 1960 was attributed by one Iranian source to Cairo's jealousy of Iran's relationship with the shaykhdoms. See *Ettelaat*, August 9, 1960.

less well aware of the nation's pride in its past, could ill afford to lag behind in any race to prove its own nationalist credentials. There is thus ample evidence of an Iranian interest in the Gulf in the late 1950's and early 1960's, at a time when Iran was unable to give concrete expression to this interest. The following quotations are from a press conference on September 27, 1958 and illustrate this interest:

Questioner: The source of our biggest income, oil, is exported through the Gulf. Moreover, we are embarking on oil extraction from the offshore areas. All these require that we should be strong in this area and that we should have a strong navy.

The Shah: Iran's supremacy over the Persian Gulf is a natural thing. We already have this and shall enhance it in the future.[5]

In a press conference a year later, the Shah was again asked whether efforts were being made to strengthen the Iranian navy. He replied: "Iran once had a first-class navy, and it is fitting that she should regain her position among maritime nations. . . ." [6] Five months later, in answering a different question, the Shah returned to the same theme: "We are doing everything we can to regain our historic and natural position in the Persian Gulf." [7] The Shah again referred to an Iranian navy in his memoirs published in 1961, where he wrote: "Since we are the dominant power in the Persian Gulf, we must rapidly strengthen our navy." [8]

These references clearly indicate the Iranian leadership's interest in Gulf affairs, which is tempered by a recognition of the material constraints that preclude a translation of that interest into an active Gulf role. They also illustrate the theme of nationalism discussed earlier. This belief in Iran's "natural right" in the Gulf, combined with glorification of Iran's earlier history, has persisted to the present day.

THE KUWAIT INCIDENT, 1961

The June 1961 assertion by Iraq of claim to Kuwait came at a time of poor Iran-Iraq relations. As a result of Britain's management of Kuwait's foreign affairs, the Iranian government had no formal ties with that state at the outbreak of the crisis. But reportedly this was

---

[5] See "Press Conferences of His Imperial Majesty Mohammad Reza Shah Pahlavi of Iran," 1958–59, p. 8. For comments on the same lines, see press conference of Jan. 24, 1959, pp. 59–60.

[6] The press conference took place on Nov. 28, 1959. See "Press Conferences," p. 48.

[7] This press conference was on April 23, 1960; see *ibid.*, 1960–61, p. 15.

[8] See the Shah's *Memoirs,* p. 311.

not for lack of trying, as Iran had attempted without success to establish a consular representative in Kuwait a few years earlier.[9] In order to allow Kuwait's diplomats to acquire experience, Britain had in practice relinquished control of Kuwait's foreign relations several months prior to the formal announcement of that state's independence in June. Thus it was in this transitional period, in February 1961, that it was announced that Iran and Kuwait would shortly establish consulates to facilitate closer cultural and commercial ties. The Egyptian government applied for permission to open a consulate in May. The announcement of Britain's relinquishment of control of Kuwait's foreign relations, and hence Kuwait's achievement of full independence in June 1961, were welcomed by the Shah in a congratulatory telegram to the Shaykh of Kuwait.[10] On July 8, 1961 an Iranian delegation visited Kuwait on a three day goodwill mission as a guest of the Kuwait ruler.[11]

The actual assertion by Iraq of a claim to Kuwait, and the subsequent repercussions of its threat to annex it to Iraq, need not detain us here. It is sufficient to note that the Iranian government supported the territorial integrity of Kuwait as far as her meager resources, domestic fragility, and preoccupations elsewhere permitted. The Iraq claim was protested by Iranian extreme nationalist groups such as the Pan-Iranist party.[12] When during June, as a result of an Iraq embargo on the sale of provisions and food to Kuwait, serious consequences appeared likely, the shortage was met by Iranian supplies of food. Between 70 and 100 launches loaded with food crossed the Gulf's waters every day. And when Iraqi naval patrols fired on these launches and threatened to block this source of supply, it was reported that the Iranian navy was instructed to protect these motor launches.[13] The Iranian government also allowed Britain the use of its airspace (as did Turkey) during the incident. It supported the move to replace British troops with those of the Arab League, and it subsequently backed Kuwait's application for membership as a sovereign state in the United Nations.

The Iranian government was also prepared to risk the consequences of recognizing Kuwait despite the Iraq Foreign Minister Hashim Jawad's warning in December 1961 that his country would reconsider

---

9 *Iran Almanac*, 1962.

10 *Tehran Journal*, June 27, 1961.

11 *Iran Almanac*, 1962, p. 144.

12 *Tehran Journal*, July 1, 1961.

13 See *Tehran Journal*, June 28, and July 1 and 3, 1961; *New York Times*, June 30, 1961.

its relations with any state establishing diplomatic relations with Kuwait. In October 1961 Iran's first ambassador to Kuwait was named.[14] On March 5, 1962, Kuwait's first ambassador arrived in Tehran, and on March 18 Iraq recalled its ambassador from Tehran in protest.[15] In June the Kuwait embassy in Tehran was officially inaugurated. That same month, on the first anniversary of Kuwait's independence, two Iranian delegations, one official and the other unofficial, visited that state. After the visits *Ettelaat* reported that the government of Kuwait was eager to establish closer relations with Iran.[16]

As far as affecting the unfolding of the Kuwait incident itself, the Iranian government's response to the Iraq claim was of minor significance—much more important were the responses of the governments of Britain and Egypt. The latter, while not supporting Britain's continued presence in the Gulf, could not concede to Iraq, its rival, the right unilaterally to acquire Kuwait or other valuable Arab land.

Iraq's claim to Kuwait surely served notice on the Iranian government of the possibility of more such claims in a future *without* a British presence in the Gulf. It may have underscored the need for a similar staking out of claims by Tehran and more attention to the Gulf. (It must be emphasized that the Iranian government has been unable to see analogies between its own historically based claims and similar claims by the Arab states.) The 1961 episode was, at the very least, a sharp reminder to Tehran of the importance of the Gulf in the future, and in particular after the British departure. At the same time, the effects of the British presence were equivocal; while probably instrumental in preventing Kuwait's annexation, it also aggravated and inflamed Arab nationalism everywhere, including Kuwait, by interjecting the question of British-Western imperialism into local politics. The failure of the Iraq governments' claim to Kuwait was due in large measure to the opposition of other Arab states. Qasim and Nasser agreed that Britain's relationship with Kuwait "was as patent a case of imperialism as could be found in any textbook," [17]

---

14 He was Mohammad Hajeb Davaloo, a 70-year-old career diplomat; see *Tehran Journal*, Oct. 23, 1961.

15 *Tehran Journal*, March 6, 1962.

16 *Ettelaat* (editorial), June 25, 1962. See also *Iran Almanac*, 1963, p. 179; *Tehran Journal*, June 18, 1962.

17 Richard Gott, "The Kuwait Incident," in D. C. Watt (ed.), *Survey of International Affairs*, 1961, pp. 522–523.

but were unable to agree on what to do about it. This might logically have raised a question on the following lines in the minds of Iranian policymakers: "What are the implications for Iranian foreign relations if Egypt and Iraq can, in the future, agree on what to do in Gulf politics?" A rerun of the Kuwait incident after a British departure, this time with Egypt supporting Iraq, would call for an Iranian response. The Kuwait incident was one precipitant of increased Iranian attention to Gulf affairs.

The second major precipitant was the war in Yemen, which started in 1962 and developed into a rivalry between Sa'udi Arabia and Egypt. Iran's relations with Egypt had been cut in 1960 (see Chapter III), and the Shah distrusted Nasser's pretensions to Arab leadership, particularly as they implied the right to export republicanism and share in the Arab oil wealth in the Persian Gulf. Iran's response was to close ranks with Sa'udi Arabia to contain Nasser's intrusion into the region. The serious threat posed by the Egyptian leader to Iran's interests, as they were understood in Tehran, spurred Iran's interest in the Gulf.

DEVELOPMENT OF THE SOUTH AND POLITICS

Apart from the historical interest in the Gulf outlined above, and the indications of renewed interest in Iran illustrated by the Shah's statements and newspaper coverage, there has been another dimension to this interest. This has taken the form, common in nationalism, of the nation's recreation of a particular past, which is imbued with a selective and symbolic mythical content—namely, Iran's past involvement in the Gulf—which is thus exaggerated and grandiosely reinterpreted to serve present political objectives. There is a strong flavor of this in contemporary discussions of Iran's former role in the Gulf, and a heady aroma of *mare nostrum* prevails in the Iranian attitude to the Gulf.

Iran's interests in the Gulf, nonetheless, are as many and as varied as they are serious and indubitable. Comprising some 1300 kilometers of Iran's coastline from the Shatt al-'Arab to the Gulf of Oman, the Gulf is Iran's only maritime outlet to the rest of the world. It is thus a vital lifeline for the country's commerce for both imports and exports (the latter for both oil and non-oil products). Unlike Iraq and Sa'udi Arabia, Iran possesses no pipeline to the Mediterranean; thus she is disproportionately dependent on transit of the Gulf for her oil exports. Secondly, and from the strategic perspective, Iran has vital interests in the Gulf. These are: to ensure the maintenance of free navigation in the Gulf; to protect vulnerable and costly oil installations (and cargoes) from damage and sabotage; and to guard against, if not prevent, the entrenchment of "unfriendly" Arab movements or regimes in the nearby Gulf states. For the successful establishment of such a movement in a Gulf state might allow interference with Gulf traffic, or become a forward base for implementing Arab claims to Khuzistan province. Finally, the Gulf was of interest to Iran both for its proximity to the rich oil fields of the southwest and for the oil-rich continental shelf that lay beneath its contested waters.

Even without its preoccupation with the Soviet Union, it is doubtful that the Iranian government had the resources or wherewithal in the early 1960's to tackle the problems involved in developing the south on other than a piecemeal basis. The terrain between Tehran and the southwestern provinces is rugged, in part mountainous, and communications were poor. The writ of the central government had rarely extended to the coastal provinces before the Reza Shah period, and there remained there the habit of autonomy. In addition to the paucity of development in the hinterland, the southern ports were inadequate for Iran's burgeoning needs. The oil industry in the south remained, in the fifties, an enclave in the economy, with little linkage to the nation's social fabric and its economic life.

The Shatt al-'Arab incidents of December 1959 and March 1961 underlined a serious problem confronting Iran's commerce. Abadan, Iran's major port for the export of oil, lay in contested waters vulnerable to Iraq pressure. In addition, because of the shallowness of the channel of the Shatt al-'Arab leading to Abadan, and tidal conditions therein, that port could not accommodate the new and increasingly used oil supertankers. As a result of these political and economic considerations, it was apparent that a new port site was needed which could at once accommodate supertankers and be under exclusive, and uncontested, Iranian sovereignty. The port of Mah-Shahr on the Khor-Musa inlet was chosen for intensive development, partially to replace Abadan; it is thus a major port for the export of refined oil products. More important was the development of Kharg island as an oil terminal. The island, some 25 miles off the Iranian coast, six miles long and two and a half miles wide, is situated close enough to the oil fields of Gachsaran and Agha Jari to contemplate its conversion into an offshore oil terminal. In 1959 work began on the construction of pipelines from the mainland fields to the island, and exports started in 1963. Today Kharg island is the world's largest oil export terminal, connected to the mainland by four 30-inch pipelines, and the island has a large storage capacity and extensive berthing facilities to accommodate the largest tankers.[18] Korramshahr, which is in the Shatt al-'Arab, remains the principal Iranian port for general (i.e., non-oil) cargo. Its principal advantage over other ports has been its ample connections to the hinterland.

With the economic boom of the mid-1960's the government was able to devote more resources to the Gulf area. As a part of its general interest in developing the economy of the region (which by the close of the decade was reflected in the development of a dam complex in Khuzistan, a sugar refinery project, a petro-chemical complex, a microwave communications system, and the development of agro-industries), it turned especially to the modernization of its southern ports which increasingly threatened to prove bottlenecks in its export trade. With the assistance of a United States (Agency for International Development) loan, a twenty-million-dollar project to develop the port of Bandar Abbas, which is situated near the strategic Hormoz straits, began in 1964. Roads linking this port to the hinterland and Afghanistan were constructed. The modernization program was intended to attract merchant shipping as well as to accommodate the projected increase in the size of the navy.[19] It was followed in August 1965 by an agreement with Dutch, Swedish, and German firms to convert Bushehr into a modern port. It was subsequently decided to expand the port still further to accommodate the berthing of large naval craft.[20] The authorities did not neglect the smaller ports (Persian, *Bandar*): Bandar Shahpur (east of Abadan), Bandari-Jask, Bandar-e-Dayyer and Bander-e-Lengeh were all developed and expanded.[21]

From the evidence available, it appears that the Shah was himself personally and enthusiastically involved in the decisions affecting the development of the south. In the records of the High Economic Council he is depicted as the principal mover for emphasis on the south. He discusses the modernization of the ports of Bushehr and Bandar Abbas and raises the question of German participation in these projects.[22] He stresses the importance of developing the southern ports for facilitating the movement of cargo and requests an expert

18 Dr. R. Ghirshman, *The Island of Kharg* (Tehran: Iranian Oil Operating Companies; 2nd ed., 1964); and D. M. Cullum, "The Kharg Story," which puts the cost of the development of Kharg up to 1968 at approximately 60 million pounds, p. 1.

19 *Middle East Economic Digest*, IX, No. 47 (Dec. 10, 1965), 555 (hereafter cited as *MEED*); also K. G. Fenelon, *The Trucial States*, p. 59.

20 *MEED*, XI, No. 11 (March 16, 1967), 244.

21 *MEED*, XI, No. 4 (Jan. 26, 1967), 78; and X, No. 36 (Sept. 30, 1966), 466. The interest in the south was reflected in the Shah's visit to Bandar Abbas. See *Keyhan*, Nov. 11, 1967.

22 *Shoray-e 'Ali-e–Eghtesadi*, I, April 14, 1965, p. 70.

study of the potential of these ports.[23] He is seen raising the possibility of the acquisition of Hovercraft or Hydro-foil (air-cushion) vessels, in the Gulf. And when a subsequent report denied the feasibility of their use in the Gulf, due to the high winds in the region, the Shah reacts skeptically comparing the report with his own personal observations elsewhere and asks for further study of the matter.[24] Iran subsequently, in the autumn of 1967, ordered ten Hovercraft for coastal patrol-work from Britain, and received these in March 1968.[25]

Iran's changed priorities and increasing interest in the Gulf, *inter alia* as a result of the political precipitants noted above, was reflected in the disposition of its armed forces. In April 1964 a joint military exercise with the United States (Operation Delaware) partially reassured Tehran of Washington's continued interest in the region. Annual military exercises under the auspices of CENTO known as MIDLINK continued with an increased Iranian naval component. In March 1965 the Shah publicly declared that Iran's military would in the future pay special attention to the Gulf. In the autumn of that year a 400-million-dollar arms appropriation was passed by the Majlis, a large proportion of which was devoted to the navy.[26] In the spring of 1967 the Iranian government announced formation of a new Third Army Corps which was to be based in the southern city of Shiraz. The modernization of the southern ports and the development of naval forces were thus well under way by January 1968. They reflected the Iranian government's newfound ability to give concrete form to its interests in the Gulf. This was made possible by a diminution of Soviet threats, a more stable domestic polity, and a buoyant economy. And it was accelerated by fear of Nasser's radicalization of the Gulf states.

Whether this response was adequate to the challenge purportedly posed in the Gulf by Nasser is questionable. The coastline of the seven trucial states extends for nearly four hundred miles from the frontier of the Sultanate of Muscat and Oman to Khor al-Odaid on the Qatar peninsula. The total area of the trucial states is approximately 36,000 square miles, and the population in 1960 numbered approximately 120,000. While all the rulers of the trucial states, as well as Qatar

---

23 *Ibid.*, I, July 11, 1966, p. 273.

24 *Ibid.*, I, Aug. 22, 1966, pp. 285–286; and II, Oct. 4, 1966, pp. 4–5.

25 Costing 3½ million pounds, eight of these were small, of the SRN-6 model, and two were BH-7, 40-ton models. See *MEED*, XI, No. 37 (Oct. 5, 1967), p. 669.

26 See *Ettelaat*, March 10 and Nov. 10, 1965; and *MEED*, X, No. 32 (Sept. 2, 1966), p. 394.

and Bahrayn, had entrusted the conduct of their foreign relations to Britain, the latter did not prohibit contact between them and friendly states.[27] The shaykhs of Dubay, Ras al-Khaymah, Ajman, and Qatar visited Iran in September–November 1959. In 1962 the shaykhs of Dubay, Abu Dhabi, and Sharjah also paid visits, the shaykh of Dubay returning again in 1965. In return, in 1962 an Iranian delegation visited Dubay to inaugurate the opening of an Iranian school in that principality.[28] Nor was it uncommon for the rulers of the Gulf shaykhdoms to spend time in southern Iran or visit the country for hunting or falconry expeditions, sometimes staying on property they owned in Shiraz or near the Caspian Sea. Relations between heads of state were marked by occasional acts of generosity such as Shaykh Shakhbut of Abu Dhabi's gift of 25,000 pounds to Iranian earthquake victims.[29]

Occasional contacts between heads of state apart, the Iranian government did not take an active interest in the development of the Gulf states. Iran's position was thus not comparable to that of Kuwait in assuming responsibility for, and interest in, the development of the poorer states (which today include 'Ajman, Ras al-Khaymah, Umm al-Qaywayn, Fujayrah, and Sharjah, but in the early sixties also included Abu Dhabi). Unlike Kuwait and later Sa'udi Arabia, Iran did not contribute to the costs of medical clinics, dispensaries, or educational costs therein. Admittedly Iranian diplomacy was handicapped at this time by its differences with Nasser, its various claims in the Gulf, and the issue of Iranian immigration. Nonetheless, there is no indication that Tehran took any interest in supporting the various development boards and agencies aimed at assisting the economic growth of the Gulf states. Iranian diplomacy was characterized, rather, by excessive and strident defensiveness which translated itself into a confused policy of asserting rights without acknowledging commensurate responsibilities. The Iran government's one, and apparently only, object was to deny the shaykhdoms to Nasser. It thus confined its diplomatic energy to actions like protesting the name proposed for a unified currency in

---

27 Donald Hawley, British political agent in Dubayy, 1958–1961, has written: "It was never part of the British policy to stand in the way of approaches which might genuinely further a ruler's interest." Hawley, *The Trucial States*, p. 183.

28 See *Saliyaneh-e Vezarat-e Omur-e Kharejeh, 1341* (1962), pp. 69–70, 72; *Iran Almanac*, 1962, p. 144, and 1963, p. 180; and *Tehran Journal*, Sept. 2, 17, and 25, Oct. 6, and Nov. 11, 1959, and Aug. 27, 1962. The Shaykh of Qatar returned again in 1963. See *Ettelaat*, Dec. 3, 1963.

29 Maj. Clarence Mann, *Abu Dhabi: Birth of an Oil Sheikhdom*, p. 113n. Shakhbut was not known for his generosity.

the shaykhdoms, "the Arabian Gulf riyal," [30] but left little of positive
achievement for the record. Given this attitude, the Iran government
was unable to accept or even privately admit that there was a side
other than an opportunist one to the Egyptian presence. Despite the
plethora of evidence that the presence of Egyptian nationals in the
shaykhdoms did not *ipso facto* indicate an Egyptian plot (any more
than Iranian immigrants in the Gulf states were instruments of Iranian
expansion), the Iran government clung to the view that Egypt could
only be attempting to take over the shaykhdoms. Thus, instead of
acknowledging that there was a real need in the shaykhdoms for the
kind of organization and skills that the Egyptians supplied, and instead of offering the Gulf states an alternative source of supply from
Iran, it limited its diplomacy until 1967 to asserting its own rights in
the Gulf.

The Iran government's official position seemed rather confused: it
asserted on the one hand that Gulf security rested on the littoral states
and that it could not tolerate the economic or political domination or
exploitation of the area "under any guise," while on the other hand
it conceded that the peoples of the area had a right to self-determina-
tion and to voluntary integration.[31] While denying Egypt the right to
cooperate with the Gulf Arab states, the Iranian government failed
to offer these states an alternative. It denied that Egyptian technicians,
as Arabs, had any right in the shaykhdoms, and viewed them as instruments of their government's annexationist policy, while remaining
oblivious to the logical analogy that uneducated Iranian immigrants
in the shaykhdoms might be open to a similar charge. In brief, Iran
conducted a shrill defensive diplomacy prior to 1967, in which there
was little evidence of constructive foresight and little assumption of
positive responsibility toward its tiny neighbors. The augmentation of
Iranian military capabilities in the Gulf replaced, even substituted for,
diplomacy in Iran's foreign relations in the Gulf. It was this general
orientation that prompted *The Economist*'s correspondent to observe
in 1966: "From the Arabian shore of the Gulf, Iran appears alien, even
irrelevant." [32] This attitude was modified in 1967–1968. Indicative of
this change was the resurrection in January 1968 of the former Persian Gulf section of the foreign ministry, which had faded into bu-

---

[30] See A. Massudi, *Didari az Shaykh-Neshinha*, p. 34; and *The Economist*, June 4,
1966, pp. 1077–1078.

[31] This confusion is reflected in the tortuous description of Iran's relations with
the Gulf states and Egypt in "Iran's Foreign Relations in 1346," (1967–68), *Vezarat-e
Kharejeh*, pp. 33–34, and in Massudi, *Didari az Shaykh-Neshinha*, pp. 103–106.

[32] *The Economist*, June 4, 1966, p. 1078.

reaucratic obscurity, and its revitalization under its present title of the ninth political section.

IRANIAN EMIGRANTS

For centuries the coastal inhabitants of the Persian Gulf had crossed from one shore to the other in the course of their commercial, fishing, or pearling activities. It was as natural for the coastal peoples to give as little thought to the concept of "frontiers" as their nomadic Bedouin brethren gave to land boundaries. With the establishment of the modern nation-state and the enhancement of the state's authority in outlying areas, and the delineation and demarcation of frontiers, the unregulated flow of peoples to and from other countries declined, but continued at a somewhat slower tempo. What to the modern bureaucrat of a central government was "illegal immigration/emigration" (i.e. entry without exit/entry visa, passport, or fee) was to the peoples of the Gulf, many of whom share a common tribal ancestry, the continued exercise of a time-honored practice, of moving to and fro between the central areas adjacent to the Gulf's waters in order to earn a livelihood.

The historical movement between the Gulf's coasts was accelerated by the discovery of oil and consequent economic boom in the coastal shaykhdoms of the Gulf. Lacking the populace and expertise, the pattern has been for the newly-thriving principality to welcome at first the floating intelligentsia, mercantile class, and mobile labor force that is found in the Gulf. These groups consist of Iranians, Indians, Pakistanis, and emigré Arabs, often Palestinians and Egyptians. By 1959 a large segment of the population of the Arab territories in the Gulf, in some cases more than half, was foreign-born. As *The Times* (London) observed: "These foreigners cannot be dispensed with, but they are tolerated rather than absorbed." [33] A decade later, except for Bahrayn where they constituted 25 percent, foreigners were reported to account for "no less than 50 percent of the total population" in the Arab oil-producing Gulf states." [34]

Although population figures in the region are notoriously unreliable, can be used to serve political ends, and probably understate the number of illegal Iranian immigrants, they nonetheless serve as general indicators of population size and composition. Of an estimated 40,000 population in 1959, Qatar was said to have 22,000 immigrants com-

---

[33] *The Times* (London), Feb. 26, 1959.
[34] Muhammad T. Sadik and William F. Snavely, *Bahrain, Qatar, and the United Arab Emirates: Colonial Past, Present Problems, and Future Prospects*, p. 28.

posed of Iranians, Indians, Palestinians, and Omanis.[35] In Dubay in
the mid-1960's, Iranians were thought to number "possibly 15,000" of
a total population of possibly four times that number.[36] In Abu Dhabi's
population of some 25,000 in the mid-1960's, at the start of the oil
boom, there was said to be an increasing expatriate and immigrant element. Although Abu Dhabi still lacked sizable communities of foreign
nationality, such as were present in Dubay, Qatar, and Kuwait, Indians and Iranian merchants "have begun to set up business as shopkeepers." [37]

A number of Iranians could also be found in the non-oil-producing
trucial shaykhdoms of Sharjah, Ajman, Ras al-Khaymah, Umm al-
Qaywayn, Fujayrah. Most of the inhabitants of the Gulf states are
Sunni Muslims (although a large number of Iranian Shi'a exist in
Dubay and Bahrayn), and except for Bahrayn, the Sunni majority and
dominance has not been challenged. The first official census of the trucial states of March–April 1968 revealed that over a third of the population had recently immigrated from abroad. It was estimated that in
March 1969 about 200 illegal immigrants were entering the trucial
states daily, and concern has been expressed that the indigenous Arabs
will soon be swamped by the newcomers.[38] The Gulf rulers are becoming concerned about this in the light of Kuwait's experience.

THE CASE OF BAHRAYN

It was principally with Bahrayn and Kuwait that the issue of Iranian immigration assumed diplomatic importance. Iran-Bahrayn relations were also strained by Tehran's claim to sovereignty over the
archipelago. In the light of this claim, the number of Iranians residing on the island could manifestly assume significant political impor-

---

[35] See *New York Times*, Nov. 25, 1959. The *New York Times*, April 8, 1964,
estimated a population comprised of 20,000 indigenous Arabs and 25 to 30,000
Iranians, Omanis, Indians, and non-Qatari Arabs. Iranian sources usually estimate
the number of Iranians higher than Western sources. Ahmad Eghtedari, *Khalij-e
Fars*, estimated that of some 50,000 Qataris, 20,000 were Iranian, p. 158. And Parviz
Mojtahedzade, *Khalij-e Fars*, gives a figure of 35,000 Iranians in a total population
of 100,000, pp. 161–162.

[36] Fenelon, *The Trucial States*, p. 48. Ahmad Eghtedari substantially agreed that
one in four of Dubay's population of 80,000 was Iranian. See *Khalij-e Fars*, p. 160.
Another Iranian source later estimated that 30 percent of a population of 80,000 was
Iranian. Mojtahedzade, *Khalij-e Fars*, p. 108.

[37] Fenelon, *The Trucial States*, pp. 36–37. Writing more than a decade after
Sanger, Fenelon seems to suggest that the presence of Iranian merchants in Abu
Dhabi is a new phenomenon, although Sanger had remarked on their existence in
1953.

[38] See *Area Handbook for the Peripheral States of the Arabian Peninsula*, p. 137.

tance if the claim were pressed, or if their numbers and residence were used as a pretext for annexation. In 1959, according to official Bahrayni statistics, there were 4,203 Iranians in the islands constituting 2.9 percent of the population; by 1965 there were 7,223, comprising 4 percent.[39] According to the 1965 census, 79 percent of the population was Bahrayni, 9 percent Sa'udi Arabian and Gulf Arab, 1.2 percent other Arabs, 5.1 percent Asian, and 1 percent European. The Iranian population is not new to the islands, some being descendants of the Persian colonists two centuries ago, yet "almost all the non-Bahrayni Arabs have entered the country since the discovery of petroleum." [40] There existed a religious dimension to Bahrayn's apprehension of Iran's claim to the islands, in that the Iranian population in Bahrayn were Shi'a Muslims. Although no official Bahrayn breakdown of the population into religious sects exists, it appears likely that at the start of the decade the Shi'a were in a slight majority, while by the end of the 1960's, as a result of (Arab) immigration, the Sunni had attained a slight edge in numbers. In the 1950's the Sunnis, while in a slight minority, had dominated the affairs of the archipelago and were afraid of losing their favored position.[41] The Sunni-Shi'a general strike in 1954 combined with the Iranian government's claim in 1957–58 caused considerable disquiet in Bahrayn about the role of the Iranians in these disturbances and their connection with Tehran's renewed claims. In general, Iranians and Arabs coexisted peacefully in Bahrayn, and many Iranians worked in the Bahrayn police force in Manamah. But owing to the Iranian claim, the ruler of Bahrayn was averse to admitting any more permanent Iranian settlers, although it proved difficult to control those who arrived at thinly-populated coastal villages. During the first two weeks of July 1960, 57 illegal immigrants from Iran were arrested, convicted, and deported. In August the Bahrayn government announced that illegal immigrants had totalled 208 in the preceding two months.[42] In the following year the Bahrayn immigration department was reportedly requested to "check the overpowering number of foreigners,

---

39 Government of Bahrayn, Population Census of 1965 as cited in Ali Humaidan, *Les Princes de l'or Noir: Evolution Politique du Golfe Persique* (Paris, 1968), p. 58. See also *New York Times*, Nov. 17, 1968.

40 *Area Handbook for the Peripheral States*, p. 135.

41 See Sir Rupert Hay, "The Impact of the Oil Industry on the Persian Gulf Shaykhdoms," pp. 362–365. In contrast, Richard Sanger, *The Arabian Peninsula*, pp. 140–141, suggests the Sunni were in a majority. David Holden, *Farewell to Arabia*, supports Hay and writes: "A strong strain of Persian blood among Bahrain's people and a majority of Shi'ite over Sunni Muslims both derive from the Persian years," p. 177. See also Fahim I. Qubain, "Social Classes and Tensions in Bahrain."

42 See *Middle East Record*, 1960, I, p. 404.

particularly Iranians" who were jeopardizing the welfare of Bahrayn.[43]

By the mid-1960's the question of immigration from whatever source assumed new importance. The growth of the Bahrayn population was outpacing revenues, and the government was running a deficit. At the same time, the political system had not been modernized and expanded to assimilate the growing numbers of educated and mobilized elements in the society. The result was a surfeit of unemployed high-school graduates who were both politically conscious and discontented.[44] For their guidance they looked neither to Riyadh nor Baghdad, but to Cairo. This segment of the populace was extremely sensitive and proud of its "Arabism" and could be expected at least to listen sympathetically to Egypt's accusations against Iran.

THE CASE OF KUWAIT

An Iranian minority has existed in Kuwait since the 1776 Persian capture of nearby Basrah. In 1950 one observer noted that in the 1915–1940 period, Persians living in Kuwait numbered as many as 10,000.[45] This Persian, Shi'a, community inhabited one port of Kuwait city, retained their own language, and rarely intermarried with the local Arabs.[46] With the oil boom in Kuwait in the postwar era, immigration rates soared and the Iranian population registered a significant increase. H. R. P. Dickson described this phenomenon for 1952–1953:

The population of Kuwait town, in 1952 a little over 160,000, rose by the end of 1953 to 250,000, an artificial increase due entirely to the enormous influx of foreign unskilled labor for carrying out of the town-development scheme. . . . The Persian community, which has increased enormously in recent years, now amounts to some 30,000 souls. There are many scores of Persian merchants and shopkeepers, but the great majority are employed as laborers.[47]

Indeed with the boom-town growth of Kuwait in the 1950's and 1960's, it was the laboring class from Iran (and other neighboring states) that was drawn there as to a magnet, and it was the mobile laborers who constituted the bulk of the waves of immigration. Kuwait was attractive not only for its employment opportunities but also for the free health, education, and social services it extended. In 1962 it was es-

---

[43] *Gulf Daily Times*, Feb. 9, 1961, as quoted in *Middle East Record*, 1961, II, p. 457.
[44] See David Holden, *Farewell to Arabia*, pp. 174–183.
[45] Mary Cubberly Van Pelt, "The Sheikhdom of Kuwait."
[46] *Area Handbook*, p. 104.
[47] H. R. P. Dickson, *Kuwait and Her Neighbours*, p. 40.

timated that there were 161,471 non-Kuwaitis resident or employed in the city. Since the total population in 1962 was 330,053, Kuwaitis accounted for only 51.6 percent of the population. By 1965, census figures indicated that Kuwaitis now constituted a minority in Kuwait and that 53 percent of a total population of 468,000 were aliens.[48] By 1968 Kuwait sources estimated that 30,000 Iranians lived in Kuwait, while Iranians put the figure much higher.[49]

The influx of foreign workers into Kuwait was a practical necessity in the 1950's and made possible Kuwait's growth and expansion. Palestinians and Egyptians were preponderant in medicine and education, Syrians and Lebanese in industry and trade, and Iraqis, Omanis, and Iranians in the unskilled labor force.[50]

In the past Iranians living in Kuwait have been for the most part politically quiescent, worked well and co-existed peacefully with their Arab counterparts.[51] Yet the increasing involvement of Kuwait in intra-Arab politics after 1961, and the phenomenon noted above of the numerical submergence of native Kuwaitis by immigrants, surely combined to create pressure for the limitation of foreign immigration. Additionally, the growing presence of large numbers of politicized Palestinians and Egyptians in professional jobs in Kuwait, and the generally known fact of Iran's trade ties with Israel, as well as Iran's claims in the Gulf, gave the limitations of Iranian immigrants an internal political dimension. At the same time Iran's rivalry with Egypt gave the question a diplomatic dimension. It being an axiom of Kuwait foreign policy not to take sides in intra-Arab or regional disputes and to avoid offense to the larger Arab states, it was perhaps natural that the Kuwait government take action to limit and restrict immigration —and if possible, to appear to limit Iranian immigration more than that of the fraternal Arab states. There is, in fact, no evidence to show

---

[48] See Raqaei el-Mallakh, "Kuwait's Economic Development and Her Foreign Aid Programmes," pp. 14–15. Between 1957, when the first census was taken, and 1965, the total population rose from 206,473 to 467,339, an increase of 126 percent in eight years with an average annual increment of 16 percent. See *Area Handbook*, pp. 101–102.

[49] *The Times* (London), Dec. 29, 1959; *Keyhan International*, Nov. 17, 1968, and *Middle East Record*, III, 1967 (1970), p. 447. Iranian sources vary considerably in their estimates. *Tehran Journal*, June 27, 1961, puts the number of Iranians at 50,000; Jan. 14, 1964, however, puts the figure at 20,000. *Ettelaat* (editorial, June 25, 1962), reports: "The Kuwaitis love the Shah and have the highest respect and admiration for him. Such a reaction appears quite ordinary and natural, as most of the original Kuwaitis are Iranians." Finally, the number of 90,000 Iranians living in Kuwait is cited in *Shoraye 'Ali-e Eghtesadi*, II, Dec. 19, 1966, pp. 45–46.

[50] *Area Handbook*, p. 102. The paragraph in the text relies heavily on this source.

[51] See Massudi, *Didari az Shaykh Neshinha*, pp. 20–21.

that Iranian immigration has been limited more than that of any other nation, but the *impression* that this was so was certainly something the Kuwait government *may* have sought in the light of domestic and intra-Arab considerations. Be that as it may, the Kuwait government for domestic reasons sought to limit and regularize immigration into the country.

Whereas previously the British political agent used to grant permanent residence to aliens, the Kuwait government in 1961 initiated a policy of restricting immigration. As a result of the availability and attraction of employment opportunities in Kuwait, and the ease of transit across the Gulf, a steady stream of Iranians seeking jobs continued to enter Kuwait illegally, either from Iran or from the nearby shaykhdoms.

To cope with the continued flow of immigrants, many of whom entered the country legally, the Kuwait national assembly decided in November 1964 to forbid entry into Kuwait of Iranians who held passports from the Arab Gulf emirates. In July 1965, as part of a measure aimed at curbing the influence of foreigners, stricter rules for work and residence permits were secretly enacted by the National Assembly. These measures were not by any means solely anti-Iranian; they were "balanced" by restrictions on pro-Nasserite groups, as we shall note in a subsequent section.

IRAN'S POLICY

The Iran government did not pursue a particularly active policy in regard to the emigration of its subjects to neighboring states. While desirous of a liberal immigration policy in Kuwait and the Gulf shaykhdoms, Tehran did not press its wishes. It sought rather to ameliorate and improve the treatment of Iranians in Kuwait. If anything, the rate of emigration was a source of embarrassment to the government and a reflection of the lack of employment opportunities in the country's south.[52] It was thus a testimony to the preoccupation of the nation's economic planners with other affairs—in the 1959–1962 period, for example, with the country's rapid inflation. At that time, as a result of a vast imbalance of imports over exports, the government instituted a series of stringent economic measures to restrict the outflow of capital. One of these measures included the imposition of a 1000 toman (approximately 120 dollars) exit fee for those who wished

---

[52] See Leonard Binder, *Iran: Political Development in a Changing Society*, pp. 332–333; and *Tehran Journal*, June 29, 1964.

to leave the country. This law, which was particularly onerous for the itinerant laborer, encouraged and promoted circumvention of the official process of departing the country through the substitution of illegal means such as bribing local officials or clandestine departure without passport or visa. In so doing, it exacerbated the existing problem of illegal emigration by rendering more precarious the status of those passportless or visaless Iranians reaching the Gulf shaykhdoms.

It was not until the mid-1960's, when the economy had picked up and the preoccupation of the leadership with security on the northern border had diminished, that attention was paid to the Gulf region. This was evident in the attention paid to the south: in the establishment of radio and television, the development of the ports of Bushehr and Bandar Abbas, in the investments in the Khuzistan region, and in new and active interest in trade relations with the Gulf states. All of these questions reached the Shah's attention.

In September 1966 the Council of Ministers authorized the Iranian embassy in Kuwait to issue passports to those Iranians already in Kuwait and, since Iran had no diplomatic representation in the Gulf shaykhdoms, to Iranians in those states as well. But the Kuwait government's legislation preventing the entry or re-entry into Kuwait of Iranians who carried Iranian passports issued in Kuwait by the Iranian embassy in effect nullified the Iranian measure to regularize retroactively the status of Iranian emigrants who had illegally departed the country. The two countries entered into negotiations on this subject in 1967.[53]

With its perception of a threat from Nasser and the possibilities of subversion in the Gulf, the issue of immigration became an important dimension of the Iranian government's evolving relations with the Gulf states that needed to be harmonized. If the Iranian government did little to allay the fears of some states that it might infiltrate and eventually dominate its tiny neighbors, it can also be said that it did not take up the question of the status of Iranian immigrants in the Gulf states or pursue their interests on a diplomatic level. The Iranian government essentially left the question of Iranian emigration to resolve itself through inaction, the natural course of time, and regional developments. There is no evidence that Iranians in the Gulf states have been used as spies, agents, or saboteurs by their government. On the other hand, there is no reason to doubt that the presence of large numbers of Iranians has facilitated the information gathering of the intelli-

---

[53] *Iran's Foreign Relations in 1346* (1967–68), p. 38.

gence agencies, especially SAVAK, which until 1968 was perhaps the
only agency involved in the Gulf region's political affairs.

IRANIAN EMIGRATION AND INTRA-ARAB POLITICS

Reference was made earlier to the question of Iranian emigration
being used as a potentially divisive instrument. Quite apart from the
genuine and legitimate apprehension that the rulers of some of the
shaykhdoms and Kuwait may have felt about the possible submergence
of their native population by waves of Arab and Asian emigrants including Iranians, this spark of suspicion was fanned by states hostile
to Iran to serve their own purposes. The Egyptian government after
1960 took the lead in such an endeavor in the face of evidence that
Iranian emigrants were welcomed in the Gulf states.[54]

Cairo had at its disposal several facts and doubts which could be
played up to further its aim: (1) Iran's *de facto* recognition of and trade
with Israel; (2) Iran's various claims in the Gulf; (3) the very size of
Iran and its large population, which could be made to appear sinister
if combined with the Palestine analogy—i.e., what passes for emigration today will become a pretext for seizure of territory tomorrow. The
Egyptian success in fully utilizing these opportunities was marred by
tension and disunity in the Arab world and a lingering suspicion of
radicalism of the more leftist Arab regimes.

Nonetheless, in intra-Arab relations the requirements of "Arabism"
and the internal pressures of politics have necessitated public criticism
of Iran at times. But there is little evidence to suggest that the Arab
states of the Gulf sought irrevocably to antagonize Iran or to become
involved in the Tehran-Cairo feud. While Cairo sought to use the immigration issue to polarize Arab and Iranian, it found this difficult to
achieve. In Iran's relations with the Gulf states, the issue of immigration has been one of legitimate concern between the neighboring states
of the Gulf and one which is a natural problem deriving from the
imbalance in populations, the economic booms of the shaykhdoms,

---

[54] See, *inter alia*, the *Economist*, June 4, 1966, pp. 1077–1078, which reports:
"Iranian immigrants, many of them building laborers, both skilled and unskilled,
are also welcome for the simple fact that they work harder than most. There is no
evidence that they, any more than the other minority groups living in the Gulf
states, are interested in anything more sinister than in making a better living than
they can at home."
See also the *Christian Science Monitor*, July 9, 1965: "Economic considerations,
more than political considerations, have decided the existence of these [minority]
groups. Arab chiefs and their tribes were happy to welcome industrious Asian
merchants and craftsmen."

and the historical ease of transit in the Gulf. There is no indication of any centrally directed emigration policy by Tehran nor of any ulterior motive in tolerating the emigration. The tardiness of the Iran government in moving to regulate it and to allay the Gulf states' fears is attributable more to bureaucratic inefficiency, insensitivity, and lack of positive political interest in the Gulf states than to any particular or sinister goal. Nasser's failure to mobilize the Gulf states against Iran was due to these states' fear of his intentions, and their consequent reluctance to antagonize Iran. It was not due to a far-sighted Iranian diplomacy which neutralized Nasser's arguments.

The emphasis in the foregoing pages on the intra-Arab dimension of the issue of Iranian emigrants has been an attempt to identify the regional context, and the political constraints with which Iran's Gulf policy has operated. Iran's diplomacy in the 1958–1967 period was essentially passive and defensive, partly due to its preoccupation elsewhere and partly as a result of a lack of means. The British presence, too, complicated a more active diplomacy, even if Iran had had such means. Iran devised no imaginative or constructive policy to win the trust of the Arab Gulf states and to counteract Nasserite propaganda. (Its rather unformed behavior toward the Gulf states at this time thus contrasts sharply with its increased engagement with the Gulf states after 1968.) Iran was however ultimately the beneficiary of intra-Arab tensions and suspicions (for example, Sa'udi Arabia's differences with Egypt over Yemen), especially since no Gulf Arab state save Iraq wished, for purely practical reasons, to irrevocably antagonize it. And if some Arab states occasionally paid lip service to the requirements of Arab nationalism, it was from a similar prudent desire not to antagonize their fellow Arabs. This need for balancing between the Iranian colossus and the Arab nationalism bandwagon has informed much of the smaller Gulf states' diplomacy, and has formed a parameter beyond which Arab-Iranian relations have been unable to develop. Iranian policy-makers have somewhat underestimated this intra-Arab constraint on the smaller Gulf states.

Chapter VI

POLICY TOWARD THE
GULF STATES

Since 1968 the Iranian government has devoted increased attention to improving commercial and cultural relations with the Gulf states. The Iranian view is that it is "natural" for Iran to assume her "historic" responsibilities in the Gulf, that these were artificially postponed by Britain's presence which rerouted Gulf trade toward India, and hence that Iran's "return to the Gulf . . . is merely correcting a situation created by the colonial presence during the past 150 years." [1]

In fulfillment of this responsibility the government embarked upon a systematic effort to open up the Gulf states to Iranian trade. Cultural exchange was also encourged, and once the British announcement about their impending withdrawal was made, the general interest in Gulf trade was transformed into a more concrete and sustained interest. It took on a political dimension and became one of the tools available to Iran's policy-makers in relations with the Gulf states. Posing as the benevolent *status-quo* power, polishing the image of the natural guardian and benevolent elder brother, Iran could productively use its size and progress to make useful commercial agreements with the Gulf states. Quite apart from agreements on trade, transit, transportation, and the like, the Iranian government could use its country's educational and manpower advantages to extend technical aid to the Gulf states.

In building up these bilateral economic relations, the Iranian government hoped to establish a more substantial and solid basis for its relations with the Gulf states, not only as a potentially rich market for its

---

[1] See Amir Taheri, "The Return of Iran," in *Keyhan International*, April 12, 1970.

exports, but also to prevent the complete economic domination of the poorer shaykhdoms by other Arab states. Finally, as a state with an interest in the continued stability of the area, Iran's assistance may be viewed as a small investment toward that goal.

THE FEDERATION: FIRST PHASE, JANUARY 1968–MARCH 1970

The announcement of the British withdrawal from the Gulf had considerable ramifications for Iran's policy toward the shaykhdoms and the Bahrayn question in particular. That Britain would leave the Gulf sometime in the future was not doubted in Tehran. But the timing of the announcement, January 16, 1968, coming just two months after the British government's assurances that it would stay until 1975, came as a surprise. Unlike neighboring Iraq, Iran had not called for a British withdrawal. Yet it had prepared itself militarily for such an eventuality in previous years by steadily augmenting its military arsenal.[2] Nonetheless, it was caught totally unprepared diplomatically. It had no Gulf or Bahrayn "policy," nor did it have the necessary diplomatic machinery either in terms of area specialists, linguists, or outlook to take an active diplomatic role immediately.

Iran's diplomacy in the next four years was thus essentially negative. It seemed to consist of what Tehran would *not* tolerate, or accept, without emphasizing the positive goals it sought, and how it wished to get there. This was true on the level of active day-to-day diplomacy as well as in the larger conceptions of the Gulf's future held by diplomats in Iran. Both deficiencies are attributable to the lack or distrust of expertise and an unwillingness to do the necessary research and analysis so basic and yet so vital to any functioning organization. Iran's diplomacy was thus personal diplomacy with all its advantages and disadvantages.

The British announcement came at a time when the Gulf states' leaders were already exchanging visits. On January 17 the Shaykh of Bahrayn concluded a three-day visit to Sa'udi Arabia, which pledged to "fully endorse and effectively support the Bahrayn government in all circumstances."[3]

---

2 For example, in February 1967 Iran ordered four destroyers from Britain, obtaining a 13¾ million pound loan for the purchase. See *The Times* (London), Feb. 16, 1967.

3 *The Times* (London), Jan. 18, 1968; the *New York Times*, Jan. 18, 1968. The text of the communiqué was broadcast by Jiddah Home Service in Arabic, Jan. 17, 1968; on BBC, Jan. 19, 1968.

Iran reacted by calling off a scheduled visit of the Shah to Sa'udi Arabia and taking a harder line regarding the division of the continental shelf.[4] But even before this, on January 28, the Iranian government had clearly indicated its differences with Sa'udi Arabia over Bahrayn and Kuwait and on the latter's references to the "Arabism" of the Gulf.[5] February 1968 witnessed much diplomatic activity on the Arabian littoral of the Gulf; the foreign minister of Kuwait visited Sa'udi Arabia; the ruler of Bahrayn went to Iraq. Cairo supported King Faysal's leadership in the Gulf and finally on February 26 a proposed union of Arabian emirates to include the trucial states, Bahrayn and Qatar, was announced. Except for Syria the Arab states welcomed this development. Iran's response was negative because the projected union included Bahrayn. On March 13 the Shah made a speech in Isfahan in which he warned certain unnamed states to honor Iran's interests in the Gulf lest the Iranian government ignore theirs.

On April 1 the Iranian government declared that Britain could not give away to others what it had obtained by force (i.e., the Bahrayn islands). It reserved Iran's rights in the Gulf and asserted that Iran would not accept this "historical injustice." The statement, which amounted to a denunciation of the federation, was followed by speculation in the press that Iran might oppose a federation which included Bahrayn.[6] Lest its position be overlooked, Tehran sent a note to the Sa'udi government on the same day saying that "it reserved its historical rights to the Gulf region." [7]

The Sa'udi Arabia and Kuwait governments continued to actively support the creation of a federation. On May 22 King Faysal told an interviewer from the *New York Times* that "There need be no vacuum in that area when the British leave in 1971 as long as the federation receives the support of the U.S. and its neighbors. We certainly support it." [8] Two days later the Shah explained in an interview that Iran's opposition to the proposed federation stemmed from its "imperialist" origins, and accused Britain of "manipulation." He insisted that its departure from the Gulf must be "genuine" and that Iran was pre-

---

[4] *Los Angeles Times,* Feb. 9, 1968.

[5] See the text of Prime Minister Hoveyda's comments on the Gulf, Jan. 28, 1968; typescript, Iran Foreign Ministry, and summarized in *The Times* (London), Jan. 29, 1968.

[6] The official text of a foreign ministry statement of April 1, 1968, is found in *Iran's Foreign Relations in 1347* (1968–69), pp. 243–244. See also *Keyhan*, April 1 and 3, 1968; *The Times* (London), April 2, 1968.

[7] *Mid-East Mirror*, April 6, 1968.

[8] *New York Times,* May 23, 1968.

pared to cooperate with other states for the defense of the Gulf, but raised a new objection to the federation by questioning its viability. "The Shah was perplexed by attempts to create a federation of oil sheikhdoms in the Persian Gulf in the light of Britain's experience with federations in South Arabia, Nigeria, and Rhodesia. He felt that tribalism and federalism were incompatible, and the Persian Gulf federation would go the way of Aden and South Arabia." [9] Despite the gap between their views, the Shah and King Faysal were personally reconciled in June, although their diplomacy continued to differ.[10]

The government's opposition to the federation did not interfere with its bilateral relations with the Gulf states. During the summer and autumn of 1968 the rulers of Fujayrah and Ras al-Khaymah, in August; Dubay, in October; and Qatar and Abu Dhabi, in November, all visited Iran and discussed the future of the Gulf.[11] Nor did it impede the Shah's official visits to Sa'udi Arabia from November 9–14 and Kuwait from November 15–17. Although contemporary accounts differed as to what agreements if any had been reached on these visits, subsequent events demonstrated a strong coincidence in timing between these visits and the Shah's speech in New Delhi in January 1969, without proving a causal relationship.[12]

In short the Shah's declaration in New Delhi on January 5 that Iran would not use force to reclaim Bahrayn and that it would listen sympathetically to the wishes of the inhabitants of the archipelago in determining their future followed hard on the heels of his visit to the principal Arab states of the Gulf.[13] It marked a turning point in that it ended or rather could have ended Iran's opposition to the federation on the basis of Bahrayn's inclusion in it.

---

[9] *The Guardian* (Manchester), May 25, 1968.

[10] King Faysal made some conciliatory remarks in May. See *Keyhan International*, May 8, 1968. The Shah stopped off at Jiddah on June 3 en route to Washington. See *The Times* (London), June 4, 1968.

[11] *Keyhan*, Aug. 25, 1968; *Ayandegan*, editorial, Aug. 18, 1968; *Keyhan International*, Nov. 4, 1968.

[12] For the text of Iran-Sa'udi Arabia and Iran-Kuwait communiqués, see "Joint Communiqués 1349" (1970–71), pp. 171–173 and 175–177, respectively. For Iranian newspaper accounts see *Ettelaat* (editorial), Oct. 28, 1968; *Seday-e Mardom*, Nov. 11, 1968; *Peygham-e Emruz*, Nov. 6 and 8, 1968; *Keyhan International*, Oct. 30 and Nov. 9, 13 and 19, 1968. See also *The Times* (London), Nov. 12 and 15, 1968; *New York Times*, Nov. 14 and 17, 1968; *Christian Science Monitor*, Nov. 5 and Dec. 5, 1968; *The Economist*, Nov. 23, 1968, p. 30.

[13] The official text of the Shah's statement is found in *Iran's Foreign Relations in 1347* (1968–69), pp. 285–287. See also *Ayandegan*, Jan. 7, 1969; *Ettelaat*, Jan. 5 and 8, 1969; *Ayandegan* (editorial), Jan. 6, 1969. Most newspapers agreed with *Keyhan International*, Jan. 6, 1969, that the Shah's statement was a "fair offer."

But this was not to be. On the contrary, it continued to insist that it would not recognize a federation which included Bahrayn. But it soon became obvious that once policy on Bahrayn had been formalized the opposition to the federation would abate. In June 1969 the Shah declared that the settlement of Bahrayn's status would end Iran's opposition to the federation. "Once the question of Bahrayn, to which Iran lays claim, is settled, there would be no objection to a federation of the shaykhdoms," the Shah insisted.[14]

This attitude created something of a problem for the federation. The federation of the nine Gulf states—that is, the seven trucial states plus Bahrayn and Qatar—which had been meeting so far could proceed in defiance of Iran and risk Tehran's displeasure. Or it could continue discussions among the eight and have Bahrayn drop out until its status was clarified. Or the construction of the federation itself could be delayed until such time as Bahrayn's status was settled, and then resume meetings with all nine states present. It cannot be doubted that Tehran's opposition had a strong influence on the federation's lack of progress.

In addition, the influence of the Gulf's "great powers," Iran, Iraq, Sa'udi Arabia, and Kuwait further complicated it. Iran was not the only state with doubts or preferences concerning the union. Sa'udi Arabia wished to include Bahrayn in the union to undercut its rival, Abu Dhabi. Kuwait also wished to have a strong union of the nine states, but preferred to have it under its own influence. Iran had a strong friend in Dubay, which could plead its case inside the union's meetings. Within the proposed union the more populous states—Bahrayn with a population of some 200,000, relatively urbanized and politicized, and Wahhabi Qatar, with a population of 100,000—competed for power. As the richest of the seven trucial states, with a total population of approximately 200,000, Abu Dhabi and Dubay were also in competition for influence.

Yet it is clear that Iran's attitude between January 1968 and March 1970 continued to delay and complicate the problems of the union. This problem was somewhat eased when the mechanisms for settling the Bahrayn dispute were announced in March 1970. Britain and Iran had agreed to allow a representative of the Secretary-General of the United Nations to ascertain the wishes of its people. The findings, made public on May 2, 1970, were unanimously endorsed by the UN Security Council on May 11 and approved by the Iranian parliament

---

14 *The Times* (London), June 10, 1969.

(186 to 4) on May 14. In the opinion of many observers at the time, the settlement was to mark a new era in Iran's Gulf relations, in that "Iran will no longer use her influence among the Gulf states to prevent the formation of the Union of Arab Emirates, UAE, of which Bahrayn is a member." [15]

The twenty-seven months between the announcement of Britain's withdrawal and the agreement to settle Bahrayn's status through the United Nations serve as a useful, and natural, division in Iran's foreign relations in the Gulf from January 1968 to December 1971. Throughout this period Iran's attitude toward the nascent union was ostensibly dependent on Bahrayn's inclusion in it. Until January 1969 there was no hint as to what form of Bahrayn settlement Tehran would accept, other than its return to Iranian sovereignty. After January 1969 it was clear that the Shah had determined to relinquish the claim gracefully, but this was not matched by a readiness to drop Iran's opposition to the federation until March 1970. Nor did Iran support the principle of a federation and encourage it, with the understanding that Bahrayn might later join it.

It was earlier suggested that the British announcement found Iran without a Bahrayn, or Gulf, policy. The Iranian leadership had consistently refused to discuss "the future of what is part of one's own country." [16] Although the Iran government admittedly did not *press* the claim prior to the announcement, it must surely be counted an unrealistic policy to have *maintained* the claim, ignored its implications for Gulf politics in the middle of the decade, and then revive it on the eve of Britain's military withdrawal. There is no need to emphasize the domestic constraints operating on the leadership on this question. [17] Doubtless they were perceived as important and real, calling

---

[15] *The Times* (London), March 30, 1970. For the same view, see *Ettelaat* (air ed.) editorials, March 31, April 1, and April 4–9, 1970; and *Le Monde* (Paris), March 31, 1970.

[16] This phrase, repeated by Foreign Ministry spokesmen in 1968, and cited earlier in the text, can be traced to a discussion the Shah had with local government officials on July 25, 1959; typescript copy from Foreign Ministry files. The phrase was repeated by the Shah in his New Delhi press conference.

[17] The Shah was subject to certain domestic political pressures on issues allegedly involving Iran's national heritage. The extreme, often xenophobic, nationalism of both Right and Left in Iran had manifestly prevented the Shah from acting on this issue at a time when he was politically weak. His perception of the domestic constraints operating on the question is attested to in an interview he gave on July 17, 1961, published in C. L. Sulzberger, *The Last of the Giants*, p. 751. Even as late as 1970, the Shah felt it essential to have a plebiscite in the archipelago, despite the obvious results, in order to protect himself. See his interview with British Labor M.P. Roebuck, excerpted in *Iran's Foreign Policy*, p. 105. The right-wing Pan-Iranist

into question the leadership's nationalist integrity. Nevertheless the Iran foreign ministry underestimated the impact of the claim on the Arab states in the mid-1950's (and in particular Sa'udi Arabia's opposition in 1957), and did not examine the practical implications of maintaining the claim in an era of Arab nationalism and Iran-Arab hostility.

The problems raised by the maintenance of the claim may be summarized thus: (1) It confirmed some of the worst fears of the smaller states about Iran's intentions, and lent credence to the charges made intermittently by Baghdad, Damascus, and Cairo. (2) It severely complicated relations with Sa'udi Arabia, given its proximity and its economic ties to the archipelago. (3) It placed moderate Arab states such as Kuwait in a difficult position. (4) If realized, the claim would have given Iran an extraordinary staging point close to the Arabian peninsula, and could interfere with the division of the Gulf's continental shelf. (5) It threatened to open up the Pandora's box of past claims and historical *irridenta* which could make a shambles of union. (6) The assertion of the claim complicated and postponed agreement on a union. For all these reasons, the rejection of Iran's claim was an issue on which all the Gulf Arab states could agree. If persevered in, it could have provoked an Iran-Arab confrontation and polarization which would have doomed any hope for a cooperative security system in the Gulf.

By mid-1968 these facts appear to have been realized by Iran, and the credibility of the claim was itself being eroded by politics in the Gulf. The notion that the issue was a purely Iran-Britain dispute was also being exposed, and clearly could not be credibly or indefinitely sustained.[18] Relinquishment of the claim was thus no surprise, and its timing is less notable than the practicality of the means chosen to jettison it.

When studied carefully it is clear that Bahrayn's inclusion in the projected federation was by no means the only basis for Iran's opposition. From the outset Iran had at least two other reservations: doubts as to its viability, and skepticism as to its proposed function as well as its parentage. The Shah voiced both these doubts in an interview with *The Guardian*, January 25, 1968. With regard to the purpose of

---

party, which had called for an Iranian invasion of Bahrayn in 1961 on the model of India's seizure of Goa (see *Tehran Journal*, Dec. 28, 1961), was quickly muzzled. See *The Times* (London), April 29 and May 14, 1970, and *Keyhan International*, April 18 and 22, 1970.

[18] One Iranian diplomat repeated the government's official and unrealistic line by maintaining that Bahrayn "is a question separate from [Iran's] desire for cooperation with the Gulf states." *Christian Science Monitor*, March 16, 1968.

the federation and Britain's alleged authorship, the Iranian leadership feared that it was only a stalking horse for British interests; the constant accusations of "imperialist manipulation" and the calls for a "genuine departure" which did not mean "Britain's withdrawal from one door and return by another door or through a window," testified to this distrust.[19]

In May 1968 the Shah told an interviewer:

As regards the Arab countries we really do not have any problems with them unless they create one. The only difficulty is that certain of these Arab countries that presently exist or are about to be created, believe that they must become the successors and heirs of Britain's ancient imperialism. If they want to follow this path we will have our difficulties. Otherwise we do not have any problems between us.[20]

An additional motivation for Iran's attitude was national pride and *amour propre*. Although difficult to document, it appears to be an unmistakable element of Iran's reaction to the sudden announcement of withdrawal. It accounts for the constant refrain that Iran would not accept a *fait accompli* in the Gulf, in its insistence on Britain's "genuine withdrawal," on its half-hearted regional initiatives, and above all on the emphasis on its responsibilities to secure the defense of the Gulf.

Thus the British announcement caught the Iranian government by surprise, without a Bahrayn or Gulf policy, and was followed by a rapid announcement on the Arabian littoral of plans to form a federation which would include Bahrayn. The Arab states then closed ranks in support of the proposed union. Uncertain as to its reaction, Tehran maintained its Bahrayn claim while attempting to devise a Gulf policy. Having opposed the federation because of Bahrayn's inclusion, it used its influence to delay the federation while it finally discarded its increasingly costly claim. At the same time it became quite unenthusiastic about a federation on quite different grounds. It did not, therefore, lend its support to the projected federation, probably because it believed that the federation, while strengthening the small Gulf states, might leave them susceptible to control by an Arab rival. And it preferred in general to deal with these states on a bilateral basis, as was indicated in the preceding discussion on trade relations.

---

[19] For numerous citations, see the section dealing with Iran's attitude toward the role of nonlittoral states in the Gulf in Chapter VIII.

[20] The interview was with A. M. Rendel of *The Times* (London), April 13, 1970; Persian text in *Ayandegan*, April 14, 1970.

THE FEDERATION: SECOND PHASE, MARCH 1970–
DECEMBER 1971

The Iranian government's skepticism of the proposed federation did
not diminish after settlement of the Bahrayn question. Indeed, the
clarification of Bahrayn's status, the ambiguity of which had been the
ostensible obstacle to Iran's support of the federation, only cleared the
way for a new objection. Tehran now insisted that its support of the
federation was contingent on Iran's possession of three long-disputed
islands, the Greater and Lesser Tumbs, and Abu Musa.

Although it surfaced as a public claim in early 1970, Iran's dormant
claim to the islands of Abu Musa and the Greater and Lesser Tumbs,
near the straits of Hormoz, had in fact been of long standing. Britain
regarded the islands as under the sovereignty of the shaykhdoms of
Sharjah and Ras al-Khaymah, respectively. Iran and Britain had had
exchanges on the islands in the 1920's and 1930's without any result,[21]
and their ownership had figured in the discussions that were launched
in the mid-1960's concerning the division of the Gulf's continental
shelf.[22]

The sovereignty of the islands was the subject of conversations with
Britain from 1968 to 1970 while the future of Bahrayn was also being
determined. Although Iran sought to obtain the return of the islands
as part of a package deal in which it relinquished its claim to Bahrayn,
no formal or explicit agreement on such a *quid pro quo* was reached.
Nevertheless, it was the Iranian government's understanding that in
the wake of the goodwill created by the Bahrayn settlement, Britain
would not actively oppose Iran's claim to the islands, and might even
bring its influence to bear on the relevant shaykhdoms on behalf of
Iran's claim.

The Iranian government's arguments in support of its claim to the
islands ranged from the purely historical to the frankly pragmatic. The
islands were Iran's, it was claimed, because they were under its
sovereignty until eighty years ago.[23] At that time, it was contended,

---

[21] For the only published work based on British documents, see R. M. Burrell,
"Britain, Iran and the Persian Gulf."

[22] See Husain M. Albaharna, *The Legal Status of the Arabian Gulf States.*

[23] It would be tedious to document each minor argument adduced by the Iranian
government between 1970 and 1971. The reader is therefore referred to the following sources which contain the most comprehensive statements on the subject made
by the Shah: *The Times* (London), May 11, 1971 (interview with Dennis Walters,

Britain interfered with the exercise of this sovereignty by using force, and subsequently claimed the islands for its wards, Sharjah and Ras al-Khaymah. The islands were thus Iran's for historical reasons, and their seizure under duress and interference by an "imperialist" power could not diminish its sovereignty. Nor could the "imperialist" country on its departure seek to perpetuate its "colonialist legacy" by ceding Iran's property to other states.

The second principal argument offered by the Iranian leadership was that of geographic strategic necessity. The islands, this view ran, are situated at a critical "choke point" near the strategic and easily blocked straits of Hormoz. Iran was vitally dependent on the free flow of oil and other commodities through these straits, and had a disproportionately large stake in free navigation in the Gulf, partly because of the length of its coastline, and partly because it has possessed no alternative means such as a pipeline by which to export its petroleum. In addition, it was argued, the Tumbs islands are situated closer to Iranian territory than to the Arab shaykhdoms claiming them. Finally it was argued, mainly for the consumption of friendly Western states, that Iran had the means to ensure freedom of navigation for all the states of the Gulf as well as for those non-Gulf states interested in the continued free flow of oil to Japan, Europe, and elsewhere. Since this navigation could be jeopardized by the seizure of one or all of the islands by "nihilists," who with "bazookas" or similarly primitive and obtainable weaponry could interfere with the oil tanker traffic and severely damage marine life in the shallow Gulf, it was in the interests of all concerned states, Gulf and non-Gulf alike, that Iran acquire the islands to prevent this.

The Shah emphasized that Iran sought the islands partly to prevent their acquiring a "nuisance value," a recurrent phrase in the hands of the enemies of the region's stability. This argument was strengthened and given a new persuasiveness after the attack on an oil tanker bound for Eilat, Israel, in June 1971. The attack was launched by a small group of the Popular Front for the Liberation of Palestine from a motor launch off Perim island in the narrow channel of waters known

---

M.P.); the Shah's interview with the editor of *Blitz* (India)—for English text see *Keyhan International*, June 26, 1971; the official Persian text is in *Akhbar va Asnad 1350 (az Farvardin ta Shahrivar)*, 1971–72, p. 65, and *Ettelaat* (air ed.), June 26, 1971. The Shah's interview with several foreign newsmen after the occupation of the islands, English text in *Keyhan International* (weekly ed.), Jan. 29, 1972; official Persian text in *Akhbar va Asnad 1350 (az Mehr ta Esfand)*, pp. 37–40; and *Ayandegan* (editorial), April 18, 1970.

as Bab el-Mandab, near the entrance to the Red Sea.[24] Finally, the Shah pointed out that the claims to Bahrayn and the islands were not analogous; in the latter case a very small number of people were involved, as compared to the much larger number living in the Bahrayn islands which had made the continued Iranian claim to the archipelago unrealistic.

In international politics, subtle and persuasive reasoning and victory in debate seldom achieve a state's aim by themselves. The Iranian government has thus relied less on the irrefutability of its claims than on the strength of its position. From the outset—that is, from April 1970 when the claim to the islands was made public—the Iranian government held that the question was a "colonial" one, and concerned only Britain and Iran. Iran hoped thereby to avoid or minimize any Iran-Arab polarization in the Gulf. The British government accepted this notion for the same reason, although it subsequently depicted its role in the question as the provider of "good offices" between Iran, on the one hand, and Sharjah and Ras al-Khaymah on the other. Sir William Luce, Britain's special envoy to the Gulf, became the principal figure in the negotiations, commuting between the two shores of the Gulf with occasional visits to London for consultations.

In order to bring Britain's perspective into line with its own, the Iranian government proceeded with a series of measures designed to communicate its earnestness and resolve in regard to the islands. In May, in deference to Iran's threat of armed intervention and to prevent an Iran-Arab confrontation, the British government directed the American company, Occidental Petroleum, not to start drilling operations some seven miles offshore, off the island of Abu Musa to which Iran laid claim.[25] The second step in the application of pressure on Britain was Iran's formal notification to Britain and the shaykhdoms in October 1970 that it would neither recognize nor support a federation until the ownership of the islands was settled.

In February 1971 the Shah publicly declared that if necessary Iran would resort to force to regain the islands. Simultaneously, and for the

---

[24] For a description of the incident, see *New York Times*, June 14–16, 1971. For a perceptive analysis of Iran's attitude towards the significance of the sealanes, see Amir Taheri, "Iran's Lifeline," *Keyhan International*, May 31, 1972.

[25] See *The Times* (London), June 1, 1970; the *Financial Times*, May 23, 1970; *The Economist*, May 30, 1970, p. 34; June 6, 1970, p. 72; *Keyhan International*, June 3, 1970. Further complicating the issue here was the dispute between Sharjah and Umm al-Qaywayn which granted overlapping concessions in the waters of Abu Musa—a question which does not concern us here.

first time, the government moved to stir up and mobilize public emotions on the issue by means of a press campaign.[26] The next step was taken in May 1971 when Iran's armed forces were ordered to fire upon British aircraft which were accused of harassing Iranian naval forces in the Gulf, particularly near the disputed islands.[27] Britain responded in placatory terms and the incident passed, but again Tehran had signaled the lengths to which it was prepared to pursue its claim to the islands.

Apart from the steady escalation of pressure on Britain, the Iranian government also aimed its diplomacy at the shaykhdoms and the regional states. To the shaykhdoms—especially the claimants of the islands, Sharjah and Ras al-Khaymah—it offered increased economic assistance. The Shah made this clear in April 1970, saying that after an agreement was reached on the islands the shaykhdoms could "count all the more on Iran's economic aid." The same point was repeated by the foreign minister in December 1970 and Iran's ambassador to London in June 1971.[28]

To counteract the Iraq government's attempt to depict the question of the islands as an Iran-Arab issue, Tehran enlisted Egypt's neutrality. This was translated into policy by supporting Egypt's position on the territories occupied by Israel both publicly and in the United Nations, while obtaining in return Cairo's agreement to abstain from interference in the Gulf.[29] Although Iran's claim and subsequently its actions were highly embarrassing to the Egyptian government, Cairo refused to involve itself in the dispute, despite pressures from such different sources as Britain, Iraq, and the shaykhdoms.[30]

There were a number of forces built into the negotiations and discussions about the islands which clearly influenced the outcome. On the Arab side there was the undoubted pressure of "Arabism," or Arab nationalism, and the specter of a violent reaction by Iraq, Syria, and

---

[26] See also *Ettelaat* (air ed.), Feb. 20, 1971, editorial of Feb. 22, 1971, and May 6, 1971; *Ayandegan*, April 4, 1972; *Keyhan* (editorial), Feb. 20, 1971; *Tehran Journal* (editorial), Feb. 23, 1971; *Keyhan International*, Oct. 23, 1971; *Keyhan International* (weekly), editorial of May 1, 1971; *The Times* (London), Feb. 12, 1971; *The Economist*, Feb. 27, 1971, p. 40.

[27] See *Ettelaat* (air ed.), May 9–13, 1971; *Keyhan International* (weekly), May 15, 1971; *The Economist*, May 15, 1971, pp. 39–40; *New York Times*, May 9, 1971.

[28] *Keyhan International*, April 13, 1970.

[29] For documentation of these points, see Chapter V. In addition, see the discussion of Foreign Minister Zahedi's visit to Cairo in *Ettelaat* (air ed.), May 18, 1971.

[30] See especially *Keyhan* (air ed.), June 24, 1971; *The Guardian* (Manchester), July 6, 1971; *The Times* (London), June 30, 1971.

perhaps other Arab states, to any agreement that could be interpreted as a cession of the Arab "homeland" to foreigners.[31] Behind every offer and counter-offer carried by Sir William Luce between Tehran and the shaykhdoms, there remained for the shaykhdoms the fear of the accusation of a "sell-out" and disloyalty to the Arab cause.

On the Iranian side there existed few domestic pressures that were not condoned by the leadership itself in its attempt to strengthen its bargaining position. The increasing hard line adopted, the timing of the settlement for support of a federation, the threat to use force, the action to prevent oil drilling in the waters of the disputed islands, the warning to British aircraft, the orchestration of official statements and mobilization of public opinion, all were designed by the steady raising of the stakes to make unmistakable Iran's determination to acquire the islands. At the same time, of course, they bound the Iranian leadership into a situation where its prestige at home and abroad was staked on the outcome of the dispute. The government also argued that its magnanimity on the Bahrayn settlement deserved to be reciprocated by Britain and the Arabs on the islands, for the Iranian people, having "given up" Bahrayn, would refuse to abandon them.[32]

There were, however, other pressures influencing Iran's policy toward the islands. Especially relevant here, as in all bargaining situations, was the deadline. The date of Britain's departure, December 31, 1971, was naturally one deadline; for it constituted the end, in practical and formal terms, of Britain's protection of the shaykhdoms. Since Iran wished to maintain the issue as an Iran-Britain dispute, the date at which Britain's legal responsibility for the protection of these shaykhdoms was terminated assumed importance. Any military action by Iran after that date would clearly be an action directed against an Arab state—dispelling once and for all the notion of an Iran-Britain dispute. Just as important, from Tehran's perspective, was the consideration that the emergence of the federation as a new Arab state, speedily recognized by the Arab League and rapidly entering the United Na-

---

31 This was evident throughout the negotiations. See especially *The Economist,* February 27, 1971, p. 40; May 6, 1971, pp. 33–34; August 21, 1971, pp. 33–34; and David Ledger, "Gulf Union."

32 Iranian sources tended to understate the number of inhabitants on the islands of Abu Musa and the Greater and Lesser Tumbs. One source gives the numbers, respectively, as 300, 85, and none. *Iran Almanac,* 1971, p. 227. An official English source gives the numbers as, respectively, 800, 150, and none. See Sir Colin Crowe's comments in *United Nations Security Council, Provisional Verbatim Records,* Dec. 9, 1971, p. 91. It should be noted that Iran's claim to the islands was supported by the Iranian Communists. Radio Iran, Courier in Persian, July 17, 1971; on BBC, July 20, 1971.

tions, would seriously complicate any unilateral Iranian action to enforce its claim to the islands. Thus the deadline in the negotiations on the islands was the date of the emergence of the new federal state of Arab shaykhdoms, which could take place any time after the July 18 announcement of agreement on the constitution, but in any case no later than the end of 1971. Iran's opposition to the federation was instrumental in persuading the shaykhs to postpone a rapid move to independence after that announcement.[33] In the meantime Britain sought to achieve a compromise agreement before its scheduled withdrawal, conscious that it would bear much of the odium whether there was an agreement or not, but preferring this to the inauguration of a new era with Iran-Arab hostilities.

On the eve of the announcement of the federation's independence, Iran and Sharjah came to an agreement on Abu Musa island, under which Iran would provide 3.75 million dollars a year in aid to that shaykhdom until the revenue realized from oil in the island or its offshore waters reached 7.5 million dollars. Thereafter, oil revenues were to be split equally. In the ambiguous agreement, neither side acknowledged the other's sovereignty, although the Shaykh of Sharjah agreed to allow Iranian troops to occupy half the island.[34] The Shaykh of Ras al-Khaymah refused a similar agreement. On November 30, the last day of formal British protection, Iranian troops occupied Abu Musa island by agreement and the still-disputed Tumbs islands by force, with the resultant loss of perhaps seven lives on the Greater Tumbs.

Although the negotiations between the parties, through Britain's good offices, were secret, it is possible to reconstruct in part the broad evolution of the discussions. From the outset Britain sought a compromise which would satisfy both parties. In the autumn of 1970 it was reported that an Iranian proposal to rent the islands from the shaykhdoms had been rejected by them.[35] Subsequently, another source reported that it was not clear whether Iran would settle for the garrisoning of troops on the islands without prejudice to the question of

---

[33] According to one source, Iran threatened not only to withhold recognition but to disrupt the federation. For this, and the related point made in the text, see the statement by the representative of the United Arab Emirates in *UN Security Council, Provisional Verbatim Records*, Dec. 9, 1971, p. 107.

[34] Britain's representative at the United Nations put it thus: "Under the agreement, neither party has given up its claim to the island, nor recognized the other's claim." See *UN Security Council, Provisional Records*, Dec. 9, 1971, p. 91. See also *Financial Times* (London), Nov. 30, 1971; *New York Times*, Dec. 1, 1971.

[35] *Financial Times* (London), Oct. 15, 1970; *The Economist*, March 6, 1971, pp. 33-34; Aug. 21, 1971, p. 34.

ultimate sovereignty.[36] On the other hand there were hints that the Iranian government was prepared to compensate the Shaykh of Sharjah, but without admitting that this in any way reflected upon its claim to the sovereignty of Abu Musa.[37] There was also discussion about an agreement on permanent demilitarization of the islands to meet Iran's fear of their use against tanker traffic in the Gulf. By early November it was clear that both parties had refused Britain's "judgment of Solomon," to divide the islands equally between the claimants.[38] It was also reported that Iran had turned down two third-party Arab suggestions: (1) to lease the islands for 99 years but recognize Arab sovereignty; or (2) to agree to a joint Iran-Arab garrison stationed on the islands.[39]

REPERCUSSIONS OF OCCUPATION OF THE ISLANDS

The assertion by Iran of its claim to the islands had had repurcussions before November 1971. Just as it has leaned toward a defense of the "Arabism" of the Gulf when Iran made its claim to Bahrayn in 1968, so did the Kuwait government do so again in 1970–71. The Kuwait government flatly rejected Iran's claim to the islands, and postponed for a month a scheduled visit by its foreign minister.[40]

Apart from Kuwait, no other Gulf state publicly sided with Iraq before the landings on the islands. Sa'udi Arabia maintained a public silence. The Gulf shaykhdoms were reportedly "puzzled" by Iran's claim to the islands. The one country that they did not for the most part fear or suspect of entertaining territorial ambitions in the Gulf was now causing severe tensions in the region and weakening the federation by pursuing its claim to the islands.[41]

The occupation of the islands by Iranian troops changed this. As expected, Egypt remained calm and moderate, refusing to support extreme measures in the Arab League, such as the severance of diplomatic relations with Iran, or sponsorship of a protest in the United Nations. It was nonetheless under considerable pressure from both states and

---

36 *The Times* (London), June 29, 1971.

37 *Daily Telegraph* (London), July 21, 1971.

38 *The Guardian* (Manchester), Nov. 3, 1971; *The Times* (London), Nov. 2, 1971.

39 The Kuwait foreign minister suggested demilitarization to the Shah on Aug. 11, 1971. See the Kuwait representative's comments, *UN Security Council, Provisional Records*, Dec. 9, 1971, p. 53. See also *The Guardian* (Manchester), Nov. 9, 1971.

40 See *Keyhan International* (weekly), June 19, 1971.

41 See especially *The Times* (London), Feb. 1, 1971, wherein the Deputy-Ruler of Ras al-Khaymah is quoted as saying that he doubted that Iran would ever harm the shaykhdoms; and *The Guardian* (Manchester), July 30, 1971.

was embarrassed by Iran's action.[42] Sa'udi Arabia, also as expected, reacted mildly, refusing to support measures designed to isolate Iran. But it too was put under a strain by Iran's action, and its silence by no means indicated consent. The reaction in the shaykhdoms was more severe; rioting occurred in Sharjah and Ras al-Khaymah, resulting in property damage to Iranians living in the shaykhdoms. The deputy ruler of Sharjah was shot, allegedly for cooperating with Iranian authorities on Abu Musa. The newly created Union of Arab Emirates which was formed on December 2, 1971, in the first statement of its Supreme Council condemned Iran's use of force. After its entry into the United Nations on December 9, its representative expressed "the deep regret felt by the people and the government of the United Arab Emirates at the action taken by Iran in forcibly occupying some Arab islands in the Gulf." [43]

The governments of Iraq and Libya reacted most severely. Iraq severed diplomatic relations with Iran and Britain, charging the latter with collusion on December 1, while Libya nationalized the British Petroleum Company in retaliation for Britain's "conspiracy" with Iran on the islands. Iraq and Libya were joined by the government of Algeria and the People's Democratic Republic of Yemen—i.e., South Yemen—in requesting an "urgent meeting of the Security Council to consider the dangerous situation in the Arabian Gulf area arising from the occupation by the armed forces of Iran of the islands. . . ."

A letter from the Shaykh of Ras al-Khaymah was also transmitted to the United Nations.[44] The governments of Kuwait and the United Arab Emirates requested permission to attend the Security Council session. It is sufficient to note that the discussion in the Council which coincided with the Indo-Pakistan hostilities resulted in no new initiatives. It was agreed to shelve the subject temporarily to allow third parties to initiate contacts with both sides to achieve by quiet diplomacy what a noisy and vituperative public session had conspicuously failed to achieve.[45]

---

[42] For a discussion of Egypt's reaction, see Ramazani, *The Persian Gulf: Iran's Role*, pp. 64–65.

[43] See *The Guardian* (Manchester), Dec. 3, 1971; and *UN General Assembly, Provisional Records*, Dec. 9, 1971, pp. 18–20. See also the representative of the United Arab Emirates' comments in the Security Council Session, Dec. 9, 1971, pp. 106–115.

[44] See the letter dated Dec. 3, 1971, from the permanent representatives of Algeria, Iraq, Libyan Arab Republic, and the People's Democratic Republic of Yemen, to the United Nations, addressed to the president of the Security Council, Dec. 3, 1971. See also the letter dated Dec. 7, 1971, from the permanent representative of Iraq to the United Nations, addressed to the secretary-general, Dec. 7, 1971.

[45] The Security Council session took place on the afternoon of December 9, 1971. See: *UN Security Council, Provisional Records*, Dec. 9, 1971.

Iran's attitude to the repercussions of its action was firm. It refused to concede that either the Arab League or the Security Council had any jurisdiction in what was a domestic matter. Its spokesman in the Security Council was unpenitent, unconciliatory, and even belligerent in defending Iran's action. He presented the case primarily for the domestic audience in Iran and refused, or was not permitted, to adopt a more diplomatic tone in the international forum.[46] Subsequently, Iran's foreign minister again emphasized that Iran's occupation of the islands was a purely internal question, thus rejecting the Security Council's "third-party" suggestion. It was also evident from Iran's behavior after the landing on Abu Musa island that the agreement with Shaykh Khalid of Sharjah had been, as far as Iran was concerned, a cover for Iran's acquisition of the island, and a face-saving formula for the Shaykh. The prime minister told an extraordinary and jubilant session of parliament that Iran had reasserted its sovereignty in the islands for the first time in eighty years.[47] On the other hand, the Iranian government rapidly recognized the new Union of Arab Emirates when Iran's support was requested in a telegram to the Shah on December 9. And the repercussions of Iran's action were not so severe as to interfere with continuation of its diplomatic relations with Bahrayn, Qatar, or Oman.

Relations with Kuwait suffered the most. Iran remained without an ambassador in that country for a year because of the government's anger at the Kuwait reaction, finally dispatching one in late 1972. Throughout 1972 Kuwait appeared to be wavering in its traditional neutrality in the Gulf and be considering an outright pro-Iraq diplomatic posture in the Gulf. Iranian newspapers cautioned Kuwait on the danger of such a policy and pointed out that it could only harm Kuwait's interests. They condemned an Iraq-Kuwait communiqué which claimed that the islands were Arab.[48]

The strength of anti-Iranian feeling that persisted after Iran's occupation of the islands is evidenced by two further phenomena. In

46 For the Iranian statement, see UN Security Council, Provisional Records, Dec. 9, 1971, pp. 78–87. The tone of the statement was a surprise to many people, including a United States ambassador at the United Nations, who remarked on it to the author.

47 For the official Persian text of the statement see: Iran's Foreign Relations in 1350 (1971–72), pp. 412–413; Ettelaat (air ed.), Nov. 30, 1971; Le Monde (Paris), Dec. 1, 1971; Keyhan International, Dec. 4, 1971. See also the Shah's comments on the agreement in his press conference of January 1972, ibid. (weekly), Jan. 29, 1972.

48 See especially Ettelaat (air ed.), editorials of May 6 and 7, 1971; Keyhan International (weekly), May 13, 1972, Sept. 2, 1972. See also Roy E. Thoman, "Iraq and the Persian Gulf Region."

February 1972 the Shaykh of Qatar was deposed while vacationing in Iran. It was reported that "informed sources believe the former ruler's trip to Iran, at a time when Arab sentiment against Tehran is strong, may have been the direct cause of the coup." [49] On July 18, 1972, fifteen Arab governments in a note to the president of the Security Council reiterated the earlier stand that "the islands are Arab and constitute an integral part of the United Arab Emirates and of the Arab home-land." [50] Iran's occupation of the islands clearly reflected the govern-ment's determination to pursue an independent policy in the Gulf and to rely on itself for defense. While its action upset its relations with its neighbors, a commonality of interests with the shaykhdoms, Kuwait and Sa'udi Arabia, in preserving the region's security, suggests that this will be temporary. Nevertheless, by the end of 1971 the discussions about a defense pact, which had taken place the previous year, appeared to belong to a different era.

OTHER ISSUES

The settlement of the disputed islands did not mark the end of the controversy about the proposed federation. Even before the resolu-tion of this dispute, other issues had been introduced concerning the federation. By February 1971 it was apparent that the original con-ception of a union of nine states was being modified. In addition to other problems,[51] an *impasse* had developed over the distribution of power in a union in which Bahrayn's population dwarfed that of the seven trucial states combined. Bahrayn's representatives wished to have its population's weight reflected in the constitution and also, having a more educated and politicized citizenry, insisted on elections for a lower house. This was resisted by the smaller and more conservative states. Since neither Bahrayn nor Qatar wished to bear the onus for breaking up the union of nine, a formal announcement of the dead-

---

[49] *New York Times*, Feb. 23, 1972.

[50] See the letter dated July 17, 1972, from the permanent representatives of Algeria, Bahrain, Egypt, Iraq, Kuwait, Lebanon, Libya, Morocco, Oman, People's Democratic Republic of Yemen, Sudan, Syrian Arab Republic, Tunisia, United Arab Emirates, and Yemen, addressed to the president of the Security Council, July 18, 1972. See also the discussion by Senator Massudi in "The Persian Gulf in the Height of International Rivalries and Provocations" (Tehran: Rotary Club pamphlet, July 17, 1972); and *Ettelaat* (air ed.), editorial of July 23, 1972.

[51] For the best single summary to date, see John Duke Anthony, "The Union of Arab Amirates." Among other differences should be mentioned the choice of a site of a capital, the number of votes alloted to each state, voting procedure in the federal assembly, the selection of the president, and the degree of centralization in monetary, tax, and defense matters.

lock was postponed after October 1970.[52] Sa'udi Arabia and Kuwait, which had both actively supported a union of nine, were reluctant to accept its failure, and attempted unsuccessfully to revive it in April 1971 by submitting joint proposals to the shaykhs.

This discrepancy between Iran's opposition to the federation, any federation, and Sa'udi Arabia and Kuwait's support for a union of nine, did not manifest itself in serious public differences between the three states. The differences on the federation, as well as Iran's claim to the islands, was nonetheless a clear indication that regional cooperation among the states on security had broken down. The reaction of Kuwait to Iran's occupation of the islands underlined this.

The formal announcement in March 1971 by the British Conservative government of its intention to honor its predecessor's decision to militarily vacate the Gulf by the end of the year created an additional incentive for the shaykhdoms to form at least some kind of union prior to the departure of the umbrella of their protection. At least on the British departure, Iran, Sa'udi Arabia, and Kuwait were in agreement. But the alacrity with which Tehran recognized the independence of Bahrayn and Qatar, and the tone of Iranian newspapers regarding attempts to postpone their independence, reemphasized the different perspectives of the states on the two shores of the Gulf. It was announced that Tehran would support their membership in the United Nations, and diplomatic relations at the ambassadorial level were agreed upon on August 29 with Bahrayn and October 16 with Qatar.

The withdrawal of Bahrayn and Qatar from the proposed union had no impact on Iran's conditions for recognizing the union, which centered on objections to any union prior to a settlement on the islands. And there was little doubt that Iran had the leverage to block the smaller union—achievement of which was in any case by no means certain.[53] In any event, the announcement on July 18, 1971, that all trucial states except Ras al-Khaymah had agreed on a constitution which would be the basis for a union, was not received with consternation in Tehran.[54]

---

[52] See *The Times* (London), Feb. 12 and July 21, 1971; *New York Times,* June 13, 1971; *Financial Times* (London), June 14, 1971; *The Economist,* July 27, 1971, p. 30.

[53] Whitehall was reported to be apprehensive that even this truncated federation would founder. See *Daily Telegraph* (London), July 21, 1971.

[54] See *Ettelaat* (air ed.), July 19, 1971; *Kayhan* (air ed.), July 20, 1971. *Ettelaat* observed that Iran would oppose a federation until the islands were settled, therefore a federation would be useless. See *Ettelaat* (air ed.), Sept. 11, 1971. On the agreement, see *The Times* (London), July 19, 1971; *The Guardian* (Manchester), July 19, 1971.

Nor did the formal inauguration of the union on December 1, 1971, present any problem for Iran. In the first place, the question of the islands had indeed been "settled," and in the second place, an agreement had been reached with Sharjah so its inclusion in the union presented no problem. Ras al-Khaymah, with which no agreement was reached, was not in the union. The Iranian government thus recognized the union on December 2, and subsequently announced its readiness to cooperate with the emirates on a basis of friendship, respect, and equality.[55]

AN EVALUATION

A constant reality in the attempts to form a union of shaykhdoms between January 1970 and November 1971 was the fact of Tehran's lack of endorsement of the project, and later its opposition to it. As was shown in this section, the Iranian government planned for a unilateral exercise of responsibility in the Gulf, and articulated its doubts as to the stability and durability of the "feudal" regimes of the region. It followed naturally that Tehran had serious reservations as to the usefulness of pooling this instability and misgivings as to how effective any union, whatever its size or degree of integration, could be in the defense of the region.[56] The inability of the shaykhs to agree on a union surely confirmed Iranian skepticism. While formally the Iranian government's position in the January 1968–March 1970 period was that it did not oppose a union or the principle of a union, but only Bahrayn's inclusion in this union,[57] the facts showed otherwise. Its claim to Bahrayn served as an obstacle to the union in the first two years. But the Bahrayn settlement saw the surfacing of a new condition. The settlement of the islands of Abu Musa and the Tumbs now became a precondition for Iran's acceptance of the union. The official position after the Bahrayn settlement was that Iran supported the principle of a federation (or confederation), and cooperation between the shaykhs in whatever way they chose to express this, provided Iran's rights in the islands were safeguarded.[58] Yet the reality was that after the settlement the Iran government accelerated its bilateral contacts with the shaykhdoms without once supporting the federation publicly,

---

[55] See *Iran's Foreign Relations in 1350* (1971–72), p. 100.

[56] Iran was skeptical of the federation's chance of success, and doubted that, even if achieved, it could be effective. See *The Times* (London), March 6, 1971.

[57] *Iran's Foreign Relations in 1347* (1968–69), p. 42.

[58] *Ibid.*, 1349 (1970–71), pp. 64–65.

even before October when it first publicly linked satisfaction of its claim to the islands with withdrawal of its opposition to the federation.

Iran's posture to the federation was an officially "correct" one; it did not seek to influence the formation of the union being discussed, nor did it express a view as to its composition or scope, nor attempt to prod the shaykhs towards a swifter union. In short, it expressed no opinion as to the type of union it would prefer to see established, nor did it at any time lend the concept of union a gesture of support. One observer at the time suggested that Iran's reticence might be based on a reluctance to jeopardize the union among the "radical" Arab states by appearing to support it; or alternatively, on a reluctance to support a union which it considered would in any case fail.[59] The latter explanation is the more tenable. But there is a difference between doubting the viability of a project and contributing through one's actions to the failure of a project.

Unsure of the chances of the union's success, and dubious of its effectiveness in security questions even in the event of its achievement, the Iran government preferred to emphasize bilateral relations. The tactic of linking settlements, first on Bahrayn, and later on the islands, with the withdrawal of its opposition to the federation, clearly demonstrated its lack of enthusiasm for the project. By exercising pressure on Britain this way, it was clearly signaling Britain that the success of the federation (which Britain considered essential for Gulf stability) was of less importance to Tehran than it was to London. This meant either that Tehran had less faith in the federation's effectiveness than London, or that it believed that it could survive quite satisfactorily without the federation. In brief, the Iran government's *quid pro quo* indicated doubts about the viability of the union and its preference for reliance on its own power. It is possible that the fear of an Arab union controlled by an unfriendly Arab state, or under the influence of a hostile Arab League, also affected the Iranian attitude.[60] Similarly it is clear that, as the dominant Gulf power, Iran could exercise more influence on the Gulf states if they remained fragmented.

---

59 *The Times* (London), June 1, 1971. The same source detected "a touch of national pride" in Iran's attitude, which was evidenced by the view that it was for the shaykhdoms to come to her for help.

60 See *Middle East Economic Digest*, IX, No. 16 (April 17, 1970), 464–466.

Chapter VII

THE SECURITY OF THE GULF

If Iran was at worst opposed to, and at best lukewarm toward, a federation of Gulf states, this was not due to the existence of a judicious, reasoned, and planned alternative arrangement held by policy-makers in Iran. Iran's foreign policy in the Gulf from 1968 to 1971 was characterized by vacillation and indecision, in particular as it related to the type of arrangement envisaged for the Gulf's security. The concept of a Gulf defense pact—preferably formalized—between the larger littoral states, combined with misgivings that this was a feasible prospect, competed for primacy with the opposing view, perhaps latently held, that Iran should gird itself for the role of sole guarantor of the region's security.

These competing concepts of a cooperative or a unilateral defense orientation were not mutually exclusive. In some ways the government's preparation for the role of Gulf guardian through arms acquisitions may be viewed as *supportive* of its *related* aim of establishing a Gulf defense pact. From this perspective, a unilateral defense posture may be viewed as a fall-back position in the event a cooperative system for ensuring Gulf security failed to materialize. Nonetheless, in Iran's Gulf policy of this period there is a detectable strain between its attempt to harmonize relations with Sa'udi Arabia and Kuwait and organize a Gulf defense arrangement with them, and a *simultaneous* lack of faith that this was a viable option, as well as a *consequent* desire to rely only on itself. The maintenance of both these threads in its policy, in a perverse dynamic, made it likelier that a clear choice would have to be made between the two.

In seeking a *formal* cooperative arrangement after the Bahrayn settlement, the Iran government was oblivious to the intra-Arab implications for its putative partners. And the Arab rejection of the plan confirmed Iranian doubts as to the reliability of the littoral states as partners. Yet in subsequently adopting an assertive go-it-alone defense posture, it only succeeded in strengthening Arab suspicions about the wisdom of the cooperative defense arrangement which Iran had proposed.

The idea of formal diplomatic cooperation between Iran and Sa'udi Arabia goes back at least to the December 1965–January 1966 discussions on an Islamic conference. Syria, Egypt, and the USSR were critical of this, labeling it an "Islamic Alliance." Given the reactions it aroused, the idea was allowed to fade away into obscurity, to be revived in a quite different political context at Rabat in September 1969. But the idea of Iran-Sa'udi cooperation had at least been raised. With the decision to withdraw its troops from the Persian Gulf, the British government examined alternative, regional means to take over its task of maintaining the region's security. With this in mind, Britain's minister of state at the foreign office, Goronwy Roberts, in his visit to the region in January 1968 put forward a suggestion for Iran-Arab cooperation in the Gulf.

Between Roberts' first visit in November 1967 and his second in January 1968, the Iran government articulated an interest in playing an active role in the Gulf's defense and announced its support for cooperation between the Gulf states in this task.[1] On January 7 Iran formally announced its readiness to participate in "any form of regional cooperation for the defense of the area." [2] Although it was clear that the Arab states of the area heard this offer, none came forward to embrace it. No reference, for instance, was made to it in the joint communiqué issued at the end of the ruler of Kuwait's four-day visit to Iran on 13 January, despite the strong presumption that it was discussed.[3] Nor was it clear what form this "regional cooperation for defense" might take.

It was reported in the British press that Mr. Roberts, on his visit to the Gulf in January, had taken with him suggestions for Arab-Iranian cooperation in the Gulf, but reports varied as to the composition of the proposed defense arrangement.[4] Indicative of British thinking, per-

---

[1] See *Keyhan* (editorial), Nov. 12 and 16, 1967; Jan. 8, 1968.

[2] *Ettelaat*, Jan. 8, 1968; *The Times* (London), Jan. 10, 1968; *Daily Telegraph* (London), Jan. 10, 1968.

[3] *Ettelaat*, Jan. 10 and 11, 1968; *Daily Telegraph* (London), Jan. 11, 1968; *The Times* (London), Jan. 11, 1968. The communiqué is found in *Joint Communiqués 1349* (1970–71), pp. 135–137

[4] *The Times* (London), Jan. 16, 1968; *The Economist*, Jan. 20, 1968, pp. 34–35. The

haps, was an article entitled "Alliance Needed Now in the Persian Gulf" written by M. P. Eldon Griffiths for a London newspaper. The author argued that "Britain should encourage a Saudi-Persian alliance by offering to extend the Saudi air defense system . . . across the Gulf to Persia. We should also help the Shah strengthen his navy." [5]

Parallel to Britain's attempts to stimulate regional cooperation, there emerged an American suggestion. Undersecretary of State Eugene Rostow, in a Voice of America interview on January 19, 1968, said that the United States relied on security groupings involving Turkey, Iran, Pakistan, Kuwait, and Sa'udi Arabia to fill the vacuum left by Britain's withdrawal from the Gulf. What *The Times* (London) characterized as the "vast irrelevancy of his [Rostow's] proposal for a kind of old-fashioned alliance grouping" was more than merely "irrelevant." It tainted the idea of a regional grouping with Western sponsorship, and imported afresh all the divisiveness of the cold war, pacts, and "imperialism" into the already fragmented region. It was, in short, the kind of help from its friends with which Tehran could have safely dispensed. The suggestion was bitterly attacked by Damascus, Baghdad, and Cairo, which viewed it as a new "imperialist" pact, similar to the Baghdad Pact.[6] The idea was also denounced by Moscow on the grounds that such a defense system would be directed against the security of the southern frontiers of the Soviet Union. In the light of this onslaught, Sa'udi Arabia and Kuwait denied any intention of joining either a military or political pact or bloc.[7]

But if Rostow's suggestion dealt the fragile concept of a regional defense a near-mortal blow, the patient was already reeling from more local causes. Iran's announcement of its readiness to participate in a regional defense arrangement was received silently on the other shore of the Gulf. Sa'udi Arabia's support for Bahrayn, and subsequent Iranian insistence on its "historical rights" in the archipelago, contributed to a temporary polarization of the Gulf. Kuwait returned to championing the Gulf's "Arabism." Iran criticized this and adopted a hard-line policy vis-à-vis the waters of the Gulf disputed with Sa'udi Arabia.

---

principal differences involved the inclusion or exclusion of Iraq. Some reports anticipated Iran-Sa'udi cooperation, others Iran, Sa'udi Arabia, Kuwait, and Iraq's cooperation.

5 *Sunday Telegraph* (London), Jan. 21, 1968.

6 See *Al-Ahram*, Nov. 10, 1968. Baghdad's view was contained in a text of an article in *Al-Masa*, Jan. 22, 1968.

7 See *Keyhan*, Jan. 24, 1968; *The Times* (London) Jan. 23, 1968; and Jiddah Radio, in Arabic, Jan. 21, 1968; on BBC, Jan. 23, 1968.

It is difficult to discern precisely whether Iran's hard-line followed the (tacit) rejection of its proposal for cooperation, or whether its proposal for cooperation was ignored because of its insistence *at the same time* on its claim to Bahrayn. But it is evident that the proposal, which was more an attempt to sound out its neighbors than a concrete plan, rested from the start on a shaky foundation. It neither took into account the impact of the pressures generated in the Arab world (and hence on its prospective partners) by such emotionally-laden issues as Western-backed pacts or defense organizations nor did it seek to ameliorate Arab suspicions about Iran's motives reinforced by the latter's persistent claim on Bahrayn.[8]

Iran did not discard the idea of defense cooperation with its neighbors. With the improvement of relations with Sa'udi Arabia in June 1968, and particularly after the Shah's November visit to Sa'udi Arabia and Kuwait, the project was quietly revived.

In May–June 1969, after the gesture of conciliation made in his New Delhi speech in January, the Shah sketched the form such a pact might take. He told Alfred Friendly of the *Washington Post* that while Iran had no desire to play the role of "grandfather" in the Gulf, it would propose the creation of a defense pact, if the littoral states were agreeable.[9] He elaborated on this to Winston S. Churchill of *The Times* (London):

We would be willing, in conjunction with Sa'udi Arabia, to provide protection for the Gulf states. Our paratroop and armored regiments at Shiraz can give them as much protection as the British forces in the area today. . . . We would like to see a common defense policy established for the area. We would propose that the Persian Gulf become a closed sea, and that the port of Bahrayn be used as a joint base.[10]

The practical implementation of such a project manifestly rested on a shared perception by the littoral states of threats to the Gulf's security, and on these states' ability to work together. Neither of these conditions were met at this time, primarily due to the Iranian government's continued claim to Bahrayn and its refusal to support a federation in advance of a settlement of this claim. Practical measures to give tangible form to a defense arrangement were thus delayed until May 1970. But the undercurrent in Iran's policy of relying on its own

---

8 See *Daily Telegraph* (London), Feb. 12, 1968; *The Economist*, Feb. 10, 1968, p. 25.

9 See the text of the interview in the *Washington Post*, May 4, 1969; official Persian translation in *Iran's Foreign Relations in 1348* (1969–70), pp. 242–243.

10 *The Times* (London), June 13, 1969. Persian text in *Iran's Foreign Relations in 1348* (1969–70), pp. 243–247. See also *Iran Tribune*, June 27, 1969.

resources was also a discernible feature of Gulf policy at this time. The official yearbook of Iran's foreign relations in 1969–70 expressed this clearly: "Iran is prepared to cooperate with any and all littoral states, but if they are unwilling, Iran is equally prepared to act on its own." [11]

In April 1970 Sa'udi Deputy Foreign Minister Omar Saqaff visited Iran, in accordance with the 1968 agreement on periodic consultations. The visit was the occasion for much speculation in the press that an agreement on a defense pact was in the offing. Although agreement was reached on the need for Britain's withdrawal on schedule, and for cooperation among the littoral states to ensure the Gulf's security, no agreement was reached on a formal defense pact.

Iran's interest in such a formal security arrangement persisted. In May the Shah told a Western journalist: "We are prepared to enter into some kind of regional cooperation treaty or pact involving anything from the closest political cooperation to the loosest. It is up to them to tell us what kind of relations they want." [12]

Thus between June 1969 and May 1970 Iran's policy toward a Gulf pact was significantly modified. Because of the lack of enthusiasm for its defense project, the Iranian government replaced its relatively concrete suggestions of June 1969 with the more passive statement that the pact offer still stood, and that it could be as loose as possible. Having in its view magnanimously discarded its claim to Bahrayn, it was clearly disappointed by the absence of Sa'udi and Kuwait enthusiasm for the Gulf defense project.[13]

Its reaction was to look to its own defenses. The Shah's April 13, 1970, interview with *The Times* (London) is a revealing illustration of the two threads of Iranian thinking noted earlier. On the one hand, the Shah left open the possibility of defense cooperation—only now it was for the Arab states to take the initiative. On the other hand, he insisted that no concrete cooperation in defense could take place until the Bahrayn dispute was resolved.

Failure to reach an agreement with Sa'udi Arabia in April 1970 was the first step in a movement toward adopting a posture of self-reliance and jettisoning the idea of formal cooperation in the Gulf's defense. Parallel to this, Iran firmly asserted its claim to the Gulf islands. In

---

11 *Iran's Foreign Relations in 1348* (1968–69), pp. 58–59.

12 *New York Times*, May 10, 1970. The foreign minister underscored the more passive Iranian attitude in *Jiddah*, May 20, 1970. See *Akhbar va Asnad 1349 (az Farvardin ta Shahrivar)*, p. 253.

13 For a report from Tehran testifying to this, see *The Times* (London), May 14, 1970.

October 1970 the idea of Iran-Arab cooperation in the Gulf's defense was dealt a final mortal blow when Tehran refused to withdraw its opposition to a federation until its claim to the islands was met.

IRAN AND THE GULF PACT: AN EVALUATION

The idea of a Gulf defense pact raised in January 1968 labored from the outset under the severest of handicaps. Like the Baghdad Pact and Islamic Conference proposal, it appeared—or was made to appear by its foes—to be "imperialist" in parentage and goals. No Arab government in the Gulf was able to withstand the pressures generated by such an issue in inter-Arab politics. Eugene Rostow's suggestion only served to increase these pressures and weaken the concept. Quite apart from this, the Iranian proposal for cooperation was severely hampered by its sponsor's ambivalence toward the project. This was evident in its alternation between a hard line (the Bahrayn claim, opposition to the federation, the oil-rig incident, the claim to the islands) and a cooperative line (Bahrayn settlement, the Gulf defense proposal, and offers of financial assistance). The same ambivalence marked the Iran government's comments, which fluctuated between the need for organizing a regional defense system and scornful comments about the reliability or durability of its prospective partners. It was also manifest in the movement from a policy of seizing the diplomatic initiative—making the proposal and attempting to rally support for it—to one of leaving the offer on the table but making unmistakably nationalist claims about self-reliance. This made it difficult for even the most well-disposed Arab states to join in any formal tie with Iran, for they could then be made to appear as supporters of Iran's claims in the Gulf.

A basic reason for the failure of the defense pact proposal was the Iran government's insufficient understanding of Arab politics. Iran's policy-makers were unable to understand the pressures working on their Arab neighbors. These pressures include the following, summarized as a set of negative propositions: No Arab state could afford to associate itself in a *formal* pact with Iran (1) if it appeared to be Western-inspired; (2) if it appeared to be directed *against* another Arab state;[14] (3) if it thereby appeared to be underwriting present or future

---

[14] In May 1970, Iranian officials were publicly expressing their concern about Iraq's threat to Kuwait's independence. The foreign minister visited Kuwait and offered it Iran's protection, much to the embarrassment of the Kuwait government. See especially *The Times* (London), July 7, 1970; *Keyhan International*, July 8, 1970, and *Ayandegan*, July 9, 1970.

Iranian claims. Negative Arab reaction is thus not difficult to comprehend.

In the first place, the suggestion came from the only state in the Gulf that was a member of a pact, a state which was militarily equipped by the West, and it coincided with Mr. Roberts' trip to Tehran. It was thus in some Arab eyes *ipso facto* a Western project, and it was treated as such by Cairo, Damascus, Baghdad, and Moscow. As a result the governments of Sa'udi Arabia and Kuwait quickly disassociated themselves from it. In the second place, the proposal could be viewed as directed against Iraq, particularly after April 1969 and the deterioration of Iran-Iraq relations. It being a cardinal principle of Kuwait foreign policy not to take sides in intra-Arab disputes, it was natural for its government to avoid taking Iran's side in Iran-Arab disputes. This even-handedness, it should be noted, extended equally to a refusal to take part in an Arab pact directed against Iran.[15] It was a measure of Iran's underestimation of the issues raised by its proposal for cooperation with the Arab states, that its press continued to insist that all the problems in the area stemmed from Nasser.[16] Finally the Iran government's claims to Bahrayn and the Gulf Islands, and its attitude toward the federation, were not conducive to creating an atmosphere of trust. Equally, it should be observed, the Arab states' reaction to its proposal served to emphasize *their* unreliability in the eyes of the Iranian leadership.

There remained a further difficulty in the proposal. A *formal* defense tie, which the government originally sought, had certain practical advantages. Informal cooperation in defense was impractical, given different languages, training methods, equipment, and so forth.[17] Iran may also have hoped that, in exchange for underwriting the costly defense of the region, a tacit understanding could be reached with the Gulf Arab oil-producing states to proportionately increase its oil production to cover some of this expenditure.[18] Both of these points are plausible and shed light on the otherwise inexplicable search for

---

15 The reference is not only to the Kuwait rejection of Iraq's proposal in July 1970—see *Keyhan,* July 20, 1970; *Ettelaat* (air ed.), July 22, 1970; *Keyhan International,* July 21, 1970; *The Guardian* (Manchester), July 22, 1970—but also to the periodic calls to defend the "Arabism of the Gulf" by means of an Arab defense pact. See especially *The Times* (London), April 5, 1968; *Los Angeles Times,* Sept. 26, 1968.

16 See *Ettelaat,* Jan. 14 and 15, 1968. See also *Keyhan,* Jan. 15, 1968.

17 *The Times* (London), May 14, 1970.

18 *The Economist,* Oct. 11, 1969, p. 43.

a *formal* defense pact. Unless defense coordination was indeed impossible informally, or there was hope in Tehran that its defense costs could be covered by some understanding with the other oil-producing states, there appears to be no convincing explanation why Iran sought a *formal* defense arrangement with the precarious governments of the Arabian littoral.

To be sure, a formal defense pact had the additional advantage to Iran of formalizing its primacy in the area and extending and legitimizing its influence on the Arabian littoral. It may have been this possibility, inherent in the military imbalance among the pact's members, which threatened to weaken Sa'udi Arabia and Kuwait's jealous influence on the shaykhdoms, that served as an additional incentive for them to rebuff it. Certainly from the vantage point of the smaller Gulf states, the proposed cure may have appeared more dangerous than the malady. A defense pact between three large Gulf states might have posed new security problems for them, problems which remained balanced or dormant in the present setting of triangular (or quadrilateral) competition between Iran, Sa'udi Arabia, Kuwait (and Iraq).[19]

THE MOVE TOWARD SELF-RELIANCE

The emphasis in Iran's recent foreign policy on reliance primarily on itself for defense, and the adoption of a stance as the responsible guardian of the Gulf, are not to be accounted for solely by the failure of a defense pact project. Underlying much of the discussion of Gulf affairs during 1968–1971 in Iran, skepticism of the reliability or durability of the shaykhdoms and the proposed federation has been evident. The Shah publicly voiced his doubts as early as May 1968.[20] Since then it has been a consistent theme in his comments. In October 1969, when asked what he considered major threats to the Gulf's stability, the Shah replied: "The threat comes from weak governments, weak countries, corrupt countries, where the element of subversion will have free ground for their activities, free hunting, if I can say so. . . . So the threat will come . . . at the beginning, and in most cases from internal struggles and strife and destruction." [21]

In April 1970 he elaborated on this theme, saying it was "high time

---

19 *Vidé* Shaykh Rashid of Dubay's comment about the security of the emirates: "The Arabs know that if they try to interfere they will have to face Iran, and Iran knows that if she tries to interfere she will have to face the Arabs. As long as both sides recognize that, there will be no trouble." *The Times* (London), Feb. 11, 1971.

20 *The Guardian* (Manchester), May 25, 1968.

21 See *NBC-TV*, "*Meet the Press*," XII, No. 41 (Oct. 26, 1969), pp. 4–5. The official text in Persian is found in *Iran's Foreign Relations in 1348* (1969–70), pp. 272–273.

to reform the medieval systems still surviving in parts of the area. . . . Rulers who blocked reform would simply have to be replaced as Shaikh Shakbut was in Abu Dhabi." [22] The following month he was asked by some French interviewers if he was anxious about the penetration and spread of Marxism in parts of the Arabian Peninsula, given Britain's withdrawal. He replied: "It must be confessed that there are signs of Maoist activities in the Persian Gulf region. But there is no opportunity for these activities to penetrate and bear fruit except in those states which still live under medieval living conditions. The danger can be recognized and easily controlled in countries where in my opinion there are serious reforms and responsible people with eyes open to life in the twentieth century." [23] In June 1970 the Shah was asked if he were pessimistic about the future of the Gulf region except for Iran. He replied he was "pessimistic if the situation remained the same and the people responsible did not open their eyes to the situation." [24] By April 1971 the Shah was expressing his doubts about, and concern for Sa'udi Arabia's stability. [25]

Paralleling the Shah's anxiety about the stability of the Gulf states was doubt as to their ability to contribute meaningfully to the Gulf's defense. In terms of practical policy, this meant that even in the event of cooperation with the Arab states in the Gulf's defense, Iran would have to bear the brunt of the defense burden, at least for the next few years. Iranian officials told Dana Adams Schmidt that the only country Iran regarded seriously as a Gulf partner was Sa'udi Arabia. Yet they noted that even in this case "It would be five or six years before Sa'udi armed forces were built up to a point where they could be taken seriously." [26]

The Shah was more explicit. He told *Associated Press* that Iran hoped for cooperation with the Gulf states but that in any case Iran was the only Gulf naval power. Since Iran could not be certain of the future course of events in the area, the Shah continued, it was prudent not to count on future developments but to proceed to assume its

---

[22] *The Times* (London), April 13, 1970; *Keyhan International*, April 16, 1970.

[23] The official Persian text of the interview of May 25, 1970, is found in *Akhbar va Asnad 1349 (az Farvardin ta Shahrivar)*, p. 229. See also *Ettelaat* (air ed.), May 27, 1970. English text is in *Keyhan International*, May 28, 1970.

[24] See *Akhbar va Asnad 1349 (az Farvardin ta Shahrivar)*, p. 223; *L'Express* (Paris), No. 987 (June 8–14, 1970), pp. 30–31; *Ettelaat* (air ed.), June 9, 1970; *Keyhan International* (editorial), June 6, 1970.

[25] See Alvin J. Cottrell, "Concern over Saudi Arabia's Viability: An Exclusive Interview with the Shah of Iran."

[26] *New York Times*, May 10, 1970.

responsibilities in the region. He particularly stressed the long lead-time necessary to acquire a navy and train its officers: "It takes twenty years to build a navy." [27] These doubts concerning the durability of the Gulf states—as well as an evaluation that they possessed, in any case, little significant military capability—partially accounts for the constant theme (a submotif until mid-1970) that Iran would rely on itself if no pact was forthcoming. The Shah put this clearly in May 1970, saying that in such an eventuality, "We will have to do the job ourselves if necessary, where defense and keeping the sea-lanes open are concerned." [28]

But skepticism about the political reliability or military effectiveness of the other Gulf states is by no means the sole explanation of Iran's emphasis on self-reliance. An important influence on the Shah's attitude has been his understanding of the role of Iran's Western friends, in particular Britain and the United States. And it is this interpretation that underlies and conditions Iran's defense posture and its view of the role of nonlittoral states in the Gulf. Basically the Shah's view of the role of Britain and the U.S. in the Gulf is informed by his reading of international politics in the past decade. There is no need to elaborate here the Shah's shock and dismay at finding little or no CENTO or SEATO aid forthcoming for Pakistan in 1965 (or again in 1971), or NATO or CENTO aid for Turkey on its Cyprus dispute. The Shah was similarly upset by Washington's rapid recognition of the Republic of Yemen and refusal to consider Nasser a serious menace to the Persian Gulf. Finally, the Shah was annoyed by Britain's failure either to provide a defense treaty with, or defend, the South Arabian federation, and by its readiness to relinquish Aden under what Tehran believed was Nasserite pressure. These shocks for the Shah, though interesting for the light they throw on the psychology of Iran's leadership—particularly as they reflect the view that these pacts were made for regional questions—do not of course explain Iran's current Gulf policy. They do, however, indicate the thinking that informs it. This can be distilled essentially to the view that the West is an unreliable ally in regional disputes.

But this was not a bitter evaluation that affected the leadership's view of the West as partners. On the contrary, the Shah welcomed the opportunity for Iran to play a more active regional role, believing that Iran had both the means and the will to do so—and in any case, no

---

27 For the Shah's AP interview of June 3, see *Ettelaat* (air ed.), June 4, 1970.
28 *New York Times,* May 10, 1970. For similar comments see *Ettelaat* (air ed.), Oct. 19, 1969; *Iran's Foreign Relations in 1348* (1969–70), pp. 57–58.

prudent alternative. The Shah has been most successful in convincing
Britain and the United States that their mutual interests dictate the
augmentation of Iran's military establishment to enable it to assume a
more active role in the region's defense. Thus both the Shah's evaluation of the West's future role in regional questions, and his assertion
of Iran's ability and willingness to assume responsibility for the Gulf's
defense, are important components affecting Iran's move to a posture
of self-reliance in the Gulf. This posture reflects, then, an evaluation
of the role of the great powers in the contemporary world and a
psychological dimension or current underlying Iran's self-assertive
policies.

As the United States' involvement in Vietnam grew in the 1960's,
and its preoccupations in that region and at home gave it less time,
resources, and inclination to pursue an activist foreign policy elsewhere on the globe, the Iranian economy grew—and, with it, the
government's military expenditures. Parallel to these trends, Britain
contracted its responsibilities, dismantled its imperial outposts, and
devalued sterling. The gradual rise in Iran's capabilities and a disposition to take a more active regional role, coincident as it was with
its Western partners' inclination to help it assume such a role, was
not an overnight phenomenon. It had at least two significant results:
(1) As a stable and relatively powerful state regionally, Iran's diplomatic hand was vastly strengthened in its relations with its Western
partners, for what its leadership was prepared to do was precisely what
the West would have liked to have it do. This gave it strong and
persuasive arguments to advance to its Western partners. (2) Since these
states shared with Iran similar interests in the stability of the region
and the continued flow of oil, the Iran government was able to extract a price for its role as guardian—that is, the passivity of the
United States and Britain in Iran's local actions.

The Shah's recognition of the change in Iran's relations with the
West dates back several years. For some purposes the 1964–1966 period,
and emphasis on an "independent national policy" and the arms agreement with the USSR, is a turning point. Certainly by 1968 a change
could be detected. The Shah told an interviewer in May of that
year: "Our relations with the West have changed in that we feel more
and more that we can now defend our interests alone." [29] In June
1969 he clearly expressed his skepticism of both the U.S. and Britain's
will to play a role in the region:

---

[29] See The Shah's interview with *Iran Tribune,* May 24, 1968.

What would happen if Iraq were to attack us tomorrow? . . . It would be like Pakistan's dispute with India. . . . When Pakistan was forced to call a cease-fire line well inside Pakistan's territory only a few miles from Lahore, what did CENTO do? *What did the United States, with whom Pakistan had a bilateral treaty, do? We cannot rely on others for our defense; that is why we are building up our forces.*

The Shah added that Iran would be able to give the Gulf shaykhdoms

as much protection as the British forces in the area today, which would probably not fight anyway if the situation became serious.[30]

The Shah subsequently elaborated on this in an interview with Edwin Newman of NBC-TV in February 1970.

The Shah: We [have] developed a sense that, well, it's very wonderful to have friends and allies; it's very wonderful to have an institution like the United Nations, but at the end, no self-respecting nation in the world would do otherwise than to first count on itself.

Edwin Newman: But a country the size of Iran obviously cannot depend on itself exclusively; there are few countries, if any any more, that can hope to be self-sufficient militarily.

The Shah: Well, that depends for what reason, Mr. Newman. That's why we have an alliance, and we are still keeping that alliance, although it's only on paper, really.

Edwin Newman: CENTO?

The Shah: Yes, and it is in the context of a global war, which seems to be so remote. But we are counting on ourselves and our military might for anything that might be local. Because I think it would be very embarrassing for the world if the big powers had to intervene in local conflicts.[31]

In addition to doubting the will of the great powers, and subsequently the sagacity of their interventions anyway, the Shah also recognized that the changing international context was decreasing the role of the hitherto ubiquitous superpowers. Thus, in January 1972, he said:

I believe that America has realized it can no longer play the role of an international gendarme and that the world's security should, in any case, be guarded by countries that can assume that duty in each region. . . . How many times can one repeat the experience of Vietnam? . . . Here we are

---

[30] *The Times* (London), June 10, 1969 (emphasis supplied). The official Persian text is found in *Iran's Foreign Relations in 1348* (1969–70), pp. 243–244.

[31] WNBC-TV, "Speaking Freely" (transcript in typescript from WNBC Community Affairs Department), Feb. 22, 1970, pp. 14–15. The official Persian text is found in *Iran's Foreign Relations in 1348*; see esp. pp. 297–298.

talking about the "superpowers" and one can say that the role of these powers will gradually become smaller.[32]

The striking similarity of this comment with the basic principles underlying the "Nixon Doctrine" and President Nixon's approach to the United States' friends around the world is evident when compared with the following quotation taken from the President's Report to Congress, 1971: "But it is no longer natural or possible in this age to argue that security or development around the globe is primarily America's concern. The defense and progress of other countries must be first their responsibility and second a regional responsibility." [33]

The Iranian leadership acted on its perception of the role of the great powers in the 1970's in the attitude it showed toward their presence in the Persian Gulf.

ROLE OF THE NONLITTORAL STATES

Consistent with its view that the United States and Britain are unreliable in regional conflicts, Iran has sought to discourage both extension of the latter's presence in the Gulf and establishment by either the United States or the Soviet Union of a substitute presence in the region. In line with its intention to become more self-reliant in regional defense, and more active in diplomacy, it has sought to convince the West that its role as guardian of the Gulf's peace could safeguard their interests as much as its own. Hence it has received support from the United States and Britain in augmenting its military establishment. This strength is intended to deter, or if necessary physically dissuade, any trouble-makers in the Gulf.

Iran's opposition to a foreign presence in the Gulf should be viewed in the light of its lack of faith in the benefits of a Western presence and a definite apprehension as to the consequences of a non-Western power's presence. Stated simply in cost/benefit terms, the Iran government doubted that the benefits of substituting the United States for the British presence would outweigh the undoubted costs this would entail in terms of the extension of superpower rivalry into the Gulf. The putative benefits of a large-scale U.S. presence, in this view, were

---

[32] The official transcript of the interview, Jan. 16, 1972, is contained in *Akhbar va Asnad, 1350 (as Mehr ta Esfand)* (1971–72), pp. 37–38; see also *Ettelaat* (air ed.), Jan. 22 and 23, 1972. For the complete English text, see *Keyhan International* (weekly), Jan. 29, 1972; excerpts in *New York Times*, Jan. 17, 1972.

[33] See the section on the Nixon Doctrine in "U.S. Foreign Policy for the 1970's: Building for Peace," *A Report to the Congress by Richard Nixon, President of the United States*, Feb. 25, 1971, p. 14, and the discussion in Chapter 10.

rendered dubious in any case by the belief that this presence would not be used (and in Iran's view would not be necessary anyway) in disputes arising between the Gulf states, and yet might provoke a Soviet intrusion into the region with serious consequences for the region's stability. It followed that if Iran, as the dominant Gulf power, could ensure the continuance of its preponderant military strength, it could guarantee the region's peace while seeking through diplomacy to avoid the intrusion of superpower rivalry by denying both superpowers a permanent presence in the Gulf.

As far as the continuation of Britain's presence was concerned, Iran would doubtless have preferred a British presence in its acknowledged and unique form for several more years. But after the January 1968 announcement, Iran came to the view that any extension or reversal of that decision would be too costly in regional terms. Long under fire in the republican Arab states, literally so in Aden and South Arabia, its presence would thereafter have been an even more conspicuous target for nationalist agitation, an incitement rather than a deterrent to extremists. It was thus perhaps the only consistent theme of Iran's Gulf diplomacy from 1968 to 1971 that Britain should withdraw on schedule, and should not be replaced by either the United States or the Soviet Union. It is to this diplomacy that we now turn.

Even before Britain's announcement, there had been signs that the Iran government wished to exclude nonlittoral states from the Gulf's affairs. In the early 1960's this had been aimed at Nasser. The announcement on January 16, 1968, of Britain's intended withdrawal was received with little public concern. Prime Minister Hoveyda emphasized that Britain's departure would not create a vacuum, and the Iran government was not worried about it.[34] Ten days later he repeated this, saying that Iran would not permit non-Gulf states to enter the Gulf, or interfere in Gulf affairs, nor would it tolerate Britain's return to the Gulf in a different form.[35] The need for Britain's "genuine" departure hereafter became a euphemism in the Iranian press to criticize Britain's support of the federation of Gulf emirates. But Britain, or Britain's support of the federation, was by no means the only source of Iran's anxiety. There still remained fear that Egypt might take an activist Gulf role, and Iran's attempts to generate broad acceptance of the principle that the Gulf's future exclusively concerned the states bordering the Gulf should be viewed in this light.

---

34 *Daily Telegraph* (London), Jan. 18, 1968.
35 *Ettelaat,* Jan. 28, 1968.

To take but one representative example, Tehran radio complained of outside interference when some of the leaders of the shaykhdoms visited Cairo in 1968: "No countries outside the Gulf area have any right to interfere in it, or determine its future. . . . Iran will not allow another colonialist power to take the place of a former one." Tehran concentrated on obtaining wide diplomatic support for the right of the Gulf states to settle the affairs of their region without outside interference. It thus sought and obtained Turkey's and Pakistan's endorsement of this proposition in December 1968, and India's in January 1969.[36]

The government throughout 1968–69 also attempted both to emphasize the littoral states' ability to manage their own affairs and cooperate, and to reject the concept of a "power vacuum" resulting from Britain's departure. The view of a panel of specialists convened at Georgetown University, that the West would need to fill the vacuum left by Britain's departure, combined with doubts as to the ability of the Gulf states to work together, was thus subjected to severe criticism by the Iranian press. It was viewed as an attempt to revive the "imperialistic era." [37]

More important, the Shah now began to make public his views about the role of outside powers in the Gulf. In January 1969, when asked by a journalist how large a role he anticipated the Soviet Union would play after Britain's departure, he replied: "This question must be settled by the countries surrounding the Persian Gulf. We do not want to see Britain leave and then come back in by the back door, still pulling strings from London. But we also don't want any big powers trying to replace Britain." [38] Two months later he told the *New York Times*' Hanson Baldwin that he opposed continuation of United States presence in Bahrayn after 1971, as well as any attempt by the great powers to fill whatever vacuum was created by Britain's withdrawal. The Foreign Minister, Zahedi, repeated this after a CENTO meeting in Tehran in May 1969.[39] In June the Shah told a British journalist: "It was your government's decision to go, and we shall not invite you back—I made this clear to Mr. Heath [the leader of the

---

[36] The text of the RCD states' communiqué of Dec. 27, 1968, is found in *Iran's Foreign Relations 1348* (1968–69) pp. 229–233, esp. 231. English summaries are found in: *The Times* (London), Dec. 28, 1968. The Iran-India communiqué is found in *Joint Communiqués* 1969–70, p. 188. See also *Keyhan International*, Jan. 5, 1969.

[37] For representative samples, see *Keyhan International* (editorial) Jan. 20 and 21, 1969; *Ayandegan*, Jan. 19, 1969.

[38] *U.S. News and World Report*, Jan. 27, 1969, p. 49.

[39] See *New York Times*, March 25 and May 28, 1969.

minority Conservative Party] when he was here. The Conservatives have made it clear that they would return only if invited. We do not intend to invite anyone, either British, Russian, or American. In fact, we would like to make the Persian Gulf a closed sea." [40] The government subsequently pointed out that what was meant by this was not a sea closed to navigation by the non-Gulf states, but rather opposition to the establishment of naval bases by foreign states in the Gulf. At the same time, the Shah expressed his doubts about both Britain's ability and its resolve to take an active role in regional disputes. Again, in an interview in September 1969 with a British member of Parliament, the Shah repeated the same theme: his opposition to an extension of Britain's presence and to any U.S. or USSR substitute for that presence, and his faith in Iran's ability to defend the area.[41] This was repeated by the foreign minister at Jiddah airport in May 1970, when he reported that Sa'udi Arabia, Kuwait, and Iran agreed on the need for Britain's withdrawal on schedule.

By mid-1970, the solution of the Bahrayn question, the new and increased contacts between Iran and the Gulf states, and Iran's increased military strength, as well as the diplomatic activity on the Arab shore of the Gulf, had all in part been stimulated by Britain's announcement in January 1968. By this time a great deal of national energy, propaganda, and diplomatic activity had been expended in the cause of a Gulf free to manage its own affairs. It was thus hardly surprising that Tehran should actively lobby against any postponement of the December 1971 deadline. The Iranian view was succinctly put by Foreign Minister Zahedi: "Once you have said you are going you must go. Otherwise staying might cause more trouble than if you went." [42] While the Labor government remained in power there was little danger of this, but the victory of a Conservative government after a sudden election in June 1970 threatened Tehran with a British reversal. In that same month the Shah twice outlined his position on this question. To a French news magazine he expressed his opposition to a substitute foreign presence in the Gulf after Britain's departure. And in a press conference in Helsinki, he warned that Britain could not unilaterally decide to extend the duration of its presence in the Gulf. If confirmation was needed by London of Tehran's attitude toward

---

40 *The Times* (London), June 10, 1969.
41 See the text of interview with Roy Roebuck, M.P., Sept. 6, 1969, in *Iran's Foreign Relations in 1348 (1969–70)*, p. 253.
42 *New York Times*, Nov. 15, 1970.

the Conservative government's reappraisal of its predecessor's Gulf policy, it came in the course of an interview of Iran's prime minister, who warned against an extension of the December 31, 1971, deadline and attempts "to turn back the hands of time." [43]

In early July 1970 the new British government announced its intention of entering into discussions with the Gulf states to ascertain their views, in order to clarify its own policy in the Gulf.[44] The Iran government immediately mounted a rapid diplomatic campaign to ensure that Kuwait and Sa'udi Arabia maintained a solid front in rejecting any extension of the British presence. Iran's foreign minister visited Kuwait on July 6 for two days and announced Kuwait's opposition to such an extension. On July 11 he visited Sa'udi Arabia for three days and succeeded in obtaining that state's opposition to an extension.[45] Meanwhile, the Shah on July 10 met Britain's foreign secretary, Alec Douglas-Home, in Brussels and informed him of Iran's opposition. Three of the largest Gulf states were thus in agreement by mid-July that Britain's departure should proceed on schedule.[46] In view of this unanimity among the major Gulf states to any reconsideration by Britain of its intention to withdraw, the Conservative government announced that it would not depart from its predecessor's schedule for quitting the Gulf.[47] The Iranian press reflected the government's exuberance at its success in coordinating the diplomacy of the littoral states on this question (as well as the importance attached to Gulf affairs) by the intensity of its coverage of Iran's Gulf policy and its editorial comments on "Iran's diplomatic victory" and Britain's "lost cause." [48]

---

[43] See respectively *Akhbar va Asnad 1349 (az Farvardin ta Shahrivar)*, (1970–71), pp. 232–233, for the Helsinki statement see *Akhbar va Asnad 1349 (az Farvardin ta Shahrivar)* (1970–71), p. 238; *Ettelaat* (air ed.), June 27 and 28, 1970 (editorial); *Keyhan International*, June 28, 1970. For the prime minister's interview, see *Ayandegan*, June 23, 1970.

[44] See *Ettelaat*, July 4, 1970. Iran had awaited this announcement. See *Keyhan International*, June 22, 1970.

[45] For Zahedi's Kuwait visit, see *Ettelaat* (air ed.), July 5 and 9, 1970; *Ayandegan*, July 6–8, 1970; *Keyhan*, July 5, 1970; *Keyhan International*, July 6, 7, 1970. For the communiqué, see *Akhbar va Asnad 1349 (az Farvardin ta Shahrivar)*, p. 251, and *Ettelaat*, July 8, 1970. For the visit to Sa'udi Arabia, see *Ayandegan*, July 12 and 15, 1970; *Keyhan International*, July 11, 13, 15, 1970.

[46] *Ayandegan*, July 14, 1970; *Keyhan International*, July 16, 1970.

[47] *The Guardian* (Manchester), July 17, 1970; *The Times* (London), July 11, 1970; *Ettelaat* (air ed.), July 11, 12, 21, 1970.

[48] See esp. *Ayandegan* (editorial), July 11 and 16, 1970; *Ettelaat* (air ed.), editorial of July 12, 1970; *Keyhan International*, editorial of July 13, 1970.

Quite apart from Iran's diplomacy, it was true that none of the independent Gulf states "could afford to be caught putting out a welcome mat for the British,"—whatever they felt about the departure. Some of the smaller Gulf states were as averse to discussion about Britain's withdrawal in 1970 as they had been in 1968, and at least one publicly regretted the decision when it was formally confirmed in March 1971.[49] But these were small states, and it was intended by London from 1968 to spur the shaykhs to cooperate and compromise in forming a union by having a definite deadline hanging over their heads.

Reflecting its eagerness to assume a more active role, the Iran government continued to show sensitivity to any sign that Britain's Gulf role might be reassessed. This is evident from the continued coverage given the issue in Iran's newspapers, the constant reiteration of the regional states' readiness to assume their responsibilities, and the coverage of Sir William Luce's activities in the Gulf and Prime Minister Heath's visit to Washington in December 1970.[50] Britain's formal reiteration in March 1971 of its decision to leave the Gulf by the end of the year was officially welcomed by Tehran as the "correct decision" and by the press as an historical watershed ending an era of "imperialism" in the Gulf.[51]

If Britain's decision to leave the Gulf on schedule satisfied Tehran as a necessary condition for Gulf security, there was no indication that it was viewed as sufficient by itself. Throughout 1971 the Shah continued to call for the exclusion of non-Gulf states from the Gulf, and particularly from a permanent presence in the Gulf. For example, he told a French newspaperman in May 1971 that it was of no benefit to the region if Britain's departure was followed by another great power's entry. Similarly, he told Parliament in September that the future of the Gulf was the responsibility of the peoples of the area only, and the defense of the security of the Gulf rested *exclusively* with the states of the region.[52]

---

[49] The phrase is from *The Economist*, July 18, 1970, p. 14. See also Shaykh Rashid of Dubay's comments in *The Times* (London), July 14, 1970, March 3, 1971.

[50] For coverage of Heath's visit to Washington, see *Ettelaat* (air ed.), Dec. 17–20, 1970, and Feb. 2, 11, 27, and 28, 1971.

[51] The government's welcome is found in *Akhbar va Asnad 1349* (*az Mehr ta Esfand*), p. 70. For articles, see *Ettelaat* (air ed.), editorials of March 3, 4, and 10, 1971. See also *The Times* (London), March 2, 1971.

[52] See the Shah's interview with *Depeche du Midi* (Toulouse), in *Akhbar va Asnad 1350* (*az Farvardin ta Shahrivar*) (1971–72), p. 54; his statement to Parliament, *ibid.*, p. 85; and his Speech from the Throne in *Keyhan International* (weekly), Sept. 4, 1971 (emphasis supplied).

Iran's continued preoccupation with the future of the Gulf and the policies adopted by the great powers toward it are quite simply explained by the ease with which a nonlittoral state could establish a presence, or a base, in the Gulf. It would merely take an invitation by a littoral state to such a power, and the extension to it of base rights, to upset much of Iran's recent diplomacy, as well as its security assumptions. Lest a foreign presence in the Gulf, whether British or American, should constitute an invitation to the Soviet Union to follow suit, the Shah has sought to assure the end of any such presence. He told *The Times* (London) correspondent in April 1970 that he had no objection to a British force "nearby but outside the Gulf itself, to guard Masirah island and the airport at Salalah in the territory of Muscat on the route to southeast Asia." The foreign minister told the same correspondent that there could be no objection to a British aircraft carrier operating in the Indian Ocean, which could exercise at times with other CENTO forces in the Gulf itself.[53]

The Shah told visitors that he hoped Britain's political presence in the region, which was beneficial, would be maintained and strengthened after the departure of the troops; and he offered to facilitate this. He told M. P. Dennis Walters: "Nobody understands the area as well as the British." [54] Britain, as the paramount power in the Gulf for the past century and a half, appears to have accepted Iran as its successor. It has assisted in building up Iran for its future role with military equipment. Apart from the sale of substantial numbers of Hovercraft and 4 Vosper MK-5 destroyers, including Seacat missiles, Britain sold Iran 400 Tiger Cat missiles and 800 Chieftain tanks.[55] There is every indication that this relationship will continue. The Shah has recently told British newsmen: "We will contribute fairly well to your balance of payments in future years." [56] This support has also been translated into Britain's diplomacy. It refused to protest, much less condemn, Iran's occupation of the Gulf islands. Thus the British representative at the United Nations, echoing his Foreign Minister's comments to the House of Commons on December 6, 1971, told the Security Council:

---

[53] *The Times* (London), April 13, 1970.

[54] *Ibid.*, May 11, 1971.

[55] For Britain's view of Iran as the "country power most likely to succeed," see Anthony Verrier, "Both Sides of Suez: New Complications Face British Withdrawal," *New Middle East*, No. 5 (February, 1969), p. 20. For the source on arms sales, see SIPRI, *The Arms Trade With the Third World*, and *Yearbook 1972*, "World Armaments and Disarmament," pp. 105–106 *et seq.*, 124–125, 170–171.

[56] *Keyhan International* (weekly), July 1, 1972.

"In the view of my government, the outcome represents a reasonable and acceptable basis for the future security of the area." [57]

Britain's *military* withdrawal from the Gulf has neither ended Britain's *political* presence in the Gulf region nor its influence in the region. It still retains overflying rights in the region, and the use of air bases in the Gulf for transit to the Far East. In addition it retains advisors in the shaykhdoms and has military officers on loan or contract in the Union army. Britain has also offered the Union the opportunity to keep close military contact through joint training exercises with British airforce and army units, and has the right to use the area for specialized desert combat training for its own troops. Finally, partly as a symbol of its new Treaty of Friendship with the Union, Bahrayn, and Qatar, Britain has promised "regular" visits to the area by the Royal Navy.[58]

Its military withdrawal (some 6,000 ground troops and air support units from Bahrayn and Sharjah) nonetheless created a new situation in the Gulf. While welcoming that withdrawal for reasons already outlined, the Iran government in all likelihood has maintained the option of future cooperation in the area with Britain. As allies in CENTO, Iran and Britain, together with the United States (as a friendly power which is not a member), in November of each year hold naval and air maneuvers in the Persian Gulf Straits of Hormoz and the vicinity of the Gulf of Oman known as Midlink exercises. These have proved valuable training in military coordination. Britain maintains important interests in the region, including large investments and dependence on the Gulf as a source of oil supply, both of which are important to it for economic and trade reasons and for vital energy requirements. Britain may be expected to continue to watch the Gulf with keen interest and to play an active diplomatic role in the region. About 180 British soldiers and officers, including Royal Air Force pilots, have not been withdrawn from the Sultanate of Oman (as the Sultanates of Muscat and Oman have been known since the palace coup of July 1970). Britain also retains the use of the strategic island of Masirah in the Arabian Sea under a lease which reportedly runs for fifteen years from the middle 1960's.[59] For a number of reasons sketched in a subsequent

---

[57] See *UN Security Council, Provisional Record*, Dec. 9, 1971, p. 93. An English newspaper reported that Britain and the United States were "delighted to see Persia and Sa'udi Arabia carving out their own spheres of influence and dividing the Gulf," provided they remained pro-Western and stable. *Daily Telegraph*, Dec. 2, 1971.

[58] *The Times* (London), March 2, 1971; *Ettelaat* (air ed.), March 4, 1971.

[59] The number of British officers is based on *Christian Science Monitor*, June 1, 1971; and "Oman: Working Paper Presented by the Secretariat," Sept. 2, 1971, p. 6.

section, there are grounds for believing that the Iran government may wish to encourage Britain's presence in Oman.

SUMMARY

It has been contended that Iran's readiness to pursue a policy of self-reliance is due to a number of trends, including its own long-standing wish to play a more active role in the Gulf. Among the trends which have facilitated and accelerated this are: (1) the contraction of Britain's responsibilities; (2) the readiness of the United States to have its regional partners assume more responsibility for local defense; (3) the growing economic strength of Iran, and the willingness of its Western partners to assist in augmenting its military arsenal; (4) the determination of the Iranian leadership to rely more on its own resources in regional affairs, as a result of recent experience, its reading of contemporary international politics, and the declining role of the superpowers; (5) the added incentive of domestic political advantage to be gained thereby, and an understanding of the symbolic dimensions of an activist Gulf role in Iranian nationalist mythology. All of these factors, in addition to the failure to forge a formal defense pact —the effectiveness of which was in any case dubious—have influenced the course of Iran's Gulf policy.

Chapter VIII

THE SUPERPOWERS AND THE GULF

THE UNITED STATES

Iran's policy toward the Gulf, as in other areas, evolved in the context of her perception of the international and regional interests of the superpowers. With the termination of the British dominant role in the Gulf, the United States and the Soviet Union became the extra-regional powers with whom Iran had to reckon.

As far as defense posture was concerned, Iran remained heavily dependent on the United States. Unable to fashion a formal defense pact with the Gulf states toward which it felt equivocal, Iran settled for the role of guardian of the Gulf. Meanwhile, desirous of excluding the non-Gulf states, particularly the great powers, it has sought to convince Britain and the United States that their interests coincide with its own, while at the same time showing the Soviet Union that these need not conflict with its interests.

"Even-handedness" in terms of Tehran's orientation toward Moscow and Washington can never be prudently even or balanced, for the geographical proximity of the former necessitates or at least encourages a compensatory leaning toward the distant balancer. Translated into Iran's Gulf policy, the foregoing serves as a cautionary reminder in assessing Tehran's apparent desire to treat the superpowers equally. In practice their equal exclusion need not have equal consequences. As the dominant Gulf power and presumably so maintained by the U.S. and Great Britain, Iran protects Western interests, which coincide to a large extent with its own, as effectively as they could themselves. British and U.S. attitudes should be viewed in this light. This coincidence of interest has created the impression of "nonalignment" of Iran's foreign policy in general. This concept has, more recently, been eroded and is scarcely distinguishable from alignment in a growingly depolarized world.

One of the first critical issues that the U.S. faced related to the gradual departure of the British presence in the Gulf. Although there was never any hint that Washington planned to substitute its presence for Britain's in 1971, some analysts thought the U.S. should favor regional alliances in the Third World. Robert E. Osgood wrote: "Ideally . . . America's interest in a reasonably orderly international environment, imposing tolerable demands on American power, would be served best if the states in the Third World would structure their relations in local balances of power by means of stable alliances among themselves." [1]

U.S. disinclination to intervene as a result of Britain's departure was evident in 1968. William D. Brewer, at that time country director for the Arabian Peninsula bureau of Near Eastern and South Asian affairs in the U.S. state department, told a conference on the Persian Gulf in October 1968: "Local leaders must and will carry on after the end of Britain's historic role. The United States will continue to do what it can to help, but there can be no question of any 'special role' in Gulf affairs." [2] This same view was formally echoed in the joint statement issued later that year at the conclusion of a visit to Washington by Iran's prime minister. The United States affirmed its intention to help Iran sustain and develop its own armed forces, and both states acknowledged that the security of the area "could be assured through the cooperation of the powers bordering the Gulf." [3] No official explanation or announcement concerning the United States' future role in Gulf affairs emanated from Washington in the next fifteen months. It was clear, however, that the emerging trend in Washington, particularly after President Nixon's declaration at Guam in June 1969, was an emphasis on self-help and regional security systems. In essence this doctrine rests on three principles:

(1) The United States will keep all its treaty commitments.
(2) [It will] provide a shield if a nuclear power threatens the freedom of a

---

1 Robert E. Osgood, *Alliances and American Foreign Policy*, p. 164.

2 William D. Brewer, "U.S. Interests in the Persian Gulf," in Cuyler T. Young (ed.), *The Middle East Focus: The Persian Gulf*, p. 174. Compare this with William D. Brewer's article elsewhere: "The countries and peoples that border the Gulf will in the future have to deal with their problems without outside tutelage or intervention." "Yesterday and Tomorrow in the Persian Gulf," p. 158.

3 For Persian text, see *Iran's Foreign Relations in 1348* (1969–70), pp. 241–242; for English text: *Department of State Bulletin*, LIX, No. 1539 (Dec. 23, 1968), 661–662.

nation allied with us or a nation whose survival we consider vital to our
security.

(3) . . . In cases involving other types of aggression, we shall furnish military
and economic assistance when requested in accordance with our treaty commitments. But we shall look to the nation directly threatened to assume
the primary responsibility of providing the manpower for its defense.[4]

The Nixon doctrine has underlined the importance of the foreign
military sales programs as well as the military assistance program in
United States foreign policy, and both are expected to increase as a
result of it.[5] Iran as a recipient of credit through the foreign military
sales program qualifies for sales not only as a friendly state *able* to
purchase and searching for new and better weapons, but also because
it meets the criterion of being *willing* to undertake its own defense in
the region. In 1971 President Nixon explained the function of "security
assistance" to Congress thus:

By fostering local initiative and self-sufficiency, security assistance enables us
. . . to reduce our direct military involvement abroad . . . [and] lessen the
need for and the likelihood of the engagement of American forces in future
local conflicts. Thus it will ease the burdens upon the United States. But
at the same time it signals to the world that the United States continues to
help and support its allies. . . .

We gave specific emphasis in our fiscal year 1971 programs to important
needs of friends and allies who are shouldering the burden of their own and
regional security.[6]

In the Persian Gulf, U.S. policy has taken the form of encouraging
cooperation between the Gulf states for regional security, while lending
a sympathetic ear to requests from Iran for credits with which to
finance arms purchases. In 1970 U. Alexis Johnson, undersecretary of
state for political affairs, testified that out of an "estimated current
annual average" of 2 billion dollars arms sales by the United States,
"30 percent go to Israel, Iran, and the Republic of China." [7] More specifically, in fiscal year 1970 the United States delivered to Iran 189.7
million dollars in foreign military sales, and in fiscal year 1971, 114.3
million dollars. This does not indicate the amount of foreign military

---

[4] "U.S. Foreign Policy for the 1970's; Building for Peace," *A Report to the Congress by Richard M. Nixon, President of the United States,* Feb. 25, 1971, pp. 12–14.
[5] U.S. Congress Joint Committee on Foreign Relations, *Foreign Military Sales Act
Amendment,* 1970, 1971, Hearing on S. 2640, S. 3429, and H.R. 15628, 91st Cong. 2nd
sess.; March 24, and May 11, 1970, p. 54.
[6] Nixon, "U.S. Foreign Policy for the 1970's," pp. 184–185.
[7] *Foreign Military Sales Act Amendment,* 1970, 1971, p. 5.

sales authorized in those years. However, an indication of the size is given by Secretary of State Rogers, who reported that in fiscal year 1971 a total of $295.8 million in Export-Import bank loans was extended to Iran "to assist in purchasing both military and commercial equipment and services in the United States." [8]

Finally, in February 1973, Iran contracted with the Pentagon to purchase 2 billion dollars worth of arms in the next five years. This agreement is only the latest in a rapid and sustained build-up of Iran's armed forces since 1969, which has been undertaken with the full support of both Washington and London. Iran now has a mobile fleet with four "ultra-rapid" frigates with sea-to-surface missiles, three refitted U.S. destroyers, the largest fleet of fast-moving Hovercraft, a squadron of minesweepers, and it may purchase the Israel-made ship-to-ship Gabriel missile. In addition it now possesses over 50 Phantom aircraft and expects to purchase four more squadrons as well as helicopter gunships.

Land forces include five infantry and two armored divisions equipped with 850 re-fitted U.S.-made T-34 tanks, and on order are 800 British-made Chieftain tanks.[9] Bandar Abbas, a port at the mouth of the Gulf, has been modernized, and there are plans to develop the port of Jask in the Gulf of Oman. It appears likely that the expansion of the navy will add *additional* expenses to the 1973 agreement made with the Pentagon, insofar as these involve purchases from other non-Communist arms suppliers.

Like its British counterpart, the U.S. government was tolerant of Iran's occupation of the Gulf islands. The secretary of state noted that: "Despite difficulties arising from the landings of Iranian forces on three small islands in the Persian Gulf, Iran's overall relations with the Persian Gulf area were constructive." By relinquishing its claim to Bahrayn and extending "friendly recognition" to the Union of Arab Emirates, Secretary Rogers reported, Iran contributed to developments which "were in the interests of all the littoral states and contributed to the U.S. goal of peace and security for the region." [10]

---

[8] The figures for foreign military sales delivered in fiscal years 1970 and 1971 are taken from "Military Assistance and Foreign Military Sales Facts" (Washington: Dept. of Defense, April, 1972), p. 16. The other figure cited is from *United States Foreign Policy 1971: A Report of the Secretary of State*, p. 106. The figure cited therein represents an increase over the 120-million dollar Export–Import loan for fiscal year 1971 cited in an earlier publication. See: *United States Foreign Policy 1969–1970: A Report of the Secretary of State*, p. 89.

[9] For reliable reports see *New York Times*, July 25, 1971 (the authenticity of this report was confirmed by the State Department; telephone interview, Aug. 2, 1971); *New York Times*, Jan. 25, 1972, and Feb. 22 and 25 (part IV), 1973.

[10] *United States Foreign Policy, 1971*, p. 106.

U.S. policy toward Iran and the Persian Gulf region as a whole should be viewed in the perspective not only of the political constraints symbolized by the Nixon Doctrine, but also in the light of its interests in the region. Quite apart from the political-strategic interest in the continued independence of the friendly states of the area, U.S. interests are considerable. (1) The Persian Gulf possesses three-fourths of the noncommunist world's oil reserves (or two-thirds of the world's oil reserves), and accounts for one-third of world production. (2) America's major allies depend on this oil, which accounts for 90 percent of Japan's oil needs and 46 percent of Europe's. Every indication is that this dependence will continue and perhaps even grow. (3) Increased energy consumption in the U.S. will necessitate dependence on the Persian Gulf region for up to, and perhaps more than, 25–30 percent of the nation's oil requirements by 1980. (4) U.S. capital investment in the oil industry of the Middle East (and North Africa) is valued at between 2 and 5 billion dollars (at depreciated book value) and 50 billion dollars or more for actual replacement value. (5) The oil industry of the region in all its operations accounts for 1.6 billion dollars per year U.S. profits, which is a healthy contribution to the U.S. balance of payments. (6) Finally, there are perhaps 12,000 U.S. citizens living or working in the Gulf region.[11]

In attempting to convince non-Gulf powers not to replace Britain's presence with one of their own, the Iran government has been confronted with an unusual situation in regard to the United States. For while Washington has had no inclination to increase its presence in the Gulf, neither has it been keen to withdraw its token presence from Bahrayn, and thereby signal its lack of interest in the region.[12] The U.S. naval presence in the Gulf, the only exception to Britain's exclusion of non-Gulf states, started in 1949 when the U.S. was allowed to share the facilities of the Jufayr base at Bahrayn. This modest U.S. force, known as the Mideast force and commanded by a rear admiral, consisted of a converted seaplane tender, the *Valcour*, which was

---

[11] These points are drawn from the statements to Congressional hearings of James E. Akins (director, office of fuels and energy, bureau of economic affairs, State Department) and John Lichtblau (oil expert, Petroleum Industry Research Foundation). See, respectively, U.S. Congress Joint Subcommittee on the Near East of the Committee on Foreign Affairs, *The Middle East, 1971: The Need to Strengthen the Peace*, 92nd Cong., 1st sess., July 15, 1971, pp. 120–124; and Joint Subcommittee on Europe and Subcommittee on the Near East, *Soviet Involvement in the Middle East and the Western Response*, 92nd Cong., 1st sess., Nov. 3, 1971, pp. 167–175.

[12] This point was made time and again by the State Department in Congressional hearings. See *U.S. Interests in and Policy Towards the Persian Gulf*, pp. 11–12, 92–93, 95.

"home-ported" in Bahrayn starting in 1966. It was supplemented by two destroyers which were assigned to it on a rotational basis from the Sixth Fleet, and since the closure of the Suez Canal, from the Atlantic Fleet. Since the principal mission of this force was showing the flag, the two destroyers remained in Bahrayn only six weeks per year.

The Shah publicly opposed the retention by the United States of its naval base facilities in Bahrayn after 1971. He told the *New York Times'* military correspondent: "Do as the Russians do; show your flag; cruise in the Persian Gulf. But base your ships on those islands in the Indian Ocean—the Seychelles or Diego Garcia." [13] The Shah's view, often expressed, is that a U.S. base in the area would only encourage Soviet countermeasures, perhaps in Iraq. It would thus open the Gulf to the direct intrusion of superpower rivalry, and exacerbate and complicate local issues. By calling for the equal exclusion of the superpowers, the Shah has attempted to demonstrate his neutrality and even-handedness so as to avoid provoking a Soviet reaction. (Parenthetically, it should be observed that a number of U.S. scholars have argued the same case in Congressional hearings.)[14] The problem posed by the Shah's desire for symmetrical abstention by the superpowers from establishing naval or military bases in the Gulf was that one superpower already had, and had had for several years, joint access to a "base."

However, the difference between Iran and the U.S. on this question has been more apparent than real. Under an Executive Agreement signed on December 23, 1971, with the Bahrayn government, the U.S. renewed its right to use the naval facilities at Jufayr. At the same time it was disclosed that the U.S. force of some 200 men would be increased by 600, for administrative duties.[15] The Iran government reiterated its opposition. The Shah observed: "We have declared before that we would not want to see any foreign presence in the Gulf—England, the United States, the Soviet Union or China—our policy hasn't changed."

---

13 *New York Times*, March 25, 1969. Construction of a communications facility on Diego Garcia, a British Indian Ocean territory, was commenced in March 1971 and is due to be completed by mid-1974. It will serve both Britain and the U.S.

14 For an interview in which he made these points, see Alvin J. Cottrell, "Concern over Sa'udi Arabia's Viability: An Exclusive Interview with the Shah of Iran," p. 23. For several scholars' similar suggestions, see the statement by Alvin J. Cottrell, U.S. Congress Joint Subcommittee on the Near East, *The Near East Conflict*, 91st Cong., 2nd sess., July 21–23, and 28–30, 1970, pp. 156–173, 181–187. Alvin Cottrell, George Rentz, and Joseph J. Malone have taken the same view, respectively, in Joint Subcommittee on the Near East, *The Middle East, 1971*, July 13 and 15 and Oct. 5, 1971, pp. 15–17, 95, and 268–269.

15 See *New York Times*, Jan. 6, 1972, and excerpts from U. Alexis Johnson's statement in *U.S. Interests in and Policy Toward the Persian Gulf*, pp. 22–24.

More critical was *Ettelaat,* which pointed out that the move might endanger the security of other nations: "The Soviets and other countries are fully justified in protesting the stationing of three American warships in the region," it editorialized.[16] But these manifestations of displeasure were for public consumption. The Shah clearly did not wish to welcome the decision openly, particularly because of the reaction of the USSR and Iraq, but also for nationalistic reasons related to the Persian Gulf. Yet there is little reason to suppose that the U.S. decision was unwelcome in Tehran.

Washington's decision on the Bahrayn facilities was clearly a compromise between a complete withdrawal and a large build-up. If the U.S. had no desire to augment its presence in the region lest it appear keen to assume Britain's mantle, it equally had no intention of signaling a lack of interest in the region by withdrawing its small token presence from the Gulf. The decision was not provocative, for it envisaged no quantitative build-up of the Mideast force. The force was upgraded qualitatively, however, in line with its mission of showing the flag, and the veteran flagship *Valcour* was retired from service in August 1972 when it was replaced by the more modern *LaSalle.* While a symbol of U.S. interest in the region and active in its present political-diplomatic role, this small force could in the face of changed circumstances such as the opening of the Suez Canal, and an increase in Soviet naval activity, combined with a change in its primary mission, become the basis for subsequent expansion. In 1971–72 the U.S. had also built up its diplomatic presence in the Gulf region. It resumed diplomatic relations with the Republic of Yemen in July 1972, and has opened up small missions in Bahrayn, the United Arab Emirates, and Oman, and has accredited its ambassador in Kuwait to these states as well as Qatar.[17]

THE SOVIET UNION

It has earlier been suggested that in the Iran government's view the major sources of instability in the region would be domestic and regional rather than external. Its assumption has been that it can deal with such threats to the peace by itself, and it has therefore concentrated its diplomacy on excluding and dissuading non-Gulf states from the establishment of bases in the region. It was contended in Chapter 1 that it was the Shah's belief that the Soviet Union could be

---

[16] See *New York Times,* Jan. 17, 1972.

[17] Joseph Sisco's statement in *U.S. Interests in and Policy Toward the Persian Gulf,* pp. 83, 85; and *Department of State Bulletin,* LXVII, No. 1732 (Sept. 4, 1972), 243.

socialized through practical cooperation and commercial relations, and that ties could eventually give the USSR a stake in the region's tranquility. This view has been reaffirmed by a recent comment attributed to the Shah. He is reported to have told an ambassador from an Asian state: "The Russians have for centuries wanted to find a way to the Persian Gulf, but now they have abandoned subversive methods—since we have provided them with a way to realize their dream—through roads, railways, and the oil pipeline: in other words, through business and mutual profits." [18]

The Iran government's assumption that the USSR can be neutralized regionally to the extent that it is reluctant to take sides between Iran on the one hand, and its Arab client, Iraq, on the other, has been realized to date. Moscow has taken no public position on the Shatt al'-Arab dispute, nor did it make known its attitude either to Iran's Bahrayn claim or its occupation of the islands in the Gulf. The Iran government, for its part, has been extremely sensitive to Moscow's wishes and careful not to annoy its northern neighbor. This consideration was evident in its opposition both to U.S. retention of the Bahrayn facilities and to the prolongation of Britain's presence in the Gulf after 1971. Less concrete, but equally illustrative of Tehran's deference to the USSR's interests, was the government's refusal to clearly quote the Soviet sources on which it partially relied to document its claim to the islands, during the Security Council session.[19]

The Soviet Union's attitude toward the federation of the Arab emirates and the Persian Gulf states has been adequately sketched by other authors.[20] It is sufficient for our purposes to note that Soviet policy has been cautious and even vacillatory. While welcoming the federation because it would mean the end of Britain's presence in the area, it has also expressed fears that the federation might be a "reactionary instrument," and has even questioned the authenticity of Britain's departure. Similarly, openly critical of Sa'udi Arabia in 1968–1969, it has more

---

[18] Quoted by Eric Rouleau in *Le Monde* (English weekly ed.), in *Manchester Guardian* (weekly), Dec. 11, 1971.

[19] After quoting British sources for the claim, the most Iran's representative would say was "in a highly authoritative encyclopaedia, published as recently as 1967 to cover the events of the last fifty years, by another major power, the Tumbs have been identified as Iranian territory." Although goaded by the Iraq representative to name the source, he refused to elaborate. *See United Nations Security Council*, Dec. 9, 1971, pp. 86, 97.

[20] See especially "The USSR and the Persian Gulf," *MIZAN*, X, No. 2 (March/April 1968), pp. 51–59; and Stephen Page, "Moscow and the Persian Gulf Countries, 1967–1970." See also O. M. Smolansky, "Moscow and the Persian Gulf: An Analysis of Soviet Ambitions and Potential."

recently relaxed this criticism and increased its trade relations with
that state. In general it has criticized Kuwait for its domestic politics
and approved of its foreign relations, while increasing its trade with
that state. Finally, it has assumed the safest posture possible in the
Gulf, and the only decisive aspect of a policy torn between ideological
distaste for the regimes of the area and the attraction of pragmatic
considerations—and this has been criticism of the departing British.[21]

Soviet foreign policy in the past has generally been opportunist,
maintaining great momentum in its outward expansion but content,
when confronted, to await a diminution in resistance before reasserting
itself. Soviet involvement in the Third World since 1945 appears to
have been marked by a similar readiness to make casual investments in
regions, mark time when necessary, and press on again when expedient.
Soviet involvement in Yemen, and particularly the provision of aircraft
pilots in that war, should serve as a constant reminder to the Tehran
government that it has been not only the Arab-Israel zone that has
seen intervention by Soviet advisors. In this connection the Soviets'
relationship with Iraq will undoubtedly be of much interest to Iran.
Although Moscow has shown no zealous support of Iraq in its regional
disputes, it maintains strong ties with that state. These include an economic link through oil agreements (reached in June–July 1969) on the
North Romaila fields, a large military aid program that puts Iraq second in the list of Soviet clients in the Arab world,[22] and more recently
a treaty of friendship and cooperation. This fifteen-year treaty, signed
in April 1972 during a five-day visit to Iraq by Premier Kosygin, envis-
ages increased military aid to Iraq and was reportedly sought by
Baghdad rather than Moscow.[23] The Soviets were at great pains to
ensure that the treaty was not interpreted by Tehran as a measure
aimed at Iran. They were thus reluctant to sign the treaty in Moscow
during a visit there by an Iraqi delegation in February, and Premier
Kosygin stressed that the pact was not aimed at any other country. The
pact was followed by agreements on Soviet participation in Iraq oil
production and also increased military assistance.[24]

---

21 In addition to the preceding citations, see G. Drambyants, "The Persian Gulf:
'Twixt the Past and Future," G. Drambyants, "Persian Gulf: the Thorny Path of
Federation," V. Zelenin, "Britain's Manoeuvres East of Suez"; and *Ettelaat* (air ed.),
July 24, 1971.

22 See Wynfred Joshua, *Soviet Penetration into the Middle East*, pp. 22–26; and
Aryeh Y. Yodfat, "Russia's Other Middle East Pasture—Iraq."

23 See "Text of the Treaty of Friendship and Cooperation Between the USSR and
the Iraqi Republic" (New York: USSR Mission to the UN, Press Release, April
10, 1972).

24 On the Soviets' sensitivity to Iran's reaction, see especially *New York Times*,

After the USSR-Iraq agreement of April 1972, the Shah was asked to comment on it. "Can you say whether this is a threat to security in the Gulf area . . . ?" He replied that anything that was in accordance with the Charter of the United Nations was not subject to debate. "But if anything goes beyond that and is outside the United Nations Charter, we reserve for ourselves the same prerogatives." [25] In October 1972 the Shah visited Moscow and succeeded in obtaining agreement from the Soviets that the Gulf states should manage their own affairs. The relevant paragraph of the joint communiqué reads thus: "The Soviet Union and Iran expressed firm belief that questions relating to the Persian Gulf area should be settled in accordance with the principles of the UN Charter by the states of the area themselves without any interference from outside." [26]

Despite this reassurance, the April 1972 Soviet-Iraq treaty remains a reminder to Tehran of the limits set to Iran's influence on the USSR and the potentially transitory nature of Soviet abstention from the region's politics. Iraq has long remained an important state in the Soviet perspective. In 1968 a Soviet analyst observed: "How important Iraq's progress is to the whole Persian Gulf area is to be felt particularly clearly in Basra, that busy Middle East crossroads. The success of the liberation movement in the eastern part of the Arab world depends largely on how things go in Iraq." [27]

In the light of Iraq's domestic instability and its lack of personnel or resources compared to Iran, and particularly in the face of Iran's massive arms purchases, Soviet support of Iraq does not at present constitute a real threat to Iran. Nor is it clear that the USSR can translate its undoubted influence in that unstable country into control. (The refusal of Iraq to support the 1970 Rogers Plan for a cease-fire in the Middle East, which the USSR backed, is but one example.)

The April 1972 Iraq-Soviet treaty has not conclusively disproven the Shah's assumption that the USSR will remain neutral in regional disputes. The problem of conflicting commitments to Iran and Iraq remains a considerable constraint on Soviet activity in the Gulf—an

---

Feb. 11 and 22 and April 10, 1972. See also: *The Times* (London), April 4, 1972. On oil agreement, see *New York Times,* June 8, 1972. On military assistance, see *The Times* (London), Sept. 20, 1972.

25 See "Press Conference by H. I. M. Shahanshah Aryamehr, London, June 24, 1972" (Tehran: Ministry of Information), p. 8.

26 Text of Joint Soviet-Iran communiqué (*New York: USSR Mission to the UN,* Press Release, Oct. 23, 1972), p. 4.

27 Dmitry Volsky, "On the Persian Gulf," *New Times* (Moscow), No. 5 (Feb. 7, 1968), p. 16.

incentive to avoid taking sides in disputes between the two states. This constraint is all the more real because of the impact a deterioration in Iran-USSR relations would have on Turkey-USSR relations (and vice versa); and also, in the future, because of the emerging political-diplomatic (but not yet military) option open to Iran of friendship with Peking. Yet, if the desire for good relations with Iran is a constraint on an activist or interventionist Gulf policy, it clearly need not remain so. For there is a question of priorities in Soviet goals involved here, and good relations with Iran need not remain as attractive as the manifold temptations and opportunities offered by a Persian Gulf-Arabian peninsula region convulsed by revolution and disorder.

OIL AND NAVAL PRESENCE

Since 1967 there has emerged considerable evidence that the Soviet Union, not hitherto a substantial net oil importer, as the leader of the Eastern bloc has become interested in obtaining inexpensive Middle East oil and gas, both for its own consumption and for that of its allies. Few experts estimate that the Soviet Union will be absolutely dependent on Persian Gulf oil for its own needs, at least until 1980. But most agree that it is becoming substantially *more* dependent on the region's oil. And there appears to be general agreement that the Soviet Union is interested in the Persian Gulf for a number of *economic* reasons: (1) its proximity to Soviet industrial centers and its inexpensiveness allows the USSR to sell its less-well-situated oil for needed hard currency in the West, or to cooperate with Japan in developing Siberian oil fields in the East; (2) it will enable the USSR to supply its Eastern-bloc allies with oil while using Persian Gulf oil itself, or alternatively by providing them with Persian Gulf oil; (3) as a long-term hedge against its own accelerated energy requirements.[28] In attempting to assess the political impact of increased Soviet interest in Persian Gulf oil, however, analysts come to different conclusions. Abraham Becker, for example, notes that the USSR encouraged the Arab states' oil blockade after the June 1967 war, and appears to suggest that Moscow might be interested in Middle East oil in order to control its flow to the West; while Marshall Goldman notes that the USSR itself con-

---

[28] See the statements by James Akins and George Rentz in Joint Subcommittee, *The Middle East, 1971,* July 15, 1971, pp. 104–107, 124; and John Lichtblau in Joint Subcommittee, *Soviet Involvement in the Middle East,* Nov. 3, 1971, pp. 135–137, 174–175.

tinued oil sales to Western nations after 1967 and emphasizes their economic-commercial stake in it.[29]

The scenario sometimes sketched by political analysts of a Soviet design to take over Persian Gulf oil and to deny it to the West by having a "hand on the tap" does not seem persuasive. (1) To be effective as an oil blockade, a Soviet denial of Middle Eastern oil would require control of the whole area, as no one or two countries are an indispensable source of supply.[30] (2) None of the oil-producing states, being dependent on oil income, are likely to cooperate voluntarily in such a project. It would require then a rapid military takeover of the whole region to be effective. The political risks and repercussions for the USSR render it extremely dubious. On the other hand, a slow political penetration of the area, and a gradual denial of oil, would be ineffective as an oil blockade, for other sources could be found by the West, and it would signal to the remainder of the region the Soviets' intentions. (3) Finally, it is unclear in such a scenario what the USSR—unable to consume the oil so diverted—would do with the oil even if it managed to obtain it and deny it to the West. In short, the scenario is unconvincing short of a general war, when it would in any case be irrelevant. The notion of a Soviet naval blockade of oil tankers in the Indian Ocean is equally unconvincing except in the case of all-out war. A more persuasive analysis is that Soviet interest in Gulf oil, as evidenced by its oil and gas agreements with Iran and Iraq, will be manifested in a policy of restraint in the region, and influenced as much by commercial as by colonial considerations.[31] In short, the Shah's assumption that practical cooperation in trade between Iran and the Soviet Union (and the latter and its other neighbors) will give Moscow a large economic stake in the peace of the area appears for the present to remain valid as regards Soviet oil needs.

A further consideration affecting Soviet policy toward Iran will be the evolution of events in the Indian Ocean and Arabian peninsula. It will be recalled that Iran's aim has been to exclude non-Gulf states from a permanent presence in the Persian Gulf. However, as an inter-

---

29 See Abraham S. Becker, "Oil and the Persian Gulf in Soviet Policy in the 1970's," pp. 23–28; Marshall I. Goldman, "Red Black Gold," p. 147.

30 Some analysts argue that the oil production of the whole region is dispensable, at least for the short term. See the provocative article by M. A. Adelman, "Is the Oil Shortage Real?"

31 See particularly John H. Berry, "Oil and Soviet Policy in the Middle East"; and "Soviet Mid-east Dilemma: Oil from the Persian Gulf," World Oil (January, 1971), pp. 69–70.

national waterway the Gulf is open to the navies of all powers. Britain's disimperialism from first Aden and now the Gulf has been paralleled by an increase in Soviet naval capability and an evident interest in the Indian Ocean area. Since 1968 this region has seen for the first time considerable Soviet naval activity manifested in a continuous naval presence. Between May 1968–November 1971, according to one calculation, the Soviet fleet made thirty visits to Persian Gulf ports: 9 in 1968, 14 in 1969, 6 in 1970 and 1 in 1971. The visits to Iraq (at Umm al-Qasr) have generally been balanced by visits to Iran (Bandar Abbas).[32] Two aspects of the Soviet naval visits in the region are striking: the tapering off of visits to the Gulf, and the numerous visits in comparison to the Red Sea ports of Berbera, Hodeida, Aden, and Massawa. The increasing Soviet naval presence in the Mediterranean and Indian oceans since 1967 has undoubtedly created a new political situation in the region. As a symbol of the Soviets' global interests and global reach, it will doubtless have a strong psychological effect on the littoral states of the area—the more since the fleet is strikingly modern and impressive. The very novelty of the presence has upset the distribution of power prevalent in the area since World War II by introducing a wholly new power factor in the political configuration of the region.

Nevertheless, there is no evidence to date (February 1973) that the Soviet navy is.equipped, or intended, for a conventional war role in the region, or that it is part of a sinister "grand design." The composition of the Soviet fleet, many analysts agree, as well as its mission, is primarily a strategic one. That is, it is oriented toward a "sea-denying" strategy aimed at counteracting the United States' *Polaris* submarine fleet. Despite increased mobility, "the Soviet navy appears to have insufficient 'spare capacity' to promote political adventuring as an end in itself. The great overstretch caused by the ASW [Anti-Submarine Warfare] commitment, the weaknesses in logistical support, the yawning gap in seaborne aviation, and the total absence of transoceanic amphibious capability will take a considerable period to eradicate." [33]

---

32 Joint Committee on Foreign Affairs, "Report on the Indian Ocean Region" (Appendix L), Australian Federal Government, Dec. 7, 1971, as cited in Geoffrey Jukes, "The Indian Ocean in Soviet Naval Policy," pp. 17, 25, 26. See also *The Times* (London), Feb. 20, 1971. Jukes' figure of one Soviet visit to the Gulf in January–November 1971 contrasts with U.S. sources, which give three visits in the entire year.

33 See John Erickson, *Soviet Military Power,* p. 60; see also pp. 52–61. For similar conclusions see Jukes, "The Indian Ocean"; Oles M. Smolansky, "Soviet Entry into the Indian Ocean: An Analysis," in Alvin Cottrell and R. M. Burrell (eds.), *The Indian Ocean: Its Political, Economic and Military Importance,* pp. 337–355; and Smolansky's statement, Joint Subcommittee, pp. 195–197.

To be sure, this does not deny that the Soviet Union will be capable of exerting strong influence on the littoral states in a flag-showing, port-calling capacity. An important spin-off of the Soviet naval build-up has already been an increase in its political influence due to its naval presence in the region. This presence now enables it to participate as an interested party in any negotiations that may take place concerning the Indian Ocean. With the construction of mobile seaborne air support,[34] the opening of the Suez Canal, and the acquisition of genuine bases in the area, its navy will be in a position to dominate many of the choke points, or key access points, such as the straits that guard entry and exit into the Indian Ocean. With the opening of the Canal, the distance from the Black Sea to the Indian Ocean would be shortened from its present Cape-route of 11,000 miles to about 3,000 miles, reducing sailing time from approximately 25 to 7 days. The Soviet Union would then be enabled to substantially increase its present naval complement, which has varied from 5 to 15 ships since 1968.[35] This, combined with the deterioration of the U.S. navy through budgetary constraints, and a failure of political will in Washington, *could* create a decided imbalance in the region favorable to the Soviet Union.

The implications of such a scenario for Iran's foreign policy need not concern us here. The point is that the area is vast, and the USSR does not now have this capability and has traditionally appeared keener to have bases in the nonaligned world dismantled than to acquire them herself. Similarly, there is every reason to assume the USSR will seek to avoid a confrontation with the U.S. in an area which has not traditionally been one of its primary interests (as compared to Europe or the Balkans, for example). At the same time, the United States still retains a powerful navy and a substantial interest in the area. It is also important, from Tehran's perspective, to contrast Soviet capability with Soviet intention. A small state cannot frame its foreign policy and react on the basis of a superpower's capability; rather it must pay close attention to the latter's shifting priorities and inclinations.

For the present Tehran does not appear to be unduly concerned about the Soviet naval build-up in the Indian Ocean. The acquisition of a naval base in the Gulf—particularly in Iraq; for example, at Umm

---

34 There is evidence that the USSR may be building a second aircraft carrier and hence moving to develop its seaborne aviation capability. At present the U.S. has 14 carriers, but is due to phase out two of these. See *New York Times,* Feb. 27, 1973.

35 For pessimistic, even alarmist, predictions see the statement by Alvin J. Cottrell, in Joint Subcommittee, *The Middle East,* 1971, July 13, 1971, pp. 2–23, *et passim.* Contrast this with John Franklin Campbell, *ibid.,* pp. 33–39 *et seq.*

al-Qasr—would change this. At present the Soviet naval intrusion into the Indian Ocean holds little prospect of such a base, and even less of a Soviet willingness to choose between Iran and Iraq. And while the USSR retains here as elsewhere in the area the option of cashing in on its investments when the time is ripe, the Soviets' naval capability poses less of a threat to the upper Gulf and Iran than it does to the Arabian peninsula. Scenarios in which the USSR is seen as assisting (or prodding) Iraq to "grab" Kuwait while neutralizing regional opposition by a naval show of force, or spurring Iraq as a "proxy" to start a regional war, appear far-fetched. For they ignore the weakness of the USSR's client, and underestimate the effectiveness of the deterrent provided by Iran's massive arms build-up. They also ignore the *political* implications for the USSR of playing the trouble-maker (i.e., the *costs* involved in terms of regional and global relations); the areas of the world in which the USSR has more important interests and stakes which preoccupy it; and finally, the USSR's commercial stake in the region's tranquility.

This is not to deny Soviet capability of interposing itself between two warring adversaries in the Gulf, or signaling a "hands-off" warning by making well-timed port calls, but rather to assert that the effect of the naval capability has been, and is likely to remain for the next five years or so, essentially political. Comparisons between the USSR's role in the Arab-Israel zone and its implications for Soviet adventurism in the Gulf are, we believe, irrelevant. Several major differences exist between the two zones which make it likely Soviet policy will be much more cautious in the Gulf: (1) The area borders on the USSR, and there is little reason to assume that Moscow would welcome a prolonged disturbance in the area. (2) There is no comparable schism between Iran and the Arab states, or even Iran and Iraq, as there is between Israel and the Arabs.

As in the Persian Gulf, the United States had adopted a policy of restraint in the Indian Ocean. As one official told a Congressional hearing in 1971: "We consider that on balance our present interests are served by normal commercial, political, and military access." [36] Yet lest

---

[36] See the statement of Ronald Spiers (director of the bureau of politico-military affairs of the State Department), in Joint Subcommittee, *The Indian Ocean: Political and Strategic Future*, July 28, 1971, p. 168. See also *Department of State Bulletin*, LXV, No. 1678 (Aug. 23, 1971), 199–203. For a critical discussion of Washington's "wait and see" attitude which stresses Soviet naval capabilities see, in addition to Cottrell's statements to Congressional committees, R. M. Burrell and Alvin J. Cottrell, "Iran, the Arabian Peninsula, and the Indian Ocean," pp. 37–44. See also T. B. Millar, "The Indian Ocean—A Soviet Sea," *New York Times*, Nov. 13, 1970; Hanson Baldwin, *ibid.*, March 20, 21, and 22, 1972.

the USSR misinterpret U.S. restraint for weakness, Washington sub-sequently announced its intention to deploy a modest naval presence in the form of task forces from the Pacific fleet into the region from time to time.[37] The "modest" presence not only signals U.S. interest in the region, and balances that of the Soviets, but reassures the littoral states of American intentions. Should the need for an increased U.S. naval commitment become evident, it is likely that Iran, like Australia and South Africa, will lobby actively for it in Washington.

SUMMARY

To sum up, in this section we have examined Soviet and American policies as they relate to Iran in the Persian Gulf. The Shah's assump-tion that the USSR can be brought to play a constructive role in the region, and neutralized in the event of regional disputes, remains valid for the present. Soviet interests in oil and assistance to both Iran and Iraq, as well as reluctance to alienate Turkey and the traditional states of the Arabian peninsula, remain considerable constraints deterring Moscow from an adventurist course in the Gulf. Increased Soviet naval capability *per se* does not appear to constitute a military threat to the region in the immediate future, although its political-psychological impact has doubtless been profound. It has also given Moscow a flexible diplomatic and military tool for future use. Soviet policy in the Gulf, and its relations with Iran, are likely to evolve in the future in the light of opportunities presented both on the global and local levels and on Moscow's priorities.

On the global level, a great deal will depend on U.S. evaluation of, and reaction to, Soviet intentions. Soviet priorities also will be partially determined by the course of its relations with the U.S. and Europe on the one hand, and the People's Republic of China on the other. On these, Iran has little influence. How events evolve on the local level, in the Gulf and the Arabian peninsula, is a quite separate matter, and it is in this environment that opportunities for covert Soviet intervention may present themselves.

---

[37] See esp. *New York Times*, Jan. 7, 16, and 18, 1972, and Nov. 4, 1971; the *Economist*, Jan. 15, 1972, pp. 38–39.

Chapter IX

OIL IN REGIONAL CONTEXT

The importance of oil to the Iran government can hardly be overstated. Its relation to Iranian foreign policy is obvious: oil revenues have permitted Iranian policy-makers to build up their armed forces, purchase modern weaponry, and increase Iran's diplomatic representation abroad. The contribution of oil to Iran's development needs little elaboration: receipts from the petroleum industry have accounted for 12 percent of Iran's gross national product and supplied between 46 and 50 percent of total government revenue. They have provided more than 60 percent of total planned expenditures of the Plan Organization and 80 percent of planned development expenditures in the Fourth Five-Year Plan (1968–1972).[1] In addition, they have provided over 65 percent of Iran's total foreign exchange earnings on current account, thus ameliorating the chronic balance-of-payments deficit (i.e., excess of imports over exports) resulting from the substantial import of goods from industrialized countries, a significant and increasing component of which has been the purchase of costly military weapons.[2]

---

[1] For these and other figures see Jahanagir Amuzegar and M. Ali Fekrat, *Iran: Economic Development under Dualistic Conditions*, pp. 113, 152. See also Fuad Rouhani, *A History of O.P.E.C.*, pp. 115–116.

[2] See Amuzegar and Fekrat, *Iran: Economic Development*, pp. 111–113; Julian Bharier, *Economic Development in Iran, 1900–1970*, pp. 115, 265. For the oil sector in the Iranian economy in 1966, see Sam H. Schurr and Paul T. Homan, *Middle Eastern Oil and the Western World: Prospects and Problems*, p. 10. They give the following figures:

Retained Value (in millions of dollars)	$757	Gross Foreign Exchange Earnings (in millions of dollars)	$986
Oil Sector as Percentage of Foreign Exchange Earnings	77%	Oil Co. Payments to Governments (in millions of dollars)	$652
Percentage of Total Government Revenue	58%		

The economic impact of such a large source of foreign exchange earnings should not obscure its domestic political importance. It has diminished the need for "backbreaking burdens on the working population or belt-tightening pressures on the consuming public." [3] Oil revenue has also provided the lubricant with which the Iranian leadership has maintained a stable and functioning government. It has enabled the leadership to dispense the patronage and rewards by which it has peacefully coopted the newly mobilized and educated elements of the society into the political system. Oil revenue has thus enabled the Iranian monarchy to coopt the "counterelite" without opening up, and/or endangering the political system. The increasing numbers of the mobilized element have required that the size of the pie (oil revenues) be steadily increased to accommodate the need for more slices. Thus from the leadership's perspective, oil revenue has had to be increased for political as well as economic reasons, for survival as well as for development. [4]

In sum, oil has had a central role in the Iranian economy. It has provided the lion's share of revenue for development and the bulk of foreign exchange earnings, enabling the country to develop and build up its armed forces without concomitant belt-tightening. It has thus financed Iran's increased military expenditures and underwritten a more active diplomacy. Finally, it has provided the Iranian leadership with means to coopt the educated, mobilized, and (potentially) politically dissident elements in the society through an elaborate system of rewards and patronage. An important corollary of this has been the political importance to the Iranian leadership of maintaining a large and increasing flow of oil revenues to Iran. This is one political explanation of the hard-line policy adopted by the Iran government toward both the oil companies and our area of principal concern here, the Gulf Arab states.

Another part of the explanation is the importance attached to oil in Iran. As a nonreplenishable resource, and as a conspicuous explanation of the great powers' interest in modern Iran, oil has taken on great nationalist-symbolic importance in the average Iranian's mind. A hard-line oil policy is a *sine qua non* for any popular leader in Iran, and it is one criterion by which a leadership's nationalist credentials are judged. This attitude coincides conveniently with the leadership's own

---

3 Amuzegar and Fekrat, *Iran: Economic Development*, p. 113.
4 For a contemporary and critical discussion of the Iranian political system, see Marvin Zonis, *The Political Elite of Iran*, and James Alban Bill, *The Politics of Iran: Groups, Classes and Modernization*.

requirements. The oil dimension of Iran's relations with the Gulf Arab states encompasses their similar status as oil-producing states and their mutual interest in preventing any interruption of the export of their oil, or oil price-cut—and hence interference with their principal source of revenue—and in reaching an agreement on the division of the continental shelf. But this overlap of common, or *cooperative,* interest is enmeshed with a *competitive* dimension: the different interests of the states regarding how the continental shelf is divided, and the interest of each state in maximizing its own revenues through increased production of *its* oil.[5]

The competitive dimension of the oil-producing states' relations was sharply burned into the Iranian government's consciousness by the oil nationalization crisis of 1951. In that year Iran lost its position as the leading oil producer of the region, a position it did not regain until 1969. "Things went so far," the Shah recently recalled, "that we had to try and sell our oil by [the] barrel, at a discount of 50 percent, and even then there weren't any buyers. . . . Meanwhile the oil companies made up for the loss of crude oil production from Iran . . . by immediately stepping up production from Iraq and Kuwait." [6]

Most observers agree that it is incontrovertible that "The crisis between Britain and Iran in 1951 . . . proved to be Kuwait's good fortune." [7] The Iranian leadership has never forgotten the lessons of this experience, namely, that oil from any *one* source is not indispensable; the ease with which the nationalized Anglo-Iranian Oil Company (later British Petroleum), which owned 50 percent of the shares of the Kuwait Oil Company, increased oil production in Kuwait amply demonstrated this. More important, it underlined the competitive dimension of the oil-producing states' relations. One state's misfortune proved to be another's windfall, one state's loss another's gain. The Iranian leadership has internalized these lessons, and they have informed Iran's oil policy ever since. A knowledgeable Iranian participant in oil affairs has put this succinctly: "It is the cardinal point of Iran's oil policy to recover

---

[5] For a theoretical discussion of cooperative-competitive, or mixed-motive, games —i.e., games involving a mixture of partnership and competition—see Thomas C. Schelling, *The Strategy of Conflict,* p. 89.

[6] The Shah's press conference, Jan. 24, 1971, reprinted in *Shahanshah of Iran on Oil, Tehran Agreement: Background and Perspectives* (London: Transorient, 1971), p. 2. For production figures clearly demonstrating this, see *Oxford Regional Economic Atlas: The Middle East and North Africa,* pp. 90, 93.

[7] Hawley, *The Trucial States,* p. 256. See also E. F. Penrose, *The Large International Firm in Developing Countries,* p. 69. The reappearance of Iranian supplies after the dispute was thus embarrassing to some. See Stephen H. Longrigg, *Oil in the Middle East,* 2nd ed., p. 288.

the leading position it enjoyed as producer before nationalization," and the Shah has made no secret of this.[8]

The lack of what in the parlance of the third world is known as "fraternal solidarity" on the part of the Arab states, in the hour of Iran's distress, has thus been neither forgotten nor forgiven. This was vividly demonstrated in 1964, more than a decade after the episode, at the height of the Arab-Iranian propaganda war. The Iranian prime minister, Hassanali Mansur, in refuting charges of Iran's territorial ambitions in the Gulf, criticized those states which had taken advantage of the stoppage of Iran's oil production during the nationalization crisis to increase their own oil exports. He said that Iran, unlike other nations, no longer considered politics a factor in determining oil policy, had set aside "outdated and tattered" attitudes over oil, and was now able to adopt a realistic policy aimed at gaining Iran the greatest possible economic benefits from petroleum.[9] The attitude that "oil is business, not politics" is reflected in Iran's adamant refusal to jeopardize its development or indeed forego any source of oil revenue by pressuring the Iranian Consortium to cease supplying oil to either Israel, Rhodesia, or South Africa. Iran's pragmatic oil policy has doubtless won it few friends in Africa or the Arab world, but it may have been satisfying to the Iranian leadership in 1967 when it had the opportunity to repay the Arab states in kind by stepping up its oil production for Europe to replace embargoed Arab oil.

If the central goal of Iran's oil policy has been to regain its former position as the region's leading oil producer, thus displacing Kuwait and Sa'udi Arabia, the Iran government has not sought this goal at the risk of contributing to cuts in the price of world oil. That is, while the Iran government has been in competition with Kuwait and Sa'udi Arabia in prevailing upon the oil companies to increase the amount of oil lifted from *its* territory, it has had in common with them the desire to avoid excessive overall oil production which might lead to the erosion of prices, and price-cutting which would affect all oil-producing states' royalties. The Iran government's concern has been with the country's interests, and these clearly are not always identical to those of the oil companies. To the *latter*, the *source* of an oil production increase is less relevant *per se* than the *costs* of its exploitation, and

---

[8] Fuad Rouhani, *O.P.E.C.*, p. 88. See the Shah's interview with Wanda Jablonski, *Petroleum Intelligence Weekly*, Dec. 9, 1960, p. 14; and *Tehran Journal*, Dec. 10, 1960.

[9] See *The Times* (London), April 23, 1964, and J. E. Hartshorn, *Politics and World Oil Economics*, p. 279.

hence its profitability; while to the government of an oil-producing state, *whose* production (and hence revenue) is increased is of central interest.

In the area where Iran's interests have converged with other oil-producing states—i.e., the maintenance of a high price for Middle East oil and progressive improvement of terms of concessions—the Iran government has cooperated with these states. Thus the governments of Iran, Iraq, Kuwait, and Sa'udi Arabia, together with Venezuela, joined together in September 1960 to establish a solid front in the Organization of Petroleum-Exporting Countries (OPEC). OPEC was intended to forestall a repetition of the type of price-cutting that had occurred in 1959–60 as a result of the overproduction of oil and its overabundance in relation to world demand. It has been successful in this endeavor, and in presenting a solid front to the oil companies has allowed the oil-producing countries to confront the cartel of oil companies with a cartel of their own.[10]

OPEC attempted to come to grips with the desire of the oil-producing states to increase their own production to the limit, without jeopardizing prices by excess supply, by setting up in 1965 a "production quota" system. These quotas, agreed upon by the member states, were intended as guidelines, although the oil companies were not obliged to meet them. The Iranian quota in 1966 was the largest single volume increase granted any country (304,000 barrels per day versus Sa'udi Arabia's 290,000 b/d), and reflected the Iran government's tenacious pursuit of primacy. Within a year of the institution of quotas, the original cooperative aim of limiting production excesses had been supplanted by the competitive aim of increasing production, albeit in an orderly manner.[11] The Iran government in its communications to the Consortium emphasized Iran's unique position, the understanding of this position by other OPEC members, the intention of OPEC not to restrict oil production but to "regulate the sources of supply within

---

[10] The most successful and publicized example of this solid front of oil-producing countries has been the February 1971 Tehran agreement. Qatar and Abu Dhabi joined OPEC in 1961 and 1967, and subsequently Algeria and Libya also joined. Illustrative of the duality of the relationship stressed in the text—that is, the cooperative-competitive relationship between Iran and the Gulf Arab states—is the founding of an Arab organization, Organization of Arab Petroleum Exporting Countries (OAPEC) in January 1968. See Zuhayr Mikdashi, *The Community of Oil Exporting Countries: A Study in Governmental Cooperation*, pp. 83–90, also pp. 69–83.

[11] See *Petroleum Intelligence Weekly*, June 13, 1966, p. 4; June 20, 1966, p. 3; Aug. 1, 1966, p. 5.

the OPEC area," and hence the necessity that the Consortium increase Iran's oil production to a maximum.[12]

Iran's interest in increasing its own revenues from stepped-up oil production has not necessarily, or always, coincided with profitability to the Consortium oil companies (which have interests elsewhere in the Gulf). Nor has it been self-evident to them that increased Iranian oil production was necessarily called for; increased production of Kuwait or Sa'udi oil has often appeared a more profitable endeavor. At these times the Iran government has resorted to a number of arguments, tactics, and devices involving political pressure, to persuade the oil companies of the seriousness with which it holds these views, supplement its weaker economic arguments, and pressure them into acceding to its demands. George Stocking has described the bargaining context within which such maneuvering occurs:

Consortium members recognize that except as demand increases or new markets develop, an increase in any one Middle East country's output must be at the expense of another's, and they also know that a concession made to one Middle East country becomes a demand of all Middle East countries. They are slow, therefore, to grant any country's demands, and frequently wait until they assume crisis proportions before effecting a compromise. That politics influences their decision can only make them unhappy; but occasionally they must bow to it.[13]

Iran's pressure on the oil companies has thus often been one facet of its competitive oil relations with Kuwait and Sa'udi Arabia. This is evident in the reaction of Sa'udi Arabia to Iran's attempt to increase production by granting offshore concessions to independent oil companies (1965) and by its exertion of pressure on the oil companies (1968). A former Sa'udi Arabian oil minister, Abdullah Tariki, bitterly attacked Iran in political terms as an "imperialist" for what he viewed as a contribution to the erosion of oil prices.[14] His successor, the present oil minister, Ahmad Zaki Yamani, reacted to the news that Iran was using political and diplomatic pressure on the Consortium to increase Iran's oil production by pointing out that the growth of Sa'udi Arabia's oil production was due to the free play of economic forces: "If, however, we see that the oil companies have allowed pressure from other host governments to interfere with the free play of these factors vis-à-vis

---

12 *Ibid.*, Nov. 29, 1965, pp. 1–2; Dec. 13, 1965, pp. 1–2.

13 George W. Stocking, *Middle East Oil: A Study in Political and Economic Controversy*, p. 192.

14 *Petroleum Intelligence Weekly*, Jan. 25, 1965, p. 1; May 3, 1965, p. 5.

Saudi offtake levels, we will at once move to safeguard our interests." [15]
Iraq and Kuwait oil spokesmen made much the same point.[16] The Iran
government in turn has balanced its interest in maintaining high prices
for oil with its interest in increasing its share of oil production in the
region. It thus viewed Sa'udi Arabia's relaxation of restrictions on
"overlifting" of oil in 1967 with interest, and followed through in
1968 with pressure on the oil companies.[17]

Another example of the competitive dimension of Iran's relations
with the Gulf Arab oil-producing states is the type of argument adduced by the Iran government to strengthen its desire for increased
production. Having a strong argument in the West's needs for a strong,
stable Iran, it can safely be assumed that the Iran government has not
foregone political arguments to enhance its case. Sometimes this has
been explicit, such as the Shah's threat to look to cheaper (Soviet)
sources for military equipment if his demands were not met;[18] but
more often, doubtless, they have remained implicit. Oblique reference
to the Gulf Arab states has also characterized Iranian arguments. In
arguing that increased oil revenues are essential for Iran's development
and that the oil companies cannot dictate how much of the country's
natural resources should be produced, the Shah has attributed Iran's
economic growth to the fact that "our oil revenues do not go into foreign banks"—an unmistakable allusion to some of the Arab states.[19]
In 1966 the Shah is reported to have told the oil companies that while
Iran produced a considerable amount of oil,

the per capita benefit to her people was negligible. With a population of
more than 28 million, which was twice the total of other Middle East oil-
exporting countries put together, Iran only received $24 per head per
annum, in contrast to the per capita income derived by Kuwait of $10,480.
Further, that, unlike in some other countries, the entire oil revenue of Iran
was spent on nation-building enterprises.[20]

---

15 *Petroleum Intelligence Weekly,* April 15, 1968, p. 3.

16 For their statements and original sources, see Stocking, *Middle East Oil,* p. 451.

17 See *Petroleum Intelligence Weekly,* Nov. 20, 1967, p. 1. In that year Iran was
particularly interested "because its production up to 12.4% so far has not risen
nearly so quickly as output in Sa'udi Arabia, up 19.1%." Nov. 14, 1966, p. 3.

18 See *ibid.,* March 21, 1966, pp. 1-2, and *Christian Science Monitor* (editorial),
May 15, 1969.

19 The comment is found in *Keyhan International,* Jan. 6, 1967. For Iranian arguments regarding oil and development, see *New York Times,* March 9, 1968; H.I.M.
Mohammed Reza Shah Pahlavi, *The White Revolution,* p. 158.

20 Quoted by Ramesh Sanghvi, *Iran: Destiny of Oil,* pp. 17–18. Schurr and
Homan, *Middle Eastern Oil and the Western World,* p. 108, give somewhat different
figures for per capita receipts from oil revenues, *viz.* $1,500 in Kuwait; $50 in Iraq;

The Iran government reportedly sponsored a more comprehensive and explicit set of arguments in support of Iran's oil demands, which included specific contrasts between Iran's need for increased oil revenues, and her wise use of them, and the waste of such revenues in the Gulf oil-producing states by "small elites" for "conspicuous personal consumption," and their accumulation of vast sums in unspent foreign exchange which "constitute a threat to international monetary stability." Reference was also made to the stability of Iran and the fact that her oil revenues were not spent on "military attacks on Iran's neighbors"—an allusion, perhaps, to Iraq's claim to Kuwait and Sa'udi Arabia's dispute with Abu Dhabi over the contested Buraimi oasis.[21]

Despite the harsh nature of the arguments and the hard-line adopted by the Iran government, the oil competition between Iran and the Arab oil-producing states has not seriously interfered with their overlapping political interests. (And in the case of Iran-Iraq relations, while the differences between the states are primarily political, these have not interfered with some cooperation in oil matters.) Nor has Iran's refusal to accept any commitments regarding oil exports to Israel interfered with their common political interests, although it undoubtedly has complicated them. Nevertheless, the area of relations pertaining to oil has, as it were, been indirect, and interaction has been through the oil companies rather than directly between governments. The area of direct interaction between the governments, OPEC, has been more positive and has emphasized the cooperative elements in the states' relations. The other area of direct interaction has involved the division of the continental shelf.

THE ISSUE OF CONTINENTAL SHELF BOUNDARIES: THE BACKGROUND

The presence of oil in the submerged and relatively shallow waters of the Persian Gulf, together with the acceptance and growth of the continental shelf doctrine since 1945, has exacerbated the already troubled problem of boundaries in the region. A breakdown of estimated world oil reserves published in January 1972 gives (in billion

---

$30 in Iran. For the economic importance of oil to the producing countries, see pp. 97–110.

21 The arguments are made in David Missen, *Iran: Oil at the Service of a Nation.* A summary of the arguments is found in Stocking, *Middle East Oil,* pp. 449–450. For corroboration that some of these arguments have been used for some time, see Hartshorn, *Politics and World Oil Economics,* p. 292.

barrels) Sa'udi Arabia 145.3, Kuwait 66, Iran 55.5, Iraq 36.0, Neutral Zone 24.4, Abu Dhabi 19.0, Qatar 6.0, and Oman 5.2.[22] It may well be that this uneven distribution of oil reserves, which is so apparent if the population of the respective Gulf states is considered, has been one of the bases for Iran's attitude toward division of the continental shelf. A hard-line or tough negotiating stance on the division of the oil-rich Gulf continental shelf might thus be motivated by the desire to increase Iran's present oil reserves, which though significant are not expected to last longer than forty years.[23]

It is not idle to speculate on the basis of these figures, and the disparity between Kuwait and Sa'udi Arabia's resources relative to their population, whether the Iran government has not convinced itself of the justice of its case and come to believe the arguments it has advanced to the oil companies concerning its "special status," its "proper use of oil revenues," and the like. Again, it is not unreasonable to question whether the Iran government's attitude on the division of the continental shelf has not been strongly influenced by the unequal distribution of oil reserves in the Gulf. Not only does Sa'udi Arabia (with a population no more than a fifth of Iran's) possess three times her reserves, but even tiny Kuwait, with a population less than one-thirtieth of Iran's, has larger reserves, and in addition both these saturated states have further reserves in the contested Neutral Zone.

The legal nature of claims to offshore oil resources, and the legal principles defining and limiting such claims, have been at best only lately worked out in the Continental Shelf doctrine.[24] Originally raised in 1945 in President Truman's proclamation, it received its authoritative formulation in the Convention on the Continental Shelf drafted in Geneva by the Conference on the Law of the Sea in 1958. Although no Gulf state is a direct party to this convention, the shelf doctrine, by reason of its wide acceptance in state practice, is part of the customary law binding on all states. By virtue of the doctrine, every coastal state is entitled to exercise sovereign rights over its continental shelf for the purpose of exploring and exploiting its natural resources. This has been the legal basis of all the offshore oil rights existing in the Gulf today beyond the limits of territorial waters.

---

22 *Oil and Gas Journal*, Dec. 27, 1971.

23 Bharier, *Economic Development in Iran*, p. 273.

24 This section leans heavily on Richard Young's paper, "Legal Problems of Offshore Concessions," presented at the Princeton University Conference on the Persian Gulf, Oct. 24, 1968 (mimeo). Mr. Young is the foremost authority on legal questions involving the Persian Gulf and has made numerous contributions on this subject to the *American Journal of International Law* in the past twenty years.

Since the continental shelf is viewed as land less than one hundred fathoms beneath the sea and adjacent to the mainland, the entire Persian Gulf because of its shallowness is "continental shelf" for the purposes of this legal doctrine. This leads to an acute legal problem of boundaries, i.e., how to allocate a common continental shelf among a number of coastal states which are either adjacent to or opposite one another. The Continental Shelf Convention has a rule on this point embodying what is known as "the principle of equidistance," which provides, in effect, that in the absence of agreement or of special circumstances, the boundary between the states on the shelf is a line equidistant throughout its length from the nearest points on the baselines (usually shorelines) from which the territorial sea of each state is measured. The rule is reasonable and has provided the basis for a number of shelf boundaries in the North Sea, and a substantially similar approach was used in reaching the boundary agreement between Sa'udi Arabia and Bahrayn in February 1958.[25] But the rule is not sufficiently precise or elaborate to provide an automatic answer or criterion when the states concerned are unable to agree on the manner of its application. The main difficulty has been in determining what baselines are to be used as points of departure for constructing the line, and particularly whether islands are to be taken into account. The Convention text is silent on this point, but it is clear that if all islands are used, a markedly inequitable apportionment of the Gulf can result. On the other hand, it might also be inequitable to ignore some islands which are closely associated with the mainland. Yet if only certain islands are to be considered as part of the mainland and to be used as baselines, the Convention rule has set forth no objective criterion for determining which. Thus it is impossible to establish through mechanical application of the Convention rule a boundary which is beyond dispute. The line can only be settled through agreement between the states concerned.

In July 1934 the Iran government passed a law establishing a *territorial waters* limit of six miles off its coasts. The British government at that time made it clear that it could neither recognize such a limit nor recognize the Iranian claim for a single belt of territorial waters to embrace a given group of islands; each island, it insisted, must stand on its own. The six-mile territorial waters limit was extended to twelve nautical miles by the Iran government in April 1959, in response to

25 See "Continental Shelf Boundary: Bahrain-Saudi Arabia," *International Boundary Study Series A, Limits in the Seas,* No. 12, U.S. State Department (Bureau of Intelligence and Research); *The Geographer,* March 10, 1970.

the Iraq government's decree of November 4, 1958, extending its territorial sea to twelve miles. The Sa'udi Arabian government had earlier,
in February 1958, replaced its Royal Decree of May 1949 setting its
limits as six nautical miles with a new claim to a twelve-mile territorial
sea. The Gulf shaykhdoms however have adopted "for the purpose of
oil concessions" a breadth of territorial sea which varies from three to
six nautical miles.[26]

The doctrine of the continental shelf first advanced by the United
States in 1945, that the riparian states should exercise authority (including that over underlying oil deposits) over the continental area of the
ocean bed off their coasts, rapidly gained ground. At the suggestion of
the British foreign office, the Persian Gulf shaykhdoms in 1949 asserted
by proclamation their claims to part of the continental shelf in the
Gulf. The Iran government drafted legislation in the same year which
was enacted into law on June 19, 1955.[27] As a result of several legal decisions, most notably the arbitration between Abu Dhabi and Petroleum
Development (Qatar) in 1951, a precedent was established that for
practical purposes the continental shelf accretion could be everywhere
considered eligible for new concessions. In the same year the Arabian
American Oil Company (ARAMCO) discovered *Al-Saffaniyah,* one of
the greatest offshore oil fields in the world.

The enactment of a new petroleum law on July 29, 1957, signaled
the beginning of a significant development in Iran's oil interest in the
Persian Gulf and provided the basis for the extension of that country's
oil operations into the continental shelf. It also coincided with the
development of a technology which made feasible the exploitation of
the resources of the (shallow) continental shelf. The Iran government
thus joined in the rush for the continental shelf in 1957 by forming a
joint company with an Italian firm, Agip Mineraria, under the acronym
SIRIP, to which it alloted three blocks totaling 23,000 square kilometers in the continental shelf at the northeast corner of the Gulf, and
on land and sea combined along the Mokran coast of the gulf of Oman.
A second grant was made to Standard Oil of Indiana and its affiliate
Pan-American Petroleum Company in a similar joint venture with the
National Iranian Oil Company, which is known as IPAC, in May 1958,
in which a 16,000-square-kilometer block was granted in the Gulf. A
third grant for an area of 1,000 square kilometers was made to a

---

26 See Husain M. Albaharna, *The Legal Status of the Arabian Gulf States,* pp.
281–282, and citations therein; see also pp. 278–311.

27 *Ibid.,* p. 279. For another discussion, consult Herbert J. Liebesny, "Documents:
Legislation on the Sea Bed and Territorial Waters of the Persian Gulf."

joint Iranian-Canadian venture (Sapphire) known as IRCAN, which covered the extreme southwest of Iran and included the onshore and offshore area.

In granting the IPAC concession, the Iran government used the island of Kharg, some 25 miles off the Iranian coast, as part of the coast-line (i.e., as a baseline). The government of Sa'udi Arabia viewed Kharg island as too distant from the coast to be considered part of the coastline. As a result of this disagreement, the concessions of IPAC and ARAMCO overlapped at certain points, as indeed did other concessions granted by Iran and Kuwait. By the beginning of the 1960's, then, the larger part of the Gulf's waters were covered by a patchwork of concessions, several of them overlapping.[28]

By 1965 the Iran government had made agreements "with nine companies, most of them jointly organized by two or more foreign companies which were newcomers to Middle East oil operations." [29] By 1967 offshore fields accounted for roughly one-eighth of all oil production in the Gulf states and were expected to continue to be an important and growing element. By 1968 there were at least 25 known offshore fields in the Gulf, with a high likelihood that more would be found. In addition, there were in 1968 at least 22 concessions, varying in type of legal arrangement, which stretched from the Shatt al-'Arab to the Straits of Hormoz, nine of these concessions lying on the Iranian side.[30] The resources of the area are not only large but also, given the shallowness of the Gulf (which averages a depth of fifty fathoms), easily accessible. The offshore areas are particularly important to Iran: they have provided the Iran government with some of its most profitable arrangements with the oil companies in the percentage of profits obtained,[31] and they are one of the keys accounting for the rapid growth of Iranian oil production.[32]

In the remainder of this section we shall attempt to describe the

---

[28] See Albaharna, *Legal Status*, pp. 292–293. See also *The Times* (London), March 18, 1961, which observed: "Offshore operations at the head of the Persian Gulf offer rich promise, but the jostling by all the countries now interested in those waters might lead to trouble." For maps of the offshore concessions up until 1960, see *Oxford Regional Economic Atlas*, pp. 41–49.

[29] Schurr and Homan, *Middle Eastern Oil*, p. 113. See also "Offshore Oil Concession Agreements in OPEC Member Countries," pp. 14–15.

[30] This figure excludes those mainland concessions which extend only to the territorial waters along the coast. See Richard Young, "Legal Problems," pp. 1–2.

[31] See *Petroleum Intelligence Weekly*, Jan. 25, 1965, pp. 1–2.

[32] *Ibid.*, Aug. 30, 1965, p. 2. The same source observes: "It is in the offshore areas that Iran has been recording the biggest percentage growth for any Middle East area." May 26, 1969, p. 1.

means utilized by the Iran government in the course of its negotiations with the Gulf Arab states to fulfill its goal of obtaining as much of the oil in the Gulf's waters as possible without unduly upsetting its relations with its neighbors. Apart from a similar status-quo orientation in international politics which all of the monarchial Gulf states (i.e., all the littoral states except Iraq) shared, there was a further "cooperative" element in the Gulf states' relations. This was the desire of all the oil-producing countries to achieve some sort of an agreement on the division of the continental shelf in order to create the security necessary for the exploration of oil. There was thus a strain toward an agreement of some sort built into the negotiations between Iran and the Gulf Arab states, since all wished to augment their income by exploiting the Gulf's riches, and none wished to postpone this indefinitely by stalling on a division. This is analogous to the oil-producing states' common interest in avoiding overproduction of oil leading to price-cutting, while each sought, *short of this,* to maximize *its own* production.

Given the novelty and vagueness of the concept of the continental shelf, even as codified in 1958,[33] and its introduction into an oil-rich region which already had its share of territorial disputes and *irridenta,* it was no surprise to find difficulties in its application. Thus one aspect of the Iran-Iraq dispute over the Shatt al-'Arab, for which the continental-shelf concept was itself inadequate, was the question of "joint exploration" of the disputed territorial waters (which overlap), to the advantage of both states. In June 1963 Iraq claimed that in opening up part of its offshore area to oil exploration, the Iran government had infringed on Iraq territorial waters. The governments of Kuwait and Sa'udi Arabia followed suit, claiming Iranian infringement of their continental shelves and concessions that they had granted.[34] Negotiations were started in October 1963 when representatives from Iran, Kuwait, Sa'udi Arabia, and Iraq met in Geneva and agreed to search for an equitable settlement of their differences.

IRAN-IRAQ NEGOTIATIONS, 1963–1969

Unlike its negotiations with other Arab states, Iran's discussions with Iraq on the continental shelf and related issues have never appeared to

---

[33] For example, the 200 meters and an "exploitability clause" in the Geneva formulation were quickly overtaken by technology, which has stretched the concept to allow exploitation in much deeper areas, even into the deep ocean. The new Law of the Sea conference in Caracas, Venezuela, and Vienna, Austria, for 1974–75 will deal with this problem, among others.

[34] See Albaharna, *Legal Status,* pp. 292–294 (and sources cited therein).

be succeeding. Progress in this area has hinged on improvement in overall relations and on trust and willingness and a domestic political ability to compromise—ingredients in short supply in Iraq's turbulent political setting. A setback in one area, say the question of the Kurds, has tended to retard progress in other areas of Iraq's relations.

Qasim's claim to the entire Shatt al-'Arab in 1959 aggravated Iran-Iraq relations. His demise in February 1963 was therefore welcomed by the Iranian press, all the more so as the new (coalition) regime in Iraq appeared to be interested in improved relations with Iran.[35] Qasim's foreign minister, Hashem Jawad, who was imprisoned by the new regime, blamed Qasim for the poor state of Iran-Iraq relations.[36] Nevertheless, the new regime lost no time in furthering its own interests. In April it made public its intention of building a 12-inch oil pipeline from Khaneghain on the Iran-Iraq border to Baghdad. The oil reserves of both Khaneghain on the Iraq side of the border, and Nafte-Shah and Khaneh on the Iranian side, were fed by a common subterranean source, and Iraq's action signaled a decision to increase to a maximum its exploitation of these (geographically joint) reserves. The decision was not, in fact, a departure from earlier practice. The Qasim regime had commenced exploitation after surreptitiously laying a pipeline, and the Iran government had reacted to this by building a pipeline on the Iranian side. Discussions were subsequently held by the two states in one of the Organization of Petroleum Exploring Countries (OPEC) conferences (presumably in Vienna) on the feasibility of joint and equitable exploitation of the reserves of the overlapping oil field.

Both this issue of the oil fields astride the Iran-Iraq border, and differences on the limits of the two states' territorial waters in the Persian Gulf, were taken up in negotiations in late July 1963 when the Iraq minister of petroleum, Dr. Abd al-Aziz Wattari, visited Tehran.[37] On the latter issue, Iraq claimed that Iran, in opening up an offshore area of 40,000 kilometers in the Gulf, had infringed on Iraq's territorial waters. But it was clear that the two states' differences on the Shatt al-'Arab border severely complicated agreement on the division of territorial waters at its mouth in the Gulf. Agreement was reached on the joint exploitation of oil resources in the border oil field; the specific volume which each state could extract annually was laid down, and

[35] See, for example, *Ettelaat* (editorial), Feb. 9, 1963, reprinted in *Tehran Journal*, Feb. 10, 1963. Newspaper attacks on Iraq (and Iraqi attacks on Iran) had been continuous until this time. See *ibid.*, Feb. 6, 1963.

[36] *Tehran Journal*, Feb. 17 and 23, 1963.

[37] See *ibid.*, April 16, May 2, June 15, and July 17, 1963.

inspection by each country of the other's operations was provided for. The two states could only reach agreement "in principle" on joint exploitation of the disputed waters in the Gulf, and the details were left for a subsequent meeting.[38]

The apparent political success of the discussions reflected and reinforced the improvement of Iran-Iraq relations. The Iraq government of February–November 1963 included a strong Ba'thist contingent which, though doctrinally opposed to the Iranian monarchy, shared with the Iranian leadership a rivalry with Nasser. This appears to have been the chief reason for the improvement in relations during this period, when after the discussions in Tehran the two states' ambassadors returned to their respective posts. But the subsequent ousting of the Ba'thist faction in November 1963 did not damage relations. Indeed it too was welcomed in general terms by the Iranian press,[39] and the new Iraq prime minister, Tahir Yahya, reciprocated by voicing the need for Iraq to strengthen relations with Muslim states in general and Iraq's two great Muslim neighbors in particular.[40]

On February 25, 1964, an Iraqi delegation led by Foreign Minister Sobhi Abd 'al-Hamid and Minister of State Abd al-Razaq Mohiuddin arrived in Tehran. The week-long visit was to clarify the issues between the states as well as to serve a "good-will" function. These issues included the ubiquitous question of the Shatt al-'Arab, the conditions of Iranians residing in Iraq, and doubtless also a clarification of the earlier agreement "in principle" on the two states' territorial waters in the Gulf.[41] The visit was cordial and included an audience with the Shah, but the vagueness of the final communiqué indicated little substantive progress on any of the contentious issues.[42] It was agreed, nonetheless, that the Iran foreign minister should return his counterpart's visit by going to Baghdad to continue discussions sometime in the future.[43]

The Iraq government's movement toward a pro-Egyptian orientation after the November 1963 anti-Ba'thist coup now caused Tehran considerable concern and complicated the two states' relations. In addition to

---

38 *Ibid.*, Aug. 5, 1963; *The Times* (London), Aug. 6, 1963.

39 See *Ettelaat* (editorial) in *Tehran Journal*, Nov. 26, 1963.

40 Baghdad Radio, Home Service in Arabic, Dec. 24, 1963. Iraq's ambassador in Tehran, Dr. Abd al-Hasan Zalzaleh, told the Iraqi News Agency that Iran-Iraq relations were good and improving. Baghdad Radio, in Arabic, Dec. 16, 1963.

41 *Tehran Journal*, Feb. 19, 24, 25, and 26, and March 4, 1964. For the statements by the two states' foreign ministers at a banquet, Radio Tehran, Home Service in Persian, Feb. 25, 1964.

42 For a critical editorial, see *Tehran Journal*, March 5, 1964.

43 "Some Facts Concerning the Dispute," p. 69.

Iran, both the Shi'a and Kurdish communities in Iraq opposed the Iraq government's movement toward Nasser and pan-Arab unity which was suggested by the Iraq-Egypt military union of March 26, 1964. This identity of interest between Iran and the Iraqi Kurds and Shi'a aroused the Iraq authorities' suspicions that Iran was actually actively encouraging the Shi'a-Sunni, the Arab-Kurd division within its borders. In response they revived Iraq and Arab claims to Khuzistan (or "Arabistan" as they called it), causing a further deterioration in relations.[44] As a result, no progress was made in the discussions in 1964 and both states again recalled their ambassadors.

As it became clear that the Abd al-Salam Arif regime was not headed for union with Egypt, relations improved. In January 1965 a Baghdad Radio broadcast signaled this improvement. It alleged that there was an overlap between areas of the Gulf which Iranian oil companies were attempting to exploit and Iraq territorial waters. But it also pointed out that Iraq had so far avoided taking steps to exploit the oil potential of the area in order to preserve its good relations with Iran and to facilitate an agreement on the division of the waters.[45]

The following month the two ambassadors returned to their respective posts in Baghdad and Tehran, and discussions were once again resumed. President Abd al-Salam Arif even invited the Shah to visit Baghdad (at an unspecified date in the future), and the Shah accepted.[46] Apart from the Kurdish question, the atmosphere of relations continued to improve during the course of Prime Minister Abd al-Rahman Bazzaz's tenure. Yet there was still no movement toward a concrete agreement on substantive issues. While Iran and Kuwait had initialed an agreement to establish a joint committee to study the question of territorial waters and the continental shelf in June 1965, and Iran and Sa'udi Arabia reached a tentative agreement in December 1965 (subsequently modified in October 1968), no progress was made on this issue by Iran and Iraq, even during the Bazzaz period, August 1965–September 1966.

With Iraq the issue was of course complicated by the intractable dispute over the rights of the two states in the Shatt al-'Arab. But the seeming ambivalence that characterized the Iraq attitude toward sub-

---

44 *The Times* (London), May 15, 1964; *Christian Science Monitor*, June 5, 1964; *Tehran Journal*, May 6, 1964. For a report of the execution of 3 of 13 Arabs accused of plotting to establish an independent state in "Arabistan" and tried before military courts, Radio Baghdad Home Service in Arabic, June 14, 1964.

45 Radio Baghdad, Home Service in Arabic, Jan. 21, 1965.

46 See *Tehran Journal*, Feb. 7, 21, 22, and 24, March 2 and 3, 1965.

stantive negotiations may reasonably be interpreted as reflecting differences of opinion in the Iraqi hierarchy.[47] The agreement reached in January 1966, after the flare-up of the Kurdish question between the states, to set up joint committees to discuss all the issues dividing them reflected this ambivalence. The formation of the committees, their selection, and their eventual meetings took place at a painfully slow, hesitant, pace.

Nevertheless, some improvement in relations was discernible following Iran Foreign Minister Aram's visit to Baghdad, December 14–19, 1966, and the conclusion of commercial, cultural, and transit agreements after Iraq President Abd 'al Rahman Arif's six-day visit in March 1967. Yet the basic impasse on the Shatt al-'Arab continued. It outlasted the subsequent visit to Tehran of Iraq's Prime Minister Tahir Yahya in June 1968, and overthrow of the Arif regime by a Ba'thist junta the following month. With the deterioration in Iran-Iraq relations following the revival of the dispute in 1969, the joint committees ceased to exist. The intensity of the differences between the two states reflected in the Shatt al-'Arab dispute has retarded any accommodation between the states on the related issues of the Khaneghain, Khaneh and Nafte-Shah oilfield and on the continental shelf and territorial waters. No progress on these areas can be anticipated until the dispute over the waterway is resolved.

On the other hand, it is of considerable interest that the dramatic deterioration in relations between Iran and Iraq from April 1969 to December 1972 characterized by almost unrelieved hostility was softened by a brief interlude. Between December 1970 and July 1971, both states ceased their radio propaganda attacks while the oil-producing states closed ranks and found common cause in a meeting of OPEC in Tehran to successfully pressure the Western oil companies for higher royalties. This overlap of mutual interest and its successful insulation from the domain of high politics was nonetheless short-lived. The Iranian claim to three islands in the Gulf was resisted by the Iraq government, and in July 1971 the propaganda truce ended, squelching reports of a possible reconciliation. The two states had by this time created a

---

[47] *The Times* (London), Jan. 11, 1966, characterizes the Iraq government's policy toward an agreement on the waters of the Gulf as ambivalent. On the one hand, it took offense at being excluded from a conference on the division of the Gulf waters in Copenhagen in the summer of 1966; on the other hand, it followed a policy of stalling in creating joint committees to discuss differences with its neighbors. See the Kuwait government's accusations to this effect in *New York Times*, April 21, 1967, and *Christian Science Monitor*, July 20, 1966.

chasm of such width between them that this limited cooperation assumed only marginal significance in their overall relations.[48]

IRAN-KUWAIT NEGOTIATIONS, 1963–1968

In April 1964 it was announced that Iran was to commence discussions with both Kuwait and Sa'udi Arabia on the offshore boundaries, after a visit to both countries by Iran's Foreign Minister Abbas Aram. Agreement was reached with Kuwait to set up joint committees to discuss the scope of territorial waters, and a protocol to this effect was signed the following year.[49] In October 1965 Shaykh Sabah of Kuwait informed the National Assembly of the agreement: "My government has recently signed an agreement with our friend, the Persian government, to form a technical committee to discuss the borders of the continental shelf between our two countries. My government approves and gives its blessing to any step which would further fraternal relations and cooperation between Arab states and other Islamic states." [50] That same month a Kuwait delegation led by Shaykh Abdullah al-Jaber al Sabah, the Kuwait minister of commerce, visited Tehran to continue discussions. The visit was repaid by an Iranian delegation headed by Nasser Yeganeh (minister without portfolio) which continued the discussions in February 1966. The following month the discussions were resumed in Tehran and continued, inconclusively, in Copenhagen during the spring and again in Tehran in August, without visible results.[51]

A serious problem complicating the agreement between Iran and

---

[48] For one such report, see *Keyhan International* (weekly ed.), Feb. 20, 1971. Cooperation in even a functionally autonomous area of mutual interest appears unlikely to recur in the immediate future. The intensity of the political rivalry has "spilled back" and politicized the area of oil cooperation. Thus in June 1972 the Shah, believing it was no longer in Iran's interest to present a solid front in backing the Iraqi oil nationalization in OPEC, served notice that Iran would assure the West of a continued oil supply. In breaking the unanimity on which the strength of OPEC depends, he undermined the impact of the Iraqi nationalization. See *The Times* (London), June 29, 1972; *New York Times,* June 26 and 27, 1972.

[49] *Tehran Journal,* March 30, April 4 (editorial) and 8, 1964; *Ettelaat* (editorial), April 5, 1964; *Chronology of Arab Politics,* II, No. 2 (April–June, 1964), 142. The agreement was signed June 9, 1965, see *ibid.,* III, No. 2 (April–June, 1965), 132; *Middle East Economic Digest,* IX, No. 22 (June 4, 1965), 253; *Petroleum Intelligence Weekly,* June 7, 1965, p. 1.

[50] Speech by H. E. Abdullah Salem Sabah, Ruler of Kuwait, at the Fourth Session of the National Assembly, from *Al-Ra'i 'Al-Am,* Oct. 27, 1965, cited in *Arab Political Documents,* 1965, p. 395.

[51] *MEED,* X, No. 32 (Sept. 2, 1966), 391, and X, No. 33 (Sept. 9, 1966), 413; *Iran Almanac,* 1966, p. 266, and 1967, p. 254.

Kuwait on a continental shelf boundary has been the lack of progress between Iran and Iraq in resolving their differences on their boundaries in the northern part of the Gulf. Since the Iran-Iraq boundary will impinge on an Iran-Kuwait boundary, lack of progress on the former has complicated and arrested progress on the latter. A further difficulty was posed by the differing claims of Iran and Kuwait to territorial waters. Iran claimed twelve miles, while Kuwait claimed only three miles. This problem was eliminated in December 1967 when Shaykh Sabah, just prior to his visit to Iran, extended Kuwait's territorial waters to twelve miles, by proclamation.[52] The final obstacle in the negotiations was resolution of the status of the islands situated in the Gulf. The Iran government insisted that Kharg island, a major oil terminal connected by pipeline to the mainland and separated from it by some 25 miles, be considered part of the coastline and hence as a baseline from which the median line in the Gulf be drawn. Kuwait was reported to have offered to accept this, provided the Iran government accept equivalent status for the island of Failaka off the Kuwait coast.[53]

The discussions were given fresh impetus by the announcement in January 1968 of Britain's intended withdrawal from the Gulf. During a visit to Tehran that same month by Shaykh Sabah, an agreement "in principle" was said to have been reached by the two states. But after the Shah's return visit to Kuwait in November 1968, it appeared that this earlier announcement had been premature, for it was then reported that the Shah and the Shaykh had only agreed "to speed up work toward the conclusion of a number of agreements, including an accord on the continental shelf of the Persian Gulf." [54] The principal problem regarding a final agreement appears to be the overlap between any Iran-Kuwait division and Iraq claims.[55] Due to the deterioration in Iran-Iraq relations since 1969, and Iran-Kuwait relations since 1971, a final, tripartite agreement for the northern triangle at the head of the Gulf remains to be achieved.

IRAN-SA'UDI ARABIAN NEGOTIATIONS, 1963–1968

Sa'udi Arabia too had protested Iran's decision to grant offshore concessions in 1963. Foreign Minister Aram's visit to Sa'udi Arabia in

---

[52] *MEED*, XII, No. 1 (Jan. 8, 1968), 8.

[53] Albaharna, *Legal Status*, pp. 295n.

[54] *Keyhan International*, Nov. 18, 1968. See also Richard Young, "Legal Problems," p. 9.

[55] Iraq is reported to have protested the Iran-Kuwait agreement. See *MEED*, XII, No. 45 (Nov. 8, 1968), 1107. See also *Guardian* (Manchester), Feb. 19, 1968.

March 1964 resulted in an agreement to exchange delegations to pursue discussions on the issue.[56] Discussions continued in Tehran, Riyadh, Geneva, and Copenhagen until December 13, 1965, when an agreement on the continental shelf was initialed. The agreement proved short-lived and was never signed or ratified by either country. Abortive though it proved, the agreement nonetheless reflected the sense of compromise and movement toward diplomatic *entente* between the major monarchial Gulf states. The identity of common interest in preserving Gulf security, which the leadership of both states viewed as jeopardized by Nasser's incursion into Yemen, and in maintaining a common front against destabilizing elements in the region, facilitated the 1965 agreement which was initialed during King Faysal's visit to Tehran.

The 1965 accord struck a compromise between Iran's desire to use Kharg island as a baseline and the Sa'udi desire to use the coast as a baseline, by giving Kharg island a half-weight status (i.e., by giving it a half-effect, a compromise between considering the island a baseline and totally ignoring it).[57] "The accord," reported one newspaper, "opens the way to harmonizing spheres of diplomatic influence as well as agreement on the ticklish subject of offshore oil exploration in the Persian Gulf." [58] There is also some evidence to suggest that the British government used its influence to bring about a speedy agreement and encouraged a diplomatic *entente* between the states as the best way to achieve stability in the region.[59]

The agreement was not ratified by Iran because shortly thereafter surveys by an Iranian concessionaire indicated that important oil deposits lay mostly on the Arabian side of the proposed dividing line. In January 1968 IPAC discovered a major oilfield in the vicinity of the proposed line, and in the same month two incidents involving the Iranian navy occurred in the area. In one case it was reported that the Iran government was using its navy to protect Iranian oil operations; in the second case, the navy seized an ARAMCO oil rig in the vicinity of the disputed line.[60] Sa'udi Arabia protested the seizure, and rela-

---

[56] *Tehran Journal,* April 4 and 7, 1964.

[57] For a technical discussion of the short-lived 1965 agreement, see Albaharna, *Legal Status,* pp. 301–311.

[58] *Christian Science Monitor,* Dec. 22, 1965. See also *The Times* (London), Dec. 15, 1965.

[59] *Ibid.,* Jan. 11, 1966, asserted that the agreement "was substantially the work of a British official in the area." Iranian newspapers vigorously denied this, probably for domestic and prestige reasons. See *Ettelaat,* Jan. 10, 1966.

[60] See *Petroleum Intelligence Weekly,* Feb. 12, 1968, p. 1; *Middle East Economic Survey* (Bayrut), No. 16 (Feb. 16, 1968), p. 1; *Los Angeles Times,* Feb. 9, 1968, and

tions deteriorated further when King Faysal gave his country's support to the visiting Emir of Bahrayn.[61] A rapprochement was subsequently effected with the help of mediators, resulting in a new agreement negotiated by the National Iranian Oil Company which was initialed on October 24, an exchange of instruments of ratification taking place in November 1968, on the occasion of the Shah's visit to Sa'udi Arabia.[62] The new agreement, which is an improvement over the 1965 draft insofar as it allocates more of the oil resources of the Gulf to Iran, is based on the concept of an "equitable distribution of oil in place" and replaces the earlier geographic criterion with an economic criterion for the division of the continental shelf.[63] It is significant not only in settling the largest single offshore boundary in the Gulf, and hence opening the way for each state to utilize the resources of the Gulf; but also in setting a precedent for subsequent agreements between the littoral states.

SA'UDI-IRANIAN AGREEMENT

On October 28, 1968, an agreement was reached between Iran and Sa'udi Arabia on two disputed islands which gave the northern one, called Farsi, to Iran and the southern one, called Arabiyeh, to Sa'udi Arabia. This compromise solution was generally welcomed by Iran as well as by Western experts on international legal issues related to territorial waters and continental shelf boundary.[63a]

NEGOTIATIONS WITH THE SHAYKHDOMS, 1966–1971

The Iran governments' negotiations with the Gulf shaykhdoms on the division of the continental shelf have involved discussions with the

---

Richard Young's authoritative "Equitable Solutions for Offshore Boundaries: The 1968 Saudi Arabia-Iran Agreement."

[61] *The Economist*, Feb. 10, 1968, p. 25; *The Times* (London), Feb. 13, 1968.

[62] *Ibid.*, June 4, 1968; *Keyhan International*, Nov. 3, 1968. According to *Time* magazine, Nov. 29, 1968, the United States was sufficiently concerned about the Iran-Sa'udi rift to send Eugene Rostow secretly to Tehran to mend the breach.

[63] The agreement entered into force Jan. 22, 1969. For a full analysis, see Richard Young's "Equitable Solutions." See also "Continental Shelf Boundary: Iran-Saudi Arabia," *International Boundary Study*, No. 24; *The Geographer*, n.d.; *MEED*, XII, No. 45 (Nov. 8, 1968), 1107; *Petroleum Intelligence Weekly*, Sept. 9, 1968, pp. 2–3. The text of the agreement is found in *International Legal Materials: Current Documents*, VIII (May, 1969), pp. 493–496; *Echo of Iran* (political ed.), Oct. 30, 1968; *Keyhan International*, Oct. 30, 1968.

[63a] Typical favorable Iranian reactions are found in *Keyhan International*, October 29, 1968, and *Iran Tribune*, Nov. 1, 1968. A discussion of legal issues is found in "Islands: Normal and Special Circumstances," *Department of State: Bureau of Intelligence and Research*, Research Study (RGES-3, Dec. 10, 1973), pp. 56–62. Also Richard Young, "Equitable Solution for Offshore Boundaries: the 1968 Sa'udi Arabia-Iran Agreement," *American Journal of International Law*, LXIV, No. 1 (January 1970), 152–157.

British officials responsible for the shaykhdoms' foreign relations. Britain, in the early part of the decade, was reluctant to go ahead and settle differences between the shaykhdoms, Kuwait and Sa'udi Arabia, without including Iran in a general settlement.[64] This presented a problem, since Iran had several claims in the area: besides Bahrayn, the Iran government claimed the islands of Abu Musa and the Greater and Lesser Tumbs.

Iran commenced discussions with the British government in January 1966. The Iranian delegation, headed by Amir Taimur, political director of the foreign ministry, discussed the boundaries pertaining to Sharjah, Ras al-Khaymah, Umm al-Qaywayn, Ajman, Dubay, Abu Dhabi, and Fujayrah. Discussions did not include the boundary line with Bahrayn because of Iran's claim to that archipelago. In addition the Iranian claim to Abu Musa and the Greater and Lesser Tumbs complicated agreement on a division with Sharjah and Ras al-Khaymah respectively. The discussions in London, and subsequently Tehran, which aimed at reaching an agreement on the principle on which a median line between Iran and the shaykhdoms could be constructed, was further complicated by the position of the large offshore Iranian island of Qishm which measures sixty miles in length and lies off the coast of Bandar Abbas near the Hormoz straits. The Iran government took the position that for the purposes of the construction of the median line, the island of Qishm (like Kharg) be considered part of the coastline and hence used as a baseline in any division of the Gulf's waters. The ruler of Abu Dhabi in turn is reported to have claimed the island of Bani Yas as part of his country's coastline. The British government appears to have preferred avoiding the use of islands as baselines altogether.[65]

The announcement of the British departure gave sharp impetus to the negotiations. An agreement with Qatar, incorporating the precedent established by the agreement with Sa'udi Arabia, was signed on September 20, 1969, and came into force May 10, 1970.[66] The resolution of the Bahrayn claim in 1970 facilitated an agreement with that state on the continental shelf, which was signed in June 1971.[67] Although discussions were still in a preliminary stage with Oman and

---

[64] See *The Economist*, Nov. 29, 1958, p. 778.

[65] See Albaharna, *Legal Status*, pp. 305–306, and citations therein. See also *MEED*, X, No. 6 (Feb. 11, 1966), 62, and X, No. 12 (March 25, 1966), 135.

[66] For text see "Continental Shelf Boundary: Iran-Qatar," *International Boundary Study*, No. 25; *The Geographer*, May 11, and July 9, 1970; *Keyhan International*, Sept. 20, 1969, and editorial, May 20, 1970.

[67] It was not ratified by December 1971. See *Keyhan International* (weekly), June 26, 1971, and *Ettelaat* (air ed.), June 13, 1970, and Dec. 10, 1971.

Dubay in mid-1971, an agreement had reportedly been reached with Abu Dhabi in September 1971.[68] Neither of these agreements had been ratified by the end of 1972. The eventual Iranian seizure of the disputed Tumbs islands, and the clouded status of the sovereignty of Abu Musa, have immensely complicated the question of territorial waters and the establishment of baselines; hence the division of the continental shelf between Iran and the new entity of the United Arab Emirates. Thus while Iran has agreements with some of the subdivisions of this federation, no agreements yet exist with the others.

SUMMARY

It has been suggested that Iran's relations with the Gulf oil-producing Arab states have had cooperative and competitive dimensions. While enjoying similar interests in maintaining the high price of oil, the improvement of concessions, and maintenance of the flow of oil, interests have diverged and the competitive dimension has intruded on the rate of production of individual countries. Throughout the decade the Iran government has sought to regain its position as the Gulf's leading oil producer and has adopted a hard-line attitude toward both the oil companies and the other producing states in pursuit of this goal. By pressuring the oil companies for increased production and by adducing political arguments to strengthen its case for production increases, it has steadily sought to increase its revenue. In pursuit of the same goal, it has granted concessions to independent oil companies in the Gulf's waters. The terms of these concessions have been unusually favorable to the Iran government, and it is a steady increase in production in these offshore concessions with independent companies that accounts for Iran's rapid growth in production.

The Iran government's hard-line in its discussions with Kuwait and Sa'udi Arabia on the status of Kharg island, and especially toward the latter after the discovery of an oil field in the Gulf, 1965–1968, reflects the importance Tehran attaches to augmenting its oil reserves and increasing its oil revenues. While it has not sought these goals at the expense of political cooperation with the Gulf states, the attitude that "oil is business, not politics" has certainly informed the Iranian position on the division of the continental shelf.

The course of relations with Sa'udi Arabia demonstrates the importance of political considerations, first in the speedy accord which was

---

68 *Ibid.* (air ed.), Sept. 5, 1971. Discussions on the continental shelf with Kuwait continued throughout 1971.

timed to coincide with Faysal's visit to Tehran, and subsequently in the exacerbation of the differences between the states which resulted from a political disagreement regarding Bahrayn. Iran's speedy "agreement in principle" with Kuwait in January 1968, after five years of negotiations, also reflected the sense of urgency of the parties to reaching an understanding in the wake of the British announcement.

Quite apart from the question of politics, there has been a "strain toward agreement" produced by the common interest of the coastal states in minimizing conflict and violence in order to allow the peaceful exploitation of their common resources.[69] It may well be that given their vast superiority in proven oil resources, and their small populations, and in the face of Iran's long coastline, large population, and adamant attitude, a "prominent solution" for the Gulf Arab states of Kuwait and Sa'udi Arabia was to compromise in an agreement to divide equitably the resources of the Gulf on an economic rather than geographic basis.

The issue of oil, though presently quiescent in Iran's relations with the Gulf states, need not necessarily remain so. Two recent events underline the importance of oil in the politics of the Gulf. One concerns Sa'udi Arabia's long-standing claim to the Buraimi oasis which Abu Dhabi also claims. In May 1970 the Sa'udi government put forward a new revised claim which included the valuable oilfield of Zarrara. The other relates to Iran's 1971 agreement with Sharjah to lease the island of Abu Musa for an annual rental. Included in the agreement was a provision that oil exploited in the offshore waters of Abu Musa would be equally shared by Iran and Sharjah. Despite the Iranian insistence that the island was vital for strategic reasons, it seems reasonable to conclude that oil, which was known to exist in the area, was an additional motive for the claim to the island.

---

[69] Thus, for example, Kuwait-Shell, which holds offshore concessions, informed Kuwait of its decision to suspend its drilling operations until an agreement with Iran on the continental shelf was achieved. See Albaharna, *Legal Status*, p. 295n.

Chapter X

CONCLUSION AND ASSESSMENT

THE EXTERNAL ENVIRONMENT

Like those of other small states, Iran's security and ability to maneuver largely depend on an international environment which it can little affect. In some instances it has been the passive beneficiary of shifts in international and regional systems to which it contributed little—e.g., Nasser's preoccupation with the West after 1967. In others, its own initiative and foresight, combined with an accurate assessment of trends in international politics, have allowed it to maneuver itself into an anticipated situation and reap the rewards of these changes. That area in which Iran's strength and security have been particularly enhanced by diplomatic skill and foresight is its relations with the superpowers.

The Shah's timely enlistment of United States aid; his diplomatic resistance to Soviet demands; his skillful use of the shield of the West to gain the necessary time to strengthen both his own position and the country's economy; his deflection of Soviet pressure, as well as his ability to withstand it; and finally, his assessment that the USSR could no longer be expansionist while it was preoccupied elsewhere with China and Europe, are all examples of a small state's successful use of the international context.

Indeed, Iran's resistance to great-power pressure by alignment and balance with another great power; its ability to correctly assess the pressuring power's diversion elsewhere, and to hold out until the pressure passed; and its accurate appraisal that good relations with it would eventually become an interest of the great power, are all classic components of small-power statecraft.

Similarly, Iran's diplomacy vis-à-vis the United States can be considered successful. The tie with the U.S., despite its costly domestic repercussions, enabled the Shah to build up his armed forces and gain U.S. diplomatic support—and, most important, bought time for himself and the country. Throughout the decade, the skillful use of this connection —as well as the knowledgeable and timely application of effective arguments and credible threats, astute personal diplomacy, and an understanding of the U.S. political system—have made the Shah a persuasive supplicant for arms and credit in Washington. To some extent, one may speak of Iran's penetration of the U.S. political system in this issue-area.

As the decade has progressed, Iran's independence has increased in the emerging multi-polar world. Yet, paradoxically, it is also more curtailed than ever. Admittedly, the Iranian government has succeeded in depoliticizing one range of issues in its relations with the West. Thus it has not confused similarity of political interests and goals with an identity of interests in commerce—and most particularly, in oil affairs. In this issue-area, Iran's bargaining hand has been strengthened by the increased consumption of oil in the world and by its reputation as a relatively stable country unlikely to use oil for patently political purposes. However, the importance of oil nationalism and an "independent" posture in oil affairs in a society which still values these images has not been overlooked. Quite the contrary, the Shah has succeeded in filling the role of nationalist in this regard.

If Iran's ability to take independent positions on political issues has been somewhat curtailed in the past decade, the reason lies in the government's reluctance to antagonize either superpower. Unlike the early cold-war era when Iran took political stands on the side of the West in the United Nations, Iran today tends to abstain or to take the least controversial stand, to avoid disconcerting either Moscow or Washington. One result has been a tendency to defer excessively on those issues which are of vital interest to *either* superpower in international forums, and to avoid the cultivation of an assertive role in international politics on issues marginal to its national interest.

A clear example of this was Tehran's reluctance to recognize the People's Republic of China before the United States moved in this direction, or to change its vote in the United Nations, despite the fact that such loyal members of NATO as Norway and Denmark had done so.[1] The scope of Iran's vital interests has been restricted, and there are

---

[1] This phenomenon is evident in even the most marginal issues in the United Nations, and represents the influence of "anticipated reaction," i.e., Iranian government officials falling into line on issues which they conceive to be of importance to the U.S. or USSR—often before these states have broached them on the issue.

very few issues on which the government is prepared to unnecessarily annoy the superpowers, and many on which it is ready, even eager, to defer. Thus while Iran's diplomacy has come of age—the Shah more mature and self-confident, the country richer and more stable, its security less threatened, and its diplomacy more diversified—Iran's reliance on the superpowers, and particularly on the West, persists.

In the past decade, the value of Iran to both superpowers has grown. As a stable prosperous state, it is a source of less anxiety to the USSR than it was as a fractured debt-ridden neighbor in the early 1960's. Economic cooperation, a model of "good neighborliness" and coexistence, and a stable frontier are thus welcomed by Moscow. In return, the USSR has carefully avoided antagonizing Iran—by, for instance, openly taking Iraq's side in their dispute. Soviet apparent neutrality in this situation, and its restraint in Dhofar, are, from Tehran's view, welcome departures from its behavior in the earlier part of the decade.

Similarly, whereas in the early 1960's Iran was a weak client and a liability in the United States camp, by the end of the decade it had become a trusted and dependable friend. This transformation in Washington's perception of Iran's status had two regional implications: (1) the U.S. has been prepared to build up Iran militarily to enable it to fill the strong regional-ally role that Tehran appears anxious to assume; and (2) the U.S. has foregone the opportunity to criticize Iran's regional policies, allowing it a free hand to pursue its own interests.

In sum, Iran's international diplomacy has been largely successful in accurately assessing trends in international politics and maneuvering accordingly. Similarly, Iran's military build-up in response to Britain's withdrawal from the Gulf augmented her regional weight and flexibility and enhanced her value to the superpowers.[2] The emergence of China as a possible second balance vis-à-vis the USSR should provide Tehran with additional leverage and security against Moscow.[3]

In its regional relations, Iran has been the beneficiary of circumstances to which it has contributed very little. Most conspicuously, Nasser's defeat in the 1967 war relieved Iran of a regional rival and gave it virtual autonomy in local affairs. Similarly, Iran's relations with

---

[2] In historical and global perspective, it is true that small states today are "less serviceable as allies" but more important as "symbols of support"; but this can be overstated if the analyst is concerned with regional affairs, and if the conflict envisaged is the limited or local war variety. See Annette Baker Fox, "The Small States in the International System, 1919–1969," p. 763.

[3] Robert L. Rothstein observes that the historical record suggests that the security of small powers, but not their opportunities, increases as the balance of power widens. *Alliances and Small Powers*, p. 257.

the Arab states have been strongly influenced by the intra-Arab constraints and cross-pressures which have limited the development of its relations with them. At the same time, Iran has also been a beneficiary of rivalry and schisms within the Arab camp, and gained from the pervasive distrust of Iraq in the shaykhdoms.

Relations with Iran are valued by the smaller Gulf states partly because of its role as balancer and partly because the leaders of these states are unwilling to commit themselves to any one state. Iran has also been a beneficiary of the Arab-Israeli conflict, to the extent that this has assumed primacy in the diplomacy of Egypt, Syria, and Iraq, has absorbed their energies, and therefore has left Iran a relatively free hand in the Gulf.

To be sure, Iran has not been totally passive in using the regional context to its own advantage. It traded diplomatic support for Egypt, in its dispute with Israel, for Egypt's neutrality in the Gulf. It used the Islamic dimension of relations with the Arab states to block polarization between Arabs and Iranians, e.g., conferences at Rabat, Jiddah, etc.[4] But in general the conduct of its diplomacy with the Arab states on the regional level was less coherent, stable, or effective than its diplomacy on the global level.

Inter alia, it seemed to have misunderstood the nature of the threat posed by Nasser; as its strength grew, it contributed to the aggravation of differences with Iraq by denouncing a treaty. Iran was also hesitant in devising a constructive policy toward the Gulf states from 1960 to 1968, and vacillated between cooperation and unilateralism between 1968 and 1971. Iran's support for its non-Arab neighbors Turkey and Pakistan has been a useful investment in relations with these states, although its success in the case of Pakistan has been minimal.

The geographical propinquity of a small power to a great power, or to a zone of great-power confrontation, lends its government a strong incentive to seriously consider the state's external orientation, but it does not determine the content of its foreign policy. It was suggested that in Iran's case, Rosenau's "individual" "role" and "governmental" sets of variables were to all intents and purposes fused into one—the Shahs perception of the world and his conception of the national interest. The only domestic constraints, it was contended, were the concrete limitations on material capacity, and the more general "societal" values held by the foreign-policy elite in Iran—values symbolized by

---

[4] A Permanent Islamic Secretariat has been set up in Jiddah since 1970, with periodic meetings of Islamic foreign ministers.

phrases such as "independence," "nationalism," "Iran's historic rights," etc. Given the perhaps unique degree to which the Shah is involved in, and controls, foreign policy, the role of the "individual" variable should not be slighted.

Clearly the Shah has been somewhat constrained by society's values and by the nation's material resources. But the constraints imposed by the latter are not self-evident, because such decisions as committing the nation's future revenue for the enhancement of today's capabilities, or allocating major resources to military weaponry, can be made with impunity. Moreover, in the post-Nixon-doctrine epoch, Washington is less convincing in pleading restraint in arms purchases, and also less disposed to do so. Today the general values of the society largely coincide with the Shah's own predilections. Glorification of the national past and the military build-up, as well as the externalization of domestic political energies, can thus be used to enhance the monarch's nationalist image. This returns us to a re-examination of several hypotheses advanced in our introduction.

DECISION-MAKING AND FOREIGN POLICY

The impact of the type of decision-making system, locus of decisions, degree of centralization, sources of inputs, policy process, role of contending bureaucracies, inter-service rivalries, interested publics, etc., have been the subject of considerable research in recent years; but little or no research has been focused on governments where decisions center in one man. Perhaps this is because it is assumed that the advantages and disadvantages of such a system are self-evident, and that such systems are unlikely to survive the transition to a highly diversified modern industrial state. Be that as it may, a brief discussion of this impact on Iran's foreign policy follows.

1. It was contended that where foreign policy is personal, it will reflect the leader's perceptions and values and tend to be as stable as the leadership's tenure and as consistent as its views.

Iran's foreign policy in broad terms has been remarkably stable, and this is due *both* to Iran's geographic location and to the long tenure of the Shah and the essential consistency of his views. It has been characterized by pragmatism rather than ideological considerations, and this is evident in economic relations with the socialist East European states and good ties with states such as Algeria.

2. Our second hypothesis was that foreign policy in this type of state will be both *less* adaptable, because the leader's prestige will be at stake, and *more* adaptable, because no need to "educate" the populace exists.

Our examination of such decisions as dropping the Bahrayn claim in the face of the costs of its retention; pursuing the claim to the Gulf islands in 1970–71; and sounding out relations with China in April 1971, demonstrated the decisiveness which comes from the absence of serious domestic constraints or of interest groups that need to be assuaged.

The Shah's almost total control of foreign and domestic policy is generally known. As a result, his negotiating hand is immeasurably strengthened. He can credibly threaten to go to Moscow for arms unless Washington offers better arms and improved credits; and more important, he has been able to go through with it, as in 1966. He can make decisions on the spot, conclude agreements that in other states might take months, and reverse himself overnight if he so chooses.

3. Our findings also support the hypothesis that, when controlled by one person, foreign policy will tend to project that person's temperament. It will tend to view other systems of government as "personal," and equate personal slights with insults to the state and personal antipathy with national rivalry.

This contention is clearly reflected in the Iranian government's attitude toward Nasser and its insistence that he "apologize" before diplomatic relations were resumed. It was again reflected in the government's treatment of relations with Kuwait and the inordinate emphasis Tehran placed on statements made by a few representatives in the former's National Assembly.

In this latter case, Iranian policy-makers appear to project their own situation abroad and assume that since the Iranian press and parliament generally reflect official views on foreign policy, this must be the case elsewhere. Hence they tend to equate the views of the press with that of the government. Similarly, little distinction appears to be made between criticisms of Iran's policy on a particular issue and criticism of Iran generally. The danger of this characteristic in a state's foreign policy is in the resultant emphasis on personality. The bestowal of personal honors and the trappings of hospitality could be confused with policy or congruence of interest.

4. It was suggested that when the personal control of foreign policy is paralleled by domination of internal affairs, there will be the temptation to use the former to enhance the leadership's prestige internationally in order to legitimize and bolster its domestic standing.

Hans Morgenthau has suggested that "a policy of prestige is an indispensable element of a rational foreign policy." [5] But clearly it cannot be a substitute for policy. The degree to which prestige is emphasized in Iran's foreign policy suggests a strong internal function.

The celebration in October 1971 of 2,500 years of monarchy; the emphasis on the most sophisticated military weapons; the extreme sensitivity to the nomenclature of the Gulf; the constant discussion of Iran's responsibilities in the Gulf; and the degree to which declaratory policy, minor initiatives, and symbolic acts are given prominence in Iran's press, all reflect a very strong emphasis on the domestic uses of foreign policy.[6]

Much of Iran's international posturing is clearly intended to legitimize and fortify the government at home. One of the results is a distinct concentration on the short-run advantage, an example being the Iranian representative's performance in the Security Council in December 1971. It is evident also in the encouragement in recent years of nationalist sloganeering in Gulf affairs, and in the regime's tendency to *mobilize* the masses on specific issues—e.g., (1) the Gulf islands, (2) "Iran's rights," (3) "Iran's historic responsibilities" without adequate recognition of the need to educate the populace for *responsible* participation.

The emphasis on the short-term dividend is exemplified by the hastily prepared and abortive 1965 continental shelf agreement with Sa'udi Arabia, which was concluded only to coincide with King Faysal's visit to Iran; by the government's reported support of the Kurds against Iraq, a tactic to which a weaker Iran has been vulnerable in the past; by the preference for acquisition of the Gulf islands rather than the Arab states' goodwill; and by the initial discouragement of a federation which might meaningfully contribute to Gulf security. More generally, Iran's emphasis on short-run issues in international politics, and its reticence to develop long-range policies, or to chart a course in the UN

---

5 Hans J. Morgenthau, *Politics Among Nations: The Struggle for Power and Peace*, p. 80.
6 See esp. *New York Times* editorials of Oct. 12 and 19, 1971; *The Times* (London), March 15, 1970.

in support of milieu goals, are characteristic of the diplomacy of a small state.[7]

5. Our fifth hypothesis was that, given its predilection to respond to the leader's priorities, this type of system will retard the professionalization of foreign policy and discourage the development of expertise and the recruitment of talented personnel.

Iran's foreign relations so far have been neither diversified enough nor beset by simultaneous crises to fully test this hypothesis. Nevertheless, potential drawbacks in Iran's day-to-day diplomacy may result from the absence of continuous policy direction, the shelving of large areas of policy until they are revived in the Palace, and the unavailability of diplomats who can *authoritatively* state Iran's position on *any* single issue until the Shah has reviewed it.

The consequences of the absence of expertise in the ministry have been particularly evident in Iran's regional relations, especially with regard to the Arab world. Since decisions are personal and often improvised to accommodate hosts or to time with visits, they tend to be based on little study. Iran's articulated support for the denuclearization of the Middle East; for an Asian collective security system, alluded to in various communiqués with the USSR; and for a UN-sponsored "zone of peace" in the Indian Ocean, are all cases in point.

The vacillation in Iran's foreign policy in the Gulf from 1968–1971 reflected the failure to prepare diplomatically for Britain's withdrawal. In the absence of policy direction or innovation from the top, no initiative or follow-up in specific areas is suggested until the leadership returns to the issue, usually as the result of a crisis.[8] By the same token, at times of great foreign affairs activity there is always the danger of a bottleneck arising from the highly centralized decision-making system.

6. Our sixth hypothesis was that where foreign and military policy are dominated by the same person, the normal "fire breaks" or gaps on the continuum between pure diplomacy and pure coercion will tend to merge, with the result that resort to the latter will come sooner than in systems where some real administrative separation is made.

Our analysis suggests that in its relations with the superpowers, Iran relies on diplomacy; but in its regional and local relations, where it is relatively strong, it prefers to emphasize might.

---

[7] See Fox, "The Small States in the International System," p. 763.

[8] For the analysis of personal diplomacy in the case of Ghana, see Scott Thompson, *Ghana's Foreign Policy, 1957–1966*, p. 420 *et seq.*

This disposition is evident in the Shatt al-'Arab dispute, the acquisition of the islands, and the constant emphasis on "preparedness" and "self-reliance." It is also apparent in the absence of planning in diplomacy or of position papers, contingency planning, the assessment of alternatives, or the projection of trends in the region. Thus, for example, the government's reaction to Nasser's campaign in Yemen was to increase arms purchases, rather than to devise a constructive policy vis-à-vis the shaykhdoms. Similarly, Tehran's initial reaction to Britain's departure from the Gulf stressed military preparation without fully exploring alternative or complementary diplomatic options.

None of these cases, of course, sustains the hypothesis that Iran's emphasis on the military facet of foreign policy and its underestimation of the diplomatic arise from its decision-making structure. But from the consistent emphasis on military hardware and derogation of diplomacy, one can at least reasonably infer that the military inputs into foreign policy are more important than those of its diplomatic counterparts.

7. Our final contention was that since there is no routinization of foreign policy-making, no formalized foreign policy process, there will be no institutionalized feedback to facilitate and encourage a learning process by the leadership so that future foreign policy can be adapted, modified, or if necessary made more congruent with "reality" in the operational environment.

In Iran, as in other comparable systems, the only learning process that can take place is a personal one—i.e., the modification of the decision-maker's perceptions and images of the external environment. Apart from its long-range inherent disadvantages, this characteristic of the decision-making process is likely to put an increasing load and consequent strain on the Iranian leadership. This is particularly so because of the growing diversification of Iran's foreign relations, combined with the many technical facets of present-day diplomacy such as international finance, the law of the sea, and disarmament, as well as the assumption of a more active and wider regional role.[9] It appears that some degree of delegation of authority and institutionalization of decision-making processes will be imperative if the efficiency and quality of Iran's diplomacy are to be maintained.

---

9 In 1970 Iran had 38 embassies abroad. See *Ettelaat* (air ed.), May 10, 1970. In that year diplomatic relations were resumed with Egypt and started with Yemen and South Africa (on a consular level). In 1971 they were started with Albania, Mongolia, Senegal, Oman, Qatar, the Union of Arab Emirates, Venezuela, and the People's Republic of China.

As for the continued concentration on military might, several considerations should be weighed. One is the inevitable apprehension of Iran's weaker neighbors, particularly in the Gulf, that enhanced military capabilities will promote expansionist tendencies. Memories of the Iranian imperial past lend credence to the belief that no state which acquires the capability to expand its influence will be indefinitely so constrained.

As we have seen in the preceding chapters, the government has repeatedly disavowed any expansionist designs once several territorial disputes were resolved. Nor does Iran believe that in the existing international system the acquisition of material wealth and power necessarily engenders expansionist tendencies. A stronger Iran would be no more inclined toward territorial expansionism than postwar Japan or West Germany have been.

A further consideration relates to the allocation of a large share of national and monetary resources to improve Iranian military capabilities. Domestic and foreign critics have maintained that the appropriation of substantial sums of foreign exchange obtained by the sale of nonreplenishable oil for arms purchases can only impede the full utilization of potentials for domestic development.

They have also pointed out that Iran is far from fully assimilating sophisticated modern weapons or developing an indigenous arms industry. Consequently, the country is totally dependent on and vulnerable to outside sources. This dependence—a characteristic of most developing countries, as pointedly demonstrated in the latest Arab-Israeli war—renders the policy of arms acquisition both dubious and wasteful. The government's chief counter-argument stresses the requirements of Iran's regional security, the inadequacy of existing security relations with the United States, and the absence of a comprehensive international disarmament agreement.[10]

Conscious of the consequences of dependence on external sources, the government has also vigorously attempted to diversify the sources of its military supplies. Indeed, this has been one of the tradeoffs of the Iran-Soviet rapprochement beginning in the third phase of postwar foreign policy developments, and has fitted well into Iran's international posture of *de facto* nonalignment. Since 1966, barter agreements with

---

[10] An experienced U.S. diplomat, Parker T. Hart, told a Congressional hearing that if Iran, Turkey, and Pakistan really believed that the 1959 bilateral pacts were intended for regional rivalries, they deluded themselves. The U.S. repeatedly made it clear that this was intended as a defense against the USSR. See U.S. Congress Joint Subcommittee, *The Indian Ocean: Political and Strategic Future*, 92nd Cong., 1st sess., July 22, 1971, p. 92.

the Soviet Union alone have procured approximately 500 million dollars worth of basically nonsophisticated equipment. Not only both
superpowers, but France, Britain, and even Israel, are today actual or
potential arms suppliers.

Above all, military preparedness is linked with independence and
nationalism, even though temporarily it requires heavy reliance on
major external powers. Although the source of threat to Iran's security
has changed over the years, the imperative of military preparedness has
never been abandoned. However, with the normalization of Iran-Soviet
ties and the resolution of most of the outstanding territorial disputes in
the Persian Gulf, the Iranian perception of security has assumed a new
dimension, i.e., the preservation of the country's impressive economic
and material gains. In this sense Iran has become a status-quo power
with no outstanding international claims requiring satisfaction through
basic structural changes in the region.[11] Indeed one may perceive even
certain similarities between the Soviet and Iranian attitude toward states
on the periphery of their boundaries. Just as the Soviet Union in the
post-Stalin era gradually acquired a stake in stability and tranquillity
of such states as Turkey and Iran, it is apparent that Iran, too, has
developed a vested interest in a similar condition in the strategic areas
adjacent to its territory. Further, the opportunities and constraints to
achieve that objective seem to be analagous even when admittedly
significant differences are recognized.

It may be that Iran's long-term security will be ensured by means
other than the accumulation of imported and rapidly obsolescent arms.
Erling Bjøl has identified an important element of a small state's power
thus:

A small country's international reputation can perhaps be enhanced by
clever propaganda, but in the long run its actual behavior is probably decisive: external behavior in the way of a nonprovocative foreign policy and a
certain talent for promoting "just settlements" of international conflicts; internal behavior in the sense of creating a civilized political and social
system.[12]

Our analysis in the preceding chapters demonstrates the relevance of
this test in assessing Iran's external behavior in the latest phase of its
foreign policy. The continuous satisfaction of this test depends largely
on the persistence of those external and internal political factors which

---

11 See Leonard Binder, *The Ideological Revolution in the Middle East*, pp. 273–
274; and Binder, *Iran: Political Development in a Changing Society*, p. 331.
12 See Erling Bjøl, "The Power of the Weak." p. 166.

have contributed to successful Iranian diplomacy. Just as a combination of these favorable conditions enabled Iran to utilize its proximity to one of the superpowers to promote a posture of virtual nonalignment, a drastic change in Soviet policy toward Iran might well reverse the advantage of proximity to Russia to a potent liability. Equally decisive would be a radical change in Iran's leadership, which could make a different kind of foreign policy an attractive alternative.

An awareness of these potentialities, as well as misgivings about the evolving détente in U.S.-Soviet relations, accounts for the continued primacy of foreign policy in Iran's scheme of priorities. The anxiety that a comprehensive and genuine détente might produce a condition of benign neglect in the United States and undermine its role as a distant but interested power has intensified Iran's vigilance. The current leadership crisis in the United States, and the prospect of diminished presidential capability to act in foreign affairs, have done little to dispel this anxiety.

Chapter XI

POSTSCRIPT

Since the bulk of this study was completed in the summer of 1973, Iran, the Middle East, and indeed the whole international system have experienced great turmoil. The Arab-Israeli October War, the energy crisis and Arab oil embargo, the growing uncertainty in the constancy and efficacy of presidential leadership in the United States and its implications for a whole range of bipolar, regional, and bilateral issues combined to accentuate Iran's search for a stable, energetic, and well-balanced foreign policy.

While we do not intend to present a detailed up-to-date or instant analysis of the effect of these developments on Iran's foreign relations, we believe a review of these in the context of our analytical framework would be useful. We also maintain that our basic conclusions and assessments require no basic alteration as a result of these developments. Indeed, their general thrust further underscores the accuracy and rigor of our analysis.

On the global level Iran's relations with both superpowers have experienced stress. In mid-summer after the Nixon-Brezhnev meeting the prospects for an expanded detente prompted the Shah's search for reassurance that matters of mutual interest to the United States and Iran will not be subordinated to the imperatives of bipolar detente. The Shah's July visit to Washington and the prime minister's August visit to the Soviet Union demonstrated a continuous concern for this possibility. They also were indicative of the delicate balancing dimension of Iran's summitry at the time that the presidency in the United States was undergoing a profound crisis.

Iran's interest in securing assurance from the superpowers could obviously not be satisfied by well-intentioned protestations of good will or pledges of continuous consultation. In particular the Soviet Union's actual behavior toward Iran and those critical areas of the Middle East which, because of geopolitical or other reasons, are intimately linked with her security had to be carefully observed and assessed. It is in this context that Soviet policy toward Iraq, Afghanistan, and Pakistan evoked a measure of suspicion in Tehran.

Iran's relations with Afghanistan have been quite stable since 1962 when the Shah's mediation between Karachi and Kabul removed the issue of Pakhtunistan as a critical and potentially dangerous thorn in the triangular ties between Pakistan, Iran, and Afghanistan. In September 1972 the prime minister and the Afghanistan chancellor, Mohammed Musa Shafigh, signed a draft treaty with two protocols concerning the authority of the bilateral commission as well as procedures for arbitration.[1] This was followed by many diplomatic exchanges, but its provisions could become operative only upon its ratification by the legislatures of the respective countries. While this poses no problem for Iran, the overthrow of Mohammad Zaher Shah on July 29, 1973, placed that approval in limbo. As of this writing (May 1974) the Afghani parliament had not approved the draft treaty. Iran's displeasure with this state of affairs was shown by a press editorial in April charging the republican regime with procrastination and even bad faith.[2]

Although the removal of yet another monarch among Iran's neighbors by itself was not cause for concern, it nonetheless presented those elements of uncertainty and ambivalence which characterize all such changes. Specifically, Iran has been worried over possible efforts to revive the Pakhtunistan dispute with Pakistan at the time that the latter had hardly recovered from the disintegrative repercussions of the 1971 war with India and the emergence of Bangla Desh. More important, the uncertainty about keeping in check the rise of Soviet influence in Afghanistan, as a result either of the new republican regime's initiative or of India's pressure on Kabul, has bothered Iran.[3] Iran's diplomacy, therefore, has been directed at assuring Kabul of its continued good-neighbor policy while watching for signs that

---

[1] *Ravabet-e Kharejeh-e Iran dar Sale 1351*, pp. 25–29.

[2] In mid-May Mohammad Naim, the brother and chief advisor of President Daud, visited Iran in what was reported by the Iranian press as a cordial and profitable visit during which matters of mutual interest such as Afghanistan oil needs and overland commercial roads to the Persian Gulf were amicably discussed. *New York Times,* May 19, 1974.

[3] *New York Times,* March 31, 1974.

increased Soviet influence will not promote a departure from Afghanistan traditional neutrality.

Similar consideration led to intense attention to post-1971 developments in Pakistan. Throughout 1973 the potentials of further disintegration of Pakistan in addition to the spread of Baluchi separatist
sentiments next to the Iranian Baluchistan and the exploitation of
these sentiments by either Iraq, Afghanistan, or India (all with close
ties with Moscow) resulted in active diplomatic interaction with
Pakistan. On several occasions the Shah used strong language in
pledging support for Pakistan if its territorial integrity was further
threatened.[4] C. L. Sulzberger of the *New York Times* has reported
that the Shah was genuinely concerned that the disintegration of
Pakistan would produce another Indochina situation. If Pakistan fell
apart, he quotes the Shah, "the least we could do in our interest would
be some kind of protective reaction in Baluchistan." This, Sulzberger
believed, would amount to, "seizing it before anyone else does, another
crude reality." [5]

During this time Iran maintained a strong military presence in the
southeastern region, in line with this declared policy. As the Bhutto
regime in Pakistan became more consolidated military concentration
shifted toward the other sensitive Iran-Iraq and Persian Gulf region.

While the Soviet attitude toward this range of issues required
assessment in a bipolar and bilateral context, it is worth noticing that
in this region the prospect of closer ties with China as a counter-
balancing weight has more recently intrigued the Iranian leadership.

Indeed, the acceptance of Iran as a replacement for Canada on the
International Control Commission to supervise the armistice in Vietnam in the summer of 1973 underscores the recognition of her
enhanced international status by both Communist powers. It is
natural for Iran, wherever external and internal environments permit,
to welcome the opportunity afforded by the gradual emergence of
China in her quest for restraining either the Soviet Union or its
close allies in the region.

THE DHOFAR REBELLION

A successful example of this aim of Iran's diplomacy was demonstrated in the summer of 1973 when Iran managed to enlist China's
support for its Persian Gulf policy. One apparent result was the
termination of Chinese support for the Dhofari rebellion in Oman, in

---

4 *Current History*, LXVI, No. 390 (February 1974), 67.
5 "Belief in 'Crude Reality,' " *New York Times*, April 22, 1973.

which Iran has been involved militarily for quite some time.[6] This involvement, which has been only recently acknowledged, is a manifestation of the Shah's determination to prevent any threat to the status quo resulting from the British departure from the area. In March Iranian paratroopers reportedly opened up the land link between Salalah, the coastal capital of Dhofar, and the rest of Oman. In December "Operation Thimble" launched by an Iranian contingent nine hundred strong helped the twelve thousand British-led troops of the Sultan to consolidate his gains. Other reports on the extent of Iran's military intervention put the size of the Iranian contingent at three "Special Force" ranger battalions, with helicopter and air support.[7]

Foreign observers have reported that Iran's military assistance is essential as long as the guerrillas of the so-called Popular Front for the Liberation of Oman and the Arab Gulf (PFLOAG) enjoy the sanctuary of the leftist regime of southern Yemen.[8]

Tehran diplomacy has been designed to neutralize foreign support for the movement as well as to offer military assistance. In addition to the Chinese promise of nonintervention, Iran endeavored to secure a similar undertaking from the Soviets. The reliability of that pledge, reaffirmed in numerous joint declarations, however, is dissipated by the Soviet ability to use such non-European communist states as Cuba or even North Korea as surrogate agents in that area.[9]

In March Sultan Qabus paid a six-day visit to Iran, during which the two countries reasserted the need and determination for keeping the Straits of Hormoz "free from foreign-inspired" subversion. Oman's ruler expressed appreciation for Iran's military contribution to his struggle against the Dhofar rebels, which he believed also had "the advantage of fortifying the stability and security of this sensitive region of the world." [10]

The Dhofar rebellion is a typical example of the dilemma that persists in Iranian-Persian Gulf relations. A policy of intervention without the request of the established authorities or in response to questionable justification by one of the shaky and feudal regimes in

---

[6] In June, Peng-fei, China's foreign minister, expressed total support for Iran's Gulf policies in a historic visit to Tehran. *Current History*, LXVI No. 390 (February 1974), 66.

[7] *Middle East Intelligence Survey* (Tel Aviv), I, No. 33 (March 1), 1974.

[8] *Christian Science Monitor*, March 7, 1974. Also the NBC Special Report on Iran's military power, March 4, 1974.

[9] See the Shah's interview in *New York Times*, Apr: 1, 1974.

[10] See "Keeping the Straits Secure," *Iran Tribune*, April 1974, p. 4.

the Gulf is fraught with complex difficulties, which we examined in our chapters on the Gulf.

The Shah told an American television audience recently that Iran would face an agonizing dilemma if chaos in this strategic area erupted and the shaykdoms did not formally request his assistance.[11] The government has therefore consistently pursued the idea of a regional defensive agreement, to which no state except Oman has yet responded. In its absence the bilateral military cooperation will continue to reinforce what may amount to a "sole guardian" role, a task that has certainly assumed a more pronounced justification since the energy crisis and oil embargo.

The struggle in that part of the Arabian peninsula has been the latest episode in Arab-Iranian relations which underwent significant stress with the outbreak of the October War. In order to participate on the Syrian side, the Baghdad regime asked Iran for restoration of diplomatic relations in mid-October. After Syria accepted the UN-sponsored cease-fire, Iraqi divisions that had been transformed from Iranian borders returned and soon after border incidents became more frequent.[12] Iran's concern with its Arab neighbor was compounded when the issue of Kurdish autonomy within Iraq came to a head in mid-March.[13]

In our chapter on Iraqi-Iranian relations we have detailed the background and the intensity of a multiplicity of issues complicating their relations. In the latest period many of these have resurfaced.

KURDISH INSURGENCY

Iran's attitude toward Kurdish autonomy contained elements of constraint as well as tempting opportunities. But primarily it is the anxiety over the Soviet attitude which looms heavily in Iran's calculations. Clearly, Iran could use its military and financial resources to promote a serious challenge to the Baghdad regime by the Pesh Merga, the Kurdish guerrilla movement. But having opposed disintegrative movements by ethnic groups as a matter of principle and being sensitive to the potential of a broader trans-territorial Kurdish separatist movement affecting her own territorial integrity, Iran has

---

[11] CBS 60 Minutes, as quoted in *New York Times*, March 3, 1974.

[12] On February 10 a major clash led to Iraq's complaint to the UN Security Council, which authorized the Secretary General to send Mexican Ambassador Luis Weckmann-Munoz on a reconciliation and fact-finding mission. In late May he reported an agreement between the two governments on mutual withdrawal of troops and early resumption of bilateral talks. *Christian Science Monitor*, May 22, 1974.

[13] See among others, *Christian Science Monitor*, March 20, 1974.

been quite restrained and largely reactive to a complex of developments, over some of which she has had scant control.

Since Barzani signed the "cease-fire" accord with Iraqi Vice President Saddam Hussein on March 11, 1970, his Kurdish Democratic
party (KDP) has remained inactive, pending the conclusion of the
four-year period for attainment of autonomy. However, when the
Baghdad regime unilaterally published the provision of the autonomy
on March 11, 1974, by granting the Kurds "legitimate national right
within the framework of a single homeland," Barzani rejected the plan
and ignored the two-week deadline for its acceptance. He objected to
the designation of Erbil as the capital of the autonomous Kurdistan
to replace the oil-rich city of Kirkuk. He was also unhappy about
alleged Iraqi tampering with the ethnic composition of Kirkuk, to the
detriment of its previously Kurdish majority, and the refusal of the
central government to allocate 50 percent of the region's oil revenue
to Kurdistan.[14]

It is obvious that apart from the delicate questions of sovereignty
and territorial integrity, the existence of valuable oil fields in Kirkuk
constitutes a major stumbling block. In desperation the Barzani
forces have sought to cultivate more active support from the United
States as well as from Iran and Turkey. Barzani told a recent interviewer that "both Turkey and Iran face the same danger from the
growing Soviet influence in Iraq. Surely the United States would gain
from backing the Kurds. We are the only force opposing the Soviet
influence in Iraq." [15]

To make this dramatic twist of orientation in Barzani's political
outlook more palatable the Kurdish leader denied any hostility
toward the Soviet Union as such and appealed for American interces-
sion on their behalf in the name of "justice and humanity."

Toward the end of the two-week deadline the Soviet Minister of
Defense and Politburo member Marshal Andrei Grechko visited Iraq
in what was reported to be a mission of reconciliation designed to
avert renewed warfare between the two sides. Soon after, however,
open hostilities broke out with the outlook for the Pesh Merga appearing somewhat grimmer than on previous occasions. This time the
privileged sanctuary in neighboring territories, except as disarmed
and resettled tribes, may be denied them. Nor will it be likely that the
United States or any other extra-regional power would venture the
risk of upsetting a complex and precarious balance of regional forces

---

14 *The Middle East Intelligence Survey* (Tel Aviv), I, No. 24 (March 15, 1974).
15 *Christian Science Monitor*, March 20, 1974.

to save the Kurds from defeat. It is true that few guerrilla movements have sustained themselves when denied these privileges. By the same token, to write off Barzani altogether may be premature. For apart from the inaccessibility of at least part of the mountainous region in their control, radical Arab and non-Arab groups including the Palestinian guerrillas have not totally abandoned the Kurds.

Irrespective of the result of the latest outbreak of Kurdish insurgency in Iraq, Tehran policy toward this crisis is likely to reckon with a further constraint in the form of the growing Turkish stakes in this issue. Turkey's interest stems from recent economic as well as older political considerations. In August 1973 Turkey and Iraq reached an agreement to build a 600-mile-long oil pipeline from Kirkuk to Dortyol on the Turkish Mediterranean coast near Iskenderun, with each country assuming responsibility for its own section of the nearly $400 million project. Once completed by 1976 its throughput will be about 25 million tons annually, rising to 35 million tons by 1983.[16] This project has augmented Turkish interest in the Kurdish region of Iraq to a degree that may not be overlooked by Iran.

These restraining influences are tempered by continuous hostility of the Ba'thist regime toward Iran. Alone among her neighbors, Iraq serves as a sanctuary for various Iranian political and tribal dissident groups actively opposing the Shah's regime. Any specific reaction to events in Iraq must be therefore informed by a complex of balancing factors involving Iran's global and regional foreign relations.[17]

OIL DIPLOMACY

The period under review catapulted the Middle East into unprecedented international and political prominence. Although Iran was neither a belligerent in the October War nor a participant in the Arab oil embargo,[18] her oil diplomacy since October 1973 has become a central focus in her international and regional relations. The vast increase in her oil revenue has accelerated economic and military development. These in turn have enhanced her capabilities to act in foreign policy. Concurrently this new-found wealth has created a new

---

[16] *Christian Science Monitor,* April 3, 1974.

[17] In the summer Iraq actively cultivated the Baluchi dissidents, to the dismay of Iran. Shahram Chubin, "Iran: Between the Arab West and the Asian East." *Survival,* XVI, No. 4 (July–August 1974).

[18] The massive resupply of the Syrian armies, necessitating Iran's permission for Soviet overflight, produced a minor diplomatic snafu between Moscow and Tehran and resulted in the reported dismissal of the deputy undersecretary of Iran's foreign ministry. *Christian Science Monitor,* Nov. 3, 1973.

range of problems related to the growing cleavage between the have and the have-not countries to which Iran could not remain impervious.

Several areas of Iran's diplomacy have been dramatically affected by this new situation. One direct result of the Arab oil embargo was that Iran, presently second to Sa'udi Arabia in annual production,[19] was called upon to fill the gap left by the embargo for several Western consumers such as the United States, the Netherlands, and Denmark.

The long-range issues of the energy crisis were also a continuous preoccupation. The Shah urged that all countries shift from gasoline and oil-burning transport and industry to electrical automobiles and other power sources to conserve oil. This should be conserved for manufacture of petrochemicals, including production of fertilizers and proteins for hungry and poorer countries.

A policy paper of the National Iranian Oil Company declared that "the decided policy of Iran is to utilize the hydrocarbon resources for conversion to petrochemicals to the maximum extent possible and thus to derive the maximum benefit of the added value. Iran does not wish to export the hydrocarbon resources in the form of energy (crude oil and natural gas) if it can be avoided."[20]

Presently about $400 million has been invested in four chemical and petrochemical complexes in Shiraz and three other centers in the Persian Gulf area, all of which operate at maximum capacity and profit. Another $1.1 billion is earmarked for such investment by 1983. Increased production of ammonia, methanol, and ethylene dichloride from plants using some of Iran's huge natural gas reserves is also considered.[21] For example, liquid recovered from the gas can be converted to olefin for export to Western industrial markets. The NIOC estimates that a special chemical refinery complex for the production of fertilizer or feedstock ingredients could use about 600,000 barrels of crude oil annually and accrue much more benefit to the country.

In March Iran agreed with West Germany on a joint-venture, 25-million-ton refinery and associated petrochemical complex worth a total of $2 billion. The new refinery, to be built at the Persian Gulf port of Bushehr, will be the second largest refinery in the oil-rich

---

[19] Six million barrels per day and projected to rise to 8 million by 1978. James Akins, "The Oil Crisis: This Time the Wolf Is Here," *Foreign Affairs*, LI, No. 3 (April 1973), 462–490.

[20] *Christian Science Monitor*, March 31, 1974.

[21] *Ibid.*

province of Khuzistan. A tri-national gas-line to carry gas to Germany via Russia is another ambitious project which when completed could ship in excess of 13,000 million cubic meters of gas to Germany annually.[22]

Total oil earning for the decade 1973–1983 is estimated by the *Middle East Economic Digest* to reach $175.8 billion, second in the world only to Sa'udi Arabia's $177.6 billion.

These opportunities required some basic changes, which could best be understood when compared with the earlier period. Iran's new oil diplomacy originated in the February 1971 agreement resulting from the Tehran OPEC oil conference. That agreement was to last five years and dramatically increased Iran's revenue. Initially the projection was an additional $3.6 billion, but soon it was revised upward because of the U.S. currency devaluation and the steady inflation in the industrialized Western states. Until fall 1973 Iran's oil policy was aimed at a steady increase in oil production compatible with its developmental needs rather than the profit considerations of oil companies.[23]

However, the necessity of expanding production as a means of increasing revenue obviously had to be examined in the context of two considerations: (1) that the unreplenishable oil should not be indiscriminately exhausted and (2) that without the control of refining and marketing facilities no producing country could really exercise a sovereign control on the disposition of its most important revenue source.

In March 1973 Iran took the decisive and ultimate action to acquire the full ownership of her oil installations. A new twenty-year agreement with the Western Oil Consortium signed in early summer signaled the acquiescence of the consortium to Iran's takeover. The main provisions of the agreements were as follows:

1. All exploration, extraction, and refining activities and installations are to come under Iranian control. A service company registered in Iran and subject to Iranian regulations will perform certain technical functions in relation to exploration and extraction for a period of five years only.

2. Control of all oil reserves is to be transferred from the former consortium to Iran. This provision "will certainly lead to an increase

---

22 *Iran Tribune,* April 1974, p. 4.
23 For an authoritative analysis of some of the above, see Jahangir Amuzegar, "The Oil Story: Facts, Fiction, and Fair Play," *Foreign Affairs,* LI, No. 4 (July 1973), 676–689.

in recoverable reserves, despite the fact that this will require massive investment."

3. Iran assumes the rights to all gas reserves in the Agreement Area and complete control of gas exports, with an option open to the former consortium to secure a 50 percent share of the operation for the export of gas through Persian Gulf ports.

4. In the event of disputes arising out of the agreement, solutions will be reached on the basis of Iranian law. Interpretation of the clause of the agreement will also be made according to Iranian law. Privileges or advantages accorded to other Persian Gulf oil-producing nations will also be applied to Iran.

5. Iran is guaranteed per-barrel profits at least equal to those secured by other Persian Gulf oil-producing states.[24]

Prime Minister Amir Abbas Hoveyda told Parliament that after twenty-three years the Nationalization Act has been implemented in its fullest sense. Additional efforts to increase Iranian revenue were undertaken. One effort through OPEC (Organization of Petroleum Exporting Countries) negotiations was designed to increase the price of oil per barrel for all member states. The other was directed at the formation of new, full-participation agreements with companies outside the consortium. Significant success was achieved on both levels when, in October 1973, the OPEC conference meeting in Kuwait approved a 17 percent increase in the posted price of crude oil per barrel.

Similarly, during his last visit to the United States, the Shah formally announced an agreement with the Ashland Oil Company of Ohio based on fifty-fifty participation in Ashland downstream operations. This agreement calls for refining 150,000 barrels of crude oil daily and marketing it "right down to the petrol pump." It gives participation to NIOC (National Iranian Oil Company) in refining and marketing as well as part ownership in Ashland's New York State operations.

The basic change in Iran's oil policy in the more recent period was therefore in favor of generating increased revenue through price hikes rather than expanding production. The October War, more than the 1967 Arab-Israeli war, helped Iran in this respect.

Several strands in Iran's oil policy in the aftermath of the October War are worth mentioning. Iran's refusal to join the Arab oil embargo stemmed from two factors. First, as a non-Arab country Iran was not

---

[24] *Iran Tribune*, August 1973, pp. 6–7.

susceptible to the kinds pressure that Arab oil states are exposed
to in the Arab-Israeli dispute. Indeed, under a comprehensive agreement worked out in early 1962 between Israeli Finance Minister Levi
Eshkol and the NIOC, Iran has supplied crude oil for Israeli consumption. The oil had been regularly transported to the Israeli port
of Elath, but the October War and the reported Egyptian blockade of
Bab-el Mandeb at the southern end of the Red Sea temporarily
stopped its flow.[25]

Second, when Iran was involved in a bitter struggle over the nationalization of oil in 1951–1953, she received no support from Arab
oil-producing countries. Several Persian Gulf states (notably Kuwait
and Iraq) more than made up for the loss of Iranian oil to the Anglo-
Oil Company by increasing production.

However, the cooperative dimension of Arab-Iranian oil relations
was also fully utilized. Sensing the great opportunity that the energy
crisis had provided for all oil-producing countries, the Shah spearheaded a move for a dramatic increase in the posted price of crude
oil. In late December the price was raised by the OPEC conference
meeting in Tehran by approximately 112 percent. Thus, in less than
a year the price of crude oil nearly quadrupled.

In announcing this latest price increase, the Shah outlined some of
his long-range plans, which are now being vigorously pursued. First,
the unavoidable impact of more expensive oil would mean problems
for the industrialized West but grave crisis for oil-less underdeveloped
countries. The West simply had to find other sources of energy and,
pending that, pay the cost of having long neglected doing so and
having exploited oil-producing countries in such indiscriminate
fashion.

The underdeveloped countries must be helped by the OPEC countries, international monetary organizations, and specifically by those
OPEC members whose countries could in no conceivable way absorb
this vast new wealth. Furthermore, since for the foreseeable future
developing countries like Iran must procure industrial commodities
from oil-importing industrial countries, a formula should be found
to prevent the inflationary trends from offsetting the increase in
purchasing power of oil-exporting countries. This was done by a consensus that periodically, April 1 and June 1, OPEC will reevaluate its
pricing policy.

In the April meeting in Vienna Iran was one of the strongest voices

---

25 Sepehr Zabih, "Iran Today," *Current History*, LXVI, No. 390 (February 1974),
66–69.

in the majority which rejected a price cut and instead pushed for a variety of schemes designed to assist poorer Afro-Asian countries facing higher costs for their oil imports. Iran attempted to achieve this by both bilateral and multilateral means. It is in the former area that Iran's oil diplomacy could complement and reinforce its regional policy. Thus, for example, the Shah could influence India's policy in the subcontinent by offering to offset its anticipated foreign exchange deficit through a generous credit or an increase in the production of the NIOC-related Madras refinery. Simultaneously, he could show his displeasure with the Pakistani government's reported cultivation of Libya's Ghaddfi by reminding the former of his option to befriend India or to offer lucrative credit to Pakistan.[26]

The international manifestation of Iran's concern for the plight of the have-not nations aggravated by the oil crisis took several forms. In February the Shah, after audiences with World Bank President Robert McNamara and International Monetary Fund President Hendrikus Johannes Witteveen, proposed the establishment of a new international fund to help stabilize the balance of payment of both developing and industrial countries affected by the oil shortage. The Shah pledged one billion dollars to the three-billion-dollar proposed initial capital of the fund and suggested that twelve OPEC countries and the twelve industrial states join the fund.[27]

To further help overcome the shortage of international liquidity Iran pledged to repay $1,000 million in outstanding foreign loans well before their due date. The Shah stressed that the new fund should take into account the developing countries' balance of payments deficits caused by the rapidly rising oil prices. Iranian funds will help increase the lending of both the IMP and the WB, thereby generating greater equilibrium in international liquidity.[28]

When the special session of the United Nations General Assembly met in April to consider the plight of what Robert Bowie has termed "the global poor," [29] Iran was afforded another international forum to expound its attitude. Jamshid Amuzegar, the Finance Minister and the current chairman of OPEC, told the session that while in the last decade the price of such essential commodities as wheat, cement, fertilizer, and sugar had trebled or quadrupled, few developed coun-

---

26 *New York Times*, March 31, 1974.

27 "Iran Launches Massive Foreign Aid Programme," *Iran Tribune*, March 1974, pp. 4–6.

28 *Ibid.*

29 *Christian Science Monitor*, April 17, 1974.

tries which supply most of these raised a protesting voice. It is when oil, which was artificially underpriced, is reaching a reasonable level that the developed countries wage a vigorous protest.[30]

During the deliberations at the UN special session Iran received support only from Algeria, Venezuela, and Libya among the OPEC member states. Sa'udi Arabia, Kuwait, Iraq, Qatar, and Abu Dhabi, which are amongst the richest yet the least populated countries amassing a large fortune from the windfall profits of price rise, showed little support. A number of them are more interested in an Arab Fund rather than a multilateral one. Nor were industrial countries any more responsive. The Common Market did not pledge support, and the United States seemed unenthusiastic about a new fund, preferring the existing UN Capital Development Fund.

Perhaps anticipating the lack of enthusiasm for a multilateral approach toward the plight of the less developed oil-less countries, Iran has been using its options bilaterally. In March the government agreed to deliver more oil to India than the Indians had purchased and to accept only one-third payment in cash. The rest will be given in credit at 2.5 percent interest. Similar deals will be offered to Tunisia, Morocco and Sudan.[31]

DOMESTIC USE OF OIL REVENUE

The projected increase in oil revenue has enabled the government to proceed with long-range armament purchases. Recent reports from American sources predict that in the fiscal year 1975 arms sales to Iran may reach between $3 and $4 billion. This would include about $1 billion for F-14 jet fighters built by Grumman, together with spare parts, ground support, missiles, and electronic fire-control equipment which may be acquired over a period of three years. The United States agreed in January to Iran's purchase of McDonnell-Douglas F-15's as they become available. About half a billion dollars are earmarked for naval crafts, notably two Spruance-class destroyers. Latest-model Hawk air-defense missiles, which proved a potent match for the Russian SA-6 missiles in the October Arab-Israel War, are also being considered. With the completion of these purchases Iran's arms deals with the United States alone will approach about $7 billion over the three fiscal years 1973, 1974, and 1975.[32] The Shah is also

---

30 *Christian Science Monitor,* April 18, 1974.
31 *Iran Tribune,* April 1974, pp. 4–6.
32 *Christian Science Monitor,* May 9, 1974.

considering ordering from Britain a "through-deck" type of mini-carrier for vertical takeoff to protect sea-lanes to the Far East.

Iran's military buildup is, among other things, linked with her desire to see the Indian Ocean as a demilitarized zone of peace. But she recognizes that this needs the collaboration of all regional and extra-regional powers. The Shah believes that India's anxiety over the influence of the United States is one-sided as long as Soviet naval strength is tolerated. He has expressed a preference for the collaboration of the coastal nations to ensure against foreign influence in the Ocean. The ability to pursue a preclusive objective in this area is restricted by extra-regional naval powers, which despite the UN designation in 1971 of the Indian Ocean as a "zone of peace," have endeavored to improve their positions in the area.

The United States plan to convert the British-owned island of Diego Garcia into a major naval and air base has been a major source of controversy since early 1974. In May a UN-appointed panel of experts concluded that the instabilities inherent in the area will not easily permit a mutual balance to be maintained by the two superpowers and that the risks of great-power conflicts interacting with the local ones and of escalation are high.

The panel noted that since the October War the naval presence of both superpowers has increased and the proposed conversion of Diego Garcia may further complicate this delicate situation. If this occurs, the other superpower will seek similar naval bases, thus generating a new strategic naval arms race.[33] India's acquisition of nuclear capability is likely to compound this question in the years to come.

As to the economic use of the burgeoning oil revenue, throughout the winter and spring 1973–1974 the Plan Organization was preoccupied with the upward revision of Iran's estimated growth during the next few years. In January the Shah declared that a 10 percent annual rate of increase in the GNP at fixed prices was anticipated in the next Five-Year Plan but that the projected augmentation of oil revenue could as much as double this rate. Likewise, the per capita income, which was expected to reach $900, is now likely to aproach $1,500. The GNP at the beginning of 1974 was about $30 billion, placing Iran among the first fifteen countries of the world.[34]

---

[33] The panel was composed of Frank Barnby, Director of Stockholm International Peace Research Institute; Shams Safavi, a retired Iranian admiral, and K. Subrahamanyam, Director of India's Institute for Defense Studies and Analysis. Summary of Report in Reuter dispatch; UN, May 11, 1974.

[34] See the Shah's interview in *Carriere della Serra,* January 4, 1974.

That the Iranian economic growth has been planned, sustained, and impressive is hardly challenged by most qualified and objective analysts. Whether the standard criteria of growth are adequate for the appraisal of socioeconomic consequences of growth is another matter. Some specialists in the field of modernization and economic development have suggested that more relevant criteria for this purpose would be the so-called *Lorenzo curve* and the *Gini Index* of income distribution.[35] Although this requires comprehensive and reliable data spread over at least three to five years, government investigations demonstrate significant gains for Iran in terms of a more equitable pattern of income distribution. It is predicted confidently that at the end of the current Five-Year Plan Iran will register even more favorably on these scales.

As this survey shows, 1973–74 has been a momentous year in the evolution of Iran's foreign relations. New opportunities have combined with new anxieties to sustain a dynamic and vigorous quest for a balanced and enlightened foreign policy. Impressed by Iran's achievement in this search such other Middle-Eastern states as Egypt have more recently endeavored to employ the instruments and tactics that have stabilized Iran's international posture.[36]

---

[35] For a discussion of these matters, see Karl W. Deutsch, *Politics and Government, How People Decide Their Fate*, Boston: 1970, Houghton Mifflin Co., pp. 88–92.

[36] In the post-October rapproachment with the United States, Egyptian officials have frequently used arguments and advocacies in favor of a "balanced" policy towards the superpowers akin to those used by Iran in the mid-6o's. For a perceptive analysis of other features of Iran's prospects consult William E. Griffith, "Iran: A New Persian Empire?" *Christian Science Monitor*, January 25, 1974.

BIBLIOGRAPHY

1. BOOKS

Achoube–Amini, Ramatollah. *Le Conflit de frontière Irako-Iranien*. Paris, 1936.

Adamiyat, Fereydoun. *Bahrein Islands: A Legal and Diplomatic Study of the British-Iranian Controversy*. New York: Frederick A. Praeger, 1952.

Adams, Thomas W., and Alvin J. Cottrell. *Cyprus Between East and West*. Baltimore: John Hopkins Press (Studies in International Affairs, No. 7), 1968.

Adamson, David. *The Kurdish War*. London: George Allen and Unwin, 1964.

Adelman, M. A. *The World Petroleum Market*. Baltimore: Johns Hopkins University Press (for Resources for the Future, Inc.), 1972.

Albaharna, Husain M. *The Legal Status of the Arabian Gulf States*. New York: Oceana Publications, 1968.

Algar, Hamid. *Religion and State in Iran, 1785–1906: The Role of the Ulama in the Qajar Period*. Berkeley and Los Angeles: University of California Press, 1969.

Almond, Gabriel, "The Comparative Study of Foreign Policy," in Roy C. Macridis (ed.), *Foreign Policy in World Politics*. Englewood Cliffs, N.J.: Prentice-Hall, 1958.

Ambrose, Stephen E. *Rise to Globalism: American Foreign Policy, 1938–1970*. Baltimore: Penguin, 1971.

Amin, Abdul Amir. *British Interests in the Persian Gulf*. Leiden, Holland: E. J. Brill, 1967.

Amuzegar, Jahangir, and M. Ali Fekrat. *Iran: Economic Development Under Dualistic Conditions*. Chicago: University of Chicago Press (Center for Middle Eastern Studies, No. 7), 1971.

Arfa, Gen. Hassan. *Under Five Shahs*. New York: William Morrow, 1965.

———. *The Kurds: An Historical and Political Study*. New York: Oxford University Press, 1966.

Aron, Raymond. *Peace and War: A Theory of International Relations*. Trans. by Richard Howard and Annette Baker Fox. New York: Doubleday, 1966.

Avery, Peter. *Modern Iran*. New York: Praeger, 1965.

Badeau, John S. *The American Approach to the Arab World*. New York: Harper and Row (Colophon Book, for the Council on Foreign Relations), 1968.

Baldwin, George B. *Planning and Development in Iran*. Baltimore: Johns Hopkins Press, 1967.

Baldwin, Hanson W. *Strategy for Tomorrow*. New York: Harper and Row (for the Center for Strategic and International Studies, Georgetown University, Washington, D.C.), 1970.

Banani, Amin. *The Modernization of Iran, 1921–1941*. Stanford, Calif.: Stanford University Press, 1961.

Bayne, E. A. *Persian Kingship in Transition: Conversations with a Monarch Whose Office Is Traditional and Whose Goal Is Modernization*. New York: American Universities Field Staff, 1968.

Be'eri, Eliezer. *Army Officers in Arab Politics and Society*. New York: Praeger, 1970.

Beichman, Arnold. *The "Other" State Department: The United States Mission to the United Nations—Its Role in the Making of Foreign Policy*. New York: Basic Books, 1967.

Benedict, Burton (ed.). *Problems of Smaller Territories*. London: The Athlone Press, University of London (for the Institute of Commonwealth Studies), 1967.

Bharier, Julien. *Economic Development of Iran, 1900–1970*. New York: Oxford University Press, 1971.

Bill, James Alban. *The Politics of Iran: Groups, Classes, and Modernization*. Columbus, Ohio: Charles E. Merrill, 1972.

Binder, Leonard. *Iran: Political Development in a Changing Society*. Berkeley and Los Angeles: University of California Press, 1962.

———. *The Ideological Revolution in the Middle East*. New York: John Wiley, 1964.

———. "The New States in International Affairs." In Robert A. Goldwin (ed.), *Beyond the Cold War: Essays in American Foreign Policy in a Changing World Environment*. Chicago: Rand McNally, 1965.

Bowles, Chester. *Promises to Keep: My Years in Public Life, 1941–1965*. New York: Harper and Row, 1971.

Brassey's Annual: Defence and the Armed Forces, 1972. Ed. by Maj. Gen. J. L. Moulton. London: William Clowes, 1972.

Brown, Seyom. *The Faces of Power: Constancy and Change in United States Foreign Policy from Truman to Johnson*. New York: Columbia University Press, 1968.

Brzezinski, Zbigniew, and Samuel P. Huntington. *Political Power: USA/USSR*. New York: Viking, 1968.

Burrell, R. M. "Britain, Iran and the Persian Gulf." In Derek Hopwood (ed.),

The Arabian Peninsula: Society and Politics. London: George Allen and Unwin, 1972.

Busch, Briton Cooper. *Britain and the Persian Gulf, 1894–1914.* Berkeley and Los Angeles: University of California Press, 1967.

Butwell, Richard (ed.). *Foreign Policy and the Developing Nation.* Lexington: University of Kentucky Press, 1969.

Cable, James. *Gunboat Diplomacy: Political Applications of Limited Naval Force.* London: Chatto and Windus (for the Institute for Strategic Studies; Studies in International Security, No. 16), 1971.

Calvocoressi, Peter. *World Order and New States: Problems of Keeping the Peace.* New York: Praeger (for the Institute of Strategic Studies; Studies in International Security, No. 4), 1962.

Campbell, John C. *Defense of the Middle East: Problems of American Policy* (rev. ed.). New York: Praeger (for the Council on Foreign Relations), 1961.

Cantori, Louis J., Jr., and Stephen L. Spiegel. *The International Politics of Regions: A Comparative Approach.* Englewood Cliffs, N.J.: Prentice-Hall, 1970.

Center for Strategic and International Studies, Georgetown University. *The Gulf: Implications of Britain's Withdrawal.* Washington, D.C. (Special Report Series, No. 8), 1969.

———. *Soviet Sea Power.* Washington, D.C. (Special Report Series, No. 10), 1969.

Chirol, Valentine. *The Occident and the Orient.* Chicago: University of Chicago Press, 1924.

Chronology of Arab Politics, I (1963), II (1964), III (1965). Bayrut: American University of Bayrut (Political Studies and Administration Dept.).

Cleveland, Harlan. *The Obligations of Power: American Diplomacy in the Search for Peace.* New York: Harper and Row, 1966.

Conolly, Violet. *Soviet Economic Policy in the East: Turkey, Persia, Afghanistan, Mongolia, and Tana Tuva, Sin Kiang.* London: Oxford University Press, 1933.

Copeland, Miles. *The Game of Nations: The Amorality of Power Politics.* New York: Simon and Schuster, 1969.

Cottam, Richard W. *Nationalism in Iran.* Pittsburgh: University of Pittsburgh Press, 1964.

———. *Competitive Interference and Twentieth Century Diplomacy.* Pittsburgh: University of Pittsburgh Press, 1967.

Cottrell, Alvin J., and R. M. Burrell (eds.). *The Indian Ocean: Its Political, Economic, and Military Importance.* New York: Praeger (for the Center for Strategic and International Studies), 1972.

Craig, Gordon A. *War, Politics, and Diplomacy: Selected Essays.* London: Weidenfield and Nicolson, 1966.

———, and Felix Gilbert (eds.). *The Diplomats, 1919–1939.* New York: Atheneum, 1967, 2 vols. (Princeton University Press, 1953).

Crankshaw, Edward. *The New Cold War: Moscow vs. Peking.* Baltimore: Penguin, 1963.

Cremeans, Charles D. *The Arabs and the World: Nasser's Arab Nationalist Policy.* New York: Praeger (for the Council on Foreign Relations), 1963.

Crick, Bernard. *In Defense of Politics.* Baltimore: Penguin, 1964.

Curzon, George N. *Persia and the Persian Question,* II. London: Frank Cass, 1966 (1892).

Dallin, David J. *Soviet Foreign Policy After Stalin.* New York: Lippincott, 1961.

Dann, Uriel. *Iraq Under Qassem: A Political History, 1958–1963.* New York: Praeger (Tel Aviv: Reuven Shiloah Research Center), 1969.

Darby, Phillip. *British Defense Policy East of Suez, 1947–1968.* London: Oxford University Press, 1973.

De Gaulle, Charles. *The War Memoirs of Charles de Gaulle: Salvation, 1944–1946.* New York: Simon and Schuster, 1960.

———. *Memoirs of Hope: Renewal and Endeavor.* New York: Simon and Schuster, 1971.

Dib, Moussa G. *The Arab Bloc in the United Nations.* Amsterdam: Djambatan, 1956.

Dickson, H. R. P. *Kuwait and Her Neighbours.* London: George Allen and Unwin, 1968 (1956).

Dinerstein, Herbert. "The Transformation of Alliance Systems." In Richard Grey (ed.), *International Security Systems: Concepts and Models of World Order.* Itasca, Ill.: Peacock, 1969.

Duncan, Raymond (ed.). *Soviet Policy in Developing Countries.* Boston: Ginn Blaisdell, 1970.

Eagleton, William, Jr., *The Kurdish Republic of 1946.* New York: Oxford University Press, 1963.

Echo of Iran, *Iran Almanac,* 1962, 1964, 1965, 1966, 1967, 1968, 1969, 1970, 1971, 1972. Tehran: Echo of Iran Press.

Eller, Ernest McNeill. *The Soviet Sea Challenge.* Chicago: Cowles, 1971.

Elwell-Sutton, L. P. *Modern Iran.* London: Routledge and Sons, 1941.

———. *Persian Oil: A Study in Power Politics.* London: Lawrence and Wishart, 1955.

Erickson, John. *Soviet Military Power.* London: Royal United Service Institute for Defence Studies, 1971.

Fairhall, David. *Russia Looks to the Sea: A Study of the Expansion of Soviet Naval Power.* London: André Deutch, 1971.

Fatemi, Nasrollah Saifpour. *Diplomatic History of Persia, 1917–1923: Anglo-Russian Power Politics in Iran.* New York: Russell F. Moore, 1952.

Feis, Herbert. *Foreign Aid and Foreign Policy.* New York: St. Martins Press, 1964.

Fenelon, K. G. *The Trucial States: A Brief Economic Study.* Bayrut: Khayats (Middle East Economic and Social Monographs, No. 1), 1967.

Fox, Annette Baker. "Small State Diplomacy." In Stephen D. Kertesz and

M. A. Fitzsimmons (eds.), *Diplomacy in a Changing World*. Notre Dame, Ind.: University of Notre Dame Press, 1959.

————. *The Power of Small States*. Chicago: University of Chicago Press, 1967 (1959).

Fox, William T. R. *The Super-Powers: The United States, Britain, and the Soviet Union—Their Responsibility for Peace*. (Institute of International Studies, Yale University.) New York: Harcourt Brace, 1944.

Ghirshman, R. *The Island of Kharg*. Tehran: Iranian Oil Operating Companies, 1964.

Goldman, Marshall I. *Soviet Foreign Aid*. New York: Praeger, 1967.

Goodrich, Leland M., and Ann P. Simons. *The United Nations and the Maintenance of International Peace and Security*. Washington, D.C.: Brookings Institution, 1952.

————. *The United Nations*. New York: Crowell, 1964.

Greaves, Rose L. *Persia and the Defence of India, 1884–1892*. London: University of London, Athlone Press, 1959.

Haddad, George. *Revolutions and Military Rule in the Middle East: The Arab States*, II. New York: Robert Speller, 1971.

Hammond, Paul Y., and Sydney S. Alexander (eds.). *Political Dynamics in the Middle East*. New York: Elsevier, 1972.

Hamzavi, Abolhôssein. *Persia and the Powers: An Account of Diplomatic Relations, 1941–1946*. London, 1947.

Hanreider, Wolfram. *Comparative Foreign Policy: Theoretical Essays*. New York: McKay, 1970.

Harriman, Averell. *The U.S. and U.S.S.R. in a Changing World*. New York: Doubleday, 1971.

Harris, George L. *Iraq*. New Haven, Conn.: Human Relations Area Files, 1958.

Hartshorn, J. E. *Politics and World Oil Economics*. New York: Praeger, 1962.

Hawley, Donald. *The Trucial States*. London: George Allen and Unwin, 1970.

Hay, Rupert. *The Persian Gulf States*. Washington, D.C.: Middle East Institute, 1959.

Heikal, Mohamed. *The Cairo Documents: The Inside Story of Nasser and His Relationship with World Leaders, Rebels, and Statesmen*. New York: Doubleday, 1973.

Henkin, Louis. *How Nations Behave: Law and Foreign Policy*. New York: Praeger (for the Council on Foreign Relations), 1968.

Heren, Louis. *No Hail, No Farewell*. New York: Harper and Row, 1970.

Herrick, Robert Waring. *Soviet Naval Strategy: Fifty Years of Theory and Practice*. Annapolis, Md.: U.S. Naval Institute, 1968.

Hirszowicz, Lukasz. *Iran, 1951–53: Nafta, Imperializm, Nacjonalizm* (Iran, 1951–53: Oil, Imperialism, Nationalism). Warsaw, 1958.

Hoffmann, Erik P. and Frederic J. Feleron. *The Conduct of Soviet Foreign Policy*. Chicago and New York: Aldine, Atherton, 1971.

Holden, David. *Farewell to Arabia*. New York: Walker, 1966.

Hopwood, Derek (ed.). *The Arabian Peninsula: Society and Politics.* (Studies on Modern Asia and Africa, No. 8.) London: George Allen and Unwin, 1972.

Hovet, Thomas. *Bloc Politics in the United Nations.* Cambridge, Mass.: Harvard University Press, 1961.

Humaidan, Ali. *Les Princes de l'Or Noir: Évolution Politique du Golfe Persique.* Paris: Futuribles No. 8, SEDEIS, 1968.

Huntington, Samuel. *Political Order in Changing Societies.* New Haven, Conn.: Yale University Press, 1968.

Hurewitz, J. C. *Diplomacy in the Near and Middle East: A Documentary Record, 1535–1914,* Vol. I; *1914–1956,* Vol. II. Princeton, N.J.: Van Nostrand, 1957.

———. *Middle East Dilemmas: The Background of U.S. Policy.* New York: Harper (for the Council on Foreign Relations), 1953.

———. *Middle East Politics: The Military Dimension.* New York: Praeger (for the Council on Foreign Relations), 1969.

——— (ed.). *Soviet-American Rivalry in the Middle East.* New York: Praeger, 1969.

Ibish, Yusuf, and Walid Khalidi (eds.). *Arab Political Documents,* 1965 and 1966. Bayrut: American University of Bayrut, 1965 and 1966.

Institute for Strategic Studies (International Institute for Strategic Studies, since 1971), London. "The Military Balance," 1961–1962, 1962–1963, 1963–1964, 1964–1965, 1968–1969, 1969–1970, 1970–1971, 1971–1972, 1972–1973, and 1973–1974.

———. "Strategic Survey," 1969, 1970, and 1971.

Issawi, Charles (ed.). *The Economic History of Iran, 1800–1914.* Chicago: University of Chicago Press, 1971. (Publications of the Center for Middle Eastern Studies, No. 8.)

———. *Oil, The Middle East, and the World.* (Washington Paper No. 4.) The Library Press, 1972.

Ivanov, M. S. *Iran Segodnya* (Iran Today). "Nauka," 1969; *idem, Rabochiy Klass Sovremennogo Irana* (The Working Class of Contemporary Iran). "Nauka," 1969.

———. *Noveyshaya Istoriya Irana* (The Recent History of Iran). 1965, pp. 246–247.

Jacobs, Norman. *The Sociology of Development: Iran as an Asian Case Study.* New York: Praeger (Praeger Special Studies in International Economics and Development), 1966.

Jakobson, Max. *The Diplomacy of the Winter War: An Account of the Russo-Finnish Conflict, 1939–1940.* Cambridge, Mass.: Harvard University Press, 1961.

———. *Finnish Neutrality: A Study of Finnish Foreign Policy Since the Second World War.* New York: Praeger, 1968.

Jennings, R. Y. *The Acquisition of Territory in International Law.* New York: Oceana, 1963.

Johnstone, William C. *Burma's Foreign Policy: A Study in Neutralism*. Cambridge, Mass.: Harvard University Press, 1963.

Joshua, Wynfred, and Stephen P. Gibert. *Arms for the Third World: Soviet Military Aid Diplomacy*. Baltimore: Johns Hopkins Press, 1969.

Kapur, Harish. *Soviet Russia and Asia, 1917–1927: A Study of Soviet Policy Towards Turkey, Iran, and Afghanistan*. Geneva: Michael Joseph, Ltd. (for Geneva Graduate Institute of International Studies), 1966.

Kauffman, William. *The McNamara Strategy*. New York: Harper and Row, 1964.

Kay, David A. *The New Nations in the United Nations*. New York: Columbia University Press, 1968.

———— (ed.). *The United Nations Political System*. New York: Wiley, 1967.

Kazemzadeh, Firuz. *Britain and Russia in Iran, 1864–1914*. New Haven, Conn.: Yale University Press, 1968.

Keddie, Nikki R. *Religion and Rebellion in Iran: The Tobacco Protest of 1891–1892*. London: Frank Cass, 1966.

Kedourie, Elie. *The Chatham House Version and Other Middle Eastern Studies*. New York: Praeger, 1970.

Kelly, J. B. *Britain and the Persian Gulf, 1795–1880*. New York: Oxford University Press, 1968.

Kerr, Malcolm H. *The Arab Cold War: Gamal 'Ab al-Nasser and His Rivals, 1958–1970* (3rd ed.). New York: Oxford University Press (for the Royal Institute of International Affairs), 1971.

Khadduri, Majid. *Republican Iraq: A Study of Iraqi Politics Since the Revolution of 1958*. New York: Oxford University Press (for the Royal Institute of International Affairs), 1969.

———— (ed). *Major Middle Eastern Problems in International Law*. Washington, D.C.: American Enterprise Institute for Public Policy Research, 1972.

Khalatbary, Abbas. *L'Iran et Le Pacte Orientale*. Paris: Pedone, 1938.

King, Gillian. *Imperial Outpost—Aden: Its Place in British Strategic Policy*. New York: Oxford University Press (Chatham House Essay No. 6 for the Royal Institute of International Affairs), 1964.

Kinnane, Derk. *The Kurds and Kurdistan*. London: Oxford University Press (for the Institute of Race Relations), 1964.

Kissinger, Henry. "Coalition Diplomacy in a Nuclear Age." In Linda B. Miller (ed.), *Dynamics of World Politics: Studies in Resolution of Conflict*. Englewood Cliffs, N.J.: Prentice-Hall, 1968.

Klieman, Arnold. *Soviet Russia and the Middle East*. Baltimore: Johns Hopkins Press, 1970.

Kolko, Gabriel. *The World and the United States Foreign Policy*. Vol. II., *The Limits of Power*, 1945–1954. New York: Random House, 1968.

Kumar, Ravinder. *India and the Persian Gulf Region*. New York: Asia Publishing House, 1965.

Lagos, Gustavo. *International Stratification and Underdeveloped Countries*. Chapel Hill: University of North Carolina Press, 1963.

Laquer, Walter. *The Soviet Union and the Middle East.* New York: Praeger, 1959.

————. *The Struggle for the Middle East: The Soviet Union in the Mediterranean.* New York: Macmillan, 1969.

Lederer, Ivo J. (ed.). *Russian Foreign Policy: Essays in Historical Perspective.* New Haven, Conn.: Yale University Press, 1962.

Lenczowski, George. *Russia and the West in Iran, 1918–1948: A Study in Big-Power Rivalry.* Ithaca, N.Y.: Cornell University Press, 1949.

————. *Soviet Advances in the Middle East.* Washington, D.C.: American Enterprise Institute for Public Policy Research, 1971.

Liska, George. *Alliances and the Third World.* Baltimore: Johns Hopkins Press (Studies in International Affairs, No. 5), 1968.

————. *Nations in Alliance: The Limits of Interdependence.* Baltimore: Johns Hopkins Press, 1962.

————. *The New Statecraft: Foreign Aid in American Foreign Policy.* Chicago: University of Chicago Press, 1960.

Little, Tom. *South Arabia: Arena of Conflict.* London: Pall Mall, 1968.

Longrigg, Stephen H. *Oil in the Middle East: Its Discovery and Development* (3rd ed.). London: Oxford University Press (for the Royal Institute of International Affairs), 1968.

Luard, Evan (ed.). *The International Regulation of Frontier Disputes.* London: Thames and Hudson, 1970.

Lukacs, John. *A New History of the Cold War* (3rd ed.). New York: Anchor Books, 1966.

McCarthy, Eugene J. *The Limits of Power: America's Role in the World.* New York: Holt, Rinehart and Winston, 1967.

MacDonald, Robert W. *The League of Arab States: A Study in the Dynamics of Regional Organization.* Princeton, N.J.: Princeton University Press, 1965.

McGuire, Michael (ed.). *Soviet Naval Developments: Capability and Context.* New York: Praeger, 1973.

Macintosh, J. M. *The Strategy and Tactics of Soviet Foreign Policy.* London: Oxford University Press, 1962.

McKay, Vernon (ed.). *African Diplomacy: Studies in the Determinants of Foreign Policy.* New York: Praeger (published for the School of Advanced International Studies, Johns Hopkins University), 1966.

Macridis, Roy C. (ed.). *Foreign Policy in World Politics* (4th ed.). Englewood Cliffs, N.J.: Prentice-Hall, 1972.

Mann, Maj. Clarence. *Abu Dhabi: Birth of an Oil Shiekhdom.* Bayrut: Khayats, 1964.

Marayati, Abd'al. *A Diplomatic History of Modern Iraq.* New York: Robert Speller, 1961.

Marlowe, John. *The Persian Gulf in the Twentieth Century.* New York: Praeger, 1962.

Martin, Bradford E. *German-Persian Diplomatic Relations, 1873–1912.* Netherlands: Mouton and Co., 1959.

Mason, Edward. *Foreign Aid and Foreign Policy*. New York: Harper and Row (for the Council on Foreign Relations), 1964.

Maxwell, Neville. *India's China War*. New York: Pantheon, 1971.

Mazour, Anatole G. *Finland Between East and West*. Princeton, N.J.: Princeton University Press, 1956.

The Middle East and North Africa, 1960–1972 (7th–19th annual editions). London: Europa.

Middle East Record, I (1960); II (1961). Tel Aviv: Israel Oriental Society.

Middle East Record, III (1967). Jerusalem: Israel Universities Press (for the Shiloah Center for Middle East and African Studies), 1971.

Mikdashi, Zuhayr. *The Community of Oil-Exporting Countries: A Study in Governmental Cooperation*. Ithaca, N.Y.: Cornell University Press, 1972.

Miller, J. D. B. *The Politics of the Third World*. New York: Oxford University Press (for the Royal Institute of International Affairs), 1967.

Miller, Linda B. (ed.). *Dynamics of World Politics: Studies in the Resolution of Conflict*. Englewood Cliffs, N.J.: Prentice-Hall, 1968.

Monroe, Elizabeth. *The Changing Balance of Power in the Persian Gulf*. (Report of an International Seminar at the Center for Mediterranean Studies, Rome, June 26-July 1, 1972.) New York: American Universities Field Staff, 1972.

Montgomery, John D. *The Politics of Foreign Aid: American Experience in Southeast Asia*. New York: Praeger (for the Council on Foreign Relations), 1962.

Morgenthau, Hans J. *Politics Among Nations: The Struggle For Power and Peace*. New York: Alfred Knopf, 1963.

Mosely, Philip. *The Kremlin in World Politics: Studies in Soviet Policy and Action*. New York: Vintage, 1960.

Nasser, Gamal 'Abd-al. *The Philosophy of the Revolution*. Buffalo, N.Y.: Economica Books, 1959.

Nollau, Gunther, and Hans Jürgen Wiehe. *Russia's South Flank: Soviet Operations in Iran, Turkey, and Afghanistan*. New York: Praeger, 1963.

Nutting, Anthony. *Nasser*. New York: Dutton, 1972.

O'Ballance, Edgar. *The War in the Yemen*. Hamden, Conn.: Archon, 1971.

Odell, Peter R. *Oil and World Power: A Geographical Interpretation*. Harmondsworth, England: Penguin, 1970.

Osgood, Robert E. *Alliances and American Foreign Policy*. Baltimore: Johns Hopkins Press, 1968.

Oxford Regional Economic Atlas: The Middle East and North Africa. London: Oxford University Press, 1960.

Page, Stephen. *The USSR and Arabia: The Development of Soviet Policies and Attitudes Towards the Countries of the Arabian Peninsula*. London: Central Asian Research Centre (in Association with the Canadian Institute of International Affairs), 1971.

Pahlavi, His Imperial Majesty Mohammed Reza Shah. *Mission for My Country*. New York: McGraw-Hill, 1961.

————. *The White Revolution.* Tehran: Keyhan, 1967.

Penrose, E. F. *The Large International Firm in Developing Countries.* Cambridge, Mass.: M.I.T. Press, 1968.

Phillips, Claude S., Jr. *The Development of Nigerian Foreign Policy.* Northwestern, Ill.: Northwestern University Press, 1964.

Proctor, Harris J. (ed.). *Islam and International Relations.* New York: Praeger, 1965.

Ralston, Jerry Wilson. *The Defense of Small States in the Nuclear Age: The Case of Sweden and Switzerland.* Geneva, Switzerland: Université de Genève Institut Universitaire des Hautes Études Internationales (Thése No. 193), 1969.

Ramazani, Rouhollah K. *The Foreign Policy of Iran, 1500–1941: A Developing Nation in World Affairs.* Charlottesville: University of Virginia Press, 1966.

————. *The Persian Gulf: Iran's Role.* Charlottesville: University of Virginia Press, 1972.

Rawlinson, Henry. *England the Russia in the East.* New York: Praeger, 1970. (London: John Murray, 1875.)

Record of the Arab World: Documents, Events, Political Opinions. Bayrut: Research and Publishing House, 1970.

Reich, Bernard, et al. *The Persian Gulf.* McLean, Va.: Research Analysis Corporation, 1971.

Rose, Leo E. *Nepal: Strategy for Survival.* Berkeley and Los Angeles: University of California Press, 1971.

Rosenau, James N. (ed.). *Linkage Politics: Essays on the Convergence of National and International Systems.* New York: Free Press, 1969.

————. *The Scientific Study of Foreign Policy.* New York: Free Press, 1971.

Rothstein, Robert L. *Alliances and Small Powers.* New York: Columbia University Press, 1968.

Rouhani, Fuad. *A History of O.P.E.C.* New York: Praeger, 1971.

Royal United Service Institution (London). *The Soviet Union in Europe and the Near East: Her Capabilities and Intentions.* (Report of a seminar sponsored jointly by Southampton University and RUSI at Melford-on-Sea, March 23–25, 1970.) London, 1970.

Russell, Ruth, and Jeanette E. Muther. *A History of the United Nations Charter: The Role of the United States, 1940–1945.* Washington, D.C.: Brookings Institution, 1958.

Russett, Bruce. *International Regions and the International System: A Study in Political Ecology.* Chicago: Rand McNally, 1967.

————. *Trends in World Politics.* New York: Macmillan, 1965.

Rustow, Dankwart A. "Foreign Policy of the Turkish Republic." In Roy Macridis (ed.), *Foreign Policy in World Politics.* Englewood Cliffs, N.J.: Prentice-Hall, 1958.

Sadik, T. Muhammad, and William P. Snavely. *Bahrain, Qatar, and the United*

Arab Emirates: Colonial Past, Present Problems, and Future Prospects. Lexington, Mass.: Heath, 1972.

Safran, Nadar. *From War to War: The Arab-Israeli Confrontation, 1948–1967.* New York: Pegasus, 1969.

Salisbury, Harrison. *War Between Russia and China.* New York: Bantam, 1970.

Sanger, Richard. *The Arabian Peninsula.* Ithaca, N.Y.: Cornell University Press, 1954.

Schelling, Thomas C. *The Strategy of Conflict.* New York: Oxford University Press, 1963.

Schmidt, Dana Adams. *Journey Among Brave Men.* Boston: Little, Brown, 1964.

————. *Yemen: The Unknown War.* New York: Holt, Rinehart and Winston, 1968.

Schou, August, and Arne Olav Brundtland (eds.). *Small States in International Relations.* (Nobel Symposium, No. 17.) New York: Wiley Interscience Division, 1971.

Schurr, Sam H., and Paul T. Homan. *Middle Eastern Oil and the Western World: Prospects and Problems.* New York: Elsevier, 1971.

Scott, Andrew M. *The Revolution in Statecraft: Informal Penetration.* New York: Random House, 1965.

Shulman, Marshall D. "Future Directions for United States Policy Toward the Soviet Union and Eastern Europe." In Robert W. Gregg and Charles W. Kegley, Jr. (eds.), *After Vietnam: The Future of American Foreign Policy.* New York: Anchor, 1971.

————. *Stalin's Foreign Policy Reappraised.* New York: Atheneum, 1969.

Singer, Marshall R. *Weak States in a World of Powers.* New York: Free Press, 1972.

Smith, Roger M. *Cambodia's Foreign Policy.* Ithaca, N. Y.: Cornell University Press, 1965.

Sorenson, Theodore. *Kennedy.* New York: Bantam, 1965.

Spector, Ivar. *The Soviet Union and the Muslim World, 1917–1956.* Seattle: University of Washington Press, 1957.

Spiro, Herbert J. *World Politics: The Global System.* Homewood, Ill.: Dorsey Press, 1966.

Sprout, Harold, and Margaret Sprout. *The Ecological Perspective on Human Affairs.* Princeton N.J.: Princeton University Press, 1965.

Stegenga, James A. *The United Nations Force in Cyprus.* Columbus: Ohio State University Press, 1968.

Stephens, Robert. *Nasser: A Political Biography.* New York: Simon and Schuster, 1971.

Stevens, Georgiana G. (ed.). *The United States and the Middle East.* Englewood Cliffs, N.J.: Prentice-Hall (for the American Assembly, Columbia University), 1964.

Stock, Ernest. *Israel on the Road to Sinai, 1949–1956, with a Sequel on the Six-Day War, 1967.* Ithaca, N.Y.: Cornell University Press, 1967.

Stockholm International Peace Research Institute. *The Arms Trade with the Third World.* New York: Humanities Press, 1971.

———. *Yearbook of World Armaments and Disarmament,* for 1968–69, 1969–70, and 1970–71. New York: Humanities Press.

Stocking, George W. *Middle East Oil: A Study in Political and Economic Controversy.* Kingsport, Tenn.: Vanderbilt University Press, 1970.

Stoessinger, John G. *The UN and the Superpowers—United States-Soviet Interaction at the United Nations.* New York: Random House, 1965.

Sulzberger, C. L. *The Last of the Giants.* New York: Macmillan, 1970.

Sviecs, V. V. *Small Nation Survival: Political Defense in Unequal Conflicts.* New York: Exposition Press, 1970.

Sykes, Percy. *A History of Persia,* II (3rd ed.). London: Macmillan, 1963 (1915).

Tadjbackshe, Gholom Reza. *Le Question des Isles Bahrein.* Paris: Pedone, 1960.

Tanzer, Michael. *The Political Economy of International Oil and Underdeveloped Countries.* Boston: Beacon Press, 1970.

Tehranian, Majid. *Iran.* In Abid Al-Marayati (ed.), *The Middle East: Its Governments and Politics.* Belmont, Calif.: Duxbury Press, 1972.

Thiam, Doudou. *The Foreign Policy of African States.* New York: Praeger, 1965.

Thomas, Lewis V., and Richard N. Frye. *The United States and Turkey and Iran.* Cambridge, Mass.: Harvard University Press, 1951.

Thompson, Scott. *Ghana's Foreign Policy, 1957–1966: Diplomacy, Ideology, and the New State.* Princeton, N.J.: Princeton University Press, 1969.

Trevelyan, Lord Humphrey. *The Middle East in Revolution.* London: Macmillan, 1970.

Ulam, Adam. *Expansion and Coexistence: The History of Soviet Foreign Policy, 1917–1967.* New York: Praeger, 1968.

Upton, Joseph M. *The History of Modern Iran: An Interpretation.* Cambridge: Harvard University Press (Harvard Middle Eastern Monographs), 1960.

Vali, Ferenc. *Bridge Across the Bosporus: The Foreign Policy of Turkey.* Baltimore: Johns Hopkins Press, 1972.

Vanderbosch, Amry. *Dutch Foreign Policy Since 1815: A Study in Small Power Politics.* The Hague: Martinus Mijhoff, 1959.

Vital, David. *The Inequality of States: A Study of the Small Power in International Relations.* Oxford: Clarendon Press, 1967.

———. *The Survival of Small States: Studies in Small Power-Great Power Conflict.* New York: Oxford University Press, 1971.

Wall, Patrick. "The Persian Gulf—Stay or Quit?" In *Brassey's Annual: Defence and the Armed Forces, 1971,* ed. by Maj. Gen. J. L. Moulton. London: William Clowes, 1971.

Walters, F. P. *A History of the League of Nations.* New York: Oxford University Press, 1965 (1952).

Warne, William R. *Mission for Peace.* New York: Bobbs-Merrill, 1956.

Waterbury, John. *The Commander of the Faithful, The Moroccan Political Elite—A Study in Segmented Politics.* New York: Columbia University Press, 1970.

Watt, D. C. (ed.). *Survey of International Affairs, 1961.* London: Oxford University Press (for the Royal Institute of International Affairs), 1965.

Wilkinson, David O. *Comparative Foreign Relations: Framework and Methods.* Belmont, Calif.: Dickenson, 1969.

Wilson, Sir Arnold T. *Persia.* London: Ernest T. Benn, 1932.

———. *The Persian Gulf: An Historical Sketch from the Earliest Times to the Beginning of the Twentieth Century.* London: George Allen and Unwin, 1959 (1928).

———. *South-West Persia: A Political Officer's Diary, 1907–1914.* London: Oxford University Press, 1941.

Wilson, David A. *The United States and the Future of Thailand.* New York: Praeger, 1970.

Wolfers, Arnold. *Discord and Collaboration: Essays on International Politics.* Baltimore: Johns Hopkins Press, 1962.

Wriggins, Howard. *The Ruler's Imperative: Strategies for Political Survival in Asia and Africa.* New York: Columbia University Press, 1969.

Yar-Shater, Ehsan (ed.). *Iran Faces the Seventies.* New York: Praeger, 1971.

Yesselson, Abraham. *United States-Persian Diplomatic Relations, 1883–1921.* New Brunswick, N.J.: Rutgers University Press, 1956.

Young, Cuyler T. (ed.). *Middle East Focus: The Persian Gulf.* Princeton, N.J.: Princeton University Conference, Oct. 24–25, 1968.

———. (ed.). *Near Eastern Culture and Society.* Princeton, N.J.: Princeton University Press, 1966 (1951).

Zabih, Sepehr. *The Communist Movement in Iran.* Berkeley and Los Angeles: University of California Press, 1966.

Zartman, I. William. *International Relations in the New Africa.* Englewood Cliffs, N.J.: Prentice-Hall, 1966.

Zonis, Marvin. *The Political Elite of Iran.* Princeton, N.J.: Princeton University Press, 1971.

2. PERIODICALS, PAMPHLETS, PAPERS

Adelman, M. A. "Is the Oil Shortage Real?" *Foreign Policy,* No. 9 (Winter, 1972–73), 69–107.

Admanov, L., and L. Teplov. "CENTO: After the Tehran Session." *International Affairs* (Moscow), No. 6 (June, 1969), 81–83.

Akhtar, S. "The Iraq-Iranian Dispute over the Shatt-el-Arab." *Pakistan Horizon,* XXII, No. 2 (1969), 213–221.

Akins, James E. "The Oil Crisis: This Time the Wolf Is Here." *Foreign Affairs*, LI, No. 3 (April, 1973), 462–490.

Alexeyev, L. "U.S. Military Mission in Iran and Iranian National Interests." *International Affairs* (Moscow), No. 7 (July, 1961), 111–114.

Alterov, F. "The Oil Consortium—Neo-Colonialism in Action." *International Affairs* (Moscow), No. 6 (June, 1962), 63–67.

Amirsadeghi, Hossein. "Iran's New Outward Look—An Authoritative Report from Tehran." *New Middle East*, No. 35 (August, 1971), 9–10.

———. "With Russia and America: the Shah's Balanced Alignment." *New Middle East*, No. 38 (November, 1971), 7–11.

Amuzegar, Jahangir. "The Oil Story: Facts, Fiction and Fair Play." *Foreign Affairs*, LI, No. 4 (July, 1973), 676–689.

Andreasyav, R. "New Aspects of Middle East Countries' Oil Policy." *International Affairs* (Moscow), No. 9 (September, 1968), 28–36.

———, and D. Penzin. "Oil and the Anti-Imperialist Struggle." *International Affairs* (Moscow), No. 8 (August, 1971), 53–59.

Anthony, John Duke. "The Union of Arab Amirates." *Middle East Journal*, XXXVI, No. 3 (Summer, 1972), 271–287.

———. "The Lower Gulf States: New Roles in Regional Affairs." In *The Great Powers, the Indian Ocean, and the Gulf.* Washington, D.C.: Middle East Institute, Panel Series IV (March 16, 1972).

Appathurai, N. "Permanent Missions to the United Nations." *International Journal*, XXV, No. 2 (Spring, 1970), 287–301.

———. "Arabia Felix and the Indian Ocean: A Study of Political Strategy." *The Roundtable*, No. 216 (September, 1964), 343–351.

Avery, Peter. "The Many Faces of Iran's Foreign Policy." *New Middle East*, No. 47 (August, 1972), 17–19.

Azadi, M. "Foreign Companies in Iran." *International Affairs* (Moscow), No. 8 (August, 1960), 113–114.

———. "Iran Today." International Affairs (Moscow), No. 9 (September, 1960), 54–59.

"A. V." "Friends and Good Neighbors." *New Times* (Moscow), No. 43 (October, 1972).

Badeau, John S. "U.S.A. and U.A.R.: A Crisis in Confidence." *Foreign Affairs*, XLIII, No. 2 (January, 1965), 281–296.

Baehr, Peter R. "The Role of the National Delegation in the General Assembly." New York: Carnegie Endowment for International Peace, Occasional Paper No. 9 (December, 1970).

Baldwin, David A. "Thinking About Threats." *Journal of Conflict Resolution*, XV, No. 1 (March, 1971), 71–78.

———. "The Costs of Power." *Journal of Conflict Resolution*, XV, No. 2 (June, 1971), 145–155.

———. "The Power of Positive Sanctions." *World Politics*, XXIV, No. 1 (October, 1971), 19–38.

————. "Inter-Nation Influence Revisited." *Journal of Conflict Resolution,* XV, No. 4 (December, 1971), 471–486.

Balfour, Paul H. G. "Recent Developments in the Persian Gulf." *Royal Central Asian Journal* (London), LVI, Part I (February, 1969), 12–19.

Ballis, William B. "Soviet-Iranian Relations During the Decade 1953–64." *Bulletin for Studies on the Soviet Union* (Munich: Institute for the Study of the USSR), XII, No. 11 (November, 1965), 9–22.

Bayne, E. A. "A Heritage from Xerxes." New York: *American Universities Field Staff Reports* (South West Asia Series, XVIII, No. 1, Iran), May, 1969.

Beasley, R. "The Vacuum That Must Be Filled—The Gulf and Iran's Military Potential Assessed." *New Middle East,* No. 32 (May, 1971), 38–40.

Beaujard, Lt. Col. "État de Forces Aeriennes dans le Golfe Persique." *Revue de Defence Nationale,* XXVII (December, 1971), 1912–1914.

Becker, Abraham S. "Oil and the Persian Gulf in Soviet Policy in the 1970's." Paper presented at a conference on the Soviet Union and the Middle East. Tel Aviv University: Russian and East European Research Center at Shiloah Center for Middle Eastern and African Studies (Dec. 26–31, 1971).

Berreby, Jean-Jacques. "La Situation Politique des Émirats du Golfe Persique." *Politique Étrangère,* XXVII, No. 6 (Summer, 1962), 567–580.

————. "Progrès et Évolution de Principautes Arabes du Golfe Persique." *Orient* (Paris), XXV (1963), 25–33.

Berry, John H. "Oil and Soviet Policy in the Middle East." *Middle East Journal,* XXVI, No. 2 (Spring, 1972), 149–160.

Binder, Leonard. "Factors Influencing Iran's International Role." RAND Corporation: Research Program on Economic and Political Problems and Prospects of the Middle East. RAND Corporation/Resources for the Future (RM-5968-FF), October, 1969.

————. "The Middle East as a Subordinate International System." *World Politics,* X, No. 3 (April, 1958), 408–429.

Bjøl, Erling. "The Power of the Weak." *Cooperation and Conflict,* III, No. 3 (1968), 157–168.

Bloomfield, Lincoln P. "Law, Politics, and International Disputes." *International Conciliation,* No. 516 (January, 1958).

————. "The UN and Vietnam." New York: Carnegie Endowment for International Peace (pamphlet), 1968.

Bochkaryov, Y. "Reactionary Plot in Iran." *New Times* (Moscow), No. 24 (June 19, 1963), 17.

————. "A Shaky Throne." *New Times* (Moscow), No. 11 (March, 1959), 11–13.

Bogushevich, O. "Southern Arabia: People Versus Reaction." *New Times* (Moscow), No. 35 (August, 1972), 6–7.

Bondrevskiy, G. L. "The Continuing Western Interest in Oman—As Seen from Moscow." *New Middle East,* No. 35 (August, 1971), 11–15.

Bowman, Larry W. "The Subordinate State System of Southern Africa." *International Studies Quarterly,* XII, No. 3 (September, 1968), 231–260.

Braun, Dieter. "The Indian Ocean in Afro-Asian Perspective." *The World Today*, XXVII, No. 6 (June, 1972), 249–256.

Brecher, Michael, Blema Steinberg, and Janice Stein. "A Framework for Research on Foreign Policy Behavior." *Journal of Conflict Resolution*, XIII (March, 1969), 75–101.

Brewer, William D. "Yesterday and Tomorrow in the Persian Gulf." *Middle East Journal*, XXII, No. 2 (Spring, 1969), 149–158.

British Information Services. "Bahrain, Qatar, and the Trucial States" (pamphlet). July, 1965.

Buchan, Alastair. "Britain in the Indian Ocean." *International Affairs* (London), XLII, No. 2 (April, 1966), 184–193.

Bull, Hedley. "Force in Contemporary International Relations." *Survival*, X (September, 1968), 300–302.

Burrell, R. M. *The Persian Gulf*. (The Washington Papers: 1. The Center for Strategic and International Studies, Georgetown University, Washington, D.C.) New York: Library Press, 1972.

———. "Politics and Participation Where Britannia Once Ruled." *New Middle East*, No. 51 (December, 1972), 32–36.

———. "Problems and Prospects in the Gulf: An Uncertain Future." *The Roundtable*, No. 246 (April, 1972), 209–219.

———. and Alvin J. Cottrell. "Iran, the Arabian Peninsula, and the Indian Ocean." New York: National Strategy Information Center, Inc. (Strategy Paper No. 14), 1972.

Busch, Briton C. "Britain and the Status of Bahrain, 1896–1899." *Middle East Journal*, XXI, No. 2 (Spring, 1967), 189–198.

Campbell, John C. "The Soviet Union and the Middle East," Part I. *Russian Review*, XXIX, No. 2 (April, 1970), 143–153, and No. 3 (July, 1970), 247–261.

Carlson, Sevinc. "Explosion of a Myth—China, the Soviet Union, and the Middle East. (1) The Chinese Intrusion." *New Middle East*, No. 27 (December, 1970), 32–40.

Centre Internationale de Documentation d'Études Petrolières. "Offshore Oil Concession Agreements in OPEC Member Countries." First International Congress on Petroleum and the Sea, Monaco, May 12–20, 1965.

Churba, Joseph. *Conflict and Tension Among the States of the Persian Gulf, Oman, and South Arabia*. Maxwell Air Force Base, Ala.: Air University Documentary Research Study (AV–204–71–IPD), December, 1971.

Colombe, Marcel. "Alliance Islamique et Golfe Persique." *Orient* (Paris), XXXVII (Spring, 1966), 175–238.

Commentator. "Provocative Imperialist Bustle in the Persian Gulf." *International Affairs* (Moscow), No. 3 (March, 1968), 75–77.

Cottam, Richard. "The U.S., Iran, and the Cold War," *Iranian Studies*, III, No. 1 (Winter, 1970), 2–22.

Cottrell, Alvin J. "British Withdrawal from the Persian Gulf." *Military Review* (June, 1970), 14–21.

————. "The U.S. and the Future of the Gulf after the Bahrain Agreement." *New Middle East*, No. 22 (July, 1970), 18–21.

————. "A New Persian Hegemony?" *Interplay*, III, No. 12 (September, 1970), 9–15.

————. "Conflict in the Persian Gulf." *Military Review* (February, 1971), 33–41.

————. "Concern over Saudi Arabia's Viability: An Exclusive Interview with the Shah of Iran." *New Middle East*, No. 31 (April, 1971), 21–23.

Cruickshank, A. A. "International Aspects of the Kurdish Question." *International Relations* (London), III, No. 6 (October, 1968), 411–430.

Cullum, D. M., "The Kharg Story." Tehran: Consortium (mimeo), 1968.

Decalo, Samuel. "Israel's Foreign Policy and the Third World." *Orbis*, XI, No. 3 (Fall, 1967), 724–745.

D'Encausse, Hélène Carrière. "L'Iran en Quête d'un Équilibre." *Revue Francaise de Science Politique*, XVII, No. 2 (April, 1967), 213–236.

Dinerstein, Herbert. "The Transformation of Alliance Systems." *American Political Science Review*, LIX, No. 3 (September, 1965), 589–601.

"D.L.M." "Soviet Interest in Middle East Oil." *Mizan* (London), X, No. 3 (May-June, 1968), 72–85.

————. "Soviet Interests in Middle East Oil." *Mizan* (London), XIII, No. 1 (August, 1971), 30–34.

Doenecke, Justus D. "Revionists, Oil, and Cold War Diplomacy." *Iranian Studies*, III, No. 1 (Winter, 1970), 23–33.

————. "Iran's Role in Cold War Revisionism." *Iranian Studies*, V, No. 2–3 (Spring-Summer, 1972), 96–111.

Dominguez, Jorge I. "Mice That Do Not Roar: Some Aspects of International Politics in the World's Peripheries." *International Organization*, XXV, No. 2 (Spring, 1971), 175–208.

Drambyantz, G. "The Persian Gulf: 'Twixt the Past and the Future." *International Affairs* (Moscow), No. 10 (October, 1970), 66–71.

————. "Persian Gulf: The Thorny Path of Federation." *International Affairs* (Moscow), No. 10 (October, 1971), 96–97.

Elm, E. "Oil Negotiations: The News from Iran." *Columbia Journal of World Business*, VI, No. 6 (November–December, 1971), 81–90.

Elwell-Sutton, L. P. "Nationalism and Neutralism in Iran." *Middle East Journal*, XII, No. 1 (Winter, 1958), 20–32.

Farmayan, Hafez F. *The Foreign Policy of Iran: A Historical Analysis, 559 B.C.-A.D. 1971.* Salt Lake City: Middle East Center, University of Utah, 1971.

Field, Michael. "The New Gulf Power." *Mid-East International*, No. 9 (December, 1971), 8–9.

————. "Oil: OPEC and Participation." *World Today*, XXVIII, No. 1 (January, 1972), 5–13.

Fox, Annette Baker. "The Small States in the International System, 1919–1969." *International Journal*, XXIV, No. 4 (Autumn, 1969), 751–764.

————. "The Small States of Western Europe in the United Nations." *International Organization*, XIX, No. 3 (Summer, 1965), 774–786.

Fuzeyev, V. "In American Harness." *International Affairs* (Moscow), No. 3 (March, 1959), 94–96.

Gaspard, J. "The East Arab Front: The Dispute Between Iraq and Iran and Its Impact on Kurdistan." *New Middle East,* No. 10 (July, 1969), 22–26.

Gerasimov, O. "Foreign Bases on the Arabian Peninsula." *International Affairs* (Moscow), No. 12 (December, 1963), 99–100.

Giniewski, Paul. "L'Iran et Ses Voisins." *Politique Étrangère,* XXV, No. 3 (1960), 285–292.

Goldman, Marshall I. "Red Black Gold." *Foreign Policy,* No. 8 (Fall, 1972), 138–148.

Gordon, Bernard. "Cambodia: Where Foreign Policy Counts." *Asian Survey,* V, No. 9 (September, 1965), 433–448.

Gordon, Edward. "Resolution of the Bahrain Dispute." *American Journal of International Law,* LXV, No. 3 (July, 1971), 560–588.

Gregoryan, K. H. "Iran: Servitors of U.S. Aggression." *International Affairs* (Moscow), No. 7 (July, 1960), 92–93.

———. "U.S. Expansion and CENTO Countries." *International Affairs* (Moscow), No. 5 (May, 1961), 118–120.

Halpern, Manfred. "Perespectives on U.S. Policy: Iran." *School of Advanced International Studies Review,* VI, No. 3 (Spring, 1962), 25–30.

Hart, Parker T. (ed.). "America and the Middle East." *The Annals,* CCCCI (May, 1972).

Hartshorn, J. E. "From Tripoli to Tehran and Back: The Size and Meaning of the Oil Game." *World Today,* XXVII, No. 7 (July, 1971), 291–301.

Hasan, Zubeida. "The Foreign Policy of Afghanistan." *Pakistan Horizon,* XVII (First Quarter, 1964), 48–57.

Hay, Sir Rupert. "The Impact of the Oil Industry on the Persian Gulf Shaykhdoms." *Middle East Journal,* IX, No. 4 (Autumn, 1955), 361–372.

Heard-Bey, Frauke. "The Gulf States and Oman in Transition." *Asian Affairs,* III (February, 1972), 14–22.

———. "Social Changes in the Gulf States and Oman." *Asian Affairs* (October, 1972), 309–326.

Heath, Air Vice Marshal M. L. "Arabian Extremities." *Royal Central Asian Journal,* XLVII, Parts 3 and 4 (July–October, 1960), 260–269.

Heller, Charles A. "The Straits of Hormoz—Critical in Oil's Future." *World Petroleum* (October, 1969), 24–26.

Hoffman, Stanley. "Restraints and Choices in American Foreign Policy." *Daedalus,* XIC, No. 4 (Fall, 1962), 668–704.

Holden, David. "The Persian Gulf: After the British Raj." *Foreign Affairs,* XIL, No. 4 (July, 1971), 721–735.

Hottinger, Arnold. "Persia II." *Swiss Review of World Affairs,* XI (November, 1959), 11–15.

———. "Consolidated Regime in Iran." *Swiss Review of World Affairs,* XVII, No. 1 (April, 1967), 5–7.

Hunter, Robert E. "The Soviet Dilemma in the Middle East. Part II: Oil and the Persian Gulf." *Adelphi Papers* (London: Institute for Strategic Studies), No. 60 (October, 1969).

International Legal Materials: Current Documents, VIII, No. 3 (May, 1969), 478–496.

Irandoust, A. "Restoring the Truth: Concerning the Memoirs of the Shah of Iran." *International Affairs* (Moscow), No. 1 (January, 1961), 69–80.

Iraq, Ministry of Foreign Affairs. "Comment on the Iranian Claims Concerning the Iraqi-Iranian Frontier Treaty of 1937, and the Legal Status of the Frontier Between the Two Countries in the Shatt al-Arab" (pamphlet). Baghdad, July, 1969.

Ivanov, K., and A. Vasilyvev. "A Slippery and Dangerous Path." *International Affairs* (Moscow), No. 2 (February, 1956), 29–39.

Ivanovsky, K. "Blow at Feudalism." *International Affairs* (Moscow), No. 3 (March, 1963), 88.

———. "A Good Start." *International Affairs* (Moscow), No. 2 (February, 1963), 82–83.

Johns, Richard. "No Peace for Kurdistan, But Will There Be War?" *New Middle East,* Nos. 52–53 (January–February, 1973), 48–50.

Joshua, Wynfred. *Soviet Penetration into the Middle East* (rev. ed.). New York: National Strategy Information Center (No. 4), 1971.

Jukes, Geoffrey. "The Indian Ocean in Soviet Naval Policy." *Adelphi Papers* (London: International Institute for Strategic Studies), No. 87 (May, 1972).

Kasatkin, D. "Assault on Oil Monopolies." *International Affairs* (Moscow), No. 1 (January, 1967), 93–94.

———. "Iran, Neighbourly Course." *International Affairs* (Moscow), No. 4 (April, 1968), 72.

Kazemzadeh, Firuz. "The West and the Middle East." *World Politics,* XII, No. 3 (April, 1959), 467–468.

Kelly, J. B. "The British Position in the Persian Gulf." *The World Today,* XX, No. 6 (June, 1964), 238–249.

———. "The Legal and Historical Basis of the British Position in the Gulf." St. Anthony's Papers, Middle East Affairs, (1958), 119–140.

———. "The Persian Claim to Bahrain." *International Affairs* (London), XXXIII, No. 1 (January, 1957), 54–70.

———. "Sovereignty and Jurisdiction in Eastern Arabia." *International Affairs* (London), XXXIV, No. 1 (January, 1958), 16–24.

Keohane, Robert O. "The Big Influence of Small Allies." *Foreign Policy,* No. 2 (Spring, 1971), 161–182.

———. "Lilliputians' Dilemmas: Small States in International Politics." *International Organization,* XXIII, No. 2 (Spring, 1969), 291–310.

———. "Political Influence in the General Assembly." *International Conciliation,* No. 557 (March, 1966).

Khadduri, Majid. "Iran's Claim to the Sovereignty of Bahrayn." *American Journal of International Law,* XLV, No. 5 (October, 1951), 631–647.

Khan, Ayub. "The Pakistan-American Alliance: Stresses and Strains." *Foreign Affairs*, XLII, No. 2 (January, 1964), 195–209.

Kinsman, John. "Kurds and Iran: Iraq's Changing Balance of Power." *New Middle East*, No. 22 (July, 1970), 25–27.

Korotkova, T. "Against Iran's Interests." *New Times* (Moscow), No. 43 (October, 1955), 9–11.

Lauterpacht, E. L. "River Boundaries: The Legal and Political Aspects of the Shatt al-Arab Frontier." *International and Comparative Law Quarterly*, IX (1960), 208–306.

Ledger, David. "Gulf Union." *Mid-East International*, No. 9 (December, 1971), 6.

Lee, Christopher D. "Soviet and Chinese Interest in Southern Arabia." *Mizan* (London), XII, No. 1 (August, 1971), 35–47.

Levy, Walter J. "Oil Power." Foreign Affairs, XLIX, No. 4 (July, 1971), 652–668.

Liebesny, Herbert J. "Documents: Legislation on the Sea Bed and Territorial Waters of the Persian Gulf." *Middle East Journal*, IV, No. 1 (January, 1950), 94–97.

Lissitzyn, Oliver J. "Treaties and Changed Circumstances (Rebus Sic Stantibus)." *American Journal of International Law*, LXI (1967), 895–922.

Lockhart, Laurence. "The Navy of Nadir Shah." *Proceedings of the Iran Society*, I, Part I (Dec. 9, 1936), 1–18.

Lowenthal, Richard. "Continuity and Change in Soviet Foreign Policy." *Survival*, XIV, No. 1 (January–February, 1972), 2–7.

Luce, Sir William. "Britain in the Gulf: Mistaken Timing over Aden." *The Roundtable*, No. 227 (July, 1967), 277–283.

———. "A Naval Force for the Gulf: Balancing Inevitable Russian Penetration." *The Roundtable*, No. 236 (October, 1969), 347–352.

———. "Britain's Withdrawal from the Middle East and Persian Gulf." *Royal United Service Institution Journal*, CXIV (March, 1969), 4–10.

Mallakh, Raqaei el-. "Kuwait's Economic Development and Her Foreign Aid Programmes." *The World Today*, XXII, No. 1 (January, 1966), 15–22.

Marlowe, John. "Arab-Persian Rivalry in the Persian Gulf." *Journal of Royal Central Asian Society*, LI, Part I (January, 1964), 23–31.

Marr, Phebe Ann. "Iraq's Leadership Dilemma: A Study in Leadership Trends, 1948–1968." *Middle East Journal*, XXIV, No. 3 (Summer, 1970), 283–301.

———. "The Iraqi Revolution: A Case Study of Army Rule." *Orbis*, XIV, No. 3 (Fall, 1970), 714–739.

Massoudi, Senator Abbas. "The Persian Gulf in the Light of International Rivalries and Provocations." Text of speech at Rotary Club, Tehran, July 17, 1972.

Mazurenko, Stella. "Tehran Summer." *New Times* (Moscow), No. 36 (Sept. 11, 1963), 23–29.

———. "Rural Iran." *New Times* (Moscow), No. 51 (Dec. 25, 1963), 27–29.

Medvedev, V. "Iran's Land Reform." *New Times* (Moscow), No. 7 (Feb. 20, 1963,) 22–23.

Melamid, Alexander. "The Shatt al-Arab Boundary Dispute." *Middle East Journal*, XX, No. 3 (Summer, 1968), 351–357.

Middle East Institute. "The Soviet Union and the Middle East: A Summary Record." *23rd Annual Conference of the Middle East Institute* (mimeo.), Washington, D.C., Oct. 10–11, 1969.

Miller, William Green. "Political Organization in Iran: From Dowreh to Political Party." Part I, *Middle East Journal*, XXIII, No. 2 (Spring, 1969), 159–167; Part II, No. 3 (Summer, 1969), 343–350.

Missen, David. *Oil at the Service of a Nation.* London: Transorient, 1969.

Mourin, Maxine. "L'Iran et les Problèmes d'Équilibre." *Revue de Defence Nationale*, XXVI (October, 1970), 1446–1461.

Nasser, Pres. Gamal Abdel. *Address on the Seventh Anniversary of Unity, at the Arab Socialist Union Rally, Feb. 21, 1965.* Cairo: Information Department.

———. *Address on the Thirteenth Anniversary of the Revolution, July 22, 1965.* Cairo: Information Department.

———. *Address on the Fourteenth Anniversary of the Revolution, June 22, 1966.* Cairo: Ministry of National Guidance (Information Administration).

———. *Address at the Arab Socialist Union at Damanhur, June 15, 1966.* Cairo: Ministry of National Guidance (Information Administration).

———. *Address at the Arab Socialist Union in Celebration of Unity Day in Cairo, Feb. 22, 1966.* Cairo: National Publication House.

———. *Address on the Anniversary of Victory Day in Port Said, Dec. 25, 1964.* Cairo; National Publication House.

———. *Historical Address on the Fourth Anniversary of the Union, Feb. 22, 1962.* Cairo: Information Department.

———. *Address on the Seventh Anniversary of Victory Day at Port Said, Dec. 23, 1963.* Cairo: Information Department.

———. *Address at the International Laborers' Day Festivities, May 1, 1968.* Cairo: Information Department.

———. *Address on the Sixth Union Day Celebration, Cairo, Feb. 27, 1964.* Cairo: Information Department.

———. *Address at Opening Meeting of the Second Session of the National Assembly, Cairo, Nov. 12, 1964.* Cairo: National Publication House.

National Broadcasting Corporation. "Meet the Press." Washington, D.C.: Merkle Press, XII, No. 41 (Oct. 26, 1969).

———, TV. "Speaking Freely." Edwin Newman, host. Feb. 22, 1970. WNBC Community Affairs Department (typescript).

Neuchterlain, Donald B. "Small States in Alliances: Iceland, Thailand, Australia." *Orbis*, XIII, No. 2 (Summer, 1969), 600–623.

New Times (Moscow). Editorial: "The Real Issue." No. 46 (November, 1958), 3.

———. Editorial: "What is the Real Danger?" No. 4 (January, 1959), 5.

———. Editorial: "The Soviet Union and Iran." No. 47 (Nov. 27, 1963), 3.

———. Editorial: "A Day to Remember." No. 29 (May 17, 1965), 23.

———. Editorial: "Good Neighbor Policy." No. 28 (July 14, 1965), 1–2.

———. "Soviet-Iranian Relations: An Interview with Ambassador Ahmad Mirfendereski." No. 6 (Feb. 9, 1966), 9–10.

———. "Iran and the USSR: Interview with Iranian M.P.'s." No. 36 (Sept. 7, 1966), 22.

———. Editorial: "The Soviet Union and Iran." No. 39 (Oct. 2, 1968), 2–3.

Ogburn, Charlton, Jr. "Divide and Rule in the Middle East." *Harper's* (December, 1957), 38–42.

Orvik, Nils. "NATO, NAFTA, and the Smaller Allies." *Orbis,* XII, No. 2 (Summer, 1968), 455–464.

———. "NATO: The Role of the Smaller Members." *International Journal,* XXI, No. 2 (Spring, 1966), 173–185.

Owen, R. P. "The British Withdrawal from the Persian Gulf." *The World Today,* XXVIII, No. 2 (February, 1972), 75–81.

Page, Martin. "The Persian Gulf." *Atlantic* (April, 1967), 39–43.

Page, Stephen. "Moscow and the Persian Gulf Countries, 1967–1970." *Mizan* (London), XIII, No. 3 (October, 1971), 72–88.

Pahlavi, Mohammed Reza Shah. *Shahanshah of Iran on Oil: Tehran Agreement: Background and Perspectives.* London: Transorient (March, 1971).

Paterson, William E. "Small States in International Politics." *Cooperation and Conflict,* IV, No. 2 (1969), 119–123.

Peck, Malcolm. "Saudi Arabia's Wealth: A Two-Edged Sword." *New Middle East,* No. 40 (January, 1972), 5–7.

Penrose, E. F. "Une Tentative de Gouvernement Civil en Irak, Septembre 1965-Août 1966." *Orient* (Paris), XXX, No. 39 (Spring, 1966), 7–34.

Penzin, D. "Oil and Independence." *International Affairs* (Moscow), No. 10 (October, 1972), 33–40.

Pin, Albert. "Iran in the Year 1346." *New Times* (Moscow), No. 26 (June 28, 1967), 26–28.

Psomiades, Harry J. "The Cyprus Dispute." *Current History,* May, 1965.

Qabain, Fahim I. "Social Classes and Tensions in Bahrain." *Middle East Journal,* IX, No. 3 (Summer, 1955), 269–286.

Reshetar, John S., Jr. "The Soviet Union and the Neutralist World." In "Nonalignment in Foreign Affairs," edited by Cecil V. Crabb, Jr., *The Annals,* CCCLXII (November, 1965).

Rodolfo, Claudine. "Le Golfe Persique: Situation Actuelle et Perspectives d'Avenir." I, *Politique Étrangère,* XXXIV, Nos. 5–6 (1969), 631–665; II, XXXV, No. 5 (1970), 547–586.

Roth, Guenther, "Personal Rulership, Patrimonialism, and Empire-Building in the New States." *World Politics,* XX, No. 2 (January, 1968), 194–206.

Rothstein, Robert L. "Alignment, Nonalignment, and Small Powers, 1945–1965." *International Organization,* XX, No. 3 (Summer, 1966), 397–418.

Rumney, Lt. Col. Mason P. "The View from Iran." *Military Review* (January, 1972), 68–74.

Russell, Ruth. "Power Politics and the United Nations." *International Journal,* XXV, No. 2 (Spring, 1970), 321–332.

Sanghvi, Ramesh. *Iran: Destiny of Oil.* London: Transorient, March, 1971.

———. *Shatt al-Arab: The Facts Behind the Issue.* London: Transorient, June, 1969.

Savid, G. "Alliance Against Progress." *International Affairs* (Moscow), No. 11 (November, 1966), 86–87.

Savory, Roger M. "The Principle of Homeostasis Considered in Relation to Political Events in Iran in the 1960's." *International Journal of Middle East Studies,* III, No. 3 (July, 1972), 282–302.

Schlesinger, Arthur, Jr. "The Historian as Participant." *Daedalus,* C, No. 2 (Spring, 1971), 339–358.

Schmidt, Dana Adams. "Recent Developments in the Kurdish War." *Royal Central Asian Journal,* LIII, Part I (February, 1961), 22–31.

Seton-Watson, Hugh. "Soviet Foreign Policy on the Eve of the Summit." *International Affairs* (London), XXXVI, No. 3 (July, 1960), 287–298.

Shatalov, I. "Iran, 1347." *International Affairs* (Moscow), No. 5 (May, 1968), 74–78.

Shulman, Marshall D. "The Future of Soviet-American Competition." *Adelphi Papers* (London: Institute for Strategic Studies), No. 66 (March, 1970).

Skuratov, L. "Oil Consortium Against Iran." *New Times* (Moscow), No. 47 (Nov. 3, 1966), 14–16.

Smolansky, Oles M. "Moscow and the Persian Gulf: An Analysis of Soviet Ambitions and Potential." *Orbis,* XIV, No. 1 (Spring, 1970), 92–108.

Solovyov, B. "U.S.A. and Britain Support Corrupt Monarchies." *International Affairs* (Moscow), No. 6 (June, 1963), 80.

"Soviet Mid-East Dilemma: Oil from the Persian Gulf." *World Oil* (January, 1917), 69–70.

"Special Issue on the Gulf." *Mid-East Forum* (Bayrut), XXXVIII, No. 7 (Summer, 1962).

Standish, J. F. "British Maritime Policy in the Persian Gulf." *Middle East Studies,* III, No. 4 (July, 1967), 324–359.

———. "Pursuit of Peace in the Persian Gulf." *World Affairs,* CXXXII, No. 3 (December, 1969), 235–244.

Starko, G. "Iran and 'Global Strategy.' " *New Times* (Moscow), No. 52 (December, 1958), 16.

Sterkina, G. "Behind the Screen of the Islamic Pact." *International Affairs* (Moscow), No. 4 (April, 1966), 86–87.

Suhrke, Astri. "Smaller Nation Diplomacy: Thailand's Current Dilemmas." *Asian Survey,* XI, No. 5 (May, 1971), 429–444.

Sullivan, Robert R. "The Architecture of Western Security in the Persian Gulf." *Orbis,* XIV, No. 1 (Spring, 1970), 71–91.

———. "Saudi Arabia in International Politics." *Review of Politics,* XXXII, No. 4 (October, 1970), 436–460.

Tekiner, Suleiman. "Soviet-Iranian Relations over the Last Half Century." *Bulletin for Studies on the Soviet Union* (Munich: Institute for Study of the USSR), New Series, VII, No. 4 (1969), 36–44.

Teplinsky, Boris. "The Persian Gulf in Imperialist Plans." *New Times* (Moscow), No. 36 (September, 1972), 23–24.

Thoman, Roy E. "Iraq and the Persian Gulf Region." *Current History* (January, 1973), 25.

"Three Islands That Could Strangle Iran's Oil Artery." *Mid-East International,* No. 5 (August, 1971), 30–31.

Törngren, Rolf. "The Neutrality of Finland." *Foreign Affairs,* XXXIX, No. 4 (July, 1961), 601–609.

Trager, Frank N. "Sino-Burmese Relations: The End of the Pauk Phaw Era." *Orbis,* XI, No. 4 (Winter, 1968), 1034–1054.

Ulman, A. H., and R. H. Dekmejian. "Changing Patterns in Turkish Foreign Policy, 1959–1967." *Orbis,* XI, No. 3 (Fall, 1967), 772–785.

———. "The USSR and the Persian Gulf." *Mizan* (London), X, No. 2 (March–April, 1968), 51–59.

USSR Mission to the United Nations. Press Release: "Text of the Treaty of Friendship and Cooperation Between the USSR and the Iraqi Republic, April 10, 1972."

———. "Text of Joint Soviet-Iran Communiqué, Oct. 23, 1972."

———. "Text of Treaty on the Development of Economic and Technical Cooperation Between the USSR and Iran, Oct. 13, 1972."

Van Pelt, Mary Cubberly. "The Sheikhdom of Kuwait." *Middle East Journal,* IV, No. 1 (January, 1950), 12–16.

Väyrynen, Raima. "On the Definition and Measurement of Small-Power Status." *Cooperation and Conflict,* VI, No. 2 (1971), 91–102.

Vellut, Jean-Luc. "Smaller States and the Problem of War and Peace: Some Consequences of the Emergence of Smaller States in Africa." *Journal of Peace Research,* No. 3 (1967), 252–269.

Verrier, Anthony. "After Aden—The Gulf?" *New Society* (Sept. 7, 1967), 329–330.

Viktorov, V. "A Harmful Policy." *International Affairs* (Moscow), No. 12 (December, 1958), 84–85.

———. "Why Evil Times Have Fallen." *International Affairs* (Moscow), No. 9 (September, 1959), 89–90.

Volodarskiy, M. I. "The Problems of Present-Day Iran as Assessed in Western Bourgeois Literature." *Narody Azii i Afriki,* No. 3, 1966, p. 154.

Volsky, Dmitry. "On the Persian Gulf." *New Times* (Moscow), No. 5 (Feb. 7, 1968), 14–16.

Voronin, A. "The Beginnings of Friendship and Neighborliness: 50th Anniversary of the Moscow Treaties with Iran, Afghanistan, and Turkey." *International Affairs* (Moscow), No. 4 (April, 1971), 48–54.

Wahlbäck, Krister. "Finnish Foreign Policy: Some Comparative Perspectives." *Cooperation and Conflict,* IV, No. 4 (1969), 282–298.

Watkins, Harold. "Neutral Iran Will Add F-40's to Strengthen Air Defense." *Aviation Week and Space Technology,* LXXXVIII, No. 6 (August, 1967), 50–62.

Watt, D. C. "The Arabs, the Heath Government, and the Future of the Gulf." *New Middle East,* No. 30 (March, 1971), 25–27.

———. "Britain and the Future of the Persian Gulf States." *World Today,* XX, No. 11 (November, 1964), 488–496.

———. "Can the Union of Arab Emirates Survive?" *World Today,* XXVII, No. 4 (April, 1971), 144–147.

———. "The Decision to Withdraw from the Gulf." *Political Quarterly,* XXXIX, No. 3 (July–September, 1968), 310–321.

———. "New Threats to Britain's Strategic Position in West Asia, Aden, and Somalia." *International Relations,* II, No. 2 (October, 1960), 86–92.

———. "Old Promises and New Dangers: The Gulf on the Eve of British Withdrawal." *New Middle East,* No. 39 (December, 1971), 8–9.

Weinstein, Franklin B. *Indonesia Abandons Confrontation: An Inquiry into the Functions of Indonesian Foreign Policy.* Ithaca, N.Y.: Cornell University Press (Interim Reports Series: Modern Indonesia Project, Southeast Asia Program), 1969.

———. "The Uses of Foreign Policy in Indonesia: An Approach to the Analysis of Foreign Policy in Less Developed Countries." *World Politics,* XXIV, No. 3 (April, 1972), 362–363.

Wenner, Lettie M. "Arab-Kurdish Rivalries in Iraq." *Middle East Journal,* XVII, Nos. 1, 2 (Winter, Spring, 1963), 68–82.

Wheeler, Geoffrey, "Soviet Interests in Iran, Iraq, and Turkey." *World Today,* XXIV, No. 5 (May, 1968), 197–203.

———. "Russia and the Middle East." *International Affairs* (London), XXXV, No. 3 (July, 1959), 295–304.

Wilcox, Wayne A. "The Influence of Small States in a Changing World." *The Annals,* CCCLXXII (July, 1967), 80–92.

——— (ed.). "Protagonists, Power, and the Third World: Essays on the Changing International System." *The Annals,* CCCLXXXVI (November, 1969).

Wilkinson, Joe R. "Denmark and NATO: The Problem of a Small State in a Collective Security System." *International Organization,* X (August, 1956), 390–401.

Wohlstetter, Albert. "On the Value of Overseas Bases." Rand Paper P-1877, Jan. 5, 1960.

Wolfers, Arnold. "In Defense of Small Countries." *Yale Review,* XXXIII (Winter, 1944), 201–213.

Wood, Robert Jefferson. "Military Assistance and the Nixon Doctrine." *Orbis,* XV, No. 1 (Spring, 1971), 247–274.

Wriggins, Howard. "Political Outcomes of Foreign Assistance: Influence, Involvement, or Intervention." *Journal of International Affairs*, XXII, No. 2 (1968), 217–230.

Yaminsky, P. "USSR-Iran: Way of Friendship and Cooperation." *International Affairs* (Moscow), No. 1 (January, 1971), 68.

Yodfat, Aryeh Y. "Russia's Other Middle East Pasture—Iraq." *New Middle East*, No. 38 (November, 1971), 26–29.

Young, Cuyler T. "Iran in Continuing Crisis." *Foreign Affairs*, XL, No. 2 (January, 1962), 275–292.

Young, Oran. "Political Discontinuities in the International System." *World Politics*, XX, No. 3 (July, 1968), 369–390.

Young, Richard. "Equitable Solutions for Offshore Boundaries: The 1968 Saudi-Arabia-Iran Agreement." *American Journal of International Law*, LXIV, No. 1 (January, 1970), 152–157.

Zabih, Sepehr. "Iran's International Posture: De Facto Nonalignment Within a Pro-Western Alliance." *Middle East Journal*, XXIV, No. 3 (Summer, 1970), 302–318.

———. "Continuity and Change in Iran's Foreign Policy in Modern Times." *World Politics*, XXIII, No. 3 (April, 1971).

———. "Irano-Soviet Ties." In "The Soviet Union and the Middle East." Middle East Institute, Washington, D.C., 1969.

———. "Contemporary Nationalism in Iran: Some Preliminary Observations." Abstracts of Papers, XXIX, *The International Congress of Orientalists*, Paris, July, 1973.

———. "Iran Today." *Current History*, LXVI, No. 390 (February, 1974), 66–69.

Zartman, I. William. "Africa as a Subordinate State System in International Relations." *International Organization*, XXI (1967), 545–564.

Zelenin, V. "Britain's Manoeuvres East of Suez." *International Affairs* (Moscow), No. 11 (November, 1972), 46–51.

Zimmerman, William. "Hierarchical Regional Systems and the Politics of System Boundaries." *International Organization*, XXVI, No. 1 (Winter, 1972), 8–36.

3. PH.D. DISSERTATIONS

Davenport, Robert W. "Soviet Economic Relations with Iran, 1917–1930." Columbia University, 1953.

Fardanesh, Mohammad Ali. "Foreign Relations and Internal Politics: A Developmental Analysis, Iran." University of Colorado, 1970.

Goreichi, Ahmad. "Soviet Foreign Policy in Iran, 1917–1962." University of Colorado, 1965.

Heravi, Mehdi. "Certain Aspects of U.S.-Iranian Relations, 1883–1945." American University, 1967.

Irani, Ghobad R. "The Azarbayjan Crisis, 1945–1946: An Options Analysis of United States Policy." University of Maryland, 1973.

Kazemzadeh, Hossein. "Iran and Postwar Political Issues: Policy Reflections in the United Nations." Princeton University, 1954.

Meister, Irene W. "Soviet Policy in Iran, 1917–1950: A Study in Techniques." Tufts University (Fletcher School of Law and Diplomacy), 1954.

Reppa, Robert B. "Israel and Iran: Their Development, Interrelationship, and Effect on the Indian Ocean Basin." University of Maryland, 1973.

Schultz, Ann Tibbitts. "The Recruitment and Behavior of Iranian Legislators: The Influence of Social Background." Yale University, 1969.

Tabari, Keyvan. "Iran's Policies Toward the U.S. During the Anglo-Russian Occupation, 1941–1946." Columbia University, 1967.

Tahir-Kheli, Shirin. "Pakistani Elites and Foreign Policy Towards the Soviet Union, Iran, and Afghanistan." University of Pennsylvania, 1972.

Weaver, Paul Elwood. "Soviet Strategy in Iran, 1941–1947." American University, 1958.

4. IRANIAN SOURCES

A. REGULAR IRANIAN FOREIGN MINISTRY PUBLICATIONS

Elamiyeh-e Moshtarak. ("Joint Communiqués.") (Idareh-e Ettela'at va Matbu'at), 1349. (Published once; supplanted by biannual publication following.)

Biannual:

Nashriyeh Omur-e Kharejeh, No. 1. ("Foreign Ministry Publication No. 1.: 3rd Period.") Doreh-e Sevom. (Ettela'at va Matbu'at), Shahrivar, 1344.

Nashriyeh Omur-Kharejeh, No. 2. ("Foreign Ministry Publication No. 2.: 3rd Period.") Doreh-e Sevom. (Ettela'at va Matbu'at), Isfand, 1344.

Nashriyeh Omur-e Kharejeh, No. 3. ("Foreign Ministry Publication No. 3.: 3rd Period.") Doreh-e Sevom. (Ettela'at va Matbu'at), Shahrivar, 1345.

Nashriyeh Omur-e Kharejeh: Az Mehr ta Isfand 1348. ("Foreign Ministry Publication: September, 1968 to March, 1969.") (Ettela'at va Matbu'at), n.d.

Nashriyeh Omur-e Kharejeh: Az Farvardin ta Shahrivar 1349. ("Foreign Ministry Publication: March, 1970 to September, 1970.") (Ettela'at va Matbu'at), n.d.

Nashriyeh Omur-e Kharejeh: Az Mehr ta Isfand 1349. ("Foreign Ministry Publication: September, 1970—March, 1971.") (Ettela'at va Matbu'at), Ordibehesht, 1350.

Nashriyeh Omur-e Kharejeh: Az Farvardin ta Shahrivar 1350 Sal-e Kurosh-e Bozorg. ("Foreign Ministry Publication: March–September, 1971.") (Ettela'at va Matbu'at), Azar, 1350.

Nashriyeh Omur-e Kharejeh. Az Mehr ta Isfand. Sal-e Kurosh-e Bozorg.

("Foreign Ministry Publication: September, 1971–March, 1972.") (Ettela'at va Matbu'at), Tir, 1351.

Ravabet-e Kharejeh-e Iran dar Sal-e 1346. ("Iran's Foreign Relations in 1967–68.") (Gozaresh-e Salianeh-e Vezarat-e Omur-e Kharejeh), Farvardin, 1347.

Ravabet-e Kharejeh-e Iran dar Sal-e 1347. ("Iran's Foreign Relations in 1968–69.") Farvardin, 1348.

Ravabet-e Kharejeh-e Iran dar Sal-e 1348. ("Iran's Foreign Relations in 1969–70.") Farvardin, 1349.

Ravabet-e Kharejeh-e Iran dar Sal–e 1349. ("Iran's Foreign Relations in 1970–71.") n.d.

Ravabet-e Kharejeh-e Iran dar Sal-e 1350: Sal-e Kurosh-e Kabir. ("Iran's Foreign Relations in 1971–72.") n.d. and (1972–1973) n.d.

Salnameh-e Vezaret-e Omur-e Kharejeh-e. ("The Foreign Ministry Yearbook." 1962–63) (Idareh-e Ettela'at va Matbu'at), 1341.

B. OTHER FOREIGN MINISTRY PUBLICATIONS IN CHRONOLOGICAL ORDER

Majmu'eh-e Gharardadha-ye Ettehad-e Jamahir-e Shoravi-e Socialisti. II. Tehran: Vezarat-e Omur-e Kharejeh 1338. (Recueil des Traites: Traites Irano-Sovietiques. Fasicule II. Tehran: Ministry of Foreign Affairs, 1959.) (In Persian and French.)

The Persian Gulf: A Name Born with History. Tehran: Bank Melli Press, 1970.

Siasat-e Beinolmelali-e Iran: Bargozideh-i az Neveshteha-ye Shahanshah Arya Mehr. ("Iran's International Diplomacy: A Collection of the Shahanshah Aryamehr's Writings.") (Ettela'at va Matbu'at), n.d.

Vajhe Tasmiyeh-e Khalij-e Fars. ("The Origins of the Word Persian Gulf.") Idareh-e Nohom-e Siasi. n.d.

"Iran's Foreign Policy: A Compendium of the Writings and Statements of His Imperial Majesty Shahanshah, Aryamehr." n.d. (1969).

Imperial Iranian Embassy, London. "Some Facts Concerning the Dispute between Iran and Iraq over the Shatt-al-Arab: The Boundary Line Between Iran and Iraq." July, 1969.

Bahrayn: Doran-e Hekhamaneshi ta Zaman-e Hal: 558 ghabl az Milad-1969 Miladi. ("Bahrayn: From the Achaemenid Period to the Present: 558 B.C. to 1969 A.D.") (Idareh-e Nohom-e Siasi), Tir, 1348.

Ministry of Foreign Affairs, Tehran. "British Official Documents Shed New Light on the Question of Shatt-al-Arab." 9th Political Department, September, 1969.

Bahrayn, (Idareh-e Nohom-e Siasi), Khordad, 1350.

Hamkari-e 'Omran-e Mantagheh'i, Iran, Pakestan, Torkiyeh. ("Regional Cooperation and Development, Iran, Pakistan and Turkey.") Tehran: Vezarat-e Omur-e Kharejeh-e (Idareh-e Hamkari-e Omran-e Mantagheh'i). Khordad, 1350.

Sarzaminha-ye Jonub-e Khalij-e Fars va Soltan Neshin-e Oman. ("The Coun-

tries of the Southern Persian Gulf and the Sultanate of Oman.") Idareh-e
Nohom-e Siasi, Shahrivar, 1350.

C. OTHER IRANIAN GOVERNMENT SOURCES

*Press Conferences of His Imperial Majesty Mohammad Reza Shah Pahlavi of
Iran. 1337.* (1958–1959) Tehran: Keyhan Press (Department of Publications
and Broadcasting, Office of Information). n.d.

*Press Conferences of His Imperial Majesty Mohammad Reza Shah Pahlavi of
Iran, 1338.* (1959–1960) Tehran: Keyhan Press (Department of Publications
and Broadcasting, Office of Information), n.d.

Khalij-e Fars. ("The Persian Gulf.") Sazman-e Sam'i-basari-e Honarha-e Ziba-e
Keshvar. 2 vols. Tehran: Idareh-e Koll-e Entesharat va Radio, n.d.

*Surat-e Jalasat-e Shora-ye Eghtesadi dar pishgah-e Shahanshah Aryamehr, ya
Majmu'eh-i az Asnad-e mo'aser-e Iran.* ("Transcripts of the Sessions of the
High Economic Council Assembled in the Shah's presence, or, a collection
of contemporary Iranian documents.") Vol. I. Az Shahrivar 1343 ta Shahrivar
1345. ("From August–September 1964 to August–September 1966.") Vol. II.
Az Shahrivar 1345 ta Shahrivar 1347. ("From August–September 1966 to
August–September 1968.") Tehran: Chapkhan-e Vezarat-e Farhang va
Honar, n.d.

Pahlavi, Mohammad Reza Shah. *Bargozideh'i az Neveshteha va Sokhanan-e
Shahan-Shah-e Aryamehr.* ("A Selection from the Writings and Speeches of
His Imperial Majesty, Shahanshah, Aryamehr.") Tehran: Chapkaneh-e
Bank-e Melli (Nashriyeh-e Ketab Khaneh-e Pahlavi.) 25 Shahrivar, 1347.

"Address of the Shahanshah Aryamehr and Reports by the Prime Minister
and the Plan Organization Managing Director at the Historic Session at
Plan Organization, Dec. 29, 1970." Tehran: Imperial Government of Iran.
n.d.

Tehran: The Plan Organization. "Report of the Prime Minister on the State
of the Iranian Economy 1347–1348 and Government Programmes for the
Year 1351." Tehran: Central Bureau of the Budget, Plan Organization, 1351.

"Text of Address Delivered by Prime Minister Amir Abbas Hoveyda to the
Majlis in Presenting the 1351 (1972–1973) National Budget." Tehran: no
publisher indicated. January 25, 1972.

"Press Conference by His Imperial Majesty Shahanshah Aryamehr, June 24,
1972." Tehran: Ministry of Information, Information Department, n.d.

Foreign Trade Statistics of Iran. March 21, 1971–March 20, 1972. Tehran:
Ministry of Finance, Bureau of Statistics, 1350.

Foreign Trade Statistics of Iran. March 21–June 21, 1972. Tehran: Ministry
of Finance, Bureau of Statistics, No. 9. 1351.

D. NON-GOVERNMENT IRANIAN SOURCES

Alam, Abdul 'amir. *Ravabet-e Siasi-e Iran va Amrika az Jang-e Dovom-e
Jahani.* ("Iran's Diplomatic Relations with the United States since WW II.")
Tehran: Amir Kabir Institute, 1939.

Amirie, Abbas. "Shoravi dar Khavare Miyaneh" (The Soviets in the Middle East). *Masael-e Jahani,* No. 5 (October, 1973), Tehran.

Ansari, Abdolhossein Masude. *Zendegani-ye man va Negahi betarikh-e Siyasi-ye Iran va Jahan.* ("My Autobiography and an Overview of Iran and World Political History.") 2 vols. Tehran: Ibne Sina Publications, 1972.

Eqhbal, Abbas. *Mutale-ati dar bab-e Bahrayn va Jazayer va Savahel-e Khalij-e Fars.* ("A Study of Bahrayn and the Islands and Coasts of the Persian Gulf.") Tehran: Majlis, 1328.

Eghtedari, Ahmad. *Khalij-e Fars.* ("The Persian Gulf.") Tehran: Ebne Sina, Ordibehesht, 1345.

Faramarzi, Ahmad. *Karim Khan-e Zand va Khalij-e Fars.* ("Karim Khan and the Persian Gulf.") Tehran: Davarpanah, Khordad, 1346.

———. *Rah-ahane Orupa va Khalij-e Fars.* ("The European Railroad and the Persian Gulf.") Tehran: Davarpanah, Aban, 1346.

———. *Shuresh-e Bardegan.* ("The Revolt of the Slaves.") Tehran: Davarpanah, Tir, 1347.

———. *Jazireh-e Khark.* ("The Kharg Island.") Tehran: Davarpanah, Tir. 1347.

Jenab, Mohammad 'Ali. *Khalij-e Fars: Āshnā'i bā Amārāt-e An.* ("The Persian Gulf: An Introduction to the Amirates.") Tehran: Melli, 1349.

Mas'udi, Senator Abbas. *Didari az Sheykh Neshinha.* ("A Visit to the Shaykhdoms.") Tehran: Iran Chap, Shahrivar, 1345.

———. *Didar-e Tazeh'i az Sheykh Neshinha: Khalij-e Fars pas az Khoruj-e Englis.* ("A New Visit to the Shaykhdoms: The Persian Gulf after Britain's Departure.") Tehran: Ettela'at Publications, Khordad, 1348.

———. "The Persian Gulf in the Light of International Rivalries and Provocations." Tehran: Rotary Club Pamphlet. 17 July 1972.

———. *Khalij-e Fars dar doran-e Sarbolandi va Shokuh.* ("The Persian Gulf in the Era of Pride and Glory.") Tehran: Ettelaat Publications, Mordad, 1352.

Mojtahedzadēh, Parviz. *Sheykh Neshinha-e Khalij-e Fars.* ("The Shaykhdoms of the Persian Gulf.") Tehran: 'Almi, 1349.

Neshat, Sadegh. *Tarikh-e Siasi-e Khalij-e Fars.* ("The Diplomatic History of the Persian Gulf.") Tehran: Sherkat-e Nesbi-ye Kanūn-e Ketab, n.d.

Sahab, A., ed. *Atlas of Geographical Maps and Historical Documents on the Persian Gulf.* Tehran: Geographic and Drafting Institute, 1971.

INDEX